## NOVELS BY LEE WILLIAMS

*IN HIS BLOOD*

*SINS OF THE FATHER*

For more information about the author,
please visit his website at www.leejwilliams.com.

# SINS

## OF THE FATHER

LEE WILLIAMS

SINS OF THE FATHER
Lee Williams

ISBN-13: 978-0615461236
Library of Congress Control Number: 2011925199

LW PUBLISHING ENTERPRISES
WESTMONT, IL

## ACKNOWLEDGEMENTS

Once again I have to thank the members of my writers' group that have had the patience to nurse me through each chapter. A special thanks goes out to members Steve Myslicki, Jon Payne, and Larry Zoeller who accepted the arduous task of completing a line-by-line edit. You did a great job guys. And I have to thank Gloria for her patience while I buried my head in the computer working on the manuscript. I would be remiss if I didn't make note of the great artwork on the cover, which was designed by Ellie Searl.

To the men and women that had the great courage to press the civil rights movement forward during a dangerous time.

# PART ONE

## CHAPTER ONE

### Rural Mississippi
### Late February 1968

Beauford Tisdale stared through the sheet of plastic that covered the kitchen window, as it snapped in the wind. Ten acres of young green shafts of winter wheat danced in the cross current as the first orange rays streaked over the eastern horizon.

His mind drifted from the thought of the $200 the wheat would bring him in June to the image of his great-grandfather, Andrew Jackson Tisdale, struggling behind a plow and mule, turning the soil of this same plot of land one hundred years ago. His great-grandfather was the first emancipated man in the Tisdale family and this farm was part of the forty acres and a mule that started his free life.

"You want breakfast? I'm making flapjacks," Nathleen said, her long slender fingers putting a match to the wood shavings in the black cast-iron stove. The kindling crackled and she put the lid back, covering the fire, and slid the coffee pot over to warm yesterday's coffee.

Beauford turned from the window to face his wife. He looked into her eyes and wanted her to look back at him the way she used to. But the color of her eyes had faded like their passion. He glanced to the floor. "No. I gotta go to Napier's to work on his barn."

"Make no sense to me." She tightened the knot in the blue bandanna covering her head. "Working for that man the way he treats us people."

Beauford knew she didn't mean it, but she hit him in that vulnerable place, between his manhood and his blackness. "Make sense eatin', don't it?" He looked out the window again. His shoulders were thick and taut. He looked down at the gaps in the wood floor. "Wheat won't be ready to harvest 'til June."

Her lips pressed together, cheeks sunk in. "You could find work somewhere else. Working for him just ain't right. If it was me, I wouldn't be doin' it."

"Well it ain't you and you ain't the one that's putting food on the table. He's got two, maybe three days of payin' work." Beauford swallowed a deep breath filling his broad chest. "I ain't got time to eat. I gotta pick up Johnny and Sherman. They workin' at Napier's too."

She stared at the stove and jerked her head up. "Ain't none of you got any pride?"

"Don't be dirt mouthin' me." Beauford walked away from his wife and past his father who slept on a cot stuck between the stove and the wall. The warmest place in the house during the winter. The wood burning stove had replaced the old fireplace but it was still connected to the chimney that had been made by his great-grandfather with rocks he had cleared from the fields where the winter wheat now grew. Beauford hoped his father wasn't awake to hear the shame his wife had poured on him.

The paint-peeled house had been the home of the Tisdales since it was a one-room shanty a hundred years earlier. Over the years, sleeping rooms had been added to one side and then the other, built from discarded rough sawn and plywood, the walls insulated with discarded newspaper. The first addition was for his father and mother and the second for him and Nathleen after they were married. His mother hadn't lived to see the children.

Beauford walked to the room on the east side and slipped inside the sheet nailed to the wall to separate the room from the kitchen. His son and daughter, William and Marlee, slept there. He leaned over the four-year old girl, kissed her on the cheek and whispered, "I love you baby." A soft smile spread across her face and he knew she was in some heavenly place that only an innocent child could visit. He tucked a worn green blanket around her body.

Beauford faced his eleven-year old son, the beds only two feet apart. The boy's eyes barely opened. "You be a good boy and listen to your momma." William's eyes closed and Beauford stroked his cheek.

He headed to their bedroom on the other side of the house to get his denim jacket. An old army blanket nailed to the doorframe provided privacy. A sagging double mattress was pushed to one side of the room. Tacked against the opposite wall was a sheet of water-stained wallpaper, faded red-tea roses against a pale-blue background.

Beauford left the cabin, closed the unpainted door behind him, and stepped onto the muddied wood pallet that was their porch. He climbed into his faded red 1955 Chevy pickup truck. The hood rattled as the engine sputtered, oily smoke belched from the exhaust, and the motor finally turned over in the chill of the morning. He pulled away and listened to the truck creak over the ruts in Poverty Road.

\*\*\*

Celeste Napier, in a white nightgown dotted with pink cherubs, stifled a yawn as she walked down the stairs from her attic bedroom to the kitchen. Red hair dangled around her sleep-puffed face.

Her father, Jimmy Napier, sat at the kitchen table. He was rail thin with brown greasy hair. Steam rose from the cup of coffee in his hand. A Salem that was one-quarter ash was clenched between his small yellow teeth. "You up early."

"Just goin' get some coffee. Goin' to take it back to my room."

Napier leaned forward resting his elbows on the table. "Like hell you will. Your momma sick and you ain't been doing a damn thing around here. That stopping today."

She scrunched her nose. "Junior ain't doing nothing."

"He only six, you almost three times older than he is. At least he's with your momma, keeping her company at her bedside."

She shook her head. "No need for both of us to be with her."

"You something else." Napier slammed his cup down and ashes fell from his cigarette onto his red flannel shirt. He brushed them off onto the linoleum. "I'm going into town. When I get back this kitchen floor better be washed and waxed. I wanna see it lookin' like it was put in yesterday. Don't forget to mop the chicken shit off that damn porch."

Celeste went to the gas stove, poured some coffee from the percolator, and started walking out of the kitchen.

"You hear me?" The cigarette waggled in his mouth.

She put her foot on the first step going upstairs.

Napier stood up, the kitchen chair screeched back, and his footfalls pounded the floor. He grabbed Celeste's arm and jerked her around. Her coffee spilled on his hand. "Ow, damn it."

"You're hurting me. Let go." She jerked her arm but couldn't break his grip.

His eyes narrowed to thin slits. "You don't give a damn about nothin' but yourself. You quittin' school, working around here full time. Doing something useful."

"Other girls my age are going to the beauty shop and dating boys. I'm stuck working around this old house and taking care of my sick momma. What kind of life is this for me?"

The skin below his right eye quivered. He squinted at her through the cigarette smoke. "Stop your whining and don't test me with your foolish talk. You'll find out I'm damn serious about that floor if it ain't done when I get back." He looked at the puddle of coffee that had dripped onto the stairs. "And you wipe this mess you caused too."

The muscles strained in her neck and her voice broke. "Why don't you just go to town and do what you have to?" She yanked her arm harder, escaping her father's grasp, and scrambled up the stairs to her attic bedroom.

He pointed a finger at her. "I'm going and you better have your chores finished by time I get back. Tisdale and a couple of other niggers are coming to work on the barn and string some fencing. They know what they suppose to do. You see 'em sittin' around, you yell at them." Napier slammed the door behind him as he left, its narrow panes of glass rattling.

"I know how to do that," Celeste pursed her lips. "Same way you yell at me." She walked into her bedroom and sat on her bed. She took a gulp of her coffee, put the cup down, and picked up a hand mirror. Celeste looked at her freckled face, puckered her lips and pretended to kiss Tommy Hays, a boy from school. She closed her eyes, lay down, and sighed, thinking about their stolen moment of passion last Friday night in Tommy's father's barn. She knew that the physical act was as much a rebellion against her father, an escape from her reality, as it was symbolic of her feelings for Tommy. But that was alright with her because Tommy Hays was her ticket out of this hell. She pressed her father out of her mind and focused on that night. She trembled when she remembered how his naked body felt on top of hers. She took a deep breath and felt her soul stir with the thought of being with him as soon as she could steal another moment. She relived that night and ran her fingers up the back of her neck and through her hair. Her chest lifted and she slid her hand across her nipple and groaned.

\*\*\*

A dozen chickens squawked and scattered as Beauford pulled his pickup next to Napier's sun-faded, sagging barn. Johnny Beverly sat next to him, over fifty, tall and lean, and not showing his age. Sherman Rule sat in the bed of the truck. He was in his early thirties, frail with thick eyeglasses and needed the work to feed his wife and young twin daughters. Beauford was younger and stronger than the other two.

"I'll start working on the barn," Beauford told them. "You guys take the tractor to the east side and start on the fence. I'll drive up and meet you for lunch. You should be able to finish that stretch of the fence."

The three men walked into the barn. The smell of damp-rotten hay filled their nostrils. Dust floated in the sunlight leaking in between the warped and cracked boards. Beverly hopped onto the seat of the old John Deere as he wedged a wad of Red Man behind his lower lip. Rule stood behind him, holding on tightly to the seat as the two men rode out of the barn.

Beauford started ripping down rotted one-by-eight-foot rough sawns, reinforcing the framing and replacing old boards. He wiped the sweat off his brow, took off his jacket, and threw it on the hay-covered floor. His sleeveless tee shirt clung on his body.

Physical labor came easy to Beauford. It allowed his mind to wander, sometimes to places he didn't want it to go. He didn't understand what was going on with Nathleen. She would disappear into her moods and they would get into an exhausting tug of war, neither one winning. Their passion had been replaced by neglect and the neglect had grown into pain.

\*\*\*

Celeste, empty coffee cup in hand, bare-footed down to the
kitchen. Her face drawn, dreading another day of her life. She put a
bucket in the sink, added soap, and turned on the hot water. She
noticed the red pickup truck parked outside the barn. "Poor man, he
gonna work you to the bone and then make you beg for your pay.
He could probably use a cup." She poured the coffee into her cup.
"No sense gettin' another one dirty. Would jus' be more for me to
wash."

She snatched a green shawl from a peg on the wall next to
the back door and slipped on a pair of brown ankle-high boots.
Outside, she stopped in the sun and filled her lungs with the brisk
air. She tilted her head back, felt the sun's rays warm her cheeks
and for moment felt a sense of hopefulness.

Crossing the trampled red clay she ambled past the
chickens pecking on their feed and left the warmth of the sun as
she entered the barn. It was dark and she felt a chill as her eyes
adjusted to the shadows. She noticed Beauford at the far end,
swinging a sledge. She watched his body twist and turn, muscles
going taut as he crashed it into a one by eight, knocking it off the
wall. A beam of light flashed into the barn. Particles of dust and
mites speckled in the light. Her eyes flinched as the brightness
danced across her face and she raised her hand to shield her eyes.
"I brought you some coffee."

\*\*\*

Beauford jerked his head around, his eyes seeing, but his
mind not believing. Her red hair falling to the shawl around her
shoulders, green eyes glistening at him, and the points of her
chilled nipples pressing against her nightgown. His initial arousal
was suddenly dampened by fear. He listened for the sound of
Napier's truck. But the day was quiet except for the light rustle of
the wind through the barn. "What you doing here?" he whispered.

"Got you a cup of coffee." She stretched out her arm,
offering the coffee.

Beauford dropped the sledge and raised both hands palms
out. "Now Miss you…you really ought to stay in the house. Your
daddy come home, he ain't gonna be too pleased."

She lowered the cup to her side. "He'll be at the Dixie Lounge getting plastered. Won't be home 'til dark and he'll be so drunk he'll sleep in his truck. What's your name?"

Beauford dragged his arm across his forehead wiping the perspiration. "Just the same, could be a lot of trouble. He come home and sees you and me alone here. Lot of people don't like that."

She stepped forward and brushed her hair off the left side of her face. "I asked you what your name was. Don't you have any manners? You're supposed to answer a woman when she asks you a question."

"Sorry miss. My name is Beauford and if you don't mind I be getting back to work. Got lotta work to do." He pointed to the empty place in the wall where he had knocked out the board.

She sighed and put her left hand on her hip. "Don't be so ignorant. You suppose to ask me my name after I ask you yours."

"Sorry miss." He shifted from one foot to the other and looked over her shoulder for her father's truck.

She stamped her foot, "Well?"

"Oh, yeah. I mean, yes ma'am. I'd be pleased to know your name." His eyes peered to one side of her and then the other.

"What're you lookin' for?"

"Nothin' ma'am." He wiped the back of his hand across his forehead.

"You supposed to look at someone when your conversating with them. Don't you know nothing about the social graces?"

"Yes, ma'am. I just got all this work to do."

"Well, fine then. My name is Celeste. You take this here coffee. Give yourself a little break. I'll head back into the house and do my chores like a good girl and you don't have to be so nervous. What is wrong with you anyway?"

Beauford took two short steps, grasped the cup, and took a sip. "I don't want you to get hurt, Miss Celeste."

She focused on his eyes. No one had ever said that to her before. She said, "How anybody gonna hurt me?"

Celeste turned and marched to the open doorway. She stopped there and felt the sun penetrating her nightgown. She glanced over her shoulder and caught Beauford focusing on her silhouette. She smiled and thought of Tommy Hays. He would be doing more than looking.

Returning to the kitchen, she lifted the bucket out of the sink. Soapy water splashed onto the floor, circling her feet. She dragged the mop across the yellow linoleum, imagining dancing with Tommy, thinking about what her life could be, should be. Her daydream interrupted by the ringing phone. "It's got to be Tommy, hello."

"Guess what, Celeste!"

"What, Cindy?"

"Tommy Hays is taking me to a movie tonight."

Her brow furrowed. "What? I don't believe you. He never even looked your way and we…." She stopped, knowing that she couldn't say any more.

"Well, apparently he did when you were admiring yourself in your compact. And he was doing more than looking. He was liking what he was seeing."

"I'm really busy. Talk to you later." She slammed the phone down and threw the mop across the kitchen. "Damn it. I hate my life."

"You swore. I'm gonna tell Daddy," Junior said, standing at the kitchen doorway in his bib overalls.

She put her hands on her hips. "Don't you step on this wet floor or I'll beat your skinny ass, you little peckerwood."

"You swore again. You better make me lunch or you're in big trouble. I'll tell Daddy you was out talking to the nigger. I was watching you from momma's window. I saw you go to the barn."

She picked up the mop and gripped it with both hands. "You do and I'll whop you across your backside."

Junior took a step forward, turned and wiggled his butt at her, "Nigger lover."

"You're asking for it." She shook her head. "You sound just like your daddy. I hope for your sake you don't grow up like him."

"Daddy said he's gonna take me to a Klan meeting for my birthday."

Celeste leaned against the mop. "God have mercy on your soul. Do not take another step into this room. Go sit at the dining room table and I'll bring you a ham sandwich. You know if Momma wants anything to eat?"

"No. She's sleeping. Is Momma going to be all right?"

Celeste went to the refrigerator, pulled out the ham, mustard, and bread and put together Junior's sandwich. "The doctor said we just got to wait and see. He thinks its pneumonia from that cold spell we had. Here you go. You eat this while I finish cleaning."

\*\*\*

Just short of noon Napier finished his errands in town. He pointed his blue Dodge Ram Charger down Floyce Street heading into the town square. He watched a mockingbird fly past the Confederate flag hanging from the flagpole near the center of the square. He remembered one morning on the Fourth of July many years ago when he raised that flag with his father. It was that same evening that he and Linda Joy listened to the concert in the square, the same evening he stole his first kiss from her. He smiled. A year later she was pregnant with Celeste and he was seventeen when they married. He pulled a sleeve of Mail Pouch out of his shirt pocket, bit off a piece, and filled his cheek.

Napier stepped on the accelerator. The engine roared and he sped past the insurance office, a general goods store with a hitching post that looked like a black jockey, several vacant storefronts, and a drug store. He stopped in front of the Bank of Ruleville, rolled down his window and stared at the institution that held two mortgages on his farm and the note on his truck. He thought of the late notices he'd been getting in the mail. He pulled over to the curb, shifted the tobacco in his mouth, holding a wad on his tongue, and spit it onto the bank window. He watched the brown goop slide down the glass and laughed. "Jew motherfuckers."

A Sunflower County sheriff's cruiser pulled along side Napier's pickup.

Napier did a double take. "Oh shit."

The smoked window on the cruiser rolled down. "Jimmy, what did you do that for?" Deputy Sheriff Uriah Bennett dropped his hands from the steering wheel and rested them on his protruding stomach that stretched the buttons on his khaki uniform shirt.

"Ah shit. You scared me, Uriah. Didn't know it was you. Some Jews must own this place. Just cause I'm a couple months behind, they keep sending me these late notices. Don't they think I know it?"

"Well, what can I say? You know those banks. Hey, I'm meeting the mayor and Albert at the Dixie. The mayor said he's got something special he wants to talk to us about." Uriah lowered his chin as if he realized he just made a mistake.

"Think I'll join you boys." Napier followed the cruiser past the square to the Dixie Lounge. It was time for him to forget about times past and bills due. He was thirsty. He hadn't had a drink since last night and his Klan brothers were just the kind he liked to wet his palate with. Men that believed they lived by God's laws, lived life the way it should be, protecting their woman and children from the spooks, Jews, and fags. He pulled across the railroad tracks into a gravel parking lot and parked on the south side of a dusty red-frame building. His pickup truck and the cruiser fit between a white Lincoln convertible and a red Ford pickup.

A white plastic sign with Dixie Lounge printed in red letters hung over the door, adorning each side of its name were Confederate flags. In smaller red print were the words, "Whites Only."

Napier and Bennett entered the lounge. The smell of stale beer and tobacco filled the air. Their Klan brothers were at the usual round table in the back corner of the bar. Josephus LeGrand, the Mayor of Ruleville and the Imperial Wizard of the Mississippi Klan, wore a beige suit coat, a red bow tie and black horn-rimmed glasses. Gray hair curled out of his ears. Next to him sat Albert Lee, the Sunflower County assessor. He had on a white string tie and a blue shirt. A Confederate flag hung on the wall behind them. Four empty longnecks were in the middle of the table.

LeGrand looked at Napier and muttered under his breath. "The redneck is here." But he was a Klansman and LeGrand leaned back in his chair, waved at Napier with forced enthusiasm and called out, "Jimmy. You and Uriah come join us."

They sat down as the bartender brought another round of beers to the table. Napier grabbed a cold bottle and took a swig.

The mayor looked at Jimmy and Uriah. "I was telling Albert we've been fighting a losing battle because we're not organized. The niggers got SNCC, NAACP, and that Southern Christian Organization. There's Jews coming down here from up north. The fuckin' FBI's been poking into our business. It's like the world's looking for somebody to blame for its problems and they picked us." He lifted the bottle and took a sip. "I've been talking to a man, a very important man, that can help our cause. He'll help us unify and overcome all these obstacles."

"Who's this?" Albert said.

The mayor leaned forward. "This man's got influence and power, and other people that agree with his viewpoint. It's because of his position he can work from the inside. For that reason he's got to remain anonymous."

Albert shook his head. "We suppose to take orders from somebody we don't know?"

The mayor poked his finger at Albert. "God damn it, listen to reason. With the information he can get, he can help us. Instead of doing the things that we're doing one by one, we can operate as part of a machine. Part of an army." LeGrand banged his fist on the table.

Everyone looked at each other.

"What if...what if this is some FBI thing to rope us in? To finally and completely get rid of us," Uriah asked.

LeGrand rubbed his thumb and forefinger on his throbbing temples and exhaled. "This is our last fuckin' chance! If we don't take steps to protect our ways, we will lose them forever." He took a deep breath. His chest expanding and contracting as he pushed his fingers through his gray hair. "I've had several long telephone conversations with this gentleman and I'm convinced he's sincere in his intent to divide this country. Let the blacks have a state, even two. Let God's law prevail. Our families, the white Christians, will be able to live together forever. And those that aren't worthy—like Jews, niggers, and fags—can create their own hell in their own state."

"So how's this gonna happen?" Napier asked.

LeGrand leaned forward. "The first thing, right here in Sunflower County, is to reclaim our land. The federal government stole land from our forefathers and gave it to the niggers after the War against the north. If we take the land back, they got to move. So the process starts right away."

Albert pulled a cigar out of his shirt pocket. He bit off the end, spat it to the floor, and rolled the cigar in his mouth. He leaned over and gritted his brown teeth. "Yeah, how we gonna do that?"

"We got everybody we need right here. We pick one nigger family, make an example out of them. Do what we have to. Make them want to leave. If that don't work we get more serious 'til they start leaving. Once they get the picture, the county will empty out. Uriah, you're a deputy sheriff, you foreclose on their properties and Albert, you change the county records showing they defaulted, or whatever, and transfer the properties to some corporation we dream up so our names don't show up. We can lease the land from the corporation and do whatever we like with it. And we'll be paying ourselves rent. That was the man's idea. He knows what he's talking about."

Jimmy laughed. "That sounds easy enough. I could use some more land. There's four nigger landowners up in my quadrant."

Each of the men grabbed a beer and clanged their bottles together.

"To the Klan, the land, and a white United States of America," LeGrand said. "God bless us."

Napier peeled the label off the Bud and stared at the bottle. "Now, Mayor, if I was listening correctly you said that was the first thing. Does this man have anything else in mind?"

LeGrand pulled a cigar out of his suit coat pocket and ran it under his veined nose. He retrieved a gold cigar cutter and butane lighter from his pants pocket, clipped one end of the panatela, pierced the other, and placed it in his mouth. His head swiveled looking at each one and pounded his index finger on the table. "This stays here."

Albert nodded and looked at Uriah, who did the same and turned to Napier, "Sure thing."

LeGrand flicked the lighter and a two-inch flame danced back and forth as he drew on the cigar. He exhaled, the smoke clouded the air and he leaned forward and whispered. "He wants a shooter. Anybody know one that could be counted on? Somebody that might be willing to leave the country if need be?"

Albert rested his chin in his hand and shook his head.

Uriah glanced down, traced his index finger through initials carved in the table and said nothing.

Napier stuffed the label into the empty beer bottle, "I know somebody like that."

The Mayor nodded at Albert and Uriah. "Excuse us."

Napier watched them saunter to the bar, slid his chair closer to the mayor and whispered. "I got this distant cousin that's running from the law. Ain't seen him for awhile myself. The man could shoot the balls off a squirrel. Probably be only too happy to leave the country."

The Mayor tugged his ear. "You think your cousin can be trusted? He'll do what he's told to do and not talk about it?"

Napier laughed. "He runnin' from the law. Don't talk to nobody. Give him cash, he'll do anything you want. What they want him to set his sights on?"

"I don't rightly know. The man asked me if I could find somebody good with a rifle and that's what I'm doing. I doubt I'll ever know more. But that's all right. You get in touch with your cousin and let me know how that fares. I'll call my man and see if I need to pursue this any further."

***

Celeste wiped the coffee off the stairs, washed and waxed the floor, and fixed supper for her and Junior. After supper she carried a bowl of chicken soup to her mother's room, gently moved her hip against the door, opening it. She looked at her mother's sallow face. "Momma would you like some soup?"

Her mother raised her hand and motioned with her fingers. "Thank you, honey. That would be nice."

Celeste put the soup down on the nightstand, fluffed a pillow, and helped her mother sit up. "How you feeling, momma?"

"I'm so tired." She swallowed a spoonful of soup and placed her hand on Celeste's arm. "I know he's hard on you, baby. He had a hard upbringing."

"Hard on me? I don't know how you put up with him. You had to raise me and Junior by yourself. He's out drinking and running around with his Klan friends."

"Shush now, don't talk like that about your father. He means well, he just don't know any better."

"Momma, I hear you the nights he don't come home…hear you crying. It ain't got to be like that." Her mother didn't respond and Celeste gave her another spoonful of soup. "You know Irma Ferris. She took her kids and left her husband. She's doing just fine." She held another spoonful up to her mother's lips.

Her mother raised her hand before her lips and shook her head. She slumped down on the pillow, pulled the blanket up to her chin, and rolled over facing the wall.

Celeste understood her mother's unspoken words. Her father had broken her mother's will and Celeste was prying into a place a daughter shouldn't go. As she returned to the kitchen she felt her face burning and her stomach roiling. She threw the bowl into the sink shattering it into pieces. "Damn him."

Winter's dusk brought a chill to the old farmhouse. Celeste stoked the black pot-belly stove in the living room and added more wood from the stack behind the house. Celeste and Junior sat next to each other covered by an army blanket on a patched sofa facing the stove. She read *Green Eggs and Ham* to her little brother until he fell asleep, and then carried him up the stairs to his bedroom across from hers in the attic.

She retired to her own room and began reading her favorite Harlequin romance story. She lived vicariously through her books. Going places she was sure she would never see. Doing things she was sure she would never do. Like falling in love.

Her dream world was interrupted by the roar of her father's truck pulling up in front of the house. She put her book on the nightstand, turned off the lamp, and sat in the dark, listening. The truck door slammed. She heard him stumble onto the porch and fumble with his keys trying to unlock the door. Finally the door opened, knocking into the wall behind it.

"Celeste, the chicken shit is still on the goddamn porch," Napier yelled. "You better get down here now and scrub it."

"Oh, shit." She heard him coming up the stairs. Her door opened, and he stood framed in the doorway. The odor of cheap whiskey and cigarette tobacco seeped into her room.

"What the hell did I tell you?" He slid his belt out from his jeans.

She pulled the cover up to her neck, "Daddy, I'm sorry. I did the floors and before I knew it, it was suppertime, Junior was hungry and then momma. It just slipped my mind."

His belt hung suspended from his hand. "I want you to scrub that porch on your hands and knees."

She crept out of bed and circled the room, her back against the wall, slipping through the narrow space between her father and the doorframe. She was one step past him when his belt buckle lashed across her back. She fell into the railing for support. Tears rushed down her face. *Damn you. I hate you so much.* Her knuckles whitened as she gripped the railing. She gritted her teeth, walked down the stairs to the kitchen for the bucket, scrub brush and hot water.

The next morning she awoke sleeping on her side. She rolled onto her back and a shooting pain from the welt left by her father's belt buckle brought tears to her eyes. Then she heard his footfalls on the steps and the door shook with a loud knock.

"We need breakfast. Get downstairs and fix it."

"Okay, Daddy." She grimaced. "I'll be down in a second."

He thumped down the stairs.

Over breakfast he said, "I got to go into town again. You check with your momma and see if she feels like eatin'. I want you to clean the bathroom and the upstairs today, and don't forget Junior's room. He's coming into town with me. And do a real good job with the bathroom. You hear?" He dropped a cigarette butt into a half-empty coffee cup and listened to it sizzle. "You know how your momma likes that bathroom cleaned. Oh, yeah, them niggers are coming back to finish up today. Shoulda been here by now. They almost move as slow as you, Celeste. I jus' might have to take a belt to them." He shook his head, "And they expect to get paid. Junior, I hope you learning from all this grief I got to go through."

"You gonna take me to a Klan meeting, Daddy?"

"I told you for your birthday. You get to meet some men that know how to stand up for what they believe."

Junior jumped up and spun around. "See, Celeste, I told you Daddy was going to take me."

Napier pushed the red hair off of hid son's face. "Gonna take you for a haircut. You don't want to look like a little girl. Do ya? He's gonna be one hell of a man when he grows up. Ain't he, Celeste?"

Celeste pursed her lips as she stood over the sink washing the dishes, "Yeah, Daddy, he's gonna be just like you."

Napier smiled at his son. "OK, Junior, get your things and let's go." He turned to his daughter, "You to take care of things here while we're gone."

She looked at him. Her stomach tightened. "Go..." she paused. She wanted to tell him, "Go to hell." But instead she took a deep breath and said. "Go ahead, Daddy, I'll take care of everything." Then she thought of what Beauford had said: "I don't want you to get hurt." No one had ever said that to her before.

# Chapter Two

Celeste watched Junior skipping behind his father. He opened the driver's door and the little boy clambered into the pickup truck and slid across to the passenger side. His father climbed in and slammed the door. The engine roared and the Ram Charger fishtailed away from the house, spiraling a cloud of red dust.

She collapsed onto the sofa, her chin sinking to her chest and eyes welling. The phone on the kitchen wall rang. She stood. "Tommy Hays, I hope that's you. I'll give you a piece of my mind and then listen as you plead with me to go out with you." Celeste slid her hands down her night gown pressing out the wrinkles, sauntered into the kitchen, and picked up the phone, "Hello."

"Guess what, Celeste? Tommy Hays gave me his ring last night."

Celeste sunk into a kitchen chair. Her head dropped and her free arm swung between her legs. "Oh…oh, that's nice, Cindy."

"You gonna be in school?"

She rubbed her palm across her eyes. "I don't know. My momma being sick and all."

"Well, girl. How you gonna graduate if you don't go to school?"

"Least of my problems right now."

"Tommy said when we get out of school in June we gonna get out of this godforsaken hick place. Goin' to Jackson, gettin' married and live in a fine house."

Celeste squeezed her eyes shut and bit her lip.

"You there?" Cindy asked.

"Yeah."

"Can you keep a secret?"

"Uh huh."

"Celeste, we did it. We went all the way."

Her face reddened and heart pounded in her throat. "You really believe him about gettin' married? That redneck told me the same thing when he tried to get in my pants. I can't believe you're so dumb to fall for that line, you little slut."

"You lyin' bitch. He told me he never even liked you. Had no interest in fucking you and—"

Celeste slammed the phone down as tears cascaded from her eyes. She covered her face with her hands.

She wandered into the living room and lay across the sofa. *I hate my goddamn life. What am I gonna do? All men are just like my father, assholes. I got to get away from here.* She needed an escape, to have some form of pleasure. Her hand slipped between her legs. She groaned and took a deep breath. Her heart hammered and her breathing quickened. She heard the sound of a truck in the distance. The rumble of the engine grew louder. "Shit."

She lifted herself from the couch and looked through the window. Her father's truck was speeding down the gravel road toward the house. "Why can't they leave me alone?"

The truck came to a skidding halt. The passenger door opened and Junior ran to the front door.

A guttural sound came from her mother's bedroom.

"Oh no," She cradled her head with both hands as the door flew open and Junior stormed in.

"Where's Momma's prescription? Daddy forgot it."

"I don't know and Momma's sick again. I got to go clean her up."

"He's in a hurry. You better help me find it."

"Celeste, I threw up, come help me!" Her voice came from the back of the house.

"I'm coming Mama. Be there in a minute." She grabbed Junior's hand and dragged him into the kitchen. "There, it's right next to his Salems. You better take them or he'll be pissed that he forgot those too."

Junior grabbed the pack and put a cigarette between his lips. "I'm gonna have a smoke on the way into town."

"It wouldn't surprise me." She grabbed the prescription and slammed it into his chest. You better take that and get out of here before Daddy comes lookin' for you."

"Ow, you hurt me. I'm gonna tell Daddy."

She clenched her teeth and pointed to the front door, "Get out."

The boy spun around and ran out of the house with the pack of cigarettes in his shirt pocket, the prescription in one hand and a Salem dangling from his mouth.

"Celeste, are you here? Come and clean me up please. This smell is making me sicker."

"I'm coming Mama." She poured water and soap into a bucket, grabbed the mop and trudged to her mother's room. The bedroom window was covered by blinds. The room was dark and a picture of Jesus hung on the wall. Her mother's emaciated body was covered by a faded yellow and blue patchwork quilt. The stench of her mother's vomit hovered in the air and her bile was splattered across the quilt and the wood floor. Celeste felt her stomach turn. "Oh, Mama. I'm gonna have to change you, the bedding, and clean the floor."

"I'm sorry." Her boney arm jutted out from under the cover and pointed at the floor." Mop that up first. Most of it's down there. You gotta get that smell out of here. Gonna make me puke again."

Celeste cleaned the floor, helped her mother out of her soiled nightgown, dressed her, and put clean sheets on the bed.

"Thanks for taking care of me, honey."

"Daddy wants me to quit school so I can take care of you and work around the farm."

"Well, honey? What good is school gonna do you? You probably gonna marry some nice local boy and start pushing out babies in a year or two."

"Momma, I want to have a life. I can't see spending the rest of it on a farm. I want to go to the city and getta job and maybe even go to college."

"Celeste, you're such a dreamer. It isn't so bad here."

"Mama, I got nothin' here. The one boy I liked turned out to be a jerk. He's gonna marry Cindy and they movin' to Jackson."

"That's jus talk. Even if they do I betcha they come back. People from here don't fit in the big city. This is the only place for us. Everything you need you can find here."

"Mama, you're as hopeless as everyone else around here." Celeste picked up the dirty bed linen and night clothes off the floor and held them under one arm and the mop and bucket with the other hand. As she passed the back room she threw the dirtied items at the washing machine. Then she dumped the water from the bucket into the toilet and flushed it. "Another great day for me. Let's see, should I hop in my Mustang convertible and drive into town to have my nails done? No, I'd much rather clean Junior's room and the bathrooms." She took an imaginary cigarette from between her lips and tapped the ashes onto the floor like her father, 'You know how your momma likes that bathroom cleaned. Them niggers coming back today. They almost move as slow as you, Celeste. I might have to take a belt to them.' She went to the kitchen sink and splashed water in the bucket, cleaning the remnants of her mother's sickness and mumbled, "Fuck you, Daddy and fuck this place."

As she rinsed the bucket, the red pickup truck pulled up next to the barn. She watched Beauford take a tool box out of the back and slip between the doors of the barn. She wondered where his two friends were.

She thought about how gentle Beauford seemed yesterday. How concerned he was about her father seeing them together and hurting her. He wasn't consumed with hatred. He was concerned about her, not a danger to her. It was ironic that her life was just like Beauford's—a prisoner of her father.

She opened the coffee can, scooped the grounds into the percolator. As the coffee brewed she realized that Beauford was the only person she knew who didn't look down on her. With two cups of coffee in hand she left the kitchen. Stepping off the porch, she felt the warmth of the sun through her nightgown and the chill of the perspiration evaporating from between her breasts.

Celeste pushed against the partially open barn door just enough to step inside. Beauford faced the back wall, building a new stall. She walked toward him, set his coffee down on the barrel, and touched his shoulder.

Beauford jerked back.

She smiled and thought of the last time she was in a barn with a man. A landslide of emotions hit her—the hurt and the excitement. Her heart quickened and she wasn't sure what she was feeling. She just knew that there was something about the contrast of her fair skin and his brown skin that was arousing and wondered what kissing his lips would be like. She wanted to live life, not be shackled by it. Her heart raced.

He stepped back. "Miss Celeste please. You better go back to the house."

"No, everybody uses me…. it's my time now. I want a life, everybody else has one. Why can't I?" Her breath quickened. *Fuck Tommy. Fuck Cindy. I'm a woman. I want to be touched like one.* She fixated on the rise and fall of his broad chest. The sweat glistening on his forehead. She stepped toward him, fascinated by his coffee colored skin.

He grasped her arms and gently pushed her away. "No, Miss Celeste, you don't want to do this."

Celeste threw her coffee cup to the ground. The handle cracked off and the contents spilled. She grabbed the shoulder of her nightgown and ripped it. "You a sweet man. Don't make me say you took me. You know that would be real bad for you." She lunged forward, put her hand behind his neck, pulled him toward her, and kissed him. The softness of his lips and the gentleness of the kiss surprised Celeste. She took a deep breath, inhaling the aroma of his body. She heard her heart throbbing in her throat. She wanted more and fingered the metal hooks on his overalls and they dropped to the floor. Celeste pulled Beauford's tee shirt over his head and he stood there, head down, arms by his side, naked.

***

Beauford trembled. He wanted to run out of the barn but he hadn't felt the passion of a woman like this for a long time. Maybe it was the danger that made it exciting. At first, he didn't know if he could resist her. Then he wanted her. In that split second he decided he needed this, something that would soothe the ache deep in his chest. Something that would give him a sense of wholeness, even if it just covered the pain for a moment.

***

Celeste pushed him away and dropped her nightgown. She reached out and lifted his chin, making him take a good look at her. Stepping forward, she put her arms around him and kissed his neck. Slowly his arms enveloped her, her back arched as he touched the swollen bruise on her back. "My father," she said. Their anger at the man they both hated intensified their passion. She pressed herself against him as hard as she could, feeling her naked body against his. She felt his arms around her waist and they kissed again. She cupped her hand between his legs and felt him harden and heard him groan. Listened to his breath—fast and short.

They went to their knees, tongues dancing together, and lay down on the straw. Celeste rolled onto her back and Beauford hovered over her, his arms extended. She wanted this to last, to make up for everything she had missed. She wanted to taste him, to smell his scent.

She felt him sucking and biting. Her nipples were in pleasure and then pain. Then his groin thrust into hers. She dug her fingernails into his back and felt his skin breaking. His hips moved faster and faster. Beauford groaned and she panted, releasing everything she felt, everything she needed, and gently he lay down on top of her before rolling to her side. Celeste rested her head on his shoulder. *Don't matter about my father or Cindy or Tommy anymore.* She closed her eyes and they lay there together for an hour.

Celeste raised her head from Beauford's shoulder. She heard the faint rumble of an engine in the distance. The rumble of a truck engine grew louder. She shook Beauford. "Get up, somebody's comin'." The engine became quiet, doors slammed shut, and gravel crunched under heavy footfalls.

They stood up, brushed the hay off their bodies, and jumped into their clothes.

"You better go and forget this ever happened," he said, shaking up the hay to remove the impressions of their bodies.

"I just wanted to have a life like everyone else."

Beauford waved his hand. "Jus go before your father comes in here and finds you."

She shook the straw from her hair and ran to the door without looking back. She stopped at the door, took a deep breath and held her head high as she walked through the chickens toward the house.

Napier stormed out of the front door. "I see that you ain't done nothing around here."

"I took a nap. I thought you'd be gone all day and I'd clean the upstairs later."

Napier's eyes shot to the red pickup. "Took a nap? Well, where the hell you coming from if you were sleeping?"

"I was checking," her eyes glanced down, "...on the nigger. See if he was working. Thought you tole me to do that."

He grabbed her arm. "You ain't done a fucking thing in the house that I told you to do. And you go prancing in front of that nigger in your nightgown like a whore. You going in the house right now and gettin' that stuff done." He grabbed her arm and dragged her into the house. He noticed the torn nightgown. A deep furrow jutted down the middle of his forehead. "You making a fool out of me? How'd your nightgown get torn?" He pushed her down to the floor.

She looked at him. The skin under his eyes quivered. "I...I bent down and it got stuck on a cabinet knob in the kitchen."

"You lyin'. I know it. Now I gotta go out there and kick that nigger's ass."

Celeste trembled as she rose from the floor. "He didn't do nothing. Leave him alone. He jus doin' what you want him to."

"No daughter of mine is flaunting herself in front of a nigger." Napier grabbed a pump shotgun from the hall closet. He jacked the slide back, grabbed four shells from the box on the closet shelf, loaded the shotgun and chambered a round. He charged out of the house.

Beauford was dropping his tool box into the back of his truck.

"Hey, fuckin' nigger where you goin'?" He brought the stock of the shotgun to his shoulder.

Beauford ran to the door and jumped into the truck.

Napier squeezed the trigger and the shotgun blasted the pickup's rear window out.

\*\*\*

Beauford was covered in glass. He leaned into the steering wheel, turned the key and the engine turned over and sputtered. He glanced over his shoulder.

Napier lowered the shotgun and strutted toward the Beauford. "You better get out of that truck, nigger."

The engine caught and oily smoke belched from the exhaust. Beauford shifted into gear and the truck rolled forward.

Napier shouldered the shotgun and squeezed off another shot. The buckshot pelted the side of the truck like a snare drum.

Beauford pushed the accelerator to the floor and sped around the back side of the house. He glanced in the rearview mirror and saw Napier running after him pulling off the last two rounds from the shotgun.

Beauford's truck headed down the gravel road.

\*\*\*

Napier mumbled, "Celeste, what did you do?"

He looked at the kitchen window and saw Celeste holding a dish cloth against her mouth. He marched into the house.

Celeste stared down at the dishes she was washing.

"What made that nigger run like that?"

Celeste was silent.

He walked behind her, grabbed her shoulder and spun her around. "Why'd that nigger run?"

Her chin dropped to her chest. "Don't know. He scared of you like everybody is."

Napier rested the shotgun against the sink and folded his arms. "You don't kick 'em around, shoot at 'em they don't respect you." He pulled the Salems out of his shirt pocket and slipped a smoke between his lips. "You ever do anything stupid you gonna be treated jus like that nigger." He flicked a match with his thumbnail and lifted it to his cigarette, inhaled and blew the smoke into Celeste's face.

He grabbed the shotgun, turned and strolled to the kitchen table. "Make me some lunch and get me that address book Momma keeps?"

Celeste had no desire to risk raising his anger again. She dried her hands, slid to the cabinet next to the sink and pulled a worn spiral notebook out of the drawer. "Here it is, Daddy."

Napier set the shotgun against the kitchen wall, grabbed the notebook and placed it on the table. He flipped halfway through the pages. "Here it is." His fingers locked on the handset and dialed the number. "Auntie Grace, this is your nephew, Jimmy Napier…How you doing?…Oh, that's too bad…How's your son?  Still running from the law? Well, I'm glad they haven't caught up with him…Can you get a word to him, ask him to gim me call? I got some friends that might be able to help him with his legal problem. And he can make some money too. Okay, and it was good talking to you too."

A vision came to Napier's mind as he hung up the phone. He stared at Celeste filling the bucket at the sink, clenched his fist and his knuckles whitened.

*** 

A few days later Celeste was at the stove preparing the family's dinner. Pork chops sizzled in a black cast iron skillet and homemade rolls baked in the oven. She poured boiled potatoes into a colander, draining the water into the white enamel sink, dumped the potatoes into a bowl, and started mashing them. Finally, she turned down the flame under a pot of simmering collard greens. Napier sat at the kitchen table playing solitaire and Junior sat across from him.

"Can I play too, Daddy?" he asked.

Napier picked up his beer, took a sip, and put the bottle down. "Not now, Junior, I'm concentrating." He looked at Celeste. "Your momma always had supper on the table at six sharp. It's a quarter past already. When we gonna eat?"

"I'm trying the best I can." Celeste wiped the sweat from her brow.

"When can I play?" Junior said.

Napier took a drag on his smoke, glanced from the cards to Junior and back at the three cards he pulled from the deck and lay on the table. The telephone rang. Napier leaned back and put his feet against the chrome table legs. "Somebody get that."

"I'm busy making dinner. Besides, if it's Cindy, I don't want to talk to her."

Napier pulled the cigarette out of his mouth, grimaced in her direction and nodded at Junior, "Make yourself useful and get the phone for Daddy."

Junior slid off his chair and scampered over to the phone. "Hello…Yeah…Daddy, it's for you."

"Who is it?" The cigarette wobbled in his mouth.

"I don't know. He didn't say."

"Can't sit down and relax for a minute." Napier stood and walked to the wall phone. "Yeah…Yeah, I called you…The guy needs to meet with you…He's the Imperial Wizard…Yeah, he said money and out of the country…I don't know. You'll have to find out from him…You close?…When can you get here?…Midnight tomorrow. My barn. All right, I'll tell him. See you then." Napier hung up the phone and returned to his chair.

"Who was that, Daddy?" Junior asked.

"A distant cousin. You don't know him." He picked up the cards, shuffled them, and drew the top three, turning over a jack of spades. "Damn it. Can't get me a red one when I need it."

"Supper's ready. Junior, set the table," Celeste said.

Junior put both elbows on the table. "What's his name?"

"You heard your sister. Go get the plates so we can finally eat." He flicked an ash to the floor.

"I wanna know his name."

Napier picked up the cards and slipped a rubber band around them. His eyes narrowed and he cracked his knuckles. "Damn it, boy, you jus like a woman. Got to know everything." Napier raised his leg, shoved the sole of his boot into his son's chest knocking him to the floor. "Now you be like a good little girl and get your butt over to the dishes and set the table so your daddy can finally get something to eat."

# Chapter Three

The mayor sat at his usual table in the Dixie Lounge, a half empty long-neck bottle in his hand and the Confederate flag hanging on the wall behind him. He glanced at his watch, 11:40 p.m. *Time to meet the shooter.* He left the bar wearing a black coat, white shirt with an open collar and the long-neck bottle in his hand. He slid into the seat of his Lincoln, slammed the door, put the bottle between his legs and leaned across the seat. He unlocked the glove compartment and pulled out a Colt Cobra .38 special with a two-inch barrel. He snapped open the cylinder to check that all six rounds were loaded. With a flick of his wrist the cylinder clicked shut, and he slipped the pistol under the waistband of his slacks on his right hip.

The temperature was only a few degrees above freezing, but he lowered the convertible top and cranked the heater on full blast, feeling the push of warm air on his face. One of his pleasures in life was feeling the wind billowing over the windshield, through his silver hair and watching the stars fill the night sky. He pulled out of the parking lot of the Dixie Lounge, headed across Railroad Street and through the town square. The quiet of the night interrupted by the clanging of the lanyard against the flagpole. He headed north on Oak Avenue through the heart of town, past juke joints that blasted honky-tonk music through plywood walls. He smelled the greasy smoke of creosote from burning railroad ties in fifty-five gallon drums that black men danced around. The gray smoke cascaded into the night sky while the men drank beer and whiskey out of bottles wrapped in brown paper bags. On the outskirts of town, Oak Avenue turned into Route 49W and he was surrounded by the flat terrain and remnants of last fall's cotton harvest. The mayor punched the accelerator. He was pushed back in his seat and listened to the engine roar as the speedometer jumped up to 100 miles per hour. He grabbed the beer between his legs, brought it up to his lips, drained it and tossed it towards the scrub cotton plants besides the road.

He rifled his hand through a cardboard box on the passenger seat, found his favorite eight-track and pushed it into the tape player. The mayor turned up the volume and shouted the lyrics with Johnny Cash to a *Ring of Fire*. He let up on the gas pedal and the Lincoln slowed to fifty. His heart quickened as the words of the song hit home and made him wonder what he was getting into meeting this shooter. He swallowed and shut off the tape. Even for the Imperial Wizard this was a step further than he'd ever gone.

Four miles up the highway, he turned east onto a gravel road and in the distance saw a light shining from Jimmy Napier's farm house. He eased up on the Lincoln so the gravel wouldn't chip the paint and pulled in front of the clapboard house.

Napier stood on the porch, a Salem dangling from his mouth and a flashlight in his left hand. He wore bib overalls tucked into brown leather boots, a red flannel shirt and a denim jacket. He flicked the cigarette onto the ground and walked to the driver's side of the car. The beam of the flashlight bounced along the ground. Napier leaned both elbows on the door. "You must be freezing your ass off."

The mayor brushed his fingers through his hair and glanced in the rearview mirror. "Nothing like fresh Mississippi night air. Very invigorating. Your boy here?"

"Don't know. Said he'd meet us in the barn. It's a little past midnight. Maybe he's in there."

"Don't see any car." The mayor said.

Napier shrugged.

The Mayor nodded toward the barn. "Let's go see."

Napier backed away from the door and the mayor climbed out. He pulled the lapels of his suit coat up around his neck and tugged at the sleeves, straightening the wrinkles out of the elbows.

They walked across the yard toward the faded red barn. The Mayor looked up at Napier. "What'd you tell him?"

"Wasn't much I could tell him. Somebody willing to pay him to shoot somebody and that man will get him out of the country."

"What's your boy's name?"

"Said he'd talk to you direct. You don't need his name 'til then."

The mayor cocked his head. "That's bullshit. You expect me to talk to somebody about something like this and not know who I'm talking to."

Napier shrugged. "Well, that's up to you."

The mayor stopped and grabbed Napier's arm. "What's his name?"

Napier shook his arm loose, pulled a pack of Salems from his shirt pocket and slipped one between his lips. "You can ask him when you see him." He leaned over, struck a match on the side of his boot and lit his smoke. "If you're not happy with that it's outta my hands."

The mayor shook his head. "I got to know his name. He's got to be checked out. He's got to be willing to do what he's told. He can't be setting the rules to his own liking. That's not going to work."

"Mayor, you asked me if I knew somebody that was good with a rifle. I said I did and arranged for you to meet him just like you asked. I can't tell the man what he's supposed to do and say."

"We're not starting off on the right foot." The mayor dragged his fingers through his hair. Let's get in there." He stepped toward the barn and mumbled, "Fuckin' rednecks."

The hinges creaked as Napier pulled the barn door open. They stepped into the barn and Napier pointed the flashlight around the interior. The beam circled past the tractor, stacks of rough sawn, the open space in the wall where Beauford Tisdale tore down the rotted pieces, bales of hay, and up at the loft. "Hey, you in here?"

There was no response.

The mayor looked at his watch. "It's 10 after. He's supposed to be here already."

Napier sat on a bale of hay. "Give him a chance. I'm sure he'll be here shortly."

SINS OF THE FATHER

The mayor pulled a cigar out of his inside jacket pocket, clipped off the end and lit it with his lighter. "This boy has got to be reliable or we're gonna have to get somebody else."

Napier blew smoke rings into the air. "I don't know anybody else and either did Uriah or Albert. Jesus Christ, Mayor. It's not like you can hang a sign in the town square, 'Looking for somebody to shoot somebody."

The mayor circled the interior of the barn for the next ten minutes dragging on his cigar and looking through the opening between the barn doors. "The man ain't gonna want somebody that's not reliable. Your friend's pissing me off."

Napier pointed to another bale of hay. "Why don't you sit a spell, give him some time."

"My reputation is on line with this man. He's not the kind of man you want to cross. He don't know you from shit or shinola but I got a reputation at stake."

Napier's face reddened. "Look, I did what you asked me to do. If it don't work out, ain't nothing I can do about it."

The mayor glanced at his watch and jabbed his cigar at Napier. "It's 12:30 and he isn't here. I told the man that I had somebody for the job. I'm going to look like a fool. He's a half-hour late and for Christ sake I bet he's not gonna show. Probably lying drunk on the floor of some juke joint and he's gonna be a shooter and get sent out of the country. You fuckin' rednecks are no better than niggers."

Napier shot off the bale of hay and jabbed his finger in the mayor's chest knocking him two feet back. "I've had it with your whining about you and the man. If you're so fuckin' important get a shooter yourself. It all sounds like horseshit to me anyway. I'm going in the house. You can do what you want." Napier shoved the flashlight in the mayor's chest and barged out of the barn.

The mayor stood there, hands wrapped around the flashlight mumbling. "What the hell am I gonna do now? This peckerwood doesn't show, the man's gonna think I'm just like the rest of these rednecks."

The mayor circled around, pointing the beam around the interior of the barn. He lowered the light to his side and exhaled.

"Douse your light." A voice said.

The mayor switched off the flashlight and a shadow of a man stepped through the open space in the back wall. A high beam glared in the mayor's face. "I know from listening to you that you didn't want any rednecks around so I waited 'til we had a little privacy, Mr. Mayor."

The mayor squinted and put his hand in front of his face blocking the glare. "You been here all this time? Making me wait?"

The man took a couple of steps forward. "I'm sure Jimmy told you I'm running from the law so I can't be too careful. Had to make sure this wasn't some kind of lawman's scheme to get me arrested. Can't trust nobody nowadays."

The man didn't smell like someone on the run. The mayor smelled the aroma of soap and Old Spice. He nodded and lowered the cigar out of his mouth. "That's good. It's good to be careful. Why don't you get that light out of my face?"

The man shut off his flashlight. "So what is it that your people want done?"

He put down his hand, lifted the cigar to his mouth, drew on it, and the ashes glowed. "I don't know. All I know is that they'll pay you $5,000 cash up front. After you finish the job, they'll give you another $5,000 and get you a couple of passports under different names so you can get out of the country."

The man pulled on his right ear. "I'm supposed to agree to this without having the slightest idea what I'm agreeing to?"

"You aren't going to decide nothing. I'm the one that's got to decide if you're the one."

The man laughed. "That so?"

"I got to know your name so I can have you checked out."

"I'll tell you my name when I think the time is right."

"Look, I'm beginning not to like you. But that isn't too important. I need to know if you can do what you supposed to do before we go any further. So, you any good with a rifle?"

The man spit a wad of tobacco to the ground. "I can shoot the balls off a squirrel at a hundred yards. Jimmy will swear to that."

"It don't really matter to me what Jimmy says. I need to see for myself."

The man nodded. "You're really impressed with yourself, ain't ya?"

The mayor folded his arms across his chest. "When I do something, I do it right."

The man tugged on his ear again. "That so? Then why you relying on a redneck like Jimmy to get ya a shooter."

"I'm liking you less and less." The mayor felt the .38 inching up on his waist. He wondered if he should end this here and look for someone else. This man's edgy. He wanted things on his terms. If he couldn't be trusted he's probably not the right man. But Jimmy was right, candidates to fill a shooter's vacancy were few and far between. "I need to see you shoot."

"You won't find a better man with a rifle."

"I know, you told me. But it don't matter what you say. If I don't see you shoot you won't be getting ten grand and you won't be getting out of the country. In fact the only thing you'll be getting is twenty years hard time in Parchman cause you a fugitive."

He cocked his head and put his hands on his hips. "You threatening me? Don't seem too smart to be threatening a man you been told is a shooter."

"You're not in the best place to be setting terms for negotiating. If you think this isn't a deal that's good for you, best turn around and get out of here. Or, if you think this is an opportunity you should take advantage of, we need to set up a time for me to see you shoot right now."

"All right. I'll meet you behind this barn at dawn. I got my own rifle and I'll show you how I shoot."

"Dawn? Shit it's 10 to 1 now."

"As you pointed out, I'm a fugitive, so I can't be running around in the daytime toting a rifle. You want to see some shootin', I'll show you some shootin'. See you at dawn." He turned and walked toward the opening in the back wall.

The Mayor's brow furrowed. "You son of a bitch. Who do you think you are telling me to meet you at dawn? Where do you think you're going? Hey, I'm not done with you. I need your name. What's your name? Where you staying at?"

The man put one leg through the opening in the wall and turned to look at the Mayor. "You ain't hired me yet. You don't need my name. I'll tell ya when and if you do."

"What if I need to get in touch with you?"

"Leave a message at the Delta Boarding House in Greenville for John Willard. I'll get it. See you at dawn." He turned around and lifted his other foot through the opening, disappearing into the night.

# CHAPTER FOUR

After a sleepless night Mayor LeGrand followed the same route he took five hours earlier. This time, shortly before sunrise, everything was different. There wasn't any music coming from the juke joints and no blacks were dancing around burning fires at the gas station; just glowing embers drifting in the wind from the remnants of burnt railroad ties. He passed dormant cotton fields going less than the speed limit.

The convertible top was up and the tape deck off. In the quiet darkness he pondered what lay ahead and if there was some way to distance himself from the hollow feeling in his gut. He felt inside his coat pocket for the envelope he had carried with him since a week before he told Uriah, Albert, and Napier that his man was looking for a shooter. It had been folded and creased in his nervous attempts to hide it from prying eyes. The envelope was next to a stainless steel flask that he had nearly drained since his first encounter with the shooter. He recalled the meeting in Jackson with the man who ordered the assassin.

"Under no circumstances are you to open this envelope. When you're absolutely certain, and I mean absolutely, that you have found the shooter. You give it to him, have him read it and then burn it. If the shooter decides it's not for him. You've got to get rid of him. You understand what I mean?"

The mayor reached for the wooden grips of the Colt 38 tucked in his waistband. Beads of sweat rolled from his armpits soaking his shirt. The grips felt hard and cold tucked against his damp shirt. He pulled his hand down his face and felt the stubble on his cheeks. He slowed down to twenty and pulled onto the gravel road leading to Napier's farm.

He doused his headlights, parked behind the barn and looked to the east. The sky was turning from black to gray, but the sun still hadn't crested over the horizon. The hands on the dashboard clock read, 6:20. Sunrise would be at 6:32.

The mayor turned the key and the engine quieted. The warm air jetting from the heater stopped. He sat in the leather seat feeling the cold creep into his bones. He pulled out the flask. The envelope stuck to the beads of condensation on the shiny steel, then peeled away and tumbled down next to the accelerator. He glanced at the envelope, unscrewed the cap on the flask and drained the whiskey. It burned his throat and churned his stomach.

He tossed the flask toward the passenger side. It clanged against the door and bounced to the floor. LeGrand tapped his index finger on the face of his watch to make sure it hadn't stopped. The gold second hand swept past the twelve, 6:22. He leaned over, clutched the envelope, exhaled and folded his arms across his chest crushing the envelope.

He shivered and turned the engine on, felt the warm air against his face and leaned back into the seat. He thought about the man he met five hours ago. He didn't seem like a man on the run. He was clean and groomed. But everything else about him was aggravating, that constant tugging at his right ear. He had that arrogant attitude of someone who couldn't cope with being told what to do. *Omens are warnings.*

He dropped the envelope onto the passenger seat, pressed on the brake and shifted the Lincoln into gear. The dashboard clock glowed, 6:29. *Three minutes, three minutes.* He looked east and saw a thin orange line breaking the horizon. He shut off the engine.

The mayor drummed his fingers on the steering wheel. *If he's late again, that's it. I'm gone.* A white ball peaked over the horizon. Golden rays stretched up and muddled through the dark shadows of the clouds. Gray streaks reached across the sky. He raised his wrist. It was 6:35. "That son of a bitch."

He swung the door open, stepped out of the car, slammed it shut, walked past the front fender and gazed down the far side of the barn, "Goddamn it." He marched back and stepped through the gap in the back wall of the barn.

"If you're in here you better get you ass out here cause I'm going in one minute."

There was no response.

The mayor stepped out of the barn. He looked over the roof of his car, eyed the empty fields and kicked the ground. A cloud of red dust had settled on the white Lincoln. He knelt beside the car and brushed off the dirt with his sleeve. He grimaced, walked past the trunk and looked down the other side of the barn. There was no one to be seen. He swirled, took a step back to the car.

Bang.

Shards of red plastic from the tail light exploded into the air and ricocheted off the mayor.

He dove to the ground in front of the rear tire. Gasping, his mouth filled with red dust. His heart raced and shoulder muscles tightened. His fingers clawed the earth. He listened for footfalls. The only sound was the wind whistling through the gaps in the barn wall. He lifted his head and looked over his shoulder; didn't see anyone. Except for his pistol that had scattered across the red earth and lay under the front tire.

LeGrand raised himself to his hands and knees, then to his haunches. He reached for the handle of the driver's door.

He heard the whang of a rifle shot.

The side view mirror exploded off the door. Shards of glass erupted into the air. Blood bubbled from the capillaries on the mayor's forehead.

He rolled on the ground, grabbed the pistol, and ran to the front of the car. He ducked behind the headlight, pulled out a white handkerchief and waved it in the air. "All right you son of bitch. I've seen enough." He yelled. There was no response. He peeked over the fender, his hand gripping the pistol shaking, and peered across the gravel road a hundred yards away. Through the blood trickling over his eyes he saw a figure jump out of a live oak. The man strutted in his direction. A rifle yoked across his shoulders. "It's that fucker." He lodged the pistol in his waistband and pressed the handkerchief against his forehead soaking up the blood.

For the first time the mayor saw the man in daylight. He was in his early thirties, slender, wore black-rimmed glasses and his blue eyes stood out against his pale skin. He had a long narrow nose, brown hair slicked back, and a receding hairline.

\*\*\*

The man stopped at the driver's door of the Lincoln. "Mr. Mayor, you can get up from behind your car. Ain't nothing gonna happen to you." He had a thin smile that twisted at the right corner of his mouth.

The mayor lowered the soaked handkerchief and looked at his blood. "You could have killed me, you son of bitch."

The man tugged on his right ear. "Only if I wanted to."

The mayor rose from his crouched position. His chest rising and falling with each breath. He brushed the dirt off his coat with his free hand.

"You wanted to see me shoot. So I was just giving you what you wanted. Good thing you ain't a squirrel. You'd be a gelding." He laughed.

Blood seeped down the mayor's nose. He brushed his fingers across his face, looked at the red smeared across his hand and blotted his forehead with the handkerchief. He glanced at the chrome mirror holder dangling from the driver's door. "Look what you did to my beautiful car. Damn you." He marched to the door pushing the man away. "You could of shot tin cans or crows. No, you had to shoot my car." He caressed the door.

The man shrugged and laughed again. He lowered the rifle off his shoulder, rested the butt plate on his boot, and gripped the barrel in his hand, standing at a makeshift parade-rest.

The mayor turned his back to the man, swallowed, placed both hands on the door. His face reddened, *I ought to whip out my pistol, poke the barrel between his eyes and yank the trigger.* "You think this is funny?"

"Yeah."

The mayor lowered his head. *If I pull out the 38 I gotta kill him now without ever knowing if he'd do the job. He can shoot.* He heard the pounding footfalls of a running man and looked over his shoulder. "Ah fuck."

Jimmy Napier was scooting from the house in gray long johns carrying his shotgun. "What the hell happened?"

"Showing the mayor I could shoot the balls off a squirrel. Said he couldn't take my word or yours."

"You shot the mayor's car? Holy shit. You shot the mayor's car." He stamped his foot on the ground.

The mayor waved his handkerchief at Napier. "Get outta here. Get back in your house. Dealing with one peckerwood is enough. Don't need for you to be here."

"Holy shit, Mayor, you're bleeding."

"No shit. Get outta here. We got business to conduct."

The mayor watched Napier walk back to his house laughing all the way. He glanced at the upstairs window and saw Celeste peering through a space in the curtains. "Too many people around here."

"I can't stand around here all day. You seen me shoot. Am I your man or ain't I."

The mayor grabbed the chrome frame of the mirror. "You're going to pay for this."

"You can take it outta my $10,000."

The mayor's jaw flexed with irritation. "We need to go someplace where we can talk." He nodded at the passenger door and got behind the steering wheel.

The man got in the seat. Put the butt of his rifle on the floor and it clanged against the flask. He leaned over and picked up the flask, its top dangling from a chain. "No wonder you're so quarrelsome. You been drinking; eyes bloodshot, stubble on your cheeks, and bloody forehead. Got a lot on your mind, mayor?"

"Don't talk to me. Just sit there until you hear what I got to say."

"You know this here Remington Gamemaster 760, 30.06 is just about the best rifle ever made."

The mayor turned the key and the engine turned over. He drove off Napier's property and headed down the gravel road away from the highway.

The man held the flask up and peered into the open top. "Coulda saved me a sip." He flipped it over his shoulder onto the back seat, laid the rifle stock between his legs and rested the barrel against his shoulder. He fidgeted with the scope. "This here is a 2X7 power Redfield variable scope. Ain't nothing I couldn't bulls eye with this."

The mayor glanced at him.

He tugged on his ear.

The mayor checked his handkerchief. The blood was dry and he dropped it between his legs to the floor. "Why do you do that?"

"Do what?"

"Do what? You're always tugging on your goddamn ear. Just another thing about you that aggravates me."

"I do? Just a thing I do I guess." He tugged again.

The mayor turned north onto a dirt road. *He says no to this, I don't have much of chance—my 38 against his rifle. I got to get him out of the car without that rifle. Give him some preliminary bull.*

"You're my man, but if you want the $10,000 you got to give me some information."

"Like what?"

"Like where'd you learn to shoot?"

"I'm a small town boy. Lived in southern Illinois mostly, Alton and Quincy. Every boy went hunting. And the Army."

"What you do in the army?"

"Was an MP."

"Where'd you serve?""

"Germany mostly. Wanted to go there cause I liked the way the Nazis did things."

"How do you know Napier?"

"We're distant cousins or something like that."

"What're you running from?"

"I was doing twenty in the Missouri State Pen for forging some postal money orders. Took me three times, but I finally snuck out of there." He laughed and slapped his knee. "Worked in the kitchen baking bread. Use to put sixty loaves in a box that was sent to the prison farm. I jumped into a bread box and had a guy stack the bread on top of me. Got to the farm and walked away. My brother met me and drove me to Chicago. Simple as that. It's almost a year now."

"Where you been all this time?"

"I've been a man on the run. Worked up in Chicago for a while. Went to Canada, made some money smuggling stuff into Detroit. Can't stay one place any too long. Went down to Birmingham, then Mexico and over to LA, New Orleans, Atlanta and places I don't even remember."

He folded his arms across his chest and turned toward the mayor. "It's time for you to tell me, what am I shootin'? I got to be moving on if we don't do this."

The mayor turned into a thick stand of tall white oaks and tulip trees and then into a clearing that had the remains of a sixteen-foot charred cross. "This is where we have our important meetings."

"I gotta put a white hood on to be on this hallowed land?"

"Get serious for once." The mayor parked fifty yards in front of the cross. He opened his door. "Let's go for a walk."

The man jerked up the handle and pushed his muddy boot against the door. He stepped out and grabbed the rifle barrel.

"You don't need that."

"Hey, you never know. Could run across a mad dog or some fool thinking we're gonna take his still." He rested the stock between his bicep and ribs and held the forearm of the rifle in his palm.

The mayor stood at the open door, one foot on the ground and the other resting on the footrest. "All the locals know about this place. Know to stay away if they're not one of us."

The man pulled the slide back and let it go. A bullet snapped into the breech. "Yeah, well, what if some lawman comes cruising through here? I got to be prepared."

"Only lawman that comes through here is gonna be one of us."

"Not if he's wearing a suit and tie. That's FBI."

"If that happens they're after me not you." The mayor curled his lower lip. He was growing tired of the debate.

"They check they're files and find I'm wanted, they'll scoop me up."

"And if you're toting that rifle you'll be getting extra time."

He tugged on his ear, "The rifle ain't registered under my name. We could say it belongs to a friend of yours." He laid the rifle across the seat and closed the door.

The mayor exhaled, slid his hand across the side of his coat to feel the pistol grip, and slammed the door shut. He walked to the front of the car and was met by the man. "Come this way." They headed toward the cross. "You know you got to tell me your name."

"I told you I will when you hire me."

The mayor reached inside his coat pocket and pulled out an envelope. "What he wants you to do is written down in here."

"Let me see it."

"Not so fast."

"What's all this bullshit? You're the Klan. What you want me to do can't be nothing I wouldn't do anyway—hate niggers and Jews." He grabbed the edge of the envelope.

The mayor didn't let go. They stood there staring at each other.

"Is there anything you wouldn't do?"

"Well, I ain't gonna hurt my momma." He laughed, "Unless you come up with a little more cash."

The mayor released the envelope and took two steps, back putting a safe distance between them. He felt the Colt .38 pressing against his side. Beads of perspiration rolled down the back of his neck. "There's something you need to know before you open that envelope. You got to commit to doing the job now or walk away. Cause once you open the envelope I can't let you walk."

"You're a real southern gentleman. Get me in the middle of nowhere, have me leave my rifle behind and then tell me I ain't walkin' away." He tugged on his ear. "I bet you got a pistol tucked in your pants or you wouldn't have the balls to say that. Well I don't walk away from nothing that's gonna make me $10,000. You think your man might send me to Rhodesia? Always wanted to go there." A grin broke across his face. The right corner of his mouth twisted up. He tapped the end of the envelope on his palm and ripped it open.

"So what's your name?"

He pulled a folded paper out of the envelope, "James."

"James what?"

He flicked his wrist and the sheet snapped open, "James Earl."

"Earl your last name?"

"Nope, that be Ray. James Earl Ray." He snorted, pulled a handkerchief out of his pants pocket, blew his nose and put it back. "You can consider it done, except for it's gonna take more than a measly $10,000. Ain't likely to be an easy thing and I'd have to lie low for a long while."

"How much?"

"Thirty g's—half up front," Ray said.

"That's lot of money."

Ray held the paper in front of him. "You want me to tell you who's name is on this sheet of paper?"

He shook his head. "No, if I was supposed to know he would have told me."

Ray pulled on his ear. "I think you ought to get back in touch with your man and tell him what my terms are. Tell him I can do this and as far as I'm concerned the sooner the better cause I'd like to get out of the country. And one other thing. Like when and where is this supposed to happen?"

"I'll find out. How do I get in touch with you?" the mayor asked. "What if he doesn't want to go for $30,000?"

"He will if he's serious about this. But I guess we'll have to wait and see. But could you do a man a favor? Could use me a little cash right now. Life on the run is tough."

The mayor pulled out his billfold and removed $200. "Here, take this to tide you over."

Ray ripped off the bottom of the sheet of paper. "If you call me I won't be there but I'll get the message. Put your telephone number on this so I can get back to you." He stretched out his arm holding a corner of the sheet of paper by his thumb and forefinger. "Nice doing business with you."

"Before you go we've got to burn that paper. Can't leave something like that around." The mayor reached in his pocket, pulled out his cigarette lighter, and flicked it.

Ray held the paper over the yellow and orange flame. They watched it curl, turn black, and the ashes slowly float to the ground.

## CHAPTER FIVE

### Late March 1968

Just past midnight the front door of Sherman Rule's three-room shanty shuddered and the walls shook.

Sherman bolted upright in his swayed mattress, eyes wide open. "What the hell."

His wife, Cassandra, wrapped her arms around him.

"Let go," Sherman whispered. He reached for the hurricane lamp on the wood barrel next to their bed, slid up the glass, struck a match and lit it. He lowered the glass and the yellow flame's hard light filled the barren room. He turned the wick down dimming the glow, leaned under the bed and grabbed a double-barrel shotgun. "You get the twins. I'll see what's goin' on."

"No," Cassandra's voice trembled. "You get the girls and bring 'em here. We all stay together."

"I'll get 'em. Then I'm going to see what that banging's about." Sherman got out of bed in a beige nightshirt.

She grabbed his wrist. "No, get the girls and you stay here with us."

He shook her grip and slid by the blue quilt hanging in the doorway. Shotgun in hand, he crept into the kitchen past the cast iron stove and into Mary and Emma's room.

The girls lay in bed their arms wrapped around each other. "Daddy, what was that?"

Sherman whispered, "I don't know, babies. But don't you be scared now. Daddy's taking yous to momma's bed and then I'll go look. Everything gonna be just fine. The wind probably tore a limb off that ole dead oak tree and it hit the roof." He carried one of the six-year-olds under each arm, firmly gripped the shotgun in hand as he ferried the girls into the bedroom and laid them next to his wife.

They scurried under the cover, clinging to their mother. "Sherman, please stay here. I ain't heard nothing else. Whatever that was is done." Cassandra said.

"Jus gonna look out the front door."

She clenched her teeth and her daughters crawled deeper under each arm. "Please stay here."

Sherman held the forearm of the shotgun in one hand and the stock under his arm. He pulled the two hammers back and they clicked into place. "Be back in a minute." He slipped past the quilt. Hunched over as if stalking a bobcat, Sherman crept to the front of the house. He opened the door and spotted a sheet of paper nailed to it.

He yanked the paper off the door and struggled through the words. "Quit Claim deed. I hereby convey all rights and privileges to—"

Two hooded, masked and robed Klansmen charged from each side of the door frame. A massive forearm knocked Sherman off his feet, the shotgun skittered away and the paper floated to the floor. One straddled him and pointed a lever-action Winchester at his chest. The other picked up the shotgun. Four more hooded men wearing leather belts with holstered pistols stampeded past him and ripped down the quilt hanging in the doorway. They rushed into the bedroom. Sherman's wife and daughters screamed.

Sherman heard his wife pleading, saw her dragged out by her hair and thrown next to him.

"Please don't hurt my little babies." She cried.

The mattress crashed against the wall and the twins tumbled to the floor. Sherman saw his little girls pulled by their slender arms and whipped down next to him and Cassandra. Mary's nightgown was wet with urine.

Four of the Klansmen stood behind the two leaders forming a semi-circle around the Rule family.

Sherman sat up. His wife and daughters huddled between him and the wall.

The man standing closest to Sherman wore a .357 magnum holstered on a black belt. He gripped the barrel of the shotgun with one hand and the butt with the other. "Stupid niggah, running around with a cocked double barrel. Somebody could get hurt." He lowered the barrels and pressed them against Sherman's cheek. The Klansman's fingers slipped down to the triggers. His forefinger pressed against the front trigger. "I smell piss, niggah. Is that you? A grown man pissing out of fear in front of his woman and children. Just like a niggah to do that."

Under the collar of the man's shirt beneath the robe Sherman saw a white string tie. The man's breath had the stench of whiskey and cigar tobacco. Sherman's voice cracked as he tried to talk with the shotgun barrels pinching his cheek. "You gonna kill me, least let my wife and daughters go. They ain't needing to be here for that."

"I ain't decided what's gonna happen to you or them—yet. It's up to you."

Sherman saw the Klansman's index finger pressure the rear trigger. His facial muscled tensed. He turned his head away from the barrels and saw that the man wore shiny black dress shoes. He closed his eyes. His heart raced. His body quivered.

"Oh God, please protect us." Cassandra cried out.

Behind them, Mary and Emma whimpered and shook.

"Open your eyes niggah. Don't be a coward."

Sherman raised his head and looked up. He saw the Klansman lower both hammers, release the triggers and pull the barrels away from his cheek.

"Thank you, Mista."

The Klansman lunged forward, crashing the butt of the shotgun into Sherman's face. Blood spilled onto his nightshirt and the worn-green linoleum floor.

Cassandra let out a low guttural scream, "Ahh. Stop. Stop. Please God, don't kill him. He wasn't going to hurt nobody. He jus' want to protect his family."

The girls screamed and their fingers dug into their mother's nightgown.

Sherman wiped the blood from his eyes with the sleeve of his nightshirt.

The other hooded man standing in the front row picked up the deed from the floor, shoved the paper and a pen in Sherman's face. "Sign this, nigra."

Sherman noticed the brown sleeve of a sheriff's uniform stretch out from under the robe's sleeve. He looked into the cold flinty eyes behind the hood. "What's that?"

"This states that you know that the federal government had no right to give this here land to your slave ancestors. You're returning the land to its rightful owners."

"This my land. Government gave it to my great granddaddy 'cause he was a slave."

The butt of the shotgun smashed across Sherman's face again, teeth spilling out of his mouth. Sherman covered his mouth with his hands. Blood gushed from between his fingers.

Cassandra pleaded, "Sign it, Sherman. This land ain't worth your life."

The Klansman holding the Winchester handed it to one of the men behind him and stepped forward. His meaty hands lifted Sherman up by the collar of his nightshirt and leaned him against the wall. A cigar wobbled through an opening in his mask, "You don't sign this we're taking your little girls with us. No telling what might happen to them."

"This land passed down in my family for a hundred years."

"You a light-skinned scrawny nigra. You know what that means. Some white man dipped his cock in your momma. You don't sign that paper we taking you and your pretty black girls out back." He reached down and caressed Cassandra's cheek.

She jerked her face away.

"She good lookin' for a nigra. You and your little girls gonna watch this pretty nigra get the same treatment your momma did. After she taste a white man she ain't ever gonna want you again."

The Klansmen laughed.

He pushed Sherman down and stroked his chin with his thumb and index finger. "Then again, maybe you won't want her."

One of the four Klansmen standing in the back pointed at Cassandra. He smiled and his small yellow teeth were visible through the mouth opening in his mask. "We gonna take turns with that pretty nigger."

The Klansman standing in front of Sherman took the cigar out of his mouth and pointed it at him. Saliva dripped from the splayed end onto Sherman's face. "Guess it won't matter much if you still want her. 'Cause then come the grand finale. Your Missus and the little girls get to watch you swing by your neck. Lessen of course, you got the sense to sign your name to that paper. Maybe I'm expectin' too much from a nigra. Probably can't write. We gonna need to put your mark on that line?"

Sherman could feel the wetness of his blood leak down his face. He looked over his shoulder at his daughters. They crouched behind their mother peeking out from each side of her, their eyes filled with terror.

Sherman's hand trembled as he scribbled his name on the deed and handed it to the Klansman.

The Klansman stuffed the deed inside his robe and stepped behind the one with the shotgun.

The man with the shotgun lunged forward, stabbing the butt into Sherman's gut.

Sherman's arms locked around his stomach.

"You best be out of this house by sundown tomorrow. Out of this state, if you're smart. Do your other niggah landowners a favor. Tell them to leave before we have to pay them a visit. They don't have to stick around to sign over the property. Be healthier for them that way."

The man with the shotgun turned toward his fellow Klansmen. "Let's leave a little reminder of our visit." The five hooded men stomped around the room, tossing a wooden table against the wall, crushing wooden chairs into splinters and slicing bags of grain and corn, before charging out of the house.

Sherman leaned back against the wall. One eye was swollen shut, a deep gash crossed his cheek, and teeth scattered across the floor.

"Emily, get me a wet dishrag from the washtub," Cassandra said.

The little girl ran to a wooden basin next to the cast iron stove, pulled out a dripping rag and carried it back in her outstretched hands.

Cassandra took the cloth and gently wiped the blood from his face. "Don't worry, Sherman, God will protect us. He'll find a new life for us. We gots our family. We don't need this old farm."

Sherman sniveled, head throbbing. "I can't believe this. Great granddaddy was a slave, spillin' his blood on this cotton field for white folks." He looked at his hands that were covered with his own blood. "A hundred years later my blood spillin' on this land just like his. We got to leave here right away. This darkness ain't ever going away."

Light exploded through the open doorway and into the house, flickering across the faces of Sherman's family. They moved closer together as a six-foot high, four-foot wide cross burned in front of their house. The odor of the kerosene-soaked-burlap wrapped around the cross filled their nostrils. The wind whipped the swirling, crackling flames and they heard the muffled laughter of the hooded men.

Sherman pushed himself against the wall and stood. He limped to the door and in the light of the flames saw the letters KKK scrawled across it. He slammed the door shut and bowed his head as tears flowed down his face.

\*\*\*

The next morning Sherman loaded the back seat and trunk of his faded green 1954 Nash with pots, pans, tools and their clothes and tied the mattress on the roof. He stood in front of their shanty, taking a last look at his family's home. The remains of the charred cross stood in front of it.

He pictured his great grandfather working the land as a slave; visualized him getting down on his hands and knees and pushing his fingers into the soil when he was told the land was his. Lifting his hands to the sky thanking God as the dirt slipped between his fingers and fell to the ground. His great grandfather looking into the future and seeing his son and his son's son toiling and sweating on this land and making something of it for their families. And now Sherman realized his legacy. He was the one who left the land behind, the one who broke the family's connection with the land.

Sherman's eye was swollen shut. The shadow of stubble and a long streak of dried blood covered one cheek. He wore blue bib overalls with patched knees, a matching jacket, and dusty battered boots. Cassandra sat proudly in the passenger seat in a long green dress that she had made from drapery discarded by a white family for whom she cleaned house. It was her best dress. The girls huddled between them, wearing matching tan dresses their mother had made.

Sherman hunched over, turned the key, and the engine coughed and grumbled. The muffler had a hole in it and the rumble of the engine was loud. He jerked the steering wheel and the bald tires rolled over the furrows of the dirt road.

Sherman's head wobbled between his shoulders as he drove down Turner Road, past the green winter wheat to Drew Ruleville Road, and onto the bridge crossing Blackhawk Bayou. The muddy water moved at a snail's pace, past scrubs and old barren trees emerging from the bayou. He felt his world drifting away. He realized that he had no control over his life and that this was one more experience proving it.

Sherman headed east and pulled in front of a dented trailer house with a green asphalt-shingle roof. Willie Cannon, a heavy dark-skinned man with deep-set eyes, came out of the shack. He walked to the Nash, leaned into the open window and nodded at the Rules, "Morning, Cassandra," and stared at Sherman's battered face. "What happened?"

"Klan jumped us last night. Beat me till I signed some paper giving them my land." Sherman opened the door and hobbled with Cannon a few steps away from his family. "They said to tell all the black landowners, you, the Beverlys, and the Tisdales that they want our land cause it ain't rightfully ours. They were gonna take my girls and rape Cassandra if I didn't sign."

"Ain't worth it. Take your family and get the hell out," Cannon said. "I was planning on heading up north anyway. This land don't mean nothing to me but work. I ain't gonna wait till I get my face kicked in like you."

Sherman bent down and picked up a handful of red soil. "I don't feel right about leaving the land. My family been on it since we be freed."

"Don't be a fool. Get out while you can."

"Yeah, guess so." Sherman stood, "We going to Greenville. Sell what we can there and take a bus to Detroit. Don't think this ole car could make the trip. Wife's brother lives there. He gots a job with Ford on da assembly line. Been trying to get us to come up there and live. I hope he really mean it."

"Ain't got no family keeping me here. I'm gone."

"Can you go by Beverly's and tell'em? Make sure he tells the Tisdales. At least we all get out alive."

"Sure enough. I'm going to pack up and head to Pittsburgh," Cannon said. "Got an uncle there. Stop by Beverly's on the way."

"We be heading out. You better be on your way before you leave any blood here. Say goodbye to them folks for us." He shook Cannon's hand, "See you, Willie." Sherman limped back to his car

\*\*\*

Willie Cannon pulled his black 1956 Buick Roadmaster to the front of his trailer. The front bumper leaned toward the ground on the driver's side and was tied to the chassis with a rope. He opened the trunk and back door. "Ain't waiting for a visit from no Klan." He ran back and forth, making several trips, filling the car with clothes, tools, two chickens in a crate, and whatever else he could stuff in it.

He jumped into his car, leaving the trailer's front door open, and squealed away. A cloud of red dust flew into the air. Cannon headed down the road five miles to Beverly's place.

Beverly was the oldest of the black landowners, somewhere in his fifties, no one knew exactly. He had two grown sons who had already left the South for Cleveland and his wife was visiting them.

Cannon turned off the county road and headed up the narrow dirt trail. His car slid from one rut to another. Branches from tupelo gums and bald cypresses scraped the Buick's doors.

The trail opened to a clearing and Cannon pressed his fading brakes, stopping in front of Beverly's shotgun house. Chickens scattered out of the way. He jumped out of his car and ran to the unpainted door. He banged on the door and screamed, "Johnny, Johnny, you in there?"

The wind rustled through the trees and a hawk glided overhead, eyeing some small prey in Beverly's wheat field. But there was no response to Cannon's plea.

Cannon stood in front of Beverly's door and looked around. Everything seemed normal—chickens pecking at feed, a pig lying in the sun, a stray hound dog trotting across the yard to greet him. Cannon pushed the door. The hinges creaked. He stepped inside, "Johnny, you here?" His voice cracked.

The wind slammed the door shut. Cannon jumped. "Shit, write him a note. I ain't staying around waiting for the Klan to kick my ass." He scribbled on the back of a feed bill and left it on the pine table in the kitchen.

Johnny,

We all got to get out of here. The Klan beat up Sherman. They want our land. I'm heading north. Make sure you tell the Tisdales.

Willie

Cannon ran out of the house to his car. The Buick fish-tailed and squealed back down the trail.

The wind gusted, blowing open the cabin's door. Cannon's note blew across the tabletop like a leaf scuttling along the ground, finding its home in a corner of the kitchen floor.

# CHAPTER SIX

## Saturday, March 30, 1968

William pulled out his chair from the kitchen table and plopped down. He gazed to his left at his father, Beauford, and his granddaddy at the head of the table. He was proud to be sitting with the men of the Tisdale house while his sister, Marlee, and his mother were busy preparing dinner on the cast iron stove.

Marlee lifted a pot of rabbit stew off the stove, quickstepped to the table, and placed it down. She stood behind her chair.

William stretched from his chair and reached for the ladle in the pot.

His father's hand clamped down on his arm.

His grandfather shook his head. His dark eyes were sharp and expressive. "You act like a gentleman and pull your sista's chair out for her before you feed your face."

William exhaled and felt his father's hand release his arm. His eyes strayed to his grandfather, who folded his arms across his chest. Then to his sister, who tilted her head as a smile spread across her face and imitated her granddaddy, folding her arms across her chest.

William pressed his hands against the table, pushing his chair back as if it took all the effort in the world. He trudged to Marlee's chair and pulled it back. Marlee stepped in front of the chair. William gave it a firm push and nodded as his sister fell into her seat. He marched back and sat down.

His mother smiled as she approached the table carrying two bowls and a plate, "Pickled okra that Marlee canned last summer, boiled potatoes, and biscuits." The aroma floated through the air.

"Bring it on down, Honey. You got three hungry men," Beauford said, knife and fork in hands.

She joined her family at the table. "Father, say grace please."

Beauford bowed his head and everyone followed his lead. "Dear Lord, we thank for this food and for keepin' us all well and safe. Amen."

William's eyes opened wide as he dipped the ladle deep into the pot of stew.

Beauford grabbed William's hand. "What did grampa tell you about taking care of the women and bein' a gentleman?" He let go of his son's hand.

William jerked his head back and stared at the ceiling. He curled his lower lip, bit down, lowered his head and gazed across the table at Marlee. "May I serve you some?"

She giggled and looked at her father. "Yes, please."

His chair screeched back. He stood and footslogged to the women's side of the table. He lifted the ladle out of the pot, spooned a cup full onto Marlee's plate and then onto his mother's. He bowed to the women. The whole family broke into laughter.

William sat down and huffed. "Now can I have some food?"

"Your learnin', boy." Grampa nodded, "Have at it."

"Ain't seen Sherman around lately," Beauford said. "I got a job clearing some land north of Minter City. Gonna take a ride after dinner see if he wants to work it with me."

"No you ain't." Nathleen said. "You coming to choir practice with me and the children tonight. You can go talk to him tomorrow."

"Oh yeah. Forgot all about that." Beauford winked and his kids laughed.

Grampa smiled. "You all go to church. I'm gonna visit Johnny Beverly. We'll have our own religious experience."

"Pa's going to worship the God of hooch," Beauford laughed, sinking his teeth into the rabbit.

"Beauford, don't talk like that in front of the children." Nathleen said.

William belched.

By 7:30 Beauford, Nathleen and the children were in the pickup, waving goodbye to grandpa as he saddled their plowing mule. Grandpa smiled and said. "I'll spend the night at Johnny's, playing checkers. See ya in the morning."

Beauford shook his head and started leading the family in a chorus of *Amazing Grace* as the pickup truck bounced over the ruts in the road to Saturday night choir practice.

\*\*\*

The family found their selves back at church Sunday morning. It was midday by time they were heading home. The warm air held a sweet aroma of blossoming magnolias. William changed from his church going white shirt and brown pants, slipped a hand-me-down T-shirt over his head and jumped into cutoff jeans. He snatched a leftover greased biscuit, ran out, latching onto his bamboo fishing pole, and hurdled down the sagging wooden steps.

"William Tisdale, don't you be goin' too far now." His mother shouted from the kitchen.

He looked over his shoulder. "I won't, Mama. I'm goin' to the bayou fishin'. I'll be back in half an hour with a stringer full of catfish you can make for supper."

Beauford sat at the kitchen table watching his son run out of the house. He loved the way his boy wanted to take care of the family. "He's a good boy."

"We're blessed, Beau. Got good kids. Good place to live and I got a good man." She looked over her shoulder at him and cocked her head.

Beauford glanced into the bottom of his coffee cup. She's in a good mood. He gulped down the last of his coffee. Ain't ever going over to Napier's again. No need to take Napier's abuse or deal with the likes of Celeste. Either one likely to ruin my life.

"Ahem, I said I got a good man."

"Oh, sorry, Honey. Was thinking of that job in Minter City. I got to go see if Sherman wants to work or line up somebody else." He stood and walked over to the sink where Nathleen was washing the breakfast dishes. "I got the best woman God ever made." He slipped his hands around her waist and nibbled on her ear. "We got some time."

"I thought you had to see Sherman about making some money?"

"Yeah, guess I better take care of that. I'll be back in a little while." Beauford kissed her neck and left for Sherman Rule's place. On the short ride to Rule's he thought about what Nathleen had said. She was right. *The kids were good. I'm lucky to have my father with us. Sometimes things are a struggle but that happens. Like the Good Book says, it just makes you stronger.*

As Beauford approached Rule's cabin he saw the charred cross. "What the hell?" He pulled in front of it, grabbed a crow bar next to his seat and got out of his truck. He walked past the cross to the unpainted front door and saw KKK painted in black on it. He swallowed and pushed it open. "Sherman, Cassandra, you here?" He paused for a response. There was none.

Beauford took a few steps into the cabin and noticed the dried pool of blood on the faded linoleum. He took a deep breath and firmed his grip on the crowbar. He saw corn and grain seed spilled across the floor; the broken kitchen table lying in a heap; noticed the shelves emptied of pots and pans. He cautiously pulled back the worn blue quilt hanging in the bedroom doorway, expecting to see the worst, and was relieved to see only open empty dresser drawers and the bed frame thrown against the wall. They must be alive. The Klan wouldn't take their things.

"I better head over to Beverly's and tell him and Daddy to be on the watch. Willie Cannon's on the way. I'll warn him too."

\*\*\*

William raced barefoot a quarter mile down dusty Turner Road with the greased biscuit in one hand and the bamboo fishing pole in the other. The road was flanked on the east by sharecroppers' wheat fields just beginning to turn brown and on the west by dogwoods and redbuds flowering white, pink, and red. William skipped down a worn path bordered by underbrush laced with white flowering honeysuckles, finally reaching Blackhawk bayou. He stood on the muddy banks and watched the stream meander past.

William rolled a piece of the greased biscuit between his fingers, squeezed it onto the hook and dropped the line into the brown water. Twenty minutes later, he laid down the bamboo pole, pulled off his T-shirt, and pushed a small raft he and his father had made to the edge of the bayou. William grabbed a broomstick they kept on the shore for poling the raft and pushed the craft into the water.

He drifted away from the smell of the dead vegetation of the bayou. He closed his eyes and let the lazy current take him on a trip to an imaginary paradise as he floated toward the Drew Ruleville Road Bridge.

\*\*\*

Beauford pushed hard on the accelerator and the engine whined. He bounced against the door as the truck slipped in and out of ruts, kicking up a wake of red dirt. The truck slid sideways as he lurched to a stop in front of Cannon's trailer. He shut off the engine and focused on Cannon's front door. It creaked, opening and closing on its hinges. He looked to the side of the trailer where Cannon parked his Buick. It wasn't there.

Beauford ran to the open front door. It was marked with the letters KKK. "Willie, you here? You ok?" There was no response. He ran through the house and once again noticed that things were gone or destroyed. Shelves had been emptied and his clothes rack was bare. An old table was crushed into pieces and the pot-belly stove was toppled over.

He ran back to his truck, cranked the engine, and roared away to Johnny Beverly's, hoping that he would find his father and Beverly. Beauford banged his fist on the steering wheel. "Damn it! Celeste musta got pissed at her father and told him. Everyone's gonna suffer cause of me." He swallowed and his knuckles whitened as he tightened his grip. "They're gonna lynch me."

Beauford drove five miles to Beverly's as hard as the pickup could take it. He was consumed by the guilt and terrified that everything that had happened was his fault. His expectations for his father and Johnny Beverly were even worse.

He sped down the narrow dirt trail to Beverly's, noticing the broken branches and scraped trunks of the cypresses and tulip trees bordering the road. All signs that someone had driven down this way in a frenzy.

"Shit!"

The pickup bounded up and down through the deep ruts in the trail. He swerved the truck out of the last turn into the clearing, screeching to a halt in front of Beverly's place. The chickens scattered about, frightened by the sound of his pickup roaring into the yard. His plowing mule was tied up to a post next to the house.

Beauford got out of his truck and trotted to Beverly's front door. The letters KKK spread across it. "Yo, Johnny. Daddy, you here?" He heard nothing. He pulled the door open and the inside was in shambles. Two legs broken off a pine table were lying on the floor amidst a small pool of dried blood. Pots and pans were pulled off the shelves and scattered across the floor. One chair from the table was lodged in the window, stuck in a broken pane of glass. Another chair was in pieces in the corner of the kitchen. The checkerboard had spilled off the table and lay upside down on the floor, checkers scattered about next to a broken bottle of Mad Dog 20/20.

Beauford looked toward the back of the shanty and saw a sheet of paper pinned to the door by a knife. He prowled through the debris on the floor to the back door, yanked down the paper, and read it. It was Willie Cannon's note to Johnny Beverly warning about the Klan.

"Sumbitch," Beauford's arms dropped to his side and the note fell to the floor.

He opened the back door and stepped out under the three-foot overhang of the tin roof. In front of him, the stiff body of Johnny Beverly hung by the neck from a hickory tree. He ran to one side of the house and then the other side yelling, "Daddy. Daddy, you here?" He heard nothing, turned around, and charged back to his truck. "Got to get Nathleen and the kids and get the hell out of here."

Beauford sped home. He now knew why Willie Cannon and the Rules had fled and Beverly was hanged. Daddy, I pray you're alive. Maybe he made it back to the house and he, Nathleen and the kids are hiding someplace.

He skidded to a stop and ran into their cabin. "Nathleen, is Daddy here? We all gots to leave."

She pushed aside the worn quilt hanging in the bedroom doorway and rushed out of the room. "Leave?"

"The Klan chased out Cannon and the Rules and hanged Johnny Beverly. They after everybody's land. Daddy wasn't at Beverly's. Can't find him. "

"Sweet Jesus. I ain't seen your Daddy. William's at the bayou."

"Put Marlee in the truck. Grab whatever you can and toss it in the back. Then we'll head down to the bayou and get William."

They threw as much as they could into the truck's bed. Clothes and kitchen utensils packed in cardboard boxes, toolbox, wood table, and some chairs, and headed down to the bayou looking for William. Nathleen held Marlee in her arms as the truck sped down Turner Road, leaving a trail of dust behind it. Beauford veered off onto the trail leading to the bayou. The old Chevy lumbered down the narrow path, leaning from one side to the other, ripping through underbrush and cracking branches and tearing white flowers off the honeysuckle vines. He pulled into a clearing short of the bayou, jumped out of the truck, and ran down the path to the water.

Beauford looked up and down the bayou for his son. The silence provoked his worst fears. His heart pounded. "William! William!" Beauford shouted. He saw William's bamboo pole and T-shirt lying on the bank but their raft was gone. Beauford ran downstream, his thick arms pumping, as the mud plopped and sucked at his shoes. His heart was beating in his throat.

*** 

William floated down the bayou on the raft, slipping into the shadow of the Drew Ruleville Bridge. His body shivered when the sun's rays no longer warmed him. He heard screaming and yelling coming from deep in the woods. He poled his raft to the shore under the cover of the bridge and jumped onto the muddy bank. He climbed a ten-foot rise, and saw through the dense woods one hundred yards away in a clearing the front end of a blue pickup truck. Two white men were laughing and drinking beer, standing near the open passenger door. They threw the empty bottles, crashing them against the trees, and grabbed two more bottles out of the cab. The men walked toward the back of the truck, slugging down their beers and then were out of sight.

William crept through the woods, using the front of the truck for cover. He stopped fifty yards away from the truck's shiny grill. His breathing quickened. His chest was heaving. He was close enough to make out their words.

"Been chasing you all night. For an old nigga you sure can run, boy."

"Jimmy, we gonna wait for Uriah or get this thing done?"

"He's looking for the old man's son with some of the boys. No tellin' when they might get here. Let's finish up. Then we can go help 'em." The man drained his beer, flipped the bottle into the woods. He walked to the driver's side, opened the door and climbed into the cab. The engine cranked and the man stared into the rear view mirror.

William drifted to his left, staying low behind bushy shrubs. He wanted to run back to the bayou but was scared they would see him. In the dark shadows of the tall oaks and tulip trees he shivered. He slipped behind an old oak tree that was wide enough to hide behind.

He took a quick glance around the tree and through the shrubs. He saw a black man standing on the truck bed, a rope around his neck strung from a tree limb. He jerked back and plastered himself against the tree. His hands grasped the bark.

He heard the truck engine reve. The tires spun in the soft mulch. The snap of a rope. The loud laughter of one of the men.

"Look at that ole boy shakin' and twisting."

"Come on, Albert. We got some more stringin' to do. Get in."

The truck's tires spun and slid through the soft earth and the sound of the engine become distant.

William peered around the tree. He saw the man hanging, torso and legs rippling with movement. The man's fingers clawing at the rope around his neck. The rope was twisting and the body slowly revolving.

William dashed out from behind the tree toward the man, facing his back. He grabbed the man's shoes and tried to hold him up. His slender arms shook from the weight of the body. He slipped in the muddy tracks left by the truck and fell to the ground. The body rotated on the rope turning toward William. He looked up at the bulging eyes and protruding tongue.

"Grampa," he wailed.

William's lips trembled. He scurried to his feet and raced through the dense woods toward the bayou. Errant branches scraped his body, tearing flesh away as he ran through shrubs, slipping and falling on the loose spring soil, scraping his knees and hands on rocks. He lunged down the bank, rolling into the bayou. He jumped up and heard his father yelling, "William."

\*\*\*

Beauford approached the bridge and saw his son's head above the water. He screamed, "William."

The boy stood trembling and began to bawl, tears streaming down his face. "Daddy, they hung Grampa."

Beauford splashed to William and grabbed his shoulders. "Who?" But he already knew the answer.

William stood speechless, snot hanging from his nose. His body shaking and slender chest heaving.

He grabbed William's shoulders and shook him, "Where is he?"

William's breath shot out of his mouth, gasping for air.

"Where is he?"

William lifted his spindly arm and pointed to the woods.

Beauford picked up William. He seemed so vulnerable and small in his arms. He carried him to the bank and laid him down. He held his boy's face with his hands. "Wait here, son. I'll be back in a minute. Then we're all getting outta here." *I got to see if he might be alive.* He raced in the direction William pointed, arms pumping, feet plopping through the dirt. The muscles in his legs burned as he rushed through the shrubs.

In the distance he could see a body hanging from a tall oak. It was twisting and turning, suspended from a rope. From ten feet away he saw the feet pointed downward, the noose tight around the neck. He rushed to his father's body, wrapped his arms around the ankles and lifted. "Breathe, Daddy, breathe," he shouted.

Beauford raised his head and looked at his father's face. The capillaries in his eyes had burst and blood filled them. His contorted, black tongue jutted out of his mouth. The air was filled with the stench of urine and excrement. The old man's chest was motionless. He released the old man's ankles and crashed to his knees, hands on his haunches and bowed his head in the shadow of his father's body. *I don't believe this. Why an old man? Never hurt no one.* He slammed his fist on the ground again and again. *I'll get your revenge. I'll get them even if it kills me!*

Beauford took a deep breath and shook his head. He climbed up the tree, pulled a pocket knife out of his jeans and cut the rope. He heard his father's body thud onto the ground. He scurried down and loosened the noose around his neck and threw the rope into the woods. "Sumbitches."

He picked up his father cradling him in his arms. He carried him through the woods and laid him on the bank under the bridge. Beauford pulled his son to his chest rocking back and forth. "William, we gots to leave. They got Johnny Beverly too."

Beauford looked at his father's body. "I promise I'll be back later to get you, Daddy." He grabbed William's hand and they ran upstream.

"Daddy, it was white men."

Beauford stopped. "How you know that?"

"I was floating down the bayou under the bridge when I heard 'em laughing, Daddy. And Daddy, they said Uriah was looking for you."

"Your mother and Marlee are waiting in the truck. We gotta be leaving this place. Anything else you remember?"

"I heard 'em call each other. There was Albert and Jimmy. Why's this happening? Why do they hate you bad enough to want to kill you? Why did they kill grampa?"

"Ain't got time to talk about that now, son." He huffed, "Anything else?"

"They had a shiny blue pickup truck."

"Jimmy, must be Jimmy Napier. He got a new blue Dodge Ram Charger."

"Why, Daddy—"

"William, I told you not now. We gots to go." They rushed to the path where they had entered the bayou. Beauford lifted his son onto the bed of the truck. William crawled into a space between two boxes and Beauford wrapped a blanket around his son.

Beauford climbed onto the threadbare seat of the pickup and looked at Nathleen's dark eyes. She sat there tightly holding Marlee in her slender arms. He fought to hold back the tears. Crying would scare his daughter, but he couldn't stop his lips from trembling. He turned the key and the engine kicked over. He shifted into first gear and said one word, "Father." Nathleen understood and slipped one hand from the embrace of their daughter and squeezed his forearm. "I have to come back tonight to bury him." Nathleen simply nodded and held Marlee even tighter.

Beauford started the truck and slowly pulled up to the clearing that met Turner Road. The bed of the tired Chevy creaked as it rocked from side to side under the load. He looked up and down the road for anyone that might be looking for him. There was no traffic and he decided to take his family north where it would be safer. Exactly where, he didn't know yet. "We best be careful, Nath. Stay on the back roads, keep off the interstate. Might be police lookin' for us."

Beauford weaved through backcountry roads for hours, passing cabins in the lowlands. He looked over at Nathleen and Marlee. The long slow ride had put both of them to sleep. The good life they had was over. Whether the Klan was moving in on them because of some scheme to take their land or if the violence was because of his entanglement with Celeste, it didn't really matter. He knew from the beginning that messing with Jimmy Napier's daughter was suicide. He could have stopped it but he didn't. Messing with any white woman was poison for him. He should never have touched her. It would crush Nathleen if she ever found out. He had to move on.

*** 

By mid-afternoon they reached Memphis. He drove through the city until he found a section seedy enough ten blocks south of Beale Street and a few blocks east of the Mississippi River. It was filled with dilapidated two-story buildings containing rooming houses, pawnshops, secondhand stores and warehouses on the edge of black Memphis.

He pulled into the south end of a motel parking lot so that the pickup was out of the sight of the motel clerk. The building was a one story rectangular structure. The man at the front desk might be reluctant to rent a room to someone with an old truck full of furniture, thinking they might bolt before paying the bill.

Beauford looked at Nathleen and Marlee. The child had been in his wife's arms for the entire trip. "I'll getta room, honey. Why don't you stretch your legs? You been holdin' that child for hours."

Nathleen slowly opened the door, placed Marlee on the worn seat, and stepped down to the grass-veined asphalt. She looked at the faded neon sign and mumbled, "Memphis Blues Motel." It was the first words she had said since leaving

Blackhawk Bayou. She took a deep breath and covered her nose with the back of her hand. "Beauford, this place stinks. We can't be staying here." She pointed to a dumpster at the end of the parking lot. "Look, there's garbage stacked so high it's falling over the side."

Beauford helped William out of the back of the truck, "We jus' stay here for the night and then be movin' on."

He wrapped his arms around his son and thanked God that he still had his wife and children. "You stay here with your mother and sister, I'll get a room." He trudged to the office at the north end of the building. The clerk was a middle-aged white man. "Like a room for the night."

The clerk slapped a registration card and a pen on the counter. "Full name, address, telephone number, vehicle type, tag number and $8 cash." His eyes were dark and dull.

Beauford filled out the card, pulled out some cash from his pocket and counted out a five and three singles. He pocketed his remaining $53.

The clerk picked up the card and held it close to his face. "You from Mississippi. What you doing up here?"

Beauford paused, not knowing what to say, "Ah, moving up north."

"Where to?"

"I gotta call some people up north. Got a couple of jobs lined up, see which one is best."

"What you do?"

"Mechanic, ah construction. I can do both." Beauford pulled his hand down his lips. "Why's all that garbage falling all over that dumpster out there?"

"You from Ruleville, hm? That's Sunflower County, ain't it? Ain't you heard about the sanitation workers' strikin'? Been going on almost two months. The whole city's stinkin'. Fools, as if the mayor's gonna give in. Ya know, I know some people down Sunflower County."

"Can I have the key? Wife needs the bathroom."

The clerk took a key off a rack on the wall and handed to Beauford. "Check out is 11:00."

Beauford hurried to the room, opened the door and Nathleen stepped in. "You in there a while. That white man ask a lot a questions to rent a room to ya?"

Beauford shrugged, to tired to respond and went back to the truck. He carried the boxes containing their clothing and a few pieces of the furniture from the truck into the room. He wanted the truck as empty as possible for his return trip to the Ruleville Bridge. All he needed was a shovel to dig his father's grave. In case something happened to him, at least Nathleen and the children would have some possessions.

After unloading the truck, Nathleen, William, and Marlee collapsed on the bed. Beauford pulled the curtains closed and looked at his family. He gazed across the room, taking in the boxes and furniture stacked against dark cinder block walls.

He shook his head. Twenty-four hours ago they had lived in the country. The air had a sweet fragrance after a spring rain, the wind rustled through the trees and the water meandered down the bayou. Their family had lived in the same home for generations. Now they had nothing. Now they were in a city where they didn't pick up the garbage and the air burned your lungs.

# CHAPTER SEVEN

Beauford sat for hours in a chair in the corner of the motel room. His gaze wandering from Nathleen and his son and daughter asleep in the bed to the cheap furniture and painted cement block walls. As time passed the sunlight that crept through the space between the blanched curtains of the motel room faded as darkness shrouded the city. He was exhausted from a lack of sleep and no food.

He looked at William. The boy's chest was heaving up and down and face twisted. He knew his son was reliving the day's events in his nightmare. He leaned over and nudged Nathleen's shoulder, "Honey, you think we should wake William? Look at him."

She stroked her son's cheek, his facial muscles relaxed, and breathing slowed.

"I'm going out to stretch my legs. Back in ten minutes," Beauford said.

"Are you sure it's safe?"

"Nobody knows we're here. I jus' going around the block. Need some air. Clear my head. Think about what I gotta do next."

"Next?" She glanced at William and Marlee and scowled back at Beauford. "Don't forget, you still got your wife and children."

"I know. Won't let you down. Do whatever I got to do to take care of my family, but I can't let Daddy's body rot under that bridge." He stood and rubbed his tired face with both hands, took a deep breath, and let himself out of the room.

He drifted north several blocks, past a fire station and two-story warehouses. Streetwalkers had replaced panhandlers. One hooker wore a red tube top, matching hot pants, knee high boots, and a large 'fro, another a leopard skin miniskirt, a see-through blouse covering a skimpy black bra, a blond wig, and silver high heels. They sashayed from the curb to the waiting cars looking for johns.

The vision of his father's lynching was locked in Beauford's mind. His life had been divided in half. Everything before today was what he had expected and the future was a dark abyss. His heart felt as if fingers were wrapped around it and squeezing. His throat pinched tight. Someone tapped his shoulder. He spun around and jerked his fist back.

"Whoa, Honey. I ain't into no rough stuff. But I can get somebody who like that," the blonde hooker said.

Beauford shook his head and felt his world tilting and spinning. He stumbled off the sidewalk onto the street. Brakes screeched, horns blared, and drivers cursed him. He scurried back to the curb, balancing himself with one hand against a storefront window and tumbling against a fifty-five gallon drum overflowing with rancid garbage. His chest tightened. Breathing quickened. He held on. The foul odor stung his nostrils.

He pushed himself away from the garbage and staggered down the sidewalk, finally collapsing on a cement stoop. He leaned back against the brick wall. He took a deep breath and blew it out. Let his breathing slow and his head clear.

He looked over his shoulder trying to regain a sense of his whereabouts. The address read 424 S. Main. He pushed his back against the brick wall and forced himself up. His eyes focused on the glass door and the inscription below the address, Canipes Amusement Company.

Beauford trudged past Bessie Brewer's Boarding House and Jimmy's Grill then headed south, back to the motel. It had been a day he'd never forget. *I got to get through this. Get my family away from this.* He took a deep breath, mustered his energy and ran the rest of the way. His muscles trembled and sweat slicked across his forehead.

He stepped into the motel room and saw the bathroom light seep around the partially open door. The children were asleep. He looked at William holding his little sister in his arms. He walked to the bathroom and whispered, "Nath, I'm back." The door opened, he stepped in, and closed it behind him. Beauford stood behind Nathleen breathing in her earthly scent and watching her reflection in the mirror as she wiped her weary face with a frayed wash cloth.

"Honey, I gotta go," he said. "Is there anything you need before I leave?"

She placed the washcloth in the tarnished sink and turned to him. "Be careful, Beau. We need you. Even with you, life is gonna be tough on these kids. If they don't have you…."

She put her arms around his shoulders and he was warmed by the strength of her embrace. He felt the moisture of her tear between their cheeks and tasted it when the droplet settled on his lips.

"Nath, I better get goin'." Beauford reached behind his neck, grasped her hands gave them a light squeeze, and slid them off. He reached into his pocket and grasped their life savings. "Here's $30. You take it. I got enough left for gas. No sense taking more than I need." He hugged her, left the bathroom, and walked to the bed.

He leaned over the children while Nathleen stood in the bathroom doorway. Her shadow covered them. Beauford kissed William and Marlee on their cheeks and caressed their faces. He walked to the door, turned and took a long look at his family and swallowed.

As Beauford drove past the motel office he saw the night clerk pick up the telephone.

\*\*\*

Beauford chose the interstate. Without the need to protect his family, it was the quickest 110 miles to Ruleville. It was closing in on midnight when he exited Interstate 55 and headed west on Route 8. Just before Minter City, about twelve miles from Ruleville, a car pulled off a dirt road and stayed three lengths behind him. Beauford slowed the truck down to 45. The car slowed to the same pace. For the next several minutes his eyes shifted from the road, to the rearview mirror, and back to the road. "Car's got lights on the roof—police."

"Turn north on 49. See if he stays with me." Beauford mumbled as he turned and the cruiser followed. The muscles in his neck went taut. A half mile up the road, flashing red and blue lights ricocheted off the rearview mirror and flickered across his face. "Shit, he called in my tags. Cluckers be here in a minute."

He pulled onto the shoulder of the road, grasped the crowbar that lay between the gearshift and his leg, and waited for the confrontation. A beam of light shot out from the squad car's spotlight, blinding Beauford. He heard the man's boot crunching on the gravel. The glare of the spotlight obscured the officer's exact position. Beauford braced his grip on the crowbar. A billy club tapped on his door. His eyes squinted in the direction of the knocking.

"License and registration," the man said.

Beauford read the gold name tag. "Yes, Sir, Deputy Elias." He reached with his left hand above the visor and retrieved the papers. He handed them to the deputy and slid the crowbar onto his lap. "I do something wrong, sir?" A bead of sweat rolled over his eyebrow and down the side of his face.

The deputy paused, looking at the documents. "Where ya headed, boy?"

"Goin' home. Been visiting some friends."

"You been drinking?"

"No, sir, I come from a God-fearing family. We don't touch no alcohol."

"Your taillight on the driver's side is out." He handed the papers back. "You know that?"

"No, sir I didn't. Thanks, Deputy. Fix it first thing in the mornin'."

"Letting you go this time. Catch you again, boy, you gonna get a ticket." The deputy tapped the door with the billy club again. "Go home."

"Yes, sir. Thank ya, sir." Beauford took a deep breath, slid the crowbar down, placed both hands on the steering wheel, and slowly pulled onto the road. His eyes cast into the rearview mirror. The cruiser made a U-turn and the red taillights grew smaller behind him. Beauford turned into the first road. He wiped the perspiration from his forehead with his sleeve, turned around and headed back to Route 8 and Ruleville. He slipped through Ruleville without any problems and headed west to Long Road.

The murmur of the wind rustled the treetops and the crescent moon hung like a sickle in the sky. He turned off Long Road and crossed the Drew Ruleville Bridge. The sinking feeling in his stomach hit him as he realized that ten hours ago he had left his father's body there. A cold sweat dripped down the back of his neck and his skin shuddered. "Stop by the house first. Only take a few minutes to see if there's anything else I take back with me."

Beauford turned north on Turner Road. He took a deep breath and caught the scent of burning wood. Turning east onto the dirt road he headed to their shotgun house. The dirt and gravel crunched beneath the tires. Where their home once stood he saw twisted timbers, flickering red embers and the scorched stone remains of a crumbling chimney. Beauford pulled the pickup near the remains of the front of the house.

He felt as if every aspect of his life was being hunted and destroyed. The Rules and Cannon gone. His father and Johnny Beverly killed. His home in ashes. He rubbed his temples with his thumb and forefinger. *What part of this is my fault? How have I failed?*

Beauford opened his door and the dome light flashed on. He quickly pulled the door toward him, careful not to slam it shut, and ripped the bare light bulb out of the socket. He shook his head as he pushed the door open and got out of the truck. He circled the charred remains. His gut twisted with anger.

Beauford stopped in the backyard where his father's wooden rocking chair remained untouched. He picked it up, intending to carry the chair to the truck and noticed the singed remains of a curled photograph lying on the ground. Beauford set the chair on the scrub grass, bent down and grasped the photograph. The corners were black and flaky. He carefully flattened the photograph in the palm of his hand. It was the seared remains of a picture taken ten years ago—a black and white snapshot of Beauford standing behind his father, who sat in his rocking chair holding one-year-old William. A tear fell from his face onto the photo. He rubbed it off with his thumb. His hand quivered as he put the photo in his shirt pocket.

As he lifted the chair in the back of his truck the warmth of his nostalgia subsided and he felt suddenly alone, vulnerable. Scuttling sounds in the darkness became louder. His eyes searched the woods and fields surrounding the charred remains of his house. An uncertainty settled that was fast becoming fear. His breathing quickened. Sweat beaded on his forehead. He needed to move fast, bury his father and get back to his family.

He headed back to Turner Road. He tried to build his courage, *Jus killing us ain't enough. They got to get rid any proof we were even here. At least I got a picture and his chair to remember him by. I'll get your revenge, Daddy.*

He turned onto Turner Road. After a short distance he pulled into the stand of shrubs and shut off the engine. The moon was more than half-way across the sky. He collapsed, resting his head and arms on the steering wheel. "Lord, please give me the strength to do this." He took two deep breaths, inhaled the sweet aroma of the honeysuckle, pushed himself away from the steering wheel and opened the door. He stepped out of the truck and slowly closed the door, careful to make as little noise as possible.

Beauford crept to the bank under the cover of the trees. The wind rustled the branches and the crescent moon dipped behind dark swirling clouds and reappeared. An owl hooted and croaking frogs became louder as he approached the mucky bank. In minutes the dark silhouette of the bridge came into sight. A yearning drew him to the bridge. His guilt exceeded his reasoning. He had to bury his father.

Approaching the bridge, Beauford saw his father's body lying on the bank. The old man's arms curled up against his chest, legs bent at the knees and thighs pressed against his forearms. A sense of relief overcame him that he could still do what he must. As he got closer he saw his father's face—fear was pressed into the skin—deep lines above his cheeks and pursed lips. He lifted the body and turned to go back to the truck. The wind stopped. The night became silent.

A beam from a high-powered flashlight blinded him. Beauford turned to run in the opposite direction and he was hit by another bolt of light. Then a third fixed on him from across the bayou.

"Put him down, boy."

Beauford squinted into the beam, making out several men in hoods and robes. "This my daddy. I wants to give him a rightful burial. Then I be gone."

"Don't think so," a voice said. The men behind the spokesman laughed.

The sound of rushing footsteps came at him from all directions, water splashing, and then the butt of a shotgun slammed against the base of his skull. Beauford crashed to the soft muddy bank and his father's body rolled in the muck. Two men jumped on him, tied his hands behind his back with duct tape and slipped a hangman's noose around his neck, and pulled it tight. They jerked him up onto his feet.

"It's a very honorable thing you came back to do," one of the hooded men said. "But, a very stupid thing, nigga." Laughter filled the air. "But, we're fair men, Beauford, and we gonna give you a choice. Would you like to hang from the tree your daddy did or would you prefer a lynching right here?"

Beauford raised his head, stared straight ahead, and stood quiet. He silently prayed for the well-being of Nathleen and the children.

"Cat gotch your tongue, boy? You don't know where you wanna die?"

Beauford listened to the voices, trying to recognize any one. He nodded his head, "Yeah," and turned in the direction of the one giving the orders. His mouth closed in a narrow tight line, temples throbbed and his rage exploded, "I wanna die in Jimmy Napier's barn where I fucked his daughter."

A man tore off his hood and splashed through the shoreline, shotgun in hand. Everything about him was red, the tinge of his skin, the color of his hair. Water dripped down his bony face. He jammed the barrel under Beauford's chin forcing his head back and up. "I'm gonna shoot your fuggin' head off, nigger. And then I'm gonna fuck your women and lynch your boy." Spit flew from his mouth. He jerked the slide back chambering a shell and jammed the barrel into Beauford's cheek. Napier smiled and his finger pressured the trigger.

Beauford glared down the barrel into Napier's eyes. "So you kill me. Don't make no difference if I die here or somewhere else. But you'll never find my family."

"Wait, Jimmy." The spokesman pulled off his hood. He was a tall and bulky man with thinning brown hair. He stepped forward, put his fingers on the shotgun barrel, and eased it down from Beauford's face. "This nigger don't deserve a fast death after what he did to you. I think we oughtta take him for a little ride behind the back of your truck. Tape his mouth. We don't want his moaning and groaning to get somebody's attention."

"Albert, that's a good idea," Napier said.

Napier wrapped duct tape around Beauford's mouth several times and noticed something in his victim's pocket. He ripped it out. "Well look at this. We got a family picture of three niggers. One dead, two to go."

Beauford's eyes bulged at the photo.

Napier ripped it into shreds and threw it at Beauford's face. "You won't need this anymore, nigger."

The torn pieces tumbled into the slow-moving stream, drifting away.

Napier pushed Beauford into the stream and tripped him.

Beauford arched back on his knees raising his head above the water, breathing in as much air as he could. As he inhaled, Napier's knee crashed into his neck, driving him under water, again spinning him onto his back. He floundered, trying to regain his footing.

The rope from the noose twisted like a water moccasin in the water. Napier grabbed it and pulled Beauford to shore. "Ain't gonna let you drown, boy. The dogs gonna eat the pieces of you that's left on the road."

Napier and a hooded man yanked the rope, dragging Beauford up the bank to the road and onto the bridge. At the rear of Napier's pickup truck they slammed him down on the wooden planks. Napier jumped onto Beauford's back. His knees held Beauford down while the other Klanners padlocked the chain around Beauford's chest and under his arms and hooked the chain to the hitch on the truck. "We're all set now, Albert."

Napier hopped in his truck.

"Jimmy, rev her up." Albert raised his meaty arm pointing up and down Ruleville Road. "Drive back and forth here so we can watch this. Not too fast though. We don't want to mess up the road with no body parts."

Napier got in the truck and started the engine. He gunned the motor a couple of times. The gears crunched as he shifted into first. He stuck his head out the window, nodded twice and gave a thumbs up. The truck lurched foreword.

Beauford's body thudded on the wooden planks of the bridge.

Albert frantically waved his hands overhead. "Stop, Jimmy. Stop."

He pointed down the road. Headlights were coming in their direction. The other Klansmen put their hoods on and readied their shotguns and pistols. A white Lincoln convertible slowed as it approached the bridge. The driver stopped next to Albert.

"Mayor LeGrand, I'm surprised to see you out in the wee hours of the morning," Albert said, his cigar sliding from one corner of his mouth to the other.

"Just finished my poker game and I thought I'd put the top down and enjoy this beautiful Mississippi night," he said, looking up and waving his cigar. "Albert, what's goin' on here?"

"You were right, Mayor. Tisdale came back. Mayor, this nigger says he messed with Jimmy's daughter. Can you believe that?"

"They're animals. You know that. I told you he'd be back, though. But, there's a change in plans." He spoke in a hushed voice. "Things are picking up. The man's getting ready to put some of his plans into action and they want a boy like this. He can go places and do things neither you or I or anybody else in our organization can."

"You telling me to let him go? After all this, we'll never see this nigga again."

"Depends."

"Depends? On what?"

"If he would like to see his little Marlee again. I think we could trust him. A friend of mine in Memphis called when he saw this pickup full of furniture with Mississippi plates from our lovely Sunflower County pull into his motel."

Albert leaned on the door of the Cadillac and whispered, "Mayor, what're we gonna tell Jimmy? How can he face these men again after what they heard?"

"Tell that redneck motherfucker to hop in my car. I'll take him home and explain the situation to him. He's got to look at the big picture. Do like I tell 'em. Make a personal sacrifice. You handle the situation here."

"What do you want me to do?"

"Unchain the nigger. Tell him to bury his old man and get right back to the the motel he was staying at. His family will be waitin' on him. Except for little Marlee. He needs to take his family to Chicago right away and see this man." Mayor LeGrand handed Albert a business card. "This man has an errand for Beauford to run. Then the nigger can get his little girl back, maybe."

# CHAPTER EIGHT

Napier ripped off his sheet and mask and threw them into the back seat of the Mayor's Lincoln. His lips pursed, eyes narrowed, and knuckles whitened as his grip drew tighter on the door handle. He looked over his shoulder. Albert was unlocking the padlock that secured the chain around Beauford's body. The other Klanners stood huddled about, discussing in a low murmur what was going on. They could only speculate what Napier could have done, or didn't do.

"Get in," the Mayor said. He took a drag on the cigar. Its tip glowed red.

Napier stood there in disbelief.

"Jimmy, get the fuck in the car!"

Napier opened the door, sat down on the white leather seat, and slammed the door shut. He folded his arms across his chest, staring at Beauford. He watched Albert help their captive to his feet. Albert tore the duct tape from Beauford's wrist and mouth. The black man raised his head, staring defiantly at Napier, and patted his chafed bloody lips with the back of his hand.

The Mayor slipped the car in gear and drove across the bridge, passing Beauford.

Napier spit at his face. "You're gonna be a dead nigger and your little monkey son, too."

LeGrand stepped on the gas. The Lincoln squealed off the bridge leaving a wake of dirt and stone. "I'll take you home, Jimmy. The boys will drop off your truck for you. But first, we got to talk."

Napier faced the Mayor. "What the hell's goin' on?"

"I'm just following orders. The man decided they needed somebody who could shield our actions, go places none of us could. This nigger was lucky he came up at the right place and the right time. Otherwise, you think I would've stopped you from killin' him?"

"Who the fuck is this man to tell us what we should be doin'?"

"The man's got a plan that's bigger than all of us, Jimmy. Sometimes you just gotta have faith that somebody is lookin' out for our interest. People that want to accomplish what we want. That know more than we do."

"I asked you who he was!"

"He called me cause I'm the Imperial Wizard. He knows where I stand. That I can be trusted. These are dangerous times; FBI, freedom fighters, uppity niggers. Trying to change the way we live. This man and his friends are people in high places and they share our beliefs in a righteous God and protecting our women and children from niggers, Jews and faggots."

"You still ain't tole me his name."

The mayor cleared his throat. "I don't know exactly."

"You don't know! What about me? I'll be the laughing stock of this county, probably the state. Everybody will know that nigger was fucking my daughter. And he's still alive cause someone whose name you don't even know told you we need him. Fuckin' A." He slammed his fist into the dashboard.

"You don't need to worry about your brothers talking about what they heard. They know you and they know that whatever happened was that nigger's fault. They'll be told that what happened on that bridge, and the things that were said, are never to be mentioned again." The Mayor glanced up. "These men respect you Jimmy, and you'll be able to look them in the eye without shame. Your brothers know that your ultimate revenge will happen. I'm telling you it'll be a far greater revenge than you would of got from killin' one lowly nigger. I can feel it, Jimmy."

"You full of all kind of shit tonight. What's gonna happen to Tisdale? He gonna be around here. What's to stop him from trying to carry on with Celeste or talkin' to people?"

"He ain't ever gonna be back here. And he ain't never gonna talk about this. We got his little girl. You don't think he wants to be responsible for anything that might happen to her?"

Napier pushed his fingers through his hair and grasped the back of his neck with both hands. "It ain't fair, Mayor. It just ain't fair. You shoulda let me kill 'im. It jus ain't fuckin' fair."

The Mayor drove Napier home in a roundabout way, past cotton fields and through woods, hoping time would calm his anger. For a half-hour they drove in tense silence until he pulled the Lincoln off the highway, onto a county road and then up the dirt road for a quarter mile to Napier's farmhouse. "I'm sorry, Jimmy. But it's the way it's got to be." He stopped in front of the white frame house, shifted into park, and turned to Napier.

Napier glared at the Mayor. He lifted the handle on the car door, kicked the interior side of the door, opening it and left a footprint on the white upholstery. He stepped out of the car, turned, slammed the door shut, and marched to his front porch.

The mayor pointed his cigar at Napier. "Jimmy, don't do nothin' foolish."

***

Beauford wiped Napier's spit off his face with his muddy shirtsleeve.

Albert looked at him. "You one lucky boy. This what the mayor told me to tell you. So listen up. You go bury your old man and do it fast. When you're done, you get right back to Memphis. Get your family, go to Chicago and see this man." He handed Beauford a business card. "That man is gonna take care of your family and he gonna send you on a little trip."

"How you know we in Memphis?"

"Listen nigger. You ain't the one to be asking questions. Some of our friends visited your family at the motel while you were coming down here. They got your little girl for safe keepin'. What's her name...Marlee?"

Beauford stepped towards Albert.

Albert put his hand up. "You better stop right where you are, boy. Don't you see all my Klansmen brothers? Step back and get your black ass down to that bayou and bury your old man." Albert folded his hands across his chest. "Or I'll have to be apologizing to the mayor for beating your head clear down through your black ass."

Beauford walked backwards to the end of the bridge watching Albert and the other hooded men. When he reached the end of the bridge he ran down the embankment, across the stream, and lifted his father's body. The pain sloshed through his head as he trudged through the muck, glancing over his shoulder to make sure none of the Klansmen were following him, and returned to his truck. He placed the body in the bed of his truck and his primordial instincts overcame him. He beat his fist into the side of the truck bed until blood dripped from his knuckles. He then drove back to the embers of what had been his family's home.

Beauford pulled the truck behind the remnants of his house near the oak tree where he'd found the rocking chair. He thought about his father passing hot summer days sitting in the rocking chair in the shade of the tall oak, sipping cold lemonade.

He grabbed a shovel from the truck and frantically stabbed it into the red clay, digging his father's grave as fast as he could. The blade of the shovel caught under a rock. Beauford jumped on the blade, jerked the handle back, and it snapped. He swung the handle against the blade again and again, finally knocking the blade away from the rock.

He fell to his knees, picked up the blade with both hands, lifted it over his head, and jabbed it into the ground, scooping out the dirt. His hands were bloodied.

When the grave was knee deep Beauford stopped digging. He stood and tossed the blade. His back ached and he wiped his bloody hands on his jeans. His body throbbed from the beating he'd gotten from the Klansmen.

He dragged himself to the truck and lifted his father's body out of the truck bed. "Daddy, I knows you understand I gotta get to my family. I'm gonna lay you down here. This usta be your favorite spot. I hope you find peace here." He staggered back and stumbled into the grave falling next to his father's body. He rose to his knees and stared at the blood on the palms of his hand. A blend of his and his father's. "If there's a God, there will be a time when we'll get revenge."

Beauford lifted himself out of the grave and hobbled to the remains of the stone chimney. One by one he picked up the scorched boulders and carried them to the grave until his father's body was covered. "Daddy, I'll say a prayer for you on the way to Memphis. I got to get my family and find out what I needs to do to get Marlee. Bye, Daddy."

\*\*\*

Napier shoved his front door open, crashing it into the wall. The door swung back and forth on its creaking hinges. He went to the living room leaving a trail of muddy footprints, turned on the TV, sat down, and rested his grimy brown boots on a hassock.

The hallway light flashed on and his wife, Linda Joy, cowered into the room in her pink chenille bathrobe. She saw the front door open and swallowed. "You all right? You wet and muddy." She grabbed a throw off the sofa, walked to the hassock, lifted his feet with her thin fingers and placed the throw under his boots.

He folded his hands behind his head and blew out a deep breath. "Get me a beer."

Linda Joy drifted to the front door, leaned into it and pushed it closed with both hands. She went to the kitchen, and returned, handing him a cold bottle of Budweiser. She twisted her chilled fingers in her bathrobe wiping off the cold beads of moisture from the bottle.

Napier grabbed the bottle and gulped down half of it with a long swig. Beer sluiced down his chin onto his navy blue tee shirt. He pulled a Salem from the pack in his shirt pocket and put it between his lips. "Junior okay?"

Napier reached into his blue jeans, pulled a Bic lighter out, and lit his smoke. He took a long deep drag, staring off to places his wife didn't know—places inhabited by anger and hatred. He exhaled the haze from his nostrils. His eyebrows flattened and forehead creased. "I asked you how Junior was."

Linda Joy sat on the corner of the hassock wringing her hands. Her lips folded inward. She swallowed and looked up, but just at his chest. "He's asleep, so's Celeste. Jimmy," she paused and glanced at the floor. "Jimmy, we got to talk."

"Talk, talk, talk. That's all you women know how to do." He jerked his head back, draining the beer. "Go get me another beer, first. Then we'll talk."

"I don't think you should have another before...."

"I tole you to get me a beer. Don't you be tellin' me what I should be doin'." His cheeks flushed. "Is that so hard for you to understand? Now get!"

She stood, shoulders rounded, tottered to the kitchen and returned with another beer. She sat on the hassock and extended her hand, holding the bottle.

He grabbed it from her and sucked down most of the bottle. "I'm tired. I don't need you jawing at me now." Napier rose from the chair and headed to the stairs. "We'll talk tomorrow. Maybe after I come back from town."

She turned on the hassock watching him set foot on the stairs. "Jimmy, Celeste is pregnant."

"God damn, bitch." He wheeled and hurled the bottle at the TV, shattering the screen. Napier ran up the stairs toward his daughter's bedroom. His wife chased after him.

"Jimmy, please don't do nothin'." Halfway up the stairs she grabbed his forearm. "Wait till the morning. We can think this over and do what's best."

"Let go a me." He jerked his arm out of her grasp. "I know what's best. No daughter of mine is gonna be some nigger's slut. She ain't my child no more. She ain't living here no more." He rushed to the top of the stairs.

Linda Joy followed him and grabbed his arm again. "Jimmy, we can't kick out our own flesh and blood. Please give her a chance."

A light from under Celeste's bedroom door shone into the hallway. Napier jerked his arm out of his wife's grasp, shoved her back, turned and rushed to Celeste's bedroom. He heard Linda Joy tumbling down the stairs. He looked over his shoulder at his wife lying on her back at the bottom of the stairs. She pushed herself up with both arms and then collapsed to the floor. Napier shook his head. "That God damn nigger. Look what he made me do." He smashed the bedroom door open. It banged against the wall like a crack of a gunshot. He heard a faint cry as he entered the room.

Celeste was sitting up in her bed, eyes wide open, body trembling, and hugging her knees against her chest.

Napier stared at her in her faded white nightgown covered with cherubs. "You got all those little angels on you but you ain't nothin' but a whore. And worse yet a nigger's whore." He grabbed her hair and dragged her from the bed down to the floor. "What you need is a whuppin' like the one I was gonna give your nigger.

But nobody has the guts to deal with them the way they need to be." Spit sprayed from his mouth.

He heard the sound of trucks pulling up in front of his house and the doors opening and slamming shut. "You slut. You're lucky. You was gonna get the beatin' of your life." He paused, taking shallow, rapid breaths. "I can't stand to look at your filth no more. I'm going out. When I come back you better be gone. Gone for good." He left, slamming her bedroom door shut.

Napier went down the hall to his son's room and picked up the six-year-old boy in his arms. "Junior, don't you be worried, you comin' with daddy. I got to protect you from this filth." Napier headed down the hallway to the top of the stairs. Looking down, he saw Linda Joy lying on the floor at the bottom of the stairs, blood oozing from her ears and pooling around her head.

He scurried down the stairs, burying his son's face in his chest so the boy couldn't see his mother. Napier knelt next to his wife, putting his ear near her nose. He heard no breathing. "Shit. That nigger killed her." He mumbled.

There was a loud pounding on the front door. "Jimmy, it's Albert and Uriah. We droppin' off your truck."

Napier panicked, *What'll I do now?*

"Jimmy, we got your keys." Albert shouted through the door.

Napier opened the door.

"Here's your…"

"He was here. That nigger was here!" Napier shouted. "He took Celeste." He looked at Junior, covered his son's ears and whispered, "That nigger killed my Linda Joy. We gotta find him. You boys take Junior to the neighbor's, and then head north. I'll check out Ruleville Road."

Albert grabbed Junior in his arms, "Son of a bitch. Jimmy, go to that nigger's shack. He's probably burying his old man there. I don't believe that nigger. He just walked away from certain death and he does this."

"That nigger deserved killin'." Napier shook his head. "And the mayor was tellin' me to calm down."

"Come on, let's go," Uriah said. They ran to their pickup and left.

Napier carried Linda Joy's body to her bed and covered the blood at the base of the stairs with a throw rug. Then he went to Celeste's room. The door was still shut and the light flooded into the hallway from under the door. He pushed the door and it creaked open, revealing his daughter. She sat on the floor leaning against her bed, traumatized and shaking.

He went to her closet, grabbed a suitcase, and stepped to her dresser. Napier pulled out the drawers, dumping the clothes into the suitcase. He grabbed jeans and a sweatshirt and threw them at her. "Get dressed, whore. You ain't a Napier no more. You ain't livin' here no more. I'm taking you to the bus station, giving you $100 so you can get outta my sight. You take a bus wherever you want. Just don't ever come back."

***

Beauford pulled into a gas station on Route 8. "Sumbitches, taking my little girl. I gots to call Nathleen. Let her know I'm on my way. Tell her we'll get Marlee back. Our baby's gonna be all right." He stopped at the pump and entered the office.

A thin black man, about his father's age, sat behind the counter. He wore thick glasses, overalls, and a raggedy tee shirt. His hair was thin and gray.

Beauford slid a five onto the counter. "Set me up for five bucks regular?"

The man cleared the pump. "You set." He frowned at Beauford. "What the hell happened to you?" The old man grabbed a pack of Winstons from his shirt pocket, slipped one between his lips and placed the pack on the counter top.

Beauford scanned the station. "Anybody else here?"

The old man reached under the counter, pulled out a revolver and stared at Beauford. "Why you askin'?" The cigarette wobbled in his mouth.

"I ain't gonna cause no trouble. I got rolled by the Klan. They after any of us that gots land. They hung my daddy and a friend of his. Took my little girl. I need to call my wife, see if she and my boy are okay."

"Fuckin' peckerwoods." He set the pistol on the counter. Spun around on his stool, grabbed a phone and set it next to the pistol.

Beauford pulled out the keychain from the motel and dialed the number printed on it. "Connect me to room 120." The phone rang again and again and there was no answer. "Shit!" He lowered the handset and moved it toward the cradle.

"Hello," a faint voice said.

Beauford jerked it up, "Nath?"

"They took our little girl, Beau. They took her," she bawled.

"I know, Honey. But everything gonna be okay. They jus want me to do something for them. We got to go to Chicago and meet some man and then we gonna get our baby back. Jus like that. You'll see." Beauford took a deep breath and prayed that he was right.

"You sure?"

"This what I want you to do jus to be safe. You take William and get outta there. Don't bother checking out. There was another motel two blocks south on the same street. You check in and wait there for me. I'll be up there in a couple of hours." He glanced at the pack of cigarettes. "Tell 'em your name is Winston. We get a little rest and then we ride up to Chicago and gettin' our little girl."

\*\*\*

An hour before sunrise, Beauford pulled his truck into the parking lot on the side of the Jackson Hotel. It was a two-story building with wood siding painted dark blue. He had cleaned up in the gas station bathroom and tried to walk without limping into the office. A heavy black man sat at the front desk. A mug of steaming coffee and three donuts sat on a paper towel in front of him.

"My wife checked in with my boy a couple of hours ago."

The clerk wiped crumbs off his lips with the back of his hand. "And you be?"

"Winston."

He reached behind him and pulled a key off a board. "Up the stairs, third room on left, 206."

Beauford grabbed the key and pulled himself up the creaking wooden steps. He was afraid the sound of the key turning in the lock would scare his wife so he knocked softly on the black door. Its paint was chipped and pealing. "Nath, it's me, open up."

The door, held by a chain lock, opened a crack. Nathleen peered through. She unchained it and let him in. A large purple bruise covered her left cheek. He saw fright in her wet eyes.

She looked at Beauford's bruised face. "Marlee," she mumbled and fell into his arms.

"Nath, are you okay? They didn't do anything to you? I mean…"

She shook her head.

He carried her into the room and laid her on the bed. "William, you here?" The bathroom door opened and William ran into Beauford's arms.

"Daddy, they took Marlee. Momma tried to stop them and they hit her. I tried to help…."

"It's okay, William. Everything gonna be all right. We gonna go up to Chicago. Get a new place to live and get Marlee back. Everything will be better than ever. Just you wait and see."

# CHAPTER NINE

## Tuesday, April 2, 1968

The sky in the east was purple, filtered through a gray mist, and a touch of orange layered the horizon. Beauford climbed behind the steering wheel. His shirt damp and skin chilled from the cold air. He turned the key and the engine sputtered and turned over. Rain drops splattered the windshield, making it look like he was gazing through antique glass. He flicked on the windshield wipers and the drops spilled to the sides. He shifted into first gear and the truck jerked forward, stopping in front of the entrance to the Jackson Hotel.

Nathleen held her jacket over her head protecting her and William as they ran from the hotel into the pickup truck. The boy sat in the middle and Nathleen in the passenger seat. His eyes were red and her bruised cheek a deep purple.

She looked at Beauford. "We gonna stop at the other place and pick up our things?"

"No, jus go straight up there." The truck roared out of Memphis heading to Chicago.

In Arkansas the rain stopped and the skies cleared. The sun shining through the glass warmed the damp occupants in the truck. They drove in silence as Beauford headed north on Interstate 55.

Nathleen put on a brave front, covering her fear. "When we get to Chicago, Marlee will be there." She looked at William and smiled. "You two can play tag and make all sorts of new friends in school." Tears began to well in her eyes. She looked through the passenger side window and brushed the sleeve of her coat across her face.

William forced a smile, leaned into his mother and tugged his father's arm.

Beauford glanced down at his boy. He knew his son's smile was a façade that covered the nightmare of his grandfather's lynching and his sister's kidnapping—events he feared would haunt his boy for the rest of his life.

Beauford thought about his own secrets. Can't tell Nath how close I was to bein' killed. Make her worry even more about Marlee. Gotta keep my mind on getting to Chicago and doing what I gotta to get my baby back. She must be so scared. Can't stop to sleep. Gots to keep goin'. If they do anything to her—he clenched his teeth.

He glanced in the rearview mirror. An Arkansas State trooper pulled in behind their pickup truck. He saw the trooper talking into his microphone. His grip on the steering wheel tightened. He approached the exit for Blytheville.

He glanced in the mirror again. Maybe I should I get off? Anything can happen on a lonely highway. Could be a Klanner. No other cars around. Who knows what he might try? He slowed down to fifty.

Nathleen caught him glimpsing in the mirror. "What's wrong?"

"There's a trooper behind us."

She squeezed his shirt sleeve. The lines in the corners of her eyes deepened. "Oh, God. What else can they do?"

William pulled himself up so he could look through the rear window.

"Sit down, son. Everybody take a deep breath. We gonna be all right." He swallowed and passed the exit. The trooper veered to the right, leaving the highway. Beauford's grip on the wheel lightened. Nathleen slid back in her seat and sighed. They crossed into Missouri and kept heading north on Interstate 55.

"It's getting close to lunch, Beau. William's getting hungry."

"Try to stay out of those big cities. Too easy to get turned around in them."

"The sign says Valley View. Why don't we try that?" Nathleen said.

Beauford pulled off the interstate and stopped at a gas station where he filled the tank. They went to a Tubby's Drive In Restaurant next door and spent the last of their cash on hamburgers and soft drinks. Beauford and Nathleen sat on the running board of the truck eating their sandwiches and William played with a stray yellow dog.

"What do we do when we get to Chicago?" Nathleen asked.

He pulled the business card Albert had given him out of his shirt pocket and handed it to Nathleen. "Here's the man we're supposed to see. The directions are on the back of the card."

"It's a strange name." Her forehead furrowed. "Hel—mut Rei—chardt, Democratic Ward Committeeman, Marquette Park Office, Chicago, Illinois. What's a ward committeeman?"

"I dunno. We just got to be careful. He got to have something to do with those people down home."

She slipped the card into his shirt pocket. "Why they putting us through all this, Beau? What'd they want?"

"I don't know. The only thing I know is this is what we got do to get Marlee. We better head on." He yawned.

"Beau, you look so tired. When're you supposed to meet this man?"

He leaned against the door and stretched his arms overhead. "They said after his office closes, after six."

"Why don't you lay down in the truck?"

"No, we ain't got time. We gotta get up there and get our girl." They climbed into the truck and headed north.

Dusk had settled on Chicago as Beauford headed northeast on Interstate 55 through the remnants of the evening's rush hour traffic and the industrial areas that lined the expressway. "I ain't ever seen so many trucks and cars."

They turned south onto the Dan Ryan Expressway and exited west driving through the neighborhoods and down to Marquette Road. Beauford glanced out his window. There were houses with singed bricks, boarded windows, and tagged with graffiti. The wind blew papers across shallow, barren front yards. Red and blue lights flashed from the neon signs of taverns. Dented cars sat on milk crates. Dark figures lingered in shadowy gangways.

Looking for the address on the card, he watched the numbers on the houses grow higher and the neighborhoods change. Shiny cars were parked in an orderly fashion and front yards were green with lush spring grass. Beauford stopped at a red light at California. He saw the sign for the ward office hanging from the building just west of the traffic light on the north side of the street. A large park covered the south side of Marquette Avenue.

He drove past the office and parked a few stores to the west. The building was a single story, red-brick storefront connected to a two-story four-flat behind it. Black burglar bars protected the front windows and door of the office. Emblazoned in large gold letters across the window was "Alderman Carl Hiedler-15$^{th}$ Ward, Democratic Ward Committee Office."

The office was dark inside except for a funnel of light from a desk lamp in the middle of the room. A man sat at the desk, his face lost in the shadows of the office, phone pressed against his ear.

Beauford looked at his wife and son. William was fast asleep leaning against his mother. Nathleen rested against the passenger door. He whispered, "Nath, got to be after six. That man in there waitin' on me. I better go."

She bit her lip and nodded.

He opened the truck door and stepped into the damp cold. A light rain thudded on his denim jacket as he walked around the truck and stopped at the front door. Beauford grabbed the doorknob and pulled, but the door was locked. He slipped his hand between the burglar bars and tapped on the glass.

The man at the desk placed the phone down, slid his chair back, and peered at the door. He stood up and reached the door in five long strides. He was a head taller than Beauford. His face was hard and lean with a strong chin. His eyes covered by thick glasses with gold metal frames. "What do you want?"

"I'm Beauford Tisdale." He slid his hand through the bars on the door and pressed the business card against the glass. "I'm supposed to see Mr. Reichardt."

The man unlocked the door and pushed it open. "I'm Reichardt." He motioned with his head. "Go back to my desk."

Beauford slinked into the office. His eyes squinted in the darkness, looking for a warning, for someone else's presence.

Reichardt peered into the night, looking up and down the street. The night was still except for the tapping of the rain. He stepped back, closed the door, locked it, marched back to his desk, and sat down.

Beauford stood in front of the desk. He watched the man pick up the phone and finish his notes on the pad of paper. Reichardt pushed up his glasses with his forefinger and brushed his hand through the blond bristles of his crew cut. He ripped off the sheet of paper from the tablet and handed it to Beauford. "This is where you'll be living, the LeClaire Courts housing project. Not too far from here. Just north of Midway Airport. The directions are on the paper."

Beauford grasped the paper, "What about my daughter ...sir?"

"I'll get to that." Reichardt lifted a burning cigarette off of the corner of his wooden desk. He took a drag, swallowed the smoke, and let it trail out of his nostrils. He crushed the cigarette into a glass ashtray next to the telephone.

"We put you on the payroll with the city, Department of Streets and Sanitation. It's not easy to get a city job, so don't screw up. You'll report here every day, for odd jobs, cleaning up around here, whatever I tell you to do."

"Yes, sir." Beauford shifted his weight from one foot to the other. "And my little girl?"

"You look like shit. Go to your apartment tonight and get some sleep. You need to be well rested, tomorrow's Wednesday. I have a delivery for you to make. The package has to be in Memphis no later than noon, Thursday. Come back tomorrow night about 10:00. You do what you're told, you'll get your girl back Friday—if everything goes right."

He slid his desk drawer open, picked up a set of keys, and tossed them to Beauford. "These are for your apartment. The place has got some furniture and stuff."

"I spent all my money coming up here. Could use some cash for food and gas for the trip."

"Shit, just like a...." He paused, cleared his throat, and mumbled. "Asking for cash before you do any work." Reichardt reached into his pocket and pulled out a roll of bills. He peeled off five twenties and threw them on his desk. "You're paying me back out of your first check. You can go now. Don't forget, ten tomorrow night." He thumped his index finger on his desk, "Right here."

Beauford scooped up the money, walked to the door, unlocked it, and pushed it open. He darted into the cold rain. He stood at the door of his truck and watched the rain run down the window of the ward office. He stared at the blurred image of Reichardt. *God help us all, if what I got to do don't get Marlee back.* He got in the truck.

Nathleen looked at him. "When do we get my baby back?"

"Sometime Friday. First, I got to make some kind of delivery for them. Leave tomorrow night."

"Deliver what? Where?" She frowned.

"Memphis, don't know what. He just gave me a key for an apartment for us and told me about a job they got lined up for me. Got to go back to the office tomorrow night to pick up whatever I gots to deliver. He said I should be back Friday morning."

"Just do it so I get my Marlee back."

"Ain't no other choice." He pulled away from the curb and headed to their new home.

***

Mayor LeGrand slid back his dining room chair and picked up the ringing phone from the high board. "The final instructions will be delivered to you by messenger. You should get it in the next half-hour. Make sure you get it to the man that you made the arrangements with immediately. You understand?"

"Yes. I'll handle it right away."

"After he reads them and understands them you're to witness that they are burned."

"Yes, sir." The phone went dead.

His new, young wife, Penelope, patted the back of her bouffant. "Who's that, honey?" She leaned forward, making sure her cleavage didn't escape his view.

The mayor stood, his mind drifting away. "Town business."

"Are you going to come back and finish dinner with me?"

"Yes, I'll be right back. I have to check something in my study and make a call." He left the dining room, crossing the main hallway past the large staircase heading to the second floor, and entered his study. He sat at his oak desk, behind him a portrait of Jefferson Davis, to the right the Confederate flag and to the left the Mississippi State flag.

He opened his leather briefcase, paged through his address book and dialed a number.

"Delta Boarding House," the voice said in a long slow drawl.

"Can you get me John Willard, please?"

"He's all the way down the hallway. Take me a minute."

"I'll wait." The mayor heard the phone thudded down followed by footsteps marching down the hallway. A few moments later the sounds of shuffling steps returned.

"Yeah."

"This John Willard?" The mayor asked.

"That's who you asked for, ain't it?"

"It's your friend from the barn."

"Thought you forgot about me."

"No sense talking 'less we have to. Sure you understand that. I'm coming up tonight, be there in an hour. Make sure you wait for me in your room. See you then." He cradled the phone.

Penelope stood in the doorway in her powder blue A-line dress, one hand on her hip. "Who you talking to now?"

"I told you its town business. I wish you would stop following me around." His lips pursed.

"What's a wife to think when her husband is telling someone to make sure they wait for him in their room?"

He walked to her and put his arm around her shoulder. "Honey, I ain't hiding nothing from you. It's a paving contractor for the streets around the town square."

The doorbell rang. She looked at him and cocked her head. "I'll get it."

"It's probably for me. I'm expecting a messenger to deliver a contract that I have to take to the paver." He watched her strut to the door and take the envelope from the messenger.

She turned and sashayed back to him and extended her hand holding the envelope.

He reached for it, and she jerked her hand back. "Now tell me who you were talking to."

"I told you it's the paving—"

"Oh, take the silly thing."

"Thank you," he grabbed the envelope and slipped it into the inside pocket of his brown teed jacket.

"Aren't you going to open it?"

"No, I know it's the contract. I have to ride out to Greenville tonight to finalize this deal. Sorry, but I have to leave soon."

"Why don't I come with you? It would be nice to get away from this old place for a night. Spend the night in Greenville like we used to on our special little getaways when you were married to Olivia." She ran her tongue around her lips.

"Penny, I'd love to, but this man's office is in the shabbiest part of Greenville and I'll probably have to be negotiating some of the final details with him for awhile. This guy's a real SOB."

"You work so hard for this silly little town. Will you do me a favor?'

"Sure, Honey."

"Just open that little envelope and let me see that silly contract."

"I can't—."

She put her hands on her hips. "Don't you dare be calling me later to tell me you got to be spending the night, 'cause you'll find all your possessions on the front lawn." She turned and sprang up the stairs.

The mayor walked out of his plantation house, past the tall white columns, entered his Lincoln, and headed for Greenville. He glanced at the envelope sitting on the passenger seat. It had been a few weeks since his meeting with John Willard or what-ever his name was. The fact that he was called to deliver "final instructions" meant that something was happening soon. He felt a rush. He was a part of something that was bigger than he had ever dreamed. Something worthwhile and dangerous. But he was also relieved. He had had the sense to protect himself. He was simply a messenger.

He headed into Greenville on Route 82. The city has a port on Lake Ferguson, a branch of the Mississippi River. The riverfront area was filled with dive bars. Their patrons, drunken stevedores and rednecks, letting their hard-earned pay slip through their fingers for liquor and women. Cheap hotels catered to all the transient trades.

The mayor exited north onto Service Road, west past the bus station, and to the railroad tracks, which stopped at Lake Ferguson. He heard a ship's horn hooting. The streets and buildings glistened with a damp shiny look. A mist hovered about the streetlights. Honky-tonk music blared from the bars. Down the street, a blue neon light flashed, "Delta Boarding House."

The mayor pulled to the curb, and the flashing light from the sign reflected off the polished hood of his Lincoln. He stepped out of the car to the front door and entered. To his right were two worn sofas facing a black-and-white television with rabbit ears antennae. Two men sat on the sofa facing the television sleeping off their afternoon drunk. A third man lay on the opposite sofa. He wore a faded baseball hat, and his glassy eyes peered at the characters from *The Mod Squad* on TV.

The mayor walked up to the counter. "Looking for John Willard."

A man looked up from a girlie magazine. His nose laced with tiny red veins. He raised his eyebrows, and gave a hearty laugh. "You a bill collector or process server?"

"What room he's in?"

"End of the hallway on the right, room 15."

"Thanks." He walked the dimly lit hallway looking at the numbers on the doors. Some were hanging by a nail and others were written with Magic Markers. White tiles ingrained with dirt peeled up from the floor and faded wallpaper with small roses covered the walls. Johnny Cash's voice leaked out from one room and from the next, curse words between a man and a woman.

He knocked on the door to room 15.

"Who's there?"

"I called you earlier. It's me."

The door opened a crack, secured by a chain on the inside. A blue eye peaked through the crack. "Hold on." The door closed, the chain was slid out of the bracket, and the mayor stepped into the dingy room and closed the door behind him.

He reached inside his jacket, grasped the envelope, and handed it to James Earl Ray. "Read this, understand exactly when and where you have to be. Then we have to burn it."

Ray ripped open the envelope and read the one page document. "Simple enough. I got it. I don't get any money 'til that day?"

"What ever it says, that's the arrangements. It's between you and the people that are paying you. I don't know anything about them. That's the way it's got to be. You understand?"

"Yeah, I got it."

The mayor pulled his lighter out of his pocket. "No questions then?"

Ray shook his head.

The mayor struck the emery wheel and the flame jumped. He moved the lighter under the edge of the page that Ray held and they watched the yellow flame consume the paper. The edge turning black as the flame climbed. The paper curling and crumbling to the floor.

"Good luck." The mayor turned and left the room. Ray stepped into the hallway with him. The door to the next room opened and a young redhead stepped out. She looked at the two men. Her eyes widened, "Mayor Le Grand, I…I'm so surprised to see you."

"What're you doing here?"

Ray smiled. "Well, Mayor LeGrand, I think I'll go back in my room and you can go about your business." He stepped back and closed the door.

"I ah…I left home. Please don't tell my father you saw me here. I mean he knows I left." She struggled for words. "I mean, we both agreed it was the best thing. We've been having fights and I can't live there anymore."

The mayor shook his head, *That fucking redneck. Throwing his daughter out.* "Celeste, you can't live in a place like this. I know a woman that lives here in Greenville who takes in young ladies. You'll be safe there. You can finish school and get a job. You don't have to deal with the likes of your drunken father." He looked away and then back. "I'm sorry, I shouldn't say that to you. I just can't believe he would throw you out of the house. Get your things I'll take you there now."

"Shouldn't you check first to see if it's all right?"

"No, it's my ex-wife. With all the money she got from me, she owes me this much." The mayor followed Celeste into her room and watched her take her clothes out of a small dresser and neatly place them in her suitcase. He opened the door and they walked down the hallway.

Ray was on the sofa in the lobby watching television. The mayor looked his way and then at the door, hoping to leave unnoticed. "Mayor LeGrand, You have a good time with your lady friend."

They got in the mayor's car and he pulled into the street. The mayor swallowed. The shooter that he had recruited now knew his name and the woman sitting next to him saw him meet with the shooter. He took a deep breath, looked at Celeste, and exhaled. "I was meeting with that man on city business."

*** 

The next morning Nathleen's eyes flashed open at the roar of a jet landing at Midway International Airport. "What kind of place is this?" She dragged herself out of bed, went to the kitchen and searched the cabinets. She found a can of Maxwell House, a coffee pot and brewed some coffee. Looking through the burglar bars that covered every window she watched the wind swirl trash across the gray landscape that was spotted with patches of brown and green weeds. Men hovered about in groups of threes and fours. One man was burning an old wooden doorframe in a 55-gallon drum to fight off the early morning chill. Two others struggled over the contents of a bottle wrapped in a brown paper bag. Another pulled a half-smoked cigarette out of his jacket pocket. His hollow cheeks sunk deeper as his shaking hand attempted to bring the lighted match to the tip of his smoke.

Nathleen took a cup of coffee back to the bedroom for Beauford. She jostled him with one hand. "Honey, here some coffee. It's black. There's no sugar or cream in the kitchen." She sat on the edge of the bed. "This ain't a good place for us."

He grasped the cup and took a sip. "What do you mean?"

"It's morning in the middle of the week and a bunch of men are jus' standing around outside, burning stuff to stay warm, fighting over liquor, and smoking. Don't they have no jobs to go to?"

"Nath, we don't have no choice 'til we get Marlee back. After that we'll see what's best. Do what we can do."

"Anything got to be better than this."

*** 

Late Wednesday night, Beauford drove to the ward office through patches of fog that misted on his windshield. He knew he had no option but to follow Reichardt's orders. He was scared. *What they want me to do that so important that they had to take Marlee?*

Beauford headed south on California Boulevard. His instincts told him to be careful. One block away from the office, he went west three blocks to Richmond, then south, parking just north of Marquette. He walked past three empty storefronts toward the ward office. His eyes scanned up and down the block. Each street light gave the foggy mist a yellow glow. He didn't know what he was looking for, and was relieved not to see anything that kindled his fear. Again, the office was dark except for the light on Reichardt's desk. He knocked on the front door.

Reichardt came to the door and let him in. "Sit in the chair by my desk. I've got to get something out of the backroom."

Beauford sat in a wooden chair. He was less tired than the night before, more aware of his surroundings. Election posters of Mayor Richard J. Daley and Alderman Heidler hung on the wall flanked on one side by an American flag and on the other by the city flag. Red, white, and blue banners streamed from corner to corner.

Reichardt returned carrying a brown paper sandwich bag. He set the bag on his desk, sat down, and scribbled a name and address on a sheet of paper.

"This is where you're going." He said, handing the paper to Beauford. "Remember, you need to be there by noon tomorrow. It's a boarding house. There's a room reserved for you. It's under the name of Robert Johnson. Stay in your room until the guy comes to pick up the bag. Give me those two little books on the table behind you."

Beauford turned and grabbed two small books that looked like the passbook he used to have for the $50 they had in a savings account at the Ruleville State Bank. He handed the books to Reichardt who dropped them in the bag.

"After this stuff is picked up, you can leave anytime you want. Call me when you get back and arrangements will be made for you to get your daughter."

"I'm on my way," Beauford said, grabbing the bag. He felt the weight and shape of the bag as he left the office. *Feels like money. I ain't gonna look. Do what I got to do to get Marlee back.* He glanced at the sheet of paper and mumbled, "Bessie Brewer's boarding house. Hmm, sounds familiar."

Beauford set the bag on the passenger seat and drove through the night taking Interstate 55 back to Memphis. The sun rising as he approached the city. This trip had a different feel to it.

He felt focused, purposeful. Not like he was running from something, but more like he was running to something. He didn't care about whatever he was taking or why. He would get his Marlee back. What else could matter?

He approached the boarding house when a newspaper boy on his bicycle shot out from between parked cars. Beauford stomped on the brakes. The tires screeched as the truck caught the back tire of the bicycle, knocking the boy to the ground and scattering his newspapers all over Main Street. Beauford jumped out of the truck and ran to the boy. "You all right?"

The young black boy sat on his haunches in the middle of the street. He rubbed one hand over his torn jeans and bloody knee. His bicycle lay ten feet away. "Oh, man. The rear wheel is bent. I'll never get the papers delivered now. I'll be in big trouble."

"I'm sorry." Beauford looked at the clock in the window of Jim's Grill near the boarding house. "It's only 6:00. Pick up your papers and I'll drive you so they get out." He picked up the boy's bike and put it in the back of the truck.

Beauford got in the truck as the boy retrieved his newspapers. The paper bag lay on the floor in front of the passenger seat, one hundred dollar bills, and the two small blue books scattered about.

"Shit!" He scooped up the money, stacked it up, and put it in the paper bag. He grabbed the books and looked at them. "Passports." He paged through the books and saw the same picture in each book, but two different names, John Willard and Ramon George Sneyd. He stuffed the passports into the bag and slid it under his seat.

The boy got in the passenger seat. He bent over and covered his face with his hands.

Beauford leaned toward the boy and put his arm on the boy's shoulders. "You okay?"

"My momma bought me the bike for my birthday. She work so hard at the laundry." He shook his head.

Beauford reached under the seat, grabbed the bag and pulled a one hundred dollar bill from the stack. "Here, get your bike fixed and buy something for your momma. Might as well be something good come from this money."

The boy's eyes opened wide. "Thank you, mister."

They finished delivering the newspapers and he dropped the boy off at his home. Beauford checked in at Bessie Brewer's boarding house. The rooms were on the second floor down a long hallway with green linoleum floors and one light bulb screwed into the ceiling. On the ground floor was Jim's Grill. The sign in the window advertised a lunch special of sausage, eggs, toast, grits and coffee for 62¢. Beauford bought an egg sandwich and coffee for breakfast, a salami sandwich and a coke for later, and went upstairs to his room.

The room smelled musty and dust motes floated in the sunlight shining through the window to the left of the single bed. He cracked open the window a few inches to let in fresh air and saw the Motel Lorraine. "That looks like a better place. With all this money they shoulda got me a room there."

Beauford locked the door with the sliding bolt, pulled the tattered shade down and lay on the sagging bed that had a mattress over bare springs. He took in a deep breath and inhaled the odor of a pine disinfectant. He tossed and turned, and spent most of the time staring at a bare light bulb spotted with dead insects hanging from the faded green ceiling and listening to the portable gas heater in the corner of the room. When he drifted off he was haunted by the unknown fate of his daughter and interrupted with nightmares of the vision of his father's lynching.

\*\*\*

That morning in Ruleville it was cloudy and warm and there was the pressing feel of moisture in the air. Linda Joy Napier was carried out of the white frame Calvary Baptist Church in a pine box. The shadow from the cross on top of the steeple fell across the casket as the pallbearers stepped down the three stairs from the front door and carried her to the cemetery in the rear of the church.

Jimmy Napier held two roses in one hand and clutched Junior's hand in the other as they walked behind the pallbearers. Following them were Napier's Klan brothers and their wives. Napier wore a powder blue suit he had purchased seventeen years ago from Sears for his and Linda's wedding. Junior wore overalls.

Napier pulled a handkerchief from the inside coat pocket of the wrinkled suit coat and wiped imaginary tears from his eyes as they approached the grave. The pallbearers placed the casket on the hoist above the grave. Napier handed Junior a red rose to place on the casket.

There was a momentary silence that was broken by the sound of the halyard clanking against the flagpole as the Confederate flag flapped in the breeze.

The Reverend Lamar Till stepped forward to the gravesite. "Let us say our final words of farewell to our dear sister who was tragically taken from this world far too early. She leaves behind her a grieving family, her loving husband James, sweet daughter Celeste, who is too grief stricken to be with us today, and a young son, Junior. We hope the young boy will have the strength of his father to help him walk through this dark period of his life." Reverend Till raised both arms to the sky. "The Lord is good, a stronghold in the day of trouble, and he knows those who trust in him." He lowered his arms, "Amen, brothers and sisters."

"Amen," the Klansmen and their wives responded.

Napier leaned over and placed his rose on the pine box. He grasped his son and held him as the young boy leaned forward placing his rose on his mother's coffin. Tears ran down the boy's face.

The casket was slowly lowered into the ground. In the seconds before the pine box settled in the dirt, Napier experienced her loss for the first time. His recollection of those things that at the time seemed ordinary now returned with special meaning. Her unfailing efforts to please him. Her soft warm skin as she lay next to him. Her gentle voice. He hadn't missed her or dealt with the sensation that he would never see her or hear her again. She was gone and anger inflamed his heart. *Beauford Tisdale, you a dead nigger.*

Napier perused the group of people who attended the funeral. As they started to walk away from the gravesite to their cars he noticed that there wasn't a white Lincoln in the parking lot. *Mayor LeGrand ain't here.*

Napier's heart raced. "If it wasn't for the mayor and that nigger, Linda Joy would be alive."

"What, Daddy?"

Napier knelt down and gazed into his son's green eyes. "Junior, you got to make a promise to me on your momma's grave."

Junior wiped a tear from his eye. "Okay, Daddy."

"If I don't kill that nigger, Beauford Tisdale, and his son before I die, that you'll promise to do that for the honor of your mother and sister. The blood in them men ain't worthy. Niggers with that blood only know one thing. How to defile white women."

The little boy grabbed his father's hand, gazed into his eyes, and silently nodded.

His father smiled, baring his small, yellow teeth.

\*\*\*

Shortly after four that afternoon there was a knock on the door, startling Beauford. He kicked his feet off the bed and looked at the door. "Who's there?"

"I'm here to get a package from you, Johnson. Open the door."

Beauford leaned over, picked the paper bag off the nightstand, walked the narrow path between the wall and the bed to the door. He slid the bolt back and opened the door. A scrawny white man with a receding hairline and a long, thin nose wearing a white shirt and black pants faced him. "How do I know that you supposed to get this? Mr. Reichardt would be mad if I didn't give it to the right person."

The man tugged at his earlobe and then pointed his finger in Beauford's face. "Look, nigger, don't give me no uppity talk. I don't know no Mr. Reichardt and I doubt if your name is Johnson. But that don't make no hill of beans to me. I guarantee you that your Mr. Reichardt will be a lot more than pissed if you don't give me what I came for. So you just hand that over and shut the fuck up."

Beauford handed the bag to the man.

The man opened the bag, peered into it, and nodded. "See ya around," and walked down the hallway.

Beauford closed the door, locked it, and lay down on the squeaky mattress. His mind wandered from thoughts of Marlee to his father when he realized, *had to be the right man. He was the one whose picture was in the passports.* He yawned, "Nap for twenty minutes. Try to get some rest before I head home to get my baby."

\*\*\*

Shouts from the parking lot behind the boarding house across Mulberry Street brought Beauford out of his sleep. He glanced at the plastic clock on the nightstand, "Shit, almost six. Damn it, didn't want to stay here that long." He swung his feet to the floor, shook his head, and rubbed his eyes. He opened the door, walked to the next room, the common bathroom to splash water on his face. Painted in red on the door was "toilet and bath." He grabbed the doorknob and pushed, but the door didn't open. "Anybody in there?" There was no answer. He grabbed the doorknob again and rattled the door against its frame. It wouldn't open. "Damn it."

Beauford returned to his room and tossed the leftover half of the salami sandwich into a paper bag to take with him. He turned to leave when he heard more shouts from the parking lot. A voice he had previously heard caught his attention. A voice that was familiar. He pulled the shade up and slid the window all the way up. "Why I'll be, Reverend King."

Beauford rested his hands on the sill and leaned out the window. A shot rung out to his left. His ears panged. He jerked his head to the left. A smoking rifle barrel lurked in the window.

Everything moved in slow motion. His eyes circled back. He took in the sky. Then Mulberry street. Then the second floor terrace of the motel. He saw Martin Luther King grab his neck—saw him crumble to the terrace floor. Cries and screams came from the entourage on the terrace.

Beauford's eyes swiveled to the left. The barrel of the rifle pulled back.

Beauford flashed back to the motel.

King's people pointed at his window. "Over there. The shot came from there."

Pandemonium broke out in the parking lot under the terrace. A crowd of Memphis policemen scurried around looking for cover and trying to find out where the shot came from.

Beauford heard footsteps scurrying in the bathroom next door and the door slam. He was stunned, and then he realized, *Got to get the hell out of here*. He scooped up the paper bag and ran out of the room.

At the end of the hallway, taking his first step down the stairs, holding a green bundle, was the white man he had given the paper bag to. The white man whose picture was in the passports.

The man smiled at Beauford. "The biggest nigger of them all is down." He ran down the stairs.

Beauford froze. *The man I gave the money to. He killed King.*

Beauford rushed down the stairs, a half flight behind the shooter. He saw the white man rush out the door. *I got to get him.* Beauford took the stairs two-at-a-time. He stopped at the sidewalk. He saw the shooter throw the bundle into the entryway one store down. Beauford ran toward him and froze. He felt his heart chill. *I get him and I never see Marlee again.* He watched the shooter dash to a white Ford Mustang. The man glanced at Beauford, got in the car, and drove away.

Beauford wondered, *Should I get the bundle?* The sirens of Memphis police cars crashed into his ears. Flashing lights illuminated the darkening sky. His eyes were jittering. *Get the hell outta here.* He ran to his truck, drove out of the city in the opposite direction of the Mustang, and headed back to Chicago.

He went over the events of the last few days. The bloodshed caused by the Klan in Mississippi. And then the bloodshed stopped, stopped at him. *Why? Because they wanted me for this. God, help me.*

His heart pounded in his chest. Sweat rushed down his brow. Tears stung his eyes. He knew one thing for sure.

They had him now.

# CHAPTER TEN

For five hundred and fifty miles Beauford had listened to the reports of King's murder on his truck radio. He heard that the murder weapon, a Remington 30.06 rifle with a Redfield scope, was found wrapped in a dirty green bedspread at the entrance to Canipes Amusement Company on the ground floor below Bessie Brewer's Boarding House. He remembered the white man he had given the paper bag to rushing down the sidewalk and tossing a green bundle he was carrying into a recessed doorway. He wiped his sleeve across his eyes, sweeping away the tears, and smelled the fleshy aroma of his sweat.

*I got to go to the police and tell 'em what I know. Martin Luther King killed and I'm the one that gave the devil his pay.*

At four in the morning he pulled into the LeClaire Court's housing project and parked on 43$^{rd}$ Street in front of their apartment. A place he didn't want to be. He longed for a time past when the only sounds he heard were croaking frogs, chirping mockingbirds, and the breeze whispering through live oaks. Instead, his ears were pierced by screeching steel wheels of freight trains from the tracks behind their apartment and the slapping of truck tires on the pavement of Interstate 55 just beyond the tracks. He saw buildings tagged with graffiti and discarded newspapers and dead leaves blown across the barren ground by the swirling north wind.

*This is my home now and the home of my wife and children. I got to protect them. If I go the police, there's too many risks. Got to bury this deep inside. No matter if it eats my soul 'til there's nothing left. I got to stay alive for them. Maybe this is the end for me—maybe they want more from me.*

He saw lights turning on in a few of the windows of the apartments. People were preparing for another day of life in the neighboring factories. He stumbled up the stoop of their apartment, unlocked the door, and entered.

He heard Nathleen rushing from the bedroom. "Honey, is that you?" She charged into the living room wearing a cotton nightgown. Her eyes reddened. "I'm so glad you're home. I was so worried." She put her arms around him and then backed away.

"What's wrong?" She raised her palm to her forehead. "I can tell something's wrong. Is it Marlee? Is she all right?"

"No. No. It's not that. I'll call Reichardt later and make arrangements to get her."

"You had me worried. So everything's okay?"

Beauford bit his lip. "The trip they sent me on. It...it was Memphis." His stomach knotted. He realized he couldn't tell her the truth. To do that he would bring to the surface the feelings he was trying to bury. And then he would have to deal with her emotions and he was too tired for the conflict that was sure to arise. "I...I saw the Reverend King shot."

"Oh, my God. I cried all night. What kind of people would do that?" Her lips trembled. "I'm so scared. I don't understand this killin'. First down home and now this."

Beauford stepped forward and tried to comfort her in his arms. "I don't know, Honey. I just don't know what kind of people would do that." He closed his eyes, took a deep breath, and swallowed.

She pushed him arms' length away. "This trip. ...it didn't have anything to do...I mean the delivery you made?"

He opened his eyes, looked into hers and then to the floor.

She waved her hands in front of her face. "Don't tell me. I'm afraid to know."

He shook his head. "No, no, it wasn't anything like that." He exhaled. "I'm tired, been up all night. I'm gonna lay down before I drop. I'll call Reichardt around nine. He should be in by then."

Her eyes narrowed and she nodded.

He walked past her through the sparsely furnished apartment and collapsed onto the bed knowing eventually the truth would become a dividing line between them.

\*\*\*

Six hours after Beauford Tisdale trudged into his apartment in the tired housing project on the southwest side of Chicago, Tom Sakich sat behind his large mahogany desk in his plush office. He picked up the *Chicago Tribune* his secretary had placed in the usual position on the corner of his desk and read the headlines—Martin Luther King Slain, Police Hunt for Killer. A smirk broke across his face.

Sakich flipped the *Trib* onto his desk and strutted to the window of his tenth floor office overlooking the gray monolith that was Chicago's city hall. He had worked his way up from a seventeen-year-old laborer hauling wheelbarrows of cement to become the deputy director of the city's Department of Transportation and his office reflected that in size and stature. A credenza that matched his desk. Walls filled with photographs of important city pols at ribbon-cutting ceremonies at various million-dollar projects across the city. The city flag in one corner and the Stars and Stripes in the other.

Sakich's salary was $18,000 a year. But his position enabled him to live the good life. He wore a tailor-made double-breasted navy-blue silk suit that hid his middle age paunch. A red silk tie contrasted with the whiteness of his shirt and imported black leather Italian shoes graced his feet. His gray hair was trimmed weekly and nails manicured at a Rush Street salon. He drove a new yellow Cadillac Sedan Deville. All this paid for with $100 bills.

He sat down behind his desk and straightened the photograph of his wife and daughter that had been moved by last night's cleaning crew. He leaned back in his swivel chair, crossed his hands behind his head, and thought, *It was a good day for Tom Sakich. The first one in a long time.*

He slid forward, put his elbows on the desk, and picked up the photograph of his wife and daughter, youthful looking blondes with hair the color of straw. He swiveled around, faced the wall away from the door to his office, away from the rest of the world.

"Amy and Chrissie, you two look more like sisters than mother and child." *Chrissie, so young, so much energy. Amy, such a beautiful wife*, he thought.

His mind drifted to that night ten months ago and his eyes welled. It was a night he had relived every day since.

*Chrissie's fiancé, Michael Pape, had finished law school at Harvard and was a clerk for a federal judge in Chicago. He was on the path to become an assistant U.S. attorney. Chrissie had graduated from Loyola and was starting her career with an ad agency on Michigan Avenue. They had recently moved into their apartment in Lincoln Park. An acceptable move since they were to be married in two weeks. A start of a beautiful life together.*

*Sakich took a deep breath, his breathing hastened, chest rising and falling.*

*He pictured the young couple, Michael's parents, Edward and Kathleen, and he and Amy at dinner that night at the Pump Room. Edward was a head taller than he, leaner, with salt-and-pepper hair slicked back. Kathleen was a striking brunette with porcelain skin.*

*Sakich's connections got them booth one, the same one usually reserved for Sinatra or a senator. Champagne toasted the upcoming wedding and the new family melded.*

*By the time they finished dinner and drinks it was close to 11 PM. Sakich left a crisp $100 bill on the table. Chrissie and Michael wanted to walk back to their apartment. The Papes were staying at the Sakich's house on the northwest side of Chicago.*

*His Cadillac was pulled into the circular drive of the Ambassador East Hotel. Sakich peeled a twenty off his roll and gave it to the valet. Goodnights were said and the four parents watched Chrissie and Michael walk away hand-in-hand.*

*He drove and Edward Pape sat in the front passenger seat. He slid his hand over the soft leather seats as Pape pulled out two glass cylinders, each containing a Cuban cigar, from his inside suit coat pocket. Pape clipped the ends off of the cigars, tossed them into the ashtray, and handed a cigar to Sakich. Pape flicked his butane lighter and the flame glowed across Sakich's face as he inhaled. The wives in the back seat waved their hands, dissipating the smoke as they headed to the Kennedy Expressway and then to the Sakiches' yellow-brick bungalow.*

*The next day, hours before dawn, the doorbell rang. Sakich sat up in bed not sure if he was dreaming or not. He slid out of bed* into his leather slippers and silk bathrobe, and rushed to the front door. He looked through the peep hole in the door and saw two tall men in off-the-rack navy blue suits, white shirts, and gray ties. *Looks like cops.*

He unlocked the deadbolt and opened the door a crack. "Waking me at this time of night. Do you guys know who I am? What do you want?"

They flashed their badges. "Special Agent James Eckhaus, FBI. This is special agent Gerald Franks. May we come in?"

Sakich swallowed. "What for?"

"Are you related to Christine Sakich?"

Sakich backed into the living room, which was filled with ornate French furniture covered in plastic. His brow furrowed. "I'm her father. What is it? Is she all right?"

Eckhaus stepped forward, followed by Franks. "Mr. Sakich, I'm afraid your daughter and a male companion were attacked late yesterday evening. Do you know a Michael Pape?"

"Attacked!" Air gushed out of his mouth. He pushed his hands through his hair. "No please, God, no. Is she okay?"

"She's in intensive care. Do you know a Michael..."

"That's my son." Edward Pape said, padding in from the back bedroom. "What's going on?"

Sakich turned to Pape, "Edward, these are FBI agents. Our kids were attacked."

Pape held his breath, words seized up in his throat, and his eyes veered from Franks to Eckhaus.

Sakich watched as Franks' eyes jolted down. He waited for Eckhaus to say something. The silence seemed like forever.

Eckhaus looked straight at Pape. "Mr. Pape, I'm sorry for your loss."

Pape dragged his hand over his face and then shook his head. "You must be mistaken. Michael could take care of himself. He was an intramural boxing champion at Harvard."

"Mr. Pape, I'm sorry to tell you this, but his justice department credentials were found at the scene."

Pape swallowed and his chin lowered to his chest.

"Because he was a federal employee, we have jurisdiction." Sakich felt Eckhaus' eyes drift to him. "Mr. Sakich, your daughter is seriously injured. She's at Northwestern University Hospital. We can take you there if you'd like." Without waiting for an answer he shifted to Pape. "Mr. Pape, despite your *son's identification I'm afraid we need you to identify your son's body. Franks can drive you to the morgue."*

*Sakich's knees buckled and he fell against the wall. The agents grabbed him by his arms.*

*"Oh, God. The six of us just had dinner together a few hours ago. The kids were getting married in two weeks. My wife, this will kill her." Sakich moaned.*

*Pape was breathing through his mouth, specks of spittle on his lips. "Give me a few minutes. I have to tell my wife." He turned and walked back to the bedroom.*

*Eckhaus took the Sakichs to the hospital in their Cadillac. Sakich sat in the back seat and held his wife in his arms rocking her back and forth. He knew that if Chrissie died he and his wife would suffer a wound that would never heal. That the only thing that would lay ahead of him until he died would be thousands of sleepless nights.*

*Amy Sakich held a handkerchief to her eyes and wailed. "Oh, my poor baby."*

*They rushed through the emergency room, Amy buried under Sakich's arm.*

*Dr. Abma, the treating physician, met them. He was tall with blonde hair over his ears. "Your daughter is unconscious. She's been the victim of a very serious attack. I should warn you before you enter her room that she has bruises and cigarette burns over most of her body."*

*"Oh, my God." Amy gasped.*

*Sakich tightened his hold on her. "Doctor, was she...?" He stopped not being able to say the word raped.*

*Abma nodded. "I'm afraid so. We've treated her for that."*

*The doctor took them to the room. The large door was closed, her chart hanging on the door. He took the chart, glanced at it, and slowly pushed the door open.*

*Sakich and Amy entered.*

*Amy covered her mouth.*

*Every visible part of Chrissie's body was marbled with bruises and cigarette burns. Her head swaddled in bandages. Her cheeks purple and eyes swollen shut. Ligature marks around her neck, wrists, and ankles.*

*Tubes came from her nose, and needles from blood and glucose IV bags pierced her flesh. Wires ran from underneath her hospital gown to a heart monitor. A catheter dripped urine into a plastic bag hung on the side of the bed. The whooshes, clicks, beeps, and crying were the only sounds of life.*

*Amy sat on the edge of Chrissie's hospital bed. Tom Sakich stood behind his wife, hands on her shoulders. Their faces were gray and haggard.*

*By the swell in her hospital gown Sakich could tell that her breast had been bandaged. He wondered how they had been mutilated.*

*Amy trembled as she bent over Chrissie, afraid to touch her daughter because it would cause more pain. She whispered. "I love you, baby. Momma's going to be with you until you get better." She turned and collapsed into her husband's arms, tears cascading down her face.*

*Edward Pape and his wife arrived at the hospital after they identified their son's body at the morgue. Pape was wearing the same clothes he had worn the night before, white shirt, sleeves rolled up to his elbows, and the slacks from his charcoal gray suit. He whispered into Sakich's ear. "I'm going to talk to Agent Eckhaus and find out what he knows about the cocksuckers that did this. Want to come?"*

*Sakich looked into Pape's eyes. "I don't want to leave Amy alone."*

*"Kathleen will stay here with her."*

*Sakich nodded and kissed Amy on the cheek. "I'll be right outside, Honey. Kathleen will be here with you. Is that okay?"*

*Amy nodded and bit her lip.*

*Pape led the way into the hallway while Sakich held the door open and kept one eye on his wife. "Agent, I appreciate everything you've done for us. I need to know every detail you have and what's being done to catch these SOBs."*

*"I'm afraid they wandered into the wrong neighborhood. It's just a few blocks from the gold coast to the ghetto. The CHA Police received an anonymous call early this morning and found them in a vacant apartment in the Cabrini Greens Housing Project. They called us when they found Michael's identification."*

*Sakich shook his head. "But who would do this? Why?"*

*Eckhaus placed his hand on Sakich's shoulder, "Mr. Sakich, I'm sorry, but until we have something solid, anything I'd say would be speculation."*

*Sakich let the door slip shut. "I can't be wondering about what happened to my daughter. I...I really have to know. I have to* have something to tell Amy to let her know you guys are tracking these assholes down." He folded his hands around his face and started bawling.

Pape's eyes welled and his head drooped. "Michael, he was...those animals tortured him...poor Chrissie..." He put his arm around Sakich.

Sakich felt his grief drifting to a lower level within his subconscious and his anger rising to take its place. "A bunch of sick motherfuckers."

Pape slammed his fist against the wall. His knuckles began bleeding. He lowered his hands to his sides, opened and closed his fist, blood dripped to the floor.

Eckhaus motioned with his head. "Why don't we go outside and get some fresh air?" They walked outside and headed down Delaware toward the lake. He pulled a pack of Camels from his inside coat pocket. "Would you like a smoke?"

"Thanks," Pape said.

Sakich shook his head.

Eckhaus tapped the pack against his palm, popped out a cigarette, put a smoke between his lips, and held the Camels in Pape's direction. Pape's hand shook as he took a cigarette and slipped it between his lips. Eckhaus pulled out his lighter, flicked the top open, and pulled his thumb over the emery wheel. He cupped the flame with his hand and lit the cigarettes.

Pape took a deep drag on his smoke, filling his lungs with nicotine and quieting his nerves. "I got to watch myself, just making it rougher on the wives."

Eckhaus dangled his cigarette at his side. "Anger's something that you have to go through. There's no other way."

"Thanks for pulling me out. Punching out the wall doesn't help things." He rubbed his hand over his bruised fist.

They walked to Lake Shore Drive and watched the first golden strips of the sun breaking over the horizon.

"I just don't understand this world. Why people do things like this," Sakich said.

"Symptom of the times." Eckhaus inhaled and blew the smoke out of his nose. "They're black militants. They hate whites, probably crazed on drugs. Animals like them don't deserve to live. A month ago they shot and killed a policeman who worked with us. Had two young kids. If there was only some way to get rid of them, this country would be better off."

Pape flicked the ashes off his cigarette. "What's your track record on catching them?"

"We have some leads. We're working on it. The apartment your son and daughter were found in was leased to a blackstone ranger six months ago. But, he's been locked up in Joliet for the last three months. Scrawled on the apartment walls were drawings of the black power salute, Malcolm X, H. Rap Brown, and Eldridge Cleaver. Only other things in the room were the chair your son was tied to and a dingy mattress." Eckhaus paused and looked at Sakich.

"These pricks shoot a cop, rob a bank to get money to finance their operations and then they go underground. Go to a safe house in Oakland or Newark for a few months. Change their names from Willie to Prince Ramadan, kill some cops there, move to Atlanta, and start the process all over again somewhere else. The country's going to hell." Eckhaus tossed his cigarette to the ground, red ashes firing into the air, and crushed it with the heel of his shoe.

"You told Tom you didn't want to speculate..."

"I'm sorry. Once I get going I can't stop. I know who you are Mr. Pape. I mean, attorney general for Mississippi. I'm sure you've experienced this kind of thing down South."

"Not really. This kind of violence only seems to happen in the North. We keep things in line in the South. We believe in action not reaction. Where're you from? I can tell it's not Chicago."

"Born and raised in Montgomery, Alabama," Eckhaus said.

"You ever get used to these big cities? The way of life up here?"

"I've got fifteen years to go before I'm eligible to retire and my office of preference is Birmingham. Hopefully the bureau will transfer me there before I hang it up. Save me the move. I guess that answers your question."

"I guess so. I want to thank you for being so kind to us during this difficult time. My poor boy. He had so much ahead of him." Pape flicked his smoke into the air. "Those damn niggers have ruined our lives." Pape's face turned red and his brow flexed angrily over his eyes. "Chrissie, she'll be scarred for life."

"This world, the sun comes up and it seems like a new day." Eckhaus shook his head. "But nothing ever really changes. Everyday there will be somebody else killed, brutalized, raped. And *for what? Sometimes it seems like with each passing day people get sicker. It doesn't make any sense."*

*They turned and headed back toward the hospital, quiet for an entire block.*

*Sakich broke his silence. "The doctors said Chrissie's going to live." Then he mumbled, "Don't know when or if she'll recover. My poor girl...They beat her, tortured her, raped her. She's got a concussion, broken ribs, internal bleeding. God knows what else." He sobbed. "There's not a fucking thing I can do. I feel so helpless. Those fucking bastards."*

*Eckhaus put another smoke between his lips. "I promise you that we'll try to track these animals down—"*

*"And then what?" Pape interrupted. "At best one of them gets a long sentence for murdering my son, maybe another gets a slap on the wrist, or if they get a jury full of niggers they'll be a hung jury or even acquitted."*

*"You know how the system works. We do the best we can."*

*"You're from the South. You know we have our own system of justice for dealing with these kinds of situations."*

*"What are you saying?"*

*"Why don't you come down to Jackson for my son's funeral? If you're interested we can talk about it then. It will be a more appropriate place and time. If need be I'll request that you attend. I have friends in the Justice Department." He looked at Sakich, "Being helpless is a choice. Not one I'm willing to make."*

***

For Sakich the vivid memory of that day shut down. He'd lived it exactly like that a thousand times. He put the photo of Amy and Chrissie down and looked out his window across LaSalle Street. A strong wind from the south was blowing the flag on top the roof of city hall. *It should be a pleasant day. A great day. Revenge is good for the soul.*

## CHAPTER ELEVEN

Sakich picked up the photo of his wife and daughter off his desk. His thoughts wandered to the week that followed the assault of Chrissie and Michael. The two days he spent in Mississippi for Michael's funeral. When everything came together. When everything made sense.

When Edward Pape told him how he could get revenge...

*After Michael's internment, Pape's antebellum home was crowded with guests—friends, relatives, and political allies and enemies that all came to pay their respects. Pape brought Sakich into his study to introduce him to a friend. Their dark suits were the uniform of the day. They entered the room through tall double doors. A large oak desk sat at the far end and hanging on wall behind it was a faded Confederate battle flag framed in a glass case. The cloth was tattered by war and littered with holes from minie balls. The walls on three sides were lined with bookcases filled with leather-bound histories of the world and biographies of famous leaders from Julius Caesar to Lyndon B. Johnson. The other wall was covered by windows that stretched from floor to ceiling, looking over a long drive that was bordered by oaks. In front of the desk were two tall leather chairs. From one of them, a gray cloud of cigar smoke curled into the air.*

*A diminutive man rose from the chair. This fellow was about Sakich's age, with gray hair curling out of his ears, a red* bow tie, and a broad smile, but underneath there was a sense of darkness about him.

"Tom, let me introduce you to a good friend of mine, Josephus LeGrand. We call him the Mayor for short."

They shook hands. The strength of LeGrand's grip belied his slender build.

"Please sit down, gentlemen," Pape said. "Can I get either of you a drink?"

Sakich took a Dewar's and water on the rocks and the Mayor had Jack Daniels, straight up.

"I've known the Mayor for a long time. Our families have been members of the same fraternal organization for generations."

Pape explained his family legacy to Sakich. "My Daddy had a dream but it came to an end with Michael's death. Our family has grown in wealth and influence as past generations overcame obstacles that seemed impossible. My grandfather told me about the acres of cotton harvested by his great-grandfathers' slaves and the War against the North. His grandfather died wearing confederate gray."

Pape turned and pointed to the battle flag on the wall behind him. "He was killed by Union soldiers while he carried this very flag. After the damn war, the Federal Government gave most of our land to our former slaves."

"My daddy climbed out of foxholes in France during World War One, survived the depression, and the Second World War. He lived for one thing. He wanted the Pape legacy to extend to Washington, D.C. My daddy knew Michael was the last chance for him to see his dream come true. He wanted to live long enough to see Michael sworn in. He was crushed last Sunday, Father's Day, when I told him that Michael had been killed. His dream of the Pape legacy died with Michael."

"I believe we have some common concerns about our country and the troubling times it's going through." Pape looked toward the Mayor. "The Mayor and I have been discussing this situation and have come up with some viable solutions."

The Mayor pulled his cigar out of his mouth and saliva dripped from the splayed end. He turned to Sakich. "I just can't imagine how terrible it must be for you and your wife. Please accept my deepest sympathies and my hope for a full recovery for your daughter."

*Sakich thanked him for his concern, looked into the glass of scotch and slowly exhaled. His eyes still hurt from the tears. "My wife hasn't slept since that night and she's hardly eaten anything. The doctor put her on serafem. It's been a struggle."*

*"Edward told me how you felt so helpless after the attack. That there was nothing you could do to avenge the brutality that was rendered upon Michael and Chrissie." The Mayor said.*

*Sakich brought the glass to his lips and sipped the scotch. "Nothing has changed. I'll feel helpless 'til the day I die."*

*The Mayor told Sakich how Edward and he had discussed these problems many a time, long before this tragedy struck. "There's a solution that even most nigas would approve of. One that could work to bring back a less violent society for those who desire to live that way. Nigas have a propensity toward violence, and Jews and Liberals from the North get great satisfaction from spurring on that kind of activity in our communities."*

*Sakich nodded. His brow furrowed. "What's your solution?"*

*"Most nigas would prefer to live among themselves. Even some of their spokesmen support that idea, whether it's a separate state in this country or returning to Africa. Are you inclined to agree with what I've said so far?" the Mayor asked.*

*"Yeah, I'd go along with that." Sakich curled his lower lip and shook his head. "But it's never going to happen." He felt the Mayor's eyes penetrating his.*

*The Mayor nodded. "We think it could. Are you willing to do something about it? Really willing?"*

*Sakich's fingers tightened around the glass. "I wish I could. I'd like to get my hands around those cocksuckers' necks, watch them beg for their lives, and then I'd squeeze the life out of them. It's the only thing that could give me pleasure. God help my little girl."*

*Pape slid his chair forward and rested his elbows on his desk. "Let me be blunt. The Mayor is being kind of philosophical because he doesn't know you as well as I do. Tom, we've been through hell together. And like you pointed out, we will suffer with this for the rest of out lives. The bottom line is, are you willing to support violence to get the blacks out of your city?"*

*Sakich gulped down the rest of his scotch. "I hate those niggers for what they did to my little girl. I would do anything to get rid of them. How'd we do this?"*

*"In the South, we have a strong base of support for a movement like this. We have the Klan and other groups that are willing to take active roles. Are there any organizations in Chicago that could become involved?" Pape asked.*

*Sakich paused and then Marquette Park came to mind. "There's an alderman I know that represents a part of the city that has a heavy Nazi movement. He might have some contacts that would be interested in this."*

*Pape nodded. "The Klan and the Nazis united. That would be quite a partnership. We can utilize people like these for our ground troops. To carry out our plans but keep us at a safe distance. We'll keep ourselves insulated. They'll never even know who's directing their moves."*

*The Mayor put his hand over Sakich's. "You're doing the right thing."*

*"One more question, Tom," Pape said. "What about Agent Eckhaus? Do you think he might join us? He could be a valuable asset."*

*"I don't know. That sounds too risky. He could do us in before we do anything. You mind if I have another drink?"*

*"Help yourself." Pape slid his chair back and watched Sakich pour three fingers of Dewar's. The ice clinked against his glass. "Eckhaus has the same heritage as the Mayor and I. I know he's not happy with the violence and the unrest. He came down here because he knew we had something to talk about."*

*The Mayor stood. His cigar wobbled in his mouth with each word. "You guys talk this over and decide. I don't know the man and I don't want him to know me. There ain't no FBI agent I'm looking forward to meetin'."*

*Sakich stood and shook the Mayor's hand. "It was good meeting you."*

*"Same here, Tom. Good luck to you and your family. I hope your daughter recovers."*

*The Mayor left the study and Sakich returned to his chair. "So how do you think we should go about doing this?"*

*"Eckhaus is smart. He won't talk about this if anyone else is present. He and I talked in generalities that night. It's probably best if I meet with him alone."*

*"You going to talk to him today?"*

*"Yes, he might be more comfortable if we went for a stroll, get away from the house and the people here. See if you can find*

him and take him out to the front porch for some fresh air. I'll meet you there. Then Eckhaus and I will go for a walk."

Sakich shook his head. "Be careful, Ed. He might play you along and then turn you in."

"I'll feel him out before I get too explicit. I've hidden a tape recorder in the gazebo. Once I get him there I'll see if he bites. I'll get it on tape. Worse possible scenario, I can use the tape to prove the FBI entrapped a father who was grieving his son's murder, or it's a tape that will keep Eckhaus in line. Just in case he agrees and later gets cold feet."

Sakich put his hands on the arms of the chair and pushed himself up. "All right. I'll get him."

Pape walked to the front of his desk and placed his hand on Sakich's shoulder. "Tom, we're going to succeed. We will get our revenge."

Sakich clinked his glass against Pape's and left the room to look for Eckhaus.

\*\*\*

Eckhaus lit a cigarette and Sakich sipped his scotch as they leaned against the tall white columns on the front porch. The sun slanted toward the backside of the sky but the heavy air of the day lingered. Sakich slipped off his suit coat. His shirt stuck to his back.

Pape opened the front door and walked onto the porch. His jacket and tie removed and shirt collar open. "Just about everybody's gone." He rubbed the back of his neck with his hand. "I appreciate all those people coming to pay their respects but that doesn't do as much for me as looking at a beautiful sunset. At times like this you learn to grasp whatever you have, appreciate it, and hope for a better future."

Eckhaus took a drag on his cigarette. "Quite a place you have, Edward."

"Thanks, Jim. It's like a sanctuary for Kathleen and me, even more so now. The memories of the past. Sorry, I've been so occupied I haven't had a chance to talk with you."

"No problem. You had a lot of people here that you've known for a long time."

"I've been in the house since the interment, could use some fresh air, mind if we go for a walk?"

*"Sounds good."*

*"You guys go ahead. I'm going to freshen up my drink,"* Sakich said.

\*\*\*

Later that evening Pape herded Sakich into his study. "Eckhaus just left. He's heading to Montgomery, Alabama, to visit his father. I want you to listen to the tape. I think he's good for us." Pape sat in his judge's chair behind his desk, slid the cassette into a tape recorder and turned it on.

*Pape: "I've got a couple of horses in the stables in the back. Michael used to love to ride."*

*Eckhaus: Laughter. "My old man had a couple of mules. Closest thing to a horse I ever rode."*

*Pape: "How's the investigation coming?"*

*Eckhaus: "We haven't had much luck. Canvassed the area but we didn't find any witnesses, at least any that were willing to talk. The apartment was rented to a guy that's been in the state pen since March, doing twenty years. We talked to him on Monday. He didn't shed any light on who might have had access to the apartment. So far we've got nothing. The first 24 hours are the most important in a case like this. Things get cold fast. I guess you know that. But we'll keep on it."*

*Pape: "That's not what I wanted to hear. But from what you told me in Chicago, I'm not surprised. Where do you go from here?"*

*Eckhaus: "My squad is putting everything into the investigation. They're double-checking every lead we have. I'm going to be out of touch for two days."*

*Pape: "Where're you going?"*

*Eckhaus: "Thought since I'm down here I'd go to Montgomery and visit my father. I haven't seen him for almost two years. What's that old saying? Something like while you're busy, life happens."*

*Pape: "That's the truth. It's important to go back to your roots. Makes you appreciate where you came from. I think you appreciate it even more when you've been away for a while. Gives you a different perspective on what you use to have, what you really value."*

*Eckhaus: "You're probably right."*

*Pape: "You want a smoke? I know you're a Camel man. All I've got are Salems."*

*Eckhaus: "No thanks, I'm trying to cut back anyway."*

*Pape: "You got a light? I must have left mine in the house."*
*Pause in the tape.*

*Pape: "Cigarette lighter with an FBI badge mounted on the side. Is that standard issue?"*

*Eckhaus: "No, tenth anniversary. Can you imagine that after ten years and you a get a cigarette lighter or a lapel pin if you don't smoke. Quite a deal, huh?"*

*Pape: "The FBI is really generous. You said you're going to visit your father. What about your mother? You didn't mention her."*

*Eckhaus: "She died a long time ago. I was just a kid." He cleared his throat. "Killed in a robbery attempt. Some black guy that was just released from jail. My father got into a struggle with him and a shot was fired that killed her. The nig...the guy was never arrested."*

*Pape: "I'm sorry, Jim."*

*Eckhaus: "Well, he didn't exactly get away. A month later he was found hung from a tree. No one ever claimed credit for it."*

*Pape: "It seems like we're all linked in this together. My family goes back a long time, a real long time. Over the generations, my family has made the transitions from slave owners to Klan leaders to respectability. Thirty years ago, my father was the Grand Dragon. We still feel that link to the Old South. The way things used to be. Frankly, there are a lot of people that aren't real happy with the changes in America today. We have a lot of pious bastards from the North trying to tell us in the South how to live. And I'm sure that they're happy that we're taking all the heat. Because the reality of America is that things are no different in the North than they are in the South."*

*Pape shut off the tape recorder and tapped a cigarette from his pack of Salems. The paper hissed as he lit it. "Tom, listen to this. This really tells you how he feels about everything." He switched the recorder back on.*

*Eckhaus: "I think it's fashionable for people like the Kennedys to find perceived injustices in someone else's backyard, even though the same problems are in their own state. You don't want to aggravate your constituents. There are a lot of red-blooded*

*Americans that work for the FBI that aren't too happy with the things they're doing in the name of Bobby Kennedy."*

*Pape: "I know you have your professional responsibilities but you also told me about your heritage, your personal perspective, and experience with this racial violence. In recent months, people that I have a great deal of respect for have been talking to me about changing the course of events. In Chicago you told me about your dislike for the militant black movement, its viciousness and sickness. Your sense of helplessness. I remember the story you told me about your policeman friend that was killed by those blacks and his wife and kids that have to live without their father. You have an opportunity to join me and some others that feel the same way we do. An opportunity to use your skills to change the direction this country is going in. Remember, you aren't going to be an FBI agent the rest of your life. But you will be a citizen of this country and the South. How do you want to live? I need to know where you stand before I go any further with this conversation."*

There was a long pause on the tape.

*Pape: "Obviously I've taken a great risk talking to you about this and I wouldn't have if I didn't feel this was where your heart was. That you know the futility of living the way we've been for the last decade in this country. And you know it's only going to get worse as time goes on if someone doesn't take the initiative to change things."*

*Eckhaus: "What are you planning?"*

*Pape: "I can only tell you that we want to take steps that will make black separatism a politically acceptable solution to today's race problems. The founding fathers of this country believed it was an acceptable movement. Thomas Jefferson proposed colonization of the blacks and even Abraham Lincoln contemplated it rather than risk dividing the country in two. Unfortunately, he didn't pursue it vigorously. Many other great Americans were members of a society that believed in separating the races and we want to carry on where they left off."*

*Eckhaus: "What happened? It never got off the ground?"*

*Pape: "It did, in 1816 the American Colonization Society was formed in Washington, D.C. Its purpose was to emigrate freed blacks to Africa. Subsequently, the federal government and various* *state governments funded the society. Congress, under President James Monroe, provided $100,000 to purchase land in Africa. The land was purchased from Sierra Leone and named Liberia. The capital, Monrovia, was named after the president. At one time there were 13,000 immigrant blacks in Liberia. So you see this is a real possibility. But, it has to be done right. I can't tell you any more than that until I know you're on board with us."*

*Eckhaus: "Say I agree with you. There are ways things will have to be done or I will not involve myself."*

*Pape: "What are those?"*

*Eckhaus: "First of all, I have to be completely anonymous. No one else would know my identity. I would communicate only through you. And there must be layers that would insulate me from any people taking action."*

*Pape: "That's exactly why I want you to join us, because you know how to manage these things. I will be totally honest with you. Tom knows that I'm talking to you about this. He's the only one, he hasn't been exposed to anyone else that's involved, and of course, no one is aware of you."*

*Eckhaus: "And if at any time I feel that I've been compromised, I'm out."*

*Pape: "I can live with those conditions."*

*Pape leaned forward and shut off the tape recorder. "What do you think?"*

*Sakich nodded. "Sounds like he's in. Just be careful."*

***

Sakich rested the photo back on his desk and hit the button on his intercom. "Sandy."

"Yes."

"I'm going to take the day off and visit my daughter. If anything important comes up, you know where you can reach me."

"Okay, Tom. Have a good day."

Sakich left the office and headed to the sanitarium where he had visited Chrissie several times a week since her release from the hospital almost nine months ago. She was diagnosed as having a depressive psychosis resulting from her attack. Her behavior varied from catatonia to explosions of anger from the nightmares and flashbacks of that night. The psychiatrist saw little hope for her recovery. Sakich went to mass every day and prayed for Chrissie's recovery, but nothing helped. He felt like he was losing everything.

And then the unbelievable happened. He returned home at 8:45 after spending the night watching Chrissie in bed. Her machines keeping her alive, totally unresponsive to his pleadings only to know when he got home Amy would be lost in a bottle of vodka. He stepped out of his Cadillac. The windows of his house were dark. He opened the door and was met with total silence. "She must be asleep." He slipped out of his shoes and crept to the bedroom. There was a shadow of what Amy use to be on the bed. He placed his hand on her shoulder and whispered. "Honey, wake up."

Their was no response. He touched her neck. It felt cold. His eyes adjusted to the dark and he saw an empty glass and a plastic bottle next to her opposite shoulder.

"Oh, my God." He laid his head on Amy's shoulder. He had lost so much. He had lost everything now.

# CHAPTER TWELVE

## Friday, April 5, 1968

At 8:00 A.M. the phone in the Tisdales' apartment rang. Beauford jumped out of bed, ran to the kitchen, and answered. "Hello."

"Meet me in Marquette Park across the street from the office at 9:30. Come alone. You understand?" Reichardt barked.

"Yeah, what about Marlee...?" The phone went dead. He turned, Nathleen was standing behind him.

"We gettin' Marlee?" Nathleen asked, her eyes deep set and filled with concern.

Beauford hung up the wall phone. "I got to meet Reichardt in the park across from his office."

"I'll get dressed. I'm coming with you." She turned away from Beauford and took a step toward the bedroom.

He grabbed her arm. "You got to stay here. He said I got to come alone."

She yanked her arm away. "Ain't no way I'm staying here. I'm gonna get my baby and ain't nobody stopping me."

"These people don't fool around. We better do it the way they say."

"How do you know they gonna give you Marlee? Maybe they want you to come alone so they can kill you like your father. What's gonna happen to me and William if you don't come back?

Maybe they gonna send somebody over here to kill us while you're gone." She stomped her foot on the floor and rushed to the bedroom. "Maybe we'll all be dead."

Beauford leaned against the wall. Everything Nathleen was saying was a possible outcome. It made sense. Why would they want him alive? He took cash from their man in Chicago and delivered it to King's assassin. What else would they need him for? It was possible that in an hour he could be dead and the only things he valued, Nathleen, Marlee, and William would follow suit. Their bodies dropped into a deep lake or burned and only ashes left. But, there were no other choices.

He went to the bedroom and slid on his jeans. Nathleen laid on their bed whimpering. Her back towards him. He sat on the bed, put his hand on her slender hip. "Nath, this what we gonna do. I'll drop you and William at the airport." He pulled cash out of his pocket. "Here's $65 I got left from the trip. You go in there and find the closest pay phone, write down the number and give it to me. As soon as I get Marlee I'll call the pay phone and let you know. Then I'll come and pick you up right where I dropped you off."

"And if you don't call me?"

"If I don't call you by 10:30, you and the boy catch a flight for where ever you can for $50. When you get there call the apartment here and if everything went all right I'll be there. Then I'll wire you some money so you can come back…or maybe Marlee and me will fly out to meet you."

"What if you don't call me or answer the phone at the apartment?" She whispered.

Beauford ran his tongue over his lips. "That'll probably mean I'm with Daddy." Nathleen turned toward him, sat up and they embraced for a silent minute. Then Beauford went to William's room. He sat on the corner of the bed and stroked his son's cheek. William's eyes opened. He yawned and turned toward his father.

"Hey boy, I gotta go to work. I'm gonna drop you and Momma off at the airport. You gonna have a lot of fun. Maybe even go for an airplane ride. You need to listen to your momma. Do whatever she asks you to do. Now go get dressed."

***

Beauford dropped off Nathleen at Midway National Airport terminal, a single story beige building. She rushed into the terminal, came back in a few minutes and gave Beauford a sheet of paper with a pay phone number. She leaned into the truck, across William and kissed her husband on the cheek. He could see the fear in her eyes, brushed a tear off her cheek and said goodbye. She backed away and grabbed William's hand as he stepped out of the truck. Beauford leaned over and closed the door. He drove away from the terminal and glanced at their images in the side-view mirror getting smaller and smaller and wondered if he would see them again.

On the ride to the park, Beauford decided it was in his best interest to make it a regular practice not to park anywhere near the ward office. *Sooner or later somebody gonna connect those people to what happened to Reverend King. They ain't gonna get nothin' on me. I'm gonna break away from them as soon as I can.* He pulled off California and parked on Richmond north of the park. He grabbed the crowbar between the seats and stepped out of the truck. He slid the two-foot piece of steel down the pant leg of his jeans and covered the top claw with his denim jacket.

The crisp fresh air of the early spring day brought a sense of cautious optimism. He knew that in a few minutes he would either be getting Marlee back or would be fighting for his life. He hoped that in a few days he would be starting a new life some place far away from Chicago.

Reichardt was waiting in the park. His long willowy shadow stretched across the ground. He looked like he was ready for war, dressed in a khaki jacket, and camouflage pants tucked into tall shiny brown boots. A cigarette hung from his narrow lips.

The crowbar forced Beauford to limp across Marquette Road into the park. He approached Reichardt and thought, I gotta be careful. *I'm jus' another nigger to this guy. No tellin' what he might do now that they got what they wanted.*

Reichardt drew the cigarette away from his mouth between two yellow fingers and flicked it onto the damp grass. He twisted the heel of his boot, crushing the cigarette.

Beauford saw a bulge under Reichardt's jacket on his right hip. He was two feet away from Reichardt when the man raised his hand, pulled down the zipper on his jacket, and braced his thumbs in his belt. Beauford stopped. His right side was away from

Reichardt blocking the man's view of the crowbar as he gripped its claw.

"You did all right down South," Reichardt said.

He stared into Reichardt's blue eyes. "You said everything go all right I get my baby back."

Reichardt nodded in the direction of Marquette Road.

A black Cadillac pulled up to the curb. Marlee sat in the front passenger seat on the lap of a heavy white woman. The little girl jumped up and down, hitting the inside of the passenger window with her fist, screaming, "Daddy! Daddy!"

Beauford took a step toward the car. Reichardt leaned into him and grabbed his left arm. Under the man's jacket Beauford saw a brown leather holster and black pistol grips.

Sweat beaded on his Beauford's forehead. He tightened his grip on the crowbar. "Let go of me. I did what you wanted and now I'm getting my little girl."

"Not yet. You got some problems we got to talk about."

"The only problem I got is I don't have my girl."

Reichardt laughed. The stench of tobacco was on his breath. "You got big problems in Mississippi. You killed somebody."

Beauford yanked his arm from Reichardt's grasp. "What? I ain't got no idea what you talking about. I ain't never killed nobody. Not like you..." Then he thought better of what he was going to say. His fingers brushed the saliva off his lips. He glanced over his shoulder to make sure the Cadillac was still there.

"There's a warrant out for you for murder and kidnapping in Sunflower County. You kill Linda Joy Napier and kidnap Celeste Napier?"

"That's bull. It's the Klan. Jimmy Napier setting me up cause...cause he wanted to kill me for owning land. He lynched my daddy."

"So what are you going to do?' Reichardt folded his arms across his chest and laughed. "Go down there and plead not guilty."

Beauford was trapped at every angle. A murder warrant in Mississippi from the Klan, his daughter held hostage by the Nazis in Chicago, and his hands dirty from the assassination of King in Memphis. "No..., can't do that," he muttered.

"You need a new name or you're going to find your ass in the slammer. Pick one out and I can get you a driver's license."

He thought, *I ain't safe anywhere.* Then it came to him. The only thing that represented any form of safety to him was the street he parked on. "Richmond." Beauford glanced at Marlee; maybe a new name would bring luck.

"There's one other thing you should know before you leave. That paper bag you took down to Memphis. Your fingerprints are on it and I'm sure the Feds found it in the boarding house. So if you're thinking of taking Marlee and disappearing with your family, it wouldn't be a good idea. Somebody might call the feds and give them your name. You'd not only have the Klan and our people looking for you. You'd also have the feds. I'm your insurance. You do whatever I say and you and your family will be taken care of. If you decide to leave, well, the best thing that could happen would be that the feds would find you. Then you'd only go to jail for a long time. Could be a lot worse."

Beauford nodded. "Can I get Marlee now?"

"Just curious, what did you do with the hundred bucks you skimmed out of the bag?" He shook his head. "Never mind, I guess you deserved it. You be in my office Monday morning, 8:00 sharp."

"Yeah. What time is it?"

Reichardt pulled up his sleeve and glanced at his gold Bulova. "10:15." He jerked his head toward the Cadillac. "Go."

Beauford ran to the Cadillac, dragging the leg along that was braced by the crowbar, and the passenger door opened. His little girl jumped out of the car, arms open, into her father's grasp. Beauford picked her up in his arms, "Oh, my little baby, it's so good to hold you again. You all right, honey?"

"Yeah. They had a nice dog to play with."

Beauford looked in the back seat and saw a 110-pound German shepherd snarling against the window.

"Where's Mommy and William? Are we going home now?"

"I'm taking you home now, honey. We don't live in Ruleville anymore." Beauford held Marlee against his chest as he hurried to his truck. "But first we got to make a phone call fast."

***

Beauford made the call, sped up Cicero Avenue and pulled in front of the terminal.

Nathleen and William rushed to them. She yanked open the truck door, grabbed Marlee and kissed her. "Is my baby alright?" William jumped into the truck bed. Nathleen hopped into the passenger seat, ripped off Marlee's red jacket and top, checked her arms, chest and back for bruises but didn't see any. She put the clothing back on her daughter and then lowered her pants to her ankles and examined her legs. Nathleen pulled the pants up, leaned into the seat and sighed.

"She seems okay, Nath." Beauford said.

"I was so afraid they'd hurt her. I didn't see any marks. Oh baby, you're here with us forever now. No one will ever take you away again." She rocked Marlee in her arms.

William peered through the rear window. A wide smile across his face.

Nathleen turned to Beauford. "Now we can get out of this city. Be through with these people."

Beauford didn't respond. He pulled out of the terminal and headed north on Cicero Avenue.

Nathleen's dark eyes shifted from Marlee to her husband. "Beau, you said we could go when we got Marlee back."

He stroked Marlee's hair. "Things came up. I'll tell you when we get to the apartment. It might be better for us to stay here."

She buried her daughter's face in the crook of her arm. Nathleen stared straight ahead, watching the oncoming traffic for the silent ride back to the apartment.

They entered the front door and Nathleen barked, "William, take your sister and watch TV while your daddy and I make lunch." They retreated to the kitchen. "We can't bring up our children here and I don't want to live in a place like this."

"It ain't that simple. There's problems for me down South and Reichardt lined me up with a job and a place for us to live." Beauford said, pulling bread and lunchmeat out of the refrigerator.

She put her hands on her hips. "What problems?"

Beauford told his wife about the phony murder warrant and Reichardt getting new identification for them. He bit his lip, refusing to mention Celeste for fear the guilt he felt would surface.

She slammed her fist on the kitchen counter. "These people killed our people, chased us out of our home, took our name, and set you up for murdering somebody, and we got to stay here because they tell us so?"

Beauford stepped toward her, put his hands on her waist, and looked into her eyes. "We ain't got a choice. I get pulled over for anything and they see I got a murder warrant, they gonna send me back to Mississippi. It'll be the last I ever see of you and the kids."

"If we get papers for a new name why can't we jus' leave?"

"Cause, if we run, Reichardt will do me in. He'll tell the police and I'll be looking over my shoulder 'til they catch me."

Nathleen put her hands on her hips. "What's to stop Reichardt from tellin' the police any time he pleases?"

Beauford stepped back from Nathleen. "It's just the way it's got to be. There's no more sense in talking about it." But he also wondered about that too and what else they might have in mind for him.

***

That night, Thomas Sakich's words came true. 'Revenge is good for the soul.' It was a night like no one had ever seen in this country. The inner city of every major metropolitan area was hit by violence and looting by angry crowds of blacks roaming the streets. In Washington, D.C., police teams shot teargas at crowds of black demonstrators. Eleven thousand members of the Tennessee National Guard were activated to protect the state's cities. In Greensboro/Raleigh, police circled the predominately black Shaw University, attempting to confine the black students on the campus.

Entire blocks were set on fire. On the West side of Chicago, firemen fighting the flames were shot at by snipers and attacked by crowds slinging a hail of stones and bricks. By 10:00 that night, 33 major fires had been set on the West side. Firefighters from eight suburbs were called to assist 2,000 Chicago firemen. Streets were littered with glass, bricks, and stones. One hundred buses from the Chicago Transit Authority were damaged.

The looting and violence continued for three days. The estimated property loss in Chicago was $10,000,000. The final count was seven dead, 500 injured, 1,449 arrested, and 1,000 homeless. The authorities used 10,500 policemen, 6,900 National Guardsmen, 5,000 soldiers from the U.S. Army, and 3,300 firemen. Pape, Sakich, and Eckhaus had exceeded their greatest expectations.

\*\*\*

That Saturday night, Jimmy Napier and his son Junior spent their first weekend on their own. As the sun slipped below the horizon, they walked down the front stairs of their house to the Dodge Ram Charger. Napier tossed a white hood, a small pillowcase, and a pair of sheets in the truck bed and headed to the deep backwoods of Mississippi.

He drove past wheat fields and down a narrow gravel road surrounded by live oaks. Finger-like shadows from the branches that intertwined overhead shimmied over his truck. He drove into a clearing in the woods and parked amidst forty trucks and cars. He jumped out of the truck, excitedly grabbed the hood, pillowcase, and sheets, and went to the passenger side, helping his son down to the ground.

Napier slipped his sheet over his head and put on his hood. He lifted the flap covering his face and slipped the sheet over Junior's head, resting it on his shoulders. "Your momma cut down this sheet for you just before that nigger killed her."

The boy raised his head and with a long face looked into his father's eyes. "Is Momma gonna be here?"

"No, Junior, your momma's dead. She gone. That nigger put her away. She ain't ever coming back." Napier gave him a hug and pulled a hunting knife from the sheath on his waist. The blade glistened in the moonlight. He slipped the pillowcase over Junior's head and with the knife slit holes for his eyes. He slid the knife back into the sheath and grabbed Junior's hand. They walked up a small embankment to where a hoard of men were gathered.

Mayor LeGrand, the Imperial Wizard, wore a white pointed hood and a robe. He stood on top of a hill. Behind him was a twenty-foot high wooden cross and to each side, ten-foot high crosses all wrapped in kerosene-soaked burlap. He lit a torch signifying the beginning of the meeting and waved it back and forth over his head. Close to a hundred men and a handful of women and children shouted and a frenzied spell spread across the field of white sheets. The mob in the field lit their torches and spun around kicking their feet in the air. The flames whirled overhead, and their shouts and jeers flooded the night with a fevered excitement. Junior's eyes opened wide. The smell of burning kerosene filled his nostrils and he inhaled the mood.

LeGrand lowered his torch and the crowd became silent. He raised his torch and the insanity became louder, reaching a maniacal intensity. He lowered the torch again and the gathering became quiet once more. LeGrand bellowed, "In a step, a single step, a devil was slain who refused to follow the laws of nature, the laws of God. Where Niggas go unpunished, they riot and loot. Look at the streets of Chicago, Oakland, and Harlem." He raised his hands to the dark sky. Gray shadowy clouds obscured the moon. The wind rippled through the flames of the torches.

Napier laughed to himself, *Look at that nigger lover talking out of the side of his mouth. He let Tisdale go and then he asking me to get a shooter. He bends whichever way the wind blows. Talking big to make himself important.*

The Klansmen shouted, "Amen. Praise the Lord." They picked up jugs of moonshine and slugged down the liquor, passing them through the crowd. Napier grabbed a jug, jerked his head back, and swallowed down three gulps. He wiped the alcohol from his chin and yanked out his hunting knife. "Come here, boy."

Napier grabbed the hood covering Junior's face, and tore the blade through the cloth uncovering his son's mouth. "Have a taste of this." He filled his palm with moonshine and poured it over his son's lips. Napier laughed as Junior gagged and pursed his lips.

LeGrand lowered his torch. "Those that are not worthy must be purged. Queers. Niggas. Jews. It's our heritage. We're at war and Martin Luther King, the king of the niggas, is dead." He put his torch to the base of the kerosene-soaked cross behind him. The flames roared up to the top, dancing with the swirling wind.

Their blood boiling, the sheeted men charged the other two crosses and ignited them. Napier danced near the flaming crosses, holding Junior's hand in one hand and a jug in the other.

Junior jerked his hand out of his father's grasp. The young boy slowly raised his hands over his head. Then he began spinning faster and faster and his soft giggle became a laughter that grew louder and louder until he tumbled to the ground. Saliva dribbled from his lips.

LeGrand walked over to Napier. "You still mad, Jimmy?"

Junior giggled, reached for his father's robe and pulled himself up.

Napier grabbed his son's hand and held him against his thigh. "My wife is dead and my daughter's kidnapped. Mad, shit there ain't a word I can think of to tell you how mad I am."

LeGrand lifted the flap covering his face. "What're you talking about?"

"Your favorite nigger came to my house after you dropped me off. Killed my wife and took Celeste. Put Linda Joy in the ground Wednesday. You trying to tell me you didn't know about it?"

"I was in Jackson and Greenville for a few days. Just got back. You talking about Tisdale?"

Napier felt his muscles tighten. His body became rigid. His eyes darted at the mayor. "Yeah, the nigger that should have been dead. But you saved him and see what he did."

"And you say he took Celeste?"

"Yeah, now it's just me and the boy." Napier turned and stomped away from the Mayor. He looked over his shoulder. "Imperial Wizard, bullshit. You a nigger lover!"

Junior looked over his shoulder and repeated his father's words. "You a nigger lover," and then he giggled.

The mayor watched them and muttered, "Liar."

***

The following Monday, April 8, an hour before sunrise in Toronto, Canada, a man stood in the shadows taking his last drag on a Salem. The tip of the cigarette glowed bright red. He threw it to the ground and crushed it with the toe of his leather shoe. He blew the smoke out of his nose in a slow stream, surveyed the empty street, and nervously tugged at his right earlobe. The man pulled up the collar of his jacket, lowered the bill of his baseball cap over his face, and walked across the street to a telephone booth on the corner. He dialed 1, then 601, the area code for Mississippi, and the remaining seven numbers and waited while the phone rang twice, three times, four, five, again and again.

Finally a woman answered in a sleepy voice, "Hello."

"Lemme talk to the mayor."

"Who's calling?"

"Jus' put him on."

The man heard hushed voices in the background, "It's some redneck hillbilly calling for you. Why's he calling at this hour?"

The mayor took the phone from his wife. "Who's this?"

"This is Mr. Willard from Greenville. You remember me?"

"Yeah, hold on. Honey, I'm gonna take this call downstairs. Hang up the phone when I pick up the line."

"Huh. Yeah, yeah."

A minute later, "Hang up now." The phone clicked. "What do you want?"

"Want do I want? I'm making good on my promise to you. Making that call for the rest of the money you owe me. That's what I want."

"It'll take a couple of days to get it. Where're you?"

"I'm in Canada."

"Where in Canada?"

"Now mayor you remember what you said to me in the barn, don't you?"

"Look, it's too early in the morning to play games—"

"You said I was a careful man. That was the kind of man you were looking for. Do you think a careful man like me would tell you right where he was? You might not be able to overcome the temptation to send me an unwanted visitor. So I'm thinking right now you don't need to know. I'll call you back in two days, Wednesday at noon, give ya the time and place to meet then. 'Til then, you get that money." He cradled the phone.

# CHAPTER THIRTEEN

## Monday, April 8, 1968

Later that same morning, the message from Canada made the rounds from Ruleville to Jackson to Chicago.

Edward Pape drove to downtown Jackson and parked next to a phone booth on Congress overlooking West Street Park. He stepped out of his black Mercedes, dropped a few coins into the pay phone and dialed a Chicago number.

"Sakich."

"Call me back at this number. I'll be waiting," Pape said, and gave him the number.

"Give me five minutes."

Pape hung up the phone and pulled a pack of Salems from his suit coat as he walked to his Mercedes. He sat on the fender, pulled out a cigarette and slipped it between his lips. He flipped open a gold Zippo lighter, flicked the emery wheel and inhaled. The warmth of the sun on his face and the nicotine settled his nerves.

\*\*\*

Sakich grabbed the envelope he had scribbled the telephone number on, left his office and took the elevator down ten floors to the lobby. There were three phone booths against the wall opposite the elevators and they were all being used. On one end was a white man with the door to his booth closed. On the other side a middle-aged white woman with an expensive salon coloring job on her blond hair. She hugged the phone close to her mouth. In the middle was a black man in a cheap off-the-rack blue suit.

Sakich paced back and forth within arms reach of the booths. The woman dressed in a navy pantsuit kept looking over her shoulder at him. Each time pursing her lips tighter. Finally, she slid the door to the booth closed and faced the wall.

Sakich felt the black man's dark eyes on him. Sakich looked at his silver Rolex. Ten minutes had passed. He raised his arm, pointed his expensive timepiece at the black man, and tapped his index finger on the watch's face.

The black man reached into his inside suit coat pocket, pulled out a pack of Lucky Strikes, tapped the pack, popping a smoke out, moved it to his lips, and dropped the pack back in his pocket.

*Son of a bitch,* Sakich thought. *Fucking nigger probably talking to one of his whores and I got serious business to conduct.* "I need to use that phone."

The man pulled the phone away from his ear. His forehead furrowed. "Can't you see I'm talking?" He shook his head, raised a Bic lighter to his cigarette and lit it. He blew a trail of smoke at Sakich and returned the phone to his ear.

Sakich flashed back to what his daughter went through. He imagined a sweaty black man with a large afro wearing a dingy cut off T-shirt standing over Amy. Her naked body tied down on a filthy mattress. A smoldering cigarette hanging from his lips. He takes a deep drag. The embers glow red. The paper sizzles. Laughter comes from deep in his gut. He twists the burning cigarette into her flesh. Her terrifying screams bring a smile to her attacker' face.

Sakich lunged forward, grabbed the man's arm and yanked him out of the booth. "You're not talking anymore. You niggers think you can live your life leeching off of white people. Not with me here. You don't realize who you're messing with." Spit flew from his mouth. He stepped into the booth, slammed the phone in the cradle and threw a handful of change from his pants pocket onto the shelf below the phone.

"Whitey, you don't realize who you're messin' with."

Sakich's face reddened. He turned and gripped the phone like a hammer ready to strike. "Listen asshole," he said and his eyes stared at a silver Chicago Police Department badge inches from his face. Then he heard the clicks of handcuffs snapped onto his wrist. "You can't do this. I got friends in the FBI. You'll be sorry." And the phone fell from his hands, dangling from its cord as he was led away.

*** 

Five hours later Sakich stood at a public wall phone on the ground floor of the First District Police Department headquarters at 11<sup>th</sup> and State and called Edward Pape's private line in his office.

"Where are you calling me from?" Pape asked.

Sakich ignored Pape's question. "You won't believe what happened."

"I know what happened. How could you be so stupid? Get arrested and on top of that try to get Eckhaus to get you out. You're not thinking clearly. Those kinds of mistakes can be costly—"

"I didn't know the nigger was a cop. I had to spend hours in a holding cell with four stinkin' drunken niggers that burned and looted their own neighborhood—"

"Don't interrupt me. I don't want to hear about the problems you created for yourself. Do you still have that number I gave you?"

"Yeah."

"It'll take me fifteen minutes to get there. Go find a pay phone and call me at that number. It's extremely important."

"Yeah, but..." The phone went dead. Sakich hung up, slid his hands in his pants pocket and stormed out of the police department. "He doesn't have to treat me like...like I'm a nigger," he mumbled.

Sakich hailed a cab and returned to his office. He figured if he had fifteen minutes he could lock his office and at least moisten his parched throat with a sip of scotch at the bar downstairs before he called Pape.

Sakich entered The Red Door lounge on the ground floor of his building. There was the usual after-work crowd: options traders, city bureaucrats, a couple of reporters looking for scoops and a handful of secretaries. The familiar smell of beer filled his nostrils. The music blasting from the jukebox barely covered the

---

cackle of the patrons. Ferns laced over pots hanging from the ceiling at the windows overlooking LaSalle Street. The other walls were covered in dark paneling and filled with paintings of partially clad women.

"Hey, Tommy, you want me to pour you one?" the bartender shouted over the crowd's noise. Thin red veins spider-webbed his nose and cheeks.

"Yeah, make it quick, Jimmy." Sakich laid a twenty on the bar. "You mind if I use the office to make a call?"

Jimmy slid a Dewar's and water on the rocks onto the bar and picked up the twenty in the same motion. "Yeah, go ahead. The boss won't be back 'til closin'."

He picked up the glass, took a sip and went through the door marked private. He slid into a creaky chair behind an old wooden desk covered with bills from liquor suppliers and food purveyors. He took another sip and searched his pockets for the envelope that he had scribbled the telephone number on, finding it stuffed in his rear pants pocket. He unfolded the crinkled envelope and kicked his feet on top of the desk. He lifted the black phone from the corner of the desk onto his lap and locked the handset between his ear and shoulder. He laid his drink on the desk and dialed. His call was answered on the first ring.

"I told you fifteen minutes. You're ten minutes late."

"Look, I've had a long day, sitting on my ass in the slammer."

"What is wrong with you?" Pape exhaled. "We need to keep a low profile. You can't be making contacts like calling our friend. He called me and if you do that again he's out."

"Oh, come on. You guys are paranoid." Sakich swiveled in the squeaky chair.

"Where are you? Are you on a pay phone?"

"Yeah, yeah, yeah."

"All right, try to keep yourself under control. What we accomplished far exceeded our expectations—"

"Yeah, Jesus Christ, can you believe those niggers burning up the cities and killin'—"

"Don't interrupt. Pay attention to what I'm going to tell you because if you don't get this right the whole thing could blow up in our faces."

Sakich scooted up in his chair. "All right, what's up?"

"We need you to get your cash together so we can make the final payment."

"Fifteen right?"

"That's correct. Get it together ASAP because we're going to be in contact with him Wednesday. The sooner we get him the money, the sooner he leaves the country for good. Best insurance for all parties concerned."

"I hear ya. I'll get it together tonight. What do I do with it?"

"Get the money to your man at the park and the final arrangements for delivery will be made on Wednesday. I'll let you know so you can tell him."

"I'll get the stuff to him on Tuesday. Won't be any holdups that way."

"Don't mess up. Just make the delivery. As soon as he gets the money, he's out of the country. He'll just disappear somewhere where no one will ever find him. And don't get any further involved than getting the money and stay out of trouble. You understand—stay out of trouble?" Pape said.

"Oh, yeah. You can trust me on that."

"I'll be out of touch for awhile until the next project comes up or if there's any extenuating circumstances. And whatever you do don't call our friend. If you have any questions, call me."

The line went dead.

Sakich slammed the phone down, drained his glass and headed to the bar for a fresh drink. "You guys treat me like I'm a nigger. All you want is my money. Fuck me. You think I can't handle this?"

*** 

After ten that night, Tom Sakich pulled his yellow Cadillac into the driveway of his bungalow in Sauganash. He kicked the car door open with his Italian leather shoes, put one hand on the door, the other on the steering wheel and pulled himself out of the car. The knot on his tie was pulled down to the middle of his chest and his collar had a lipstick smear from a bar floozy. He scuffled to the side door of the house and with his shaky hand tried three times to insert the key into the lock before he succeeded.

Sakich pulled the door open, stepped in, and it slammed behind him. "Oops,' he laughed. "Think I need a drink before I go to bed." He looked at the four stairs going up to the main level of the house and the five stairs going down to the rec room. "Easier going down than up and then I can get a drink and the money." Saliva bubbled in the corner of his mouth.

He flicked the light switch, leaned into the wall and gripped the rail, easing himself down the stairs. The paneled room had a bar with four stools near the stairs, and a pool table in the center of the room. Two pinball machines and a one-armed bandit graced the wall opposite the bar. Posters of 'The Rat Pack' and Al Capone separated the machines. The room had been built by a city vendor showing his appreciation for a juicy contract. The slot machine was a comp from a Las Vegas casino, showing their appreciation for the cash Sakich had lost.

Sakich stumbled his way behind the bar and poured three fingers of Dewar's into a Manhattan glass. He brought the glass to his lips and sluiced down half of the amber liquid down. "Gotta get the money."

He braced himself against the bar, strolled to the front and climbed one of the stools. He pushed aside a white perforated ceiling tile and reached for one of the three shoe boxes hidden above the suspended ceiling. "Just get one of these babies down." The box tumbled out of his hands, bounced on the bar and hundred-dollar bills scattered over the bar and tile floor. "Oh, shit."

Sakich climbed down the bar stool onto his hand and knees. He grabbed a fistful of hundreds, threw them into the air and watched them float to the floor. He laughed and then was struck by the realization of how alone he was. *All this money and for what? My little girl will never be herself. Seeing her like that is worse than if she had died. My wife gone.* A tear ran from the corner of his eye, down his cheek and across his lips. He lay on the floor, rested his head on the fallen shoe box and closed his eyes.

The next morning he woke at 9:30 on the tile floor. His eyes were dried, temples throbbing, hands shaking, and he had the insatiable desire for another drink. He peeled himself off the floor, filled his glass with scotch and called in to take another sick day.

Then he scraped the hundreds together and rubber banded three stacks of hundreds into $5,000 bundles. Sakich downed the scotch and dragged his hands down his shirt and slacks trying to press the wrinkles out. He struggled up the stairs and went out the side door to his car. "Shit, I left the car door open."

He lumbered into the car, closed the door and finger-combed his hair as he glanced into his rearview mirror. He backed out of his driveway and headed to a Denny's a few blocks from his house. He picked up a *Sun-Times* sitting on the counter, went to a pay phone, dropped a dime in and dialed while he read the front page.

"First Photo of Assassination. Aides pointing out to police where the fatal shot came from." He laughed under his breath. "The fatal shot came from me." There was a voice on the phone.

"Oh, hello, Alderman. It's Sakich. You need to come by tonight to pick up the package…..No, it's got to be you. I don't want to deal with anyone else….We'll find out tomorrow afternoon when and where the delivery has to be made….All right, see you eight tonight."

***

For thirty years Alderman Heidler had been pocketing cash from constituents requesting favors from zoning changes to new garbage cans, taking his cut and funneling the rest to the right people to get the deeds done. His chauffer, Vinnie, parked his black Olds 98 in front of Sakich's house. Vinnie hopped out of the car and helped the alderman out of the back seat. He groaned as his fleshy body was hauled out of the car. He gasped for air as he pulled himself up the six steps to the front door. His cane clicking on each step. As he rang the doorbell Sakich pushed the door open.

Heidler stepped into the house. The door closed behind him. The alderman wore a black suit, a thin black tie, and black wingtips. The living room was filled with French provincial furniture covered in plastic. Heidler pushed his black horn rimmed glasses up the bridge of his nose with his index finger and gazed at the room. "Nice place."

"My wife fixed it up." Sakich stirred his scotch and water with his finger. "She had a good eye for decorating." He walked over to the console television and picked up the envelope containing the $15,000.

The alderman slipped the envelope into his inside coat pocket. "I'll tell Reichardt —"

Sakich held up his hands and shook his head. "No names. I don't want to know who touches that envelope after you leave here, and don't tell anybody who you got it from."

Heidler raised his hands, palms up. "Relax, no problem. I'll stop at the ward office tonight and put it in the safe."

"I'll call you tomorrow afternoon so you can get the stuff where it needs to be." Sakich jerked his chin toward the door. "You better get on your way." He watched Heidler toil down the stairs and into his car. Sakich closed the door, drained his glass of scotch, and went to make another drink.

***

Mayor LeGrand was in his study and grabbed the phone on the first ring. "That's better service than the first time I called," James Earl Ray said.

"Let's keep this short. How're we doing this?"

"I want only one person handling this. I'll be watching. So if I see something that don't look right, it wouldn't be too smart. Then I might have to pay you a visit."

"Cut the bullshit. A deal's a deal. We're stand-up people. Besides, who knows, we might need your services again."

"I want that same boy that made the first delivery to me. Cause I know his face. Just him and only him. I see somebody I don't know with the boy, it'll be too bad for them. Tell him to be at the meat counter in Loblaw's Groceteria in Toronto this Friday at 2:00 p.m. Remember, I'll be watching the place so don't do nothin' stupid like sending somebody to do me."

"That doesn't give us much time to get ready."

"You been planning this a long time. You don't need any more. I'll see your boy then."

***

Thursday morning Beauford parked his pickup truck on Richmond and looked at the street sign that bore his new name. It reinforced the feeling of a new beginning for him. A chance to regroup and leave the recent past behind. Maybe he could find the man he once was and become him all over again. He headed down the sidewalk bordering Marquette Road to the ward office.

As he touched the door handle, he realized that it had been exactly one week since his trip to Memphis. He took a deep breath and felt a heavy shadow overcoming him. The violent act he had participated in and the destruction that resulted had sapped his energy. He felt a numbness that put everything far away.

He picked up his job list from Reichardt's desk. He saw that his day would consist of serving the regular list of local Democratic Party favorites; aldermen, ward committeemen, and a few major party contributors. He took a twenty out of petty cash from Reichardt's desk so he could pick up the supplies he would need for the day and walked to the door.

Reichardt came out of the backroom. "Hold it! Get back here."

Beauford flinched, did an about-face and lumbered back to the desk where Reichardt had sat down. Reichardt held out his hand. "Gimme that work list."

Beauford handed it to him, put one hand on his waist and scratched his eyebrow with the other. "That looks like more than I can get done all ready. You gonna gimme more?"

"No. Change of plans. This list is for Monday now. Got a delivery for you to make out of town. Reichardt unlocked his center desk drawer, pulled out a manila envelope about an inch thick, a road map, and held it toward Beauford.

Beauford's arms dropped to his sides.

"Take it. You got to be in Toronto, Canada, tomorrow afternoon."

He curled his lower lip. "Don't know how to get there."

"The routes marked in red on the map. Just go to Detroit and then head east. It's about a ten-hour drive."

Beauford swayed from one foot to the other.

Reichardt sat, his hand grasping the envelope and map pointed at Beauford. "Take it!"

"Can't somebody else do this?" Beauford mumbled. "I did your dirty work last week."

"You don't want us to get somebody else. Someone might figure we don't need you anymore." Reichardt shook his head and leaned forward. "You just do what I tell you. If it wasn't for me they'd be hauling your ass down to Mississippi. Getting the gas chamber ready for you. So don't give me any lip."

Beauford focused on the envelope. He felt like he had walked into a trap that squeezed him so tight he could barely breathe.

"Here's a hundred for expenses. You don't have to be back here until Monday morning. I'm talking to you."

Beauford took the envelope and stuffed it in the pocket of his overalls.

"You're going to meet that guy from Memphis on Friday at 2:00 in the afternoon. He'll be at the meat counter of the grocery store written on the envelope. Just give him that envelope. That's all you got to do."

"Yeah, I do what I gotta do." He pursed his lips, turned and left the office.

\*\*\*

Two o'clock Friday morning Beauford walked through the silence of the brisk spring air to his truck. With each step the envelope stuffed in his overalls bounced against his chest, each time reminding him of the face of the man he would meet once again. The light from the full moon glittered in the puddles of the housing project parking lot from rain that had stopped an hour ago. He opened the door, climbed into his truck, and headed north on Cicero Avenue, then eastbound on the Stevenson Expressway.

Beauford's mind wandered back to last week when he awoke from his nap and hurried to leave so he could get home and pick up his daughter. But this time there would be no reward for him. There was no motivation to make this delivery. He turned on the radio, flipping through stations hoping to find something to occupy his mind. Each station revealed a snippet of news before he could change it.

*...King's body was flown to Atlanta on a plane supplied by Bobby Kennedy...At the funeral on Tuesday, King's body was carried on a mule-drawn farm wagon for four miles through the city to its resting-place in the South View Cemetery...Riots in 125 cities across the country resulted in thirty deaths, scores injured, and property damage in excess of $30 million....This must be a conspiracy. How could one man have possibly....How could anyone have done this?*

Beauford twisted the radio dial and drove in silence, watching the beams from his headlights stare at the yellow line dividing the highway. He was driving into Detroit on Interstate 94 as the sun broke over the horizon. On both sides of the expressway were burnt ruins left over from the riots after King's murder. National Guard vehicles scattered across the neighborhoods and armed soldiers protected the burned-out ghettos.

He crossed into Canada and headed east on 401 driving straight through to Toronto, arriving just after noon, stopped and bought a hamburger at a fast-food joint for lunch and got directions to Loblaws. Beauford parked across the street from the store at 1:45 and entered.

\*\*\*

James Earl Ray sat in a diner across the street from Loblaws. He watched the man he knew as Robert Johnson enter the grocery store. Ray pulled the brim of his fedora down, shadowing his face, and took a sip of his coffee. He drummed his fingers on the table top and waited ten minutes. He glanced at his watch. No one who looked suspicious entered the store before or after his delivery boy. He was satisfied that Beauford was alone and it was time to get his cash. He raised the cup to his lips and drained his coffee. He tugged on his right earlobe. *Just go in there, get my money and leave.*

He tossed a dollar on the table, trotted across the street, entered the store and walked down the first aisle past bakery, fruits, and vegetables toward the rear of the store, making a sharp left turn, going for the meat counter. He saw Johnson talking to an armed white man in a blue security guard uniform and dropped back into the aisle he had just left. *Fucking security guard, may be a setup. Could be a cop.*

Ray's head swiveled, looking down the aisle to see if anyone was creeping up behind him. No one but a young mother, who held an apple in one hand, inspecting it for bruises, and with the other hand held her son's.

He pulled a .38 Smith & Wesson snub nose from his waist and slipped it into his right coat pocket. His finger pressed against the trigger. "Don't have time to fuck around. I gotta move on," he muttered, and walked out of the aisle towards his delivery boy.

He saw the black man look over the security guard's shoulder. Ray tightened his grip and planted his hand deep in the pocket of his black sport coat. His eyes met Johnson's and he jerked his head to the left and turned down the next aisle. Johnson parted from the guard and followed him.

Ray stood next to shelves of white bread, the bulge in his coat pocket pointing at Johnson. "Who's that?"

There was a crash behind Ray. He spun around, pressuring the trigger, pointing his coat pocket in the direction of the noise. Standing in front of him was the young boy. His grocery cart was next to a fallen stack of cans of beans. Ray dropped his hand to his side and blew air out of his mouth. "Get the fuck outta here. Go find your momma."

The boy left the cart and ran down the aisle crying.

"Who's that guy?"

"Guard that works here. He's hassling me cause he don't like a black man hanging around his store."

Ray looked over Tisdale's shoulder at the guard. "Got my stuff?"

"In an envelope stuffed in my overall pocket up here." Beauford nodded pointing with his chin toward his chest pocket.

Ray grabbed the envelope. "Turn around and go back to the meat counter and stay there for ten minutes. Order yourself a sandwich or something." He watched Beauford head to the counter. Ray smiled and strolled out of the store. "Got everything I need to start a new life."

***

On Saturday, April 20<sup>th</sup>, Beauford left their apartment early on his way to paint Alderman Heidler's garage. He stopped at a restaurant just the north of the Stevenson on Archer and Cicero Avenues.

A heavy set Greek wearing a greasy apron and a day-old beard stepped behind the cash register that rested on a glass counter holding boxes of cigars, chewing gum and candy bars. "Watcha want?"

"A black coffee and two donuts."

"That'll be a buck." He went down the counter to the coffee machine and pulled the lever, filling a Styrofoam cup.

Beauford glanced at the *Sun-Times* on the counter. The headlines read, *Galt Unmasked: Dr. King Suspect Escaped Convict*. Next to the headlines staring back at him was a photo and sketch of a man. *Shit, that's him. The man I met in Memphis and Toronto*. He picked up the newspaper and read the article that started on page one, "The FBI identified fingerprints of Eric Starvo Galt as James Earl Ray who is wanted in connection with the slaying of Martin Luther King."

"Hey, if you're gonna read it you hafta buy it." The counterman shouted putting a lid on the cup.

Beauford ignored him, flipped the paper open to page 14, continued reading the article and saw two more photos that eliminated any doubt he had. *That was him, Ray. The man that killed King. The man I delivered the money to.*

The Greek came down the counter with the coffee and a paper bag with the donuts. He slammed his open hand down on the paper. "You buying it or what?"

"Sorry, got to go." Beauford put a dollar on the counter, grabbed his coffee and the bag and went to a pay phone outside the restaurant. His hand shook as he put a dime in and dialed the number. *What if they catch him? The Feds will get me for givin' the money to him and then Mississippi will get me for murdering Napier's wife.*

"Yeah."

"Mr. Reichardt, It's me, Beauford."

"Do you know what the fuck time it is? It's 6:30 on a Saturday morning."

"There's trouble. The guy's picture is in the paper. The guy I gave the stuff to in Memphis and Toronto." Beauford quivered.

"This isn't the time or place to talk about that. Don't you talk to anybody about it. You understand."

"But what if they catch him?"

"I said, don't talk about it! What needs to be done will be done." The line went dead.

# CHAPTER FOURTEEN

Eckhaus called a meeting at the Knoxville Holiday Inn for Saturday, June 1, with the usual instructions. "Pay cash for your ticket and fly under an alias, no unnecessary contacts with anyone in public, including their selves and he would always be the first one in the room to check for bugs." He walked up to registration. "You should have a room for me, Kenneth Kaiser."

"Yes sir. Would like to give us a credit card?" The clerk asked.

"No." He laid $50 on the counter and stood there holding a bag from Bloomingdales of New York.

"Thank you Mr. Kaiser. Here's your change and key for room 204."

He arrived an hour before Pape or Sakich were due, entered the room and laid the bag on the bed. He pulled on latex gloves, pulled the curtains closed and searched the room for bugs—looking under the mattress, checking all the drawers, the alarm clock, curtains, telephone, TV and turned on the radio to create background noise.

Pape arrived and sat at the table near the window across from Eckhaus.

Fifteen minutes later Sakich entered the room and sat on the bed. He reached for the bag.

Eckhaus jumped out of his seat. "Don't touch that!"

Sakich withdrew his hand.

"We don't need any amateur mistakes." The FBI agent pulled the box out of the bag and took the top off.

Sakich looked at the polka dot dress. "Not my taste. I like my women to wear something slutty."

"You ever hear of Al Fatah?"

Pape and Sakich both shook their heads.

"It's a radical Arab group, very anti-Israel. Very advanced in the way they train their assassins. Frequently their assignments are suicide missions."

Sakich laughed and pointed at the contents of the box, "So you've got an assassin that's going to wear a polka dress."

"No." Eckhaus shook his head. "Al Fatah uses a key phrase or item to activate a hypnotic trance—it's a subliminal switch that activates a command that the subject was given under hypnosis. And the best thing about it is that the subject has no recollection of the command or its source."

Pape nodded. "The dress is the key for the trance."

"Right."

"So who's the target?" Sakich asked.

"I've researched this very carefully and have picked the best target meeting our political needs, meshing that with the security utilized by the target and his propensity to violate security."

"And the winner is?" Sakich said

Eckhaus tapped his forefinger against his temple. "That's up here."

Sakich stood up from the bed, hitched his belt up with both hands and pointed his forefinger at Eckhaus. "We're in this together—"

Pape raised his hand. "Tom, we've got to trust Jim with this. He has contacts we don't and they must be kept secure. We need to do what we can to support him."

"Oh yeah. What are you gonna do?" Sakich jerked his head at Pape. "I betcha I know what he wants me to do. How much money is this going to cost me?"

Eckhaus looked at Sakich. "I need you to do two things. Take this package to you man in Chicago and have him make arrangements to get it to Los Angeles by 6:00 p.m. this Tuesday, that's June 4. My friends in Al Fatah have reserved a room at the

Ambassador Hotel under the name of Muhammad Hasan. The name's written inside a match book that's in the box. Make sure the courier gets it so there won't be any mistakes getting the room. He's got to stay in the room until the dress is picked up." He leaned forward and put the lid on the box and slid it into the bag.

"You said you needed me to do two things. What's the second?" Sakich asked.

"I need you to give me $20,000 cash from your stash so I can pay the Al Fatah people."

Sakich put his hands on his hips. "You're not taking a little cut out of my cash for yourself are Jimmy boy?"

Eckhaus pursed his lips and leaned back in his chair.

Pape jumped in. "Tom, you're the only one of us that has an untraceable source of cash. If James or I had we would help out."

"Yeah, yeah, yeah." Sakich picked up the Bloomnigdales' bag. "He pointed at Eckhaus. "I'd rather leave the cash at the alderman's office. You can have Lawrence of Arabia pick it up there." He walked out of the room.

***

On Monday morning, June 3, Beauford arrived at the ward office. Reichardt was handing an envelope to a dark skinned man wearing a turban. He left the office stuffing the envelope in the inside pocket of his suit coat. Beauford had learned not to ask any questions about the comings and goings on at the ward office.

He approached Reichardt at his desk. "Here for my work order for the day."

Reichardt handed him a sheet of paper. "Just a half day today cause we need you to go on a trip tomorrow."

Beauford's forehead wrinkled. "What kind of trip?"

"You ever fly?"

"No."

"Some queer that lives here is a friend of a movie producer that made a movie in Chicago. They're finishing it in Hollywood. The queer designed a dress that the producer is going to use in the movie and they need it out there right away. They asked the alderman for a favor. I was going to do it myself but I'm tied up. So you lucked out."

"Wait 'til I tell the wife."

"You can't tell anyone. It's some kind of high priced fashion original so security is real high. If anybody asks you tell them you're a courier for city documents that need original signatures." Reichardt opened his desk drawer. "Here's a round trip ticket to LA. The plane leaves tomorrow morning 9:30 from O'Hare and the return leaves LA Wednesday morning at 9:00."

Beauford grabbed the tickets.

"You got hotel reservations at the Ambassador Hotel. You have to wait in the room until they pick up the dress. After that you're free. Oh, the reservations and the airline tickets are under the queer's name, Muhammad Hasan. They wrote it down in this matchbook so you don't forget." He took a roll of cash out of his pocket and pealed off five twenties. "Here's for your expenses." He wrapped the cash around the matchbook and handed him the package.

"Thanks, Mr. Reichardt."

***

Beauford boarded a plane for the first time in his life. He wore his going-to-church clothes, a white shirt, dark-blue slacks, and black spit-shined shoes. The plane taxied to the runway, the engines roared and his body was pushed into the seat as the plane lifted off the ground. His fingers tightened on the arms of his seat and his stomach flipped. Looking out the window the cars and buildings below appeared to be no more than toys. The plane leveled above the clouds.

The stewardess began beverage service. She was slender and wore a blue blouse and skirt with United stitched across her shirt pocket. She smiled at Beauford. "Coffee, juice or a soft beverage?"

He took a cup of coffee, nodded at her, and leaned back in his seat. The aroma of the coffee and the warmth of the cup in his hand comforted him. He closed his eyes, enjoyed the moment, and escaped from the sense of evil that had invaded him on the other trips.

Beauford rested his other hand on his right trouser leg and felt the matchbook in his pant's pocket. He slipped it out of his pocket. The cover read, "Holiday Inn, Knoxville, Tennessee," and on the inside, "Muhammad Hasan," was written in black ink. He stretched his leg as he slid the matchbook back into his pocket and with his foot nudged the paper bag containing the box with the dress. His hand trembled and coffee spilled over the side of the cup as he brought it to his lips. The brown liquid dribbled onto his white shirt.

*** 

At noon Beauford caught a taxi at LA International Airport. The driver was a young white man and he filled the trip with stories of his acting aspirations and the stars he had met. Beauford felt uneasy. For the first time in his life he was being chauffeured by a white man. The car zipped through traffic and finally headed down a long drive bordered by palm trees and an expansive lawn toward the seven-story Ambassador Hotel.

It pulled up to the circular canopy at the main entrance, stopping behind a red Cadillac convertible with the top down. Several porters were hovering around the car removing a multitude of suitcases. A blonde woman in a low-cut tight dress wearing large sunglasses and a scarf left the car and strutted into the hotel.

Beauford handed the cabby a twenty. A black man in a green uniform with gold epaulets and white gloves opened the door. "Welcome to the Ambassador Hotel, sir."

Beauford glanced at the cabby who nodded at the open door as he pocketed the twenty. He shook his head and stepped out of the cab onto a plush red carpet with a large "A" inscribed on it.

"May I get your luggage?" The porter asked.

Beauford stood there numbed by the extravagance. He brought his hand to his forehead shielding his eyes from the sun and gazed back at the long row of palm trees.

"Sir, may I get your luggage?"

"Ain't, I mean don't have any."

"Yes, sir. Welcome to the Ambassador and have a pleasant stay."

The doorman quick stepped to the entrance and held the door open for Beauford. He walked into a cavernous main lobby with a fountain spraying water ten-feet high, furnished with white leather sofas, coffee tables with white marble tops, lamps and tear-drop chandeliers.

He headed to the front desk. "I have a reservation." He pulled the matchbook out of his pocket, held it open in the palm of his hand, out of the sight of the clerk, and read it to make sure he got the name right. "Name is Muhammad Hasan."

The clerk handed him his key and placed the registration card in front of him, "Room 602. Please sign the registration card. Your reservation is for one night only and has been prepaid. Do you plan on staying any longer?"

"No, just the night."

"Is there any luggage, Mr. Hasan?"

"No, just what I got," he said, nodding at the bag tucked under his arm. He picked up the pen and copied the name in the matchbook onto the card. He noticed there was already a New York City address listed for him.

Beauford stepped to the elevator. Its doors were black with gold circular emblems. He stepped in, the doors silently closed behind him and in seconds it stopped at the 6th floor. The hallway carpeting was red and deep. He put the key in the lock, pushed the door open, and walked to the end of the room looking at a powdery blue sky through the large window. His eyes glanced down, taking in the lawn and tree-lined drive that he had come up.

Turning, he faced the interior. A king-size bed covered with a flowery bedspread, two matching chairs, and a large TV on the dresser. He walked into the bathroom, took off his shirt, rinsed the coffee off it and hung it on a hanger over the shower rod. He walked out of the bedroom, took off his slacks and laid them over one of the chairs. He plopped onto the bed, fluffed the pillows behind him, pressed the remote, and turned on the TV. "One day me and Nath coming to a place like this."

\*\*\*

Jimmy Napier turned the Dodge onto Harrison Street heading toward the Dixie Lounge. He pulled into the gravel lot on the side of the dusty red-brick building that bordered the tracks and parked between two pickup trucks. Napier left his truck and walked to the wooden screen door on the side of the establishment. Junior scrambled down out of the truck and was three steps behind his father. They entered and Napier saw Albert, Uriah, and two other men he had not seen since the night on the Ruleville Road Bridge.

He ambled to the bar, which was scarred with gouges and cigarette burns. "Set me up with a shot of Jack and a draft." Napier grabbed the shot glass, put it to his lips, and threw it down. He could feel the eyes of the men at the table watching him and heard his name in the undertones of their conversation. His lips smacked, shaking off the first shot of the day, and he lifted Junior sitting him on the bar. "Get me a glass of sweet tea for mah boy."

The barkeep wore a yellowed T-shirt and his hairy belly stuck out over his jeans. He held a glass up to the light, swiped a smudge off the glass with a towel, and set a tall glass of iced tea in front of the little boy.

Napier grasped his beer and clicked his son's glass. "Here's to the Napiers, m' boy. We alls that left." He downed his beer and wiped the foam off his mouth with the back of his hand. "Gim'me another set up." Napier repeated this ritual, leaving a collection of empty beer bottles in front of him.

He heard a car skid into the parking lot, its tires crunching over gravel. The door slammed shut, the screen door creaked open, and whacked closed. Boots scuffled on the wood floor and stopped.

Napier turned around. His anger seethed at the sight of the mayor. "Junior, there's that nigger lover that's responsible for your momma's killing."

The mayor stood inside the door. "You've no right to talk to me like that."

"My wife's dead cause you kissed that nigger's ass." He stepped toward the mayor and shoved the man's shoulder. "My boy lost his mama causa you."

The mayor flicked his fingers brushing the dust from Napier's hand off his beige sport coat. "You're drunk as usual and you don't know what you're saying." He took three steps toward the corner table.

Napier darted after him. "What'd you do with your nigger? Why'd you pick him over me?"

The mayor stopped and turned. His face inches from Napier's. "He ain't my nigger and I didn't..." He shook his head. "Why don't you just give it up, Jimmy? Just give it up."

Then it came to Napier. For the first time, he made the connection. He lowered his voice. "I know why you want me to give it up. You put that nigger and my cousin, Jimmy Earl, up to it. Didn't you?"

"I don't know what you're talking about. But, if I was you I wouldn't infer anything like that. In these times, you say something like that it could cause somebody a lot of trouble."

"You musta forgot." His voice went low and he smirked. "You asked me for a shooter and I gotcha Jimmy Earl. And now it's all over the radio and TV. He did it. He shot King. And my cousin and the nigger you protected ain't around. I bet you know where they are."

"I told you, don't talk like that. You talk like that could only end hurting people, maybe even you or your boy. You don't want anything to happen to your boy?"

"It don't make no difference to me if you had my cousin kill King. It only makes me proud that he was the one. Me and my boy ain't gonna cause you no trouble over that. But that nigger is another story. Cause you see, we gotta pact. Gonna find your nigger. Gonna kill 'em. And if I don't, my boy gave me his word over his mother's grave that he'll kill 'em." He stepped back to the bar and patted Junior on his head. The boy smiled.

The mayor held his ground, chewed on his lower lip, and stared at Napier.

The bartender moved down the bar, stopping across from Napier. "Jimmy, why don't you take your boy and head home. He's lookin' tired."

"Fuckin' nigger lovers." Napier glanced at Junior, grabbed a beer bottle and threw it at LeGrand.

The mayor raised his arm and ducked. The bottle flew just past his ear.

Napier jumped at him, threw him to the floor, thrusting his fist into the Mayor's face. "My wife dead causa you!"

The bartender leaped over the bar and the four men from the table rushed over. Three of them picked up Napier and held him while Albert punched him in the gut again and again. Napier bent at the waist, clutching his stomach and Albert lifted Napier off his feet with an uppercut to his jaw. Napier crashed to the dirty floor.

The bartender helped the mayor up, dusted him off, and walked him toward the table.

Junior jumped down off the bar and reached as high as he could, locking his arms around one of Albert's legs.

Albert lifted Junior by the front of his shirt, holding him suspended in mid air. "You little redneck. You're no fucking good, just like your old man. Wish you were ten years older so I could teach you a fuckin' lesson."

"Let me down. Let me down." Junior screamed, his legs swinging attempting to kick the man.

Albert opened his hand letting go of Junior and the boy thudded to the floor next to his father.

Junior crawled to his father and wiped the blood off his old man's mouth with his T-shirt. "Daddy, lets go. I don't like this place."

The mayor leaned against the table and pointed at Napier. "You should listen to your son. He's got more sense than you." LeGrand slid into a chair.

Napier crawled to a bar stool, braced himself, and stood. He wobbled as he wiped the blood running over his lips with his shirtsleeve. He thrust his forearm across the bar, knocking over the empty beer bottles and stormed out, the door crashing behind him. The six-year old stood alone glaring at the men at the table. "Fuckin' nigger lovers." Then he ran after his father.

\*\*\*

LeGrand, Albert, Uriah, and the others watched Junior run out of the bar. LeGrand turned and faced the men seated at the table. "We got to be careful. The fucking FBI are all over the place. Freedom fighters down here from up North. Too many people that don't belong here. Don't any of you boys go talking about anything we got planned or anything we already did."

"Yeah, especially Napier," Albert said. "If he try to meet up with any of you guys, don't trust him. I wouldn't be surprised if he was wearing a wire for the FBI. You talk to him you'll find your ass in jail."

"The only people we can trust are those sitting right here," Uriah said. "Remember we have a vow of secrecy to our brothers. The only ones we can rely on are each other."

\*\*\*

There was a pounding on Beauford's door. His room was dark except for the light cascading from the TV screen. He shook his head and focused his eyes on the clock on the nightstand, 11:35

p.m. He stood and turned on the lamp on the nightstand. The knocking came again, but louder. "All right, be there in a second."

"Hurry up," a woman's voice came back through the door.

He slipped on his pants and shoes and opened the door.

A white woman with dark hair wearing a raincoat barged past him into the room. "Where is it?"

"What?"

"Don't give me shit. The dress, God damn it."

"It's in the bag on the floor underneath the table." He pointed and closed the door.

She flew past the bed, bent down, picked up the bag, ripped the box out, and threw the bag to the floor. She dropped her raincoat on top of the bag and stood there in black panties and a bra.

Beauford stepped to the foot of the bed and stared at her.

"What're you looking at? Look the other way."

He turned his head but sneaked a glance at the almost-naked woman.

She flipped the top of the box off and grabbed the polka dot dress. She caught him staring at her again. Her eyes narrowed and lips pursed. "I told you don't look at me."

He jerked his head away.

She stepped into the dress, and turned. "Zip me up!"

Beauford stepped around the bed, pushed her dark hair away and touched her skin. It was soft and he thought of that time with Celeste in her father's barn. His heart pounded. *What was this going to lead to?*

Her head jerked around. Her eyes flared. "What're you waiting for? Zip me up!"

He did and she barged out of the room.

It was like it never happened. He shook his head, bent down, picked up the raincoat, bag and box and placed them on the bed. "Good, I'm done. Did what I was told to do. Get outta here. Away from this place."

Beauford walked into the bathroom, filled the sink with cold water, and splashed it on his face. He grabbed a white, plush towel off the rack and patted his face dry. His lungs filled with air and he blew it out. He was done and free. But apprehension clutched at his chest.

He grabbed his shirt off the hanger on the shower rod and put it on. He left his room, got on the elevator and pushed the lobby button.

The elevator stopped on the second floor. His finger reached for the close button when a loud cheer and applause came from a room nearby. There was a muffled montage of a speech engulfed by cheers. A voice that he remembered hearing not long ago but couldn't place. He stepped out of the elevator, drawn by the voice and went down the hallway. Stopping in front of double doors he read the lettering, "The Embassy Room."

He pulled open the door and entered a large banquet room filled with eighteen hundred people. A speaker at distant podium, surrounded by his entourage, was continuing.

> "…What I think is quite clear is that we can work together in the last analysis to overcome the division, the violence, the disenchantment with our society, the division between black and white…."

Beauford threaded his way through the crowd, getting closer to the speaker. The man wore a blue suit, white shirt and a navy tie with gray stripes.

> "…We are a great country, an unselfish country, a compassionate country…."

The cheers engulfed the hall. Beauford was on the speaker's left side, 80 feet away. He thought, *The President's brother. Thank God, there's some hope. Listen to what the man has to say.*

> "…The people in the Democratic Party and the people in the United States want change…. We want to deal with our problems in our own country…. So my thanks to all of you and now off to Chicago and let's win there."

Kennedy raised his arms in victory.

The crowd cheered, "We want Bobby! We want Bobby!"

Beauford could feel his chest swelling with emotion and he joined the chant, "We want Bobby! We want Bobby!" He moved toward Kennedy and shouted louder and louder, "We want Bobby! We want Bobby!" The network cameras behind the candidate filmed the frenzied crowd. Beauford saw Kennedy's pregnant wife standing next to the senator clapping her hands and chanting with the crowd.

Kennedy started exiting to the right side of the stage. Someone yelled, he looked back and changed direction, turning to the door at the rear of the stage.

The deafening chanting continued, "We want Bobby! We want Bobby!" The supporters in front of the stage followed the candidate. Beauford was caught in the flow. Supporters, reporters, cameramen, and hotel employees crammed into a narrow pantry. Close to 100 people. Balloons popping under foot, cheering, pushing, screaming, and shoving to get a look at the famous candidate, chaos prevailing. Beauford was swept in by the crowd and the emotion.

His eyes caught a glimpse of something familiar. Thirty feet ahead a polka dot dress. *Must be another one just like it.* His spine chilled. The dress disappeared into the crowd. He pushed his way forward looking for what he didn't want to see. *The dark hair. Looks the same.* She disappeared into the crowd again, not more than 15 feet ahead of him. He forced himself through the throng toward her.

She turned and looked over her shoulder. Her eyes narrowed, teeth clenched and she stepped away from Beauford as she pushed through the dense mass of people. She glanced back again and their eyes met.

He saw her glaring at him.

Someone shouted. "Kennedy, you son of bitch." The thick air blistered with the blast of gun shots. There was a pause and shots rang out again.

People rushed in every direction, some to the senator, some away, crashing into each other.

Shouts went out, "Get the gun! Get the Gun! Oh my God, the senator is shot."

The woman in the polka dot dress broke away from the mania. Beauford fought the crowd trying to follow her but she increased the distance between them. He saw her meet with a man and they went to an exit. He heard her shout. "We shot him! We shot him! We shot Senator Kennedy." Then they went out the door and it slammed shut.

Beauford rushed to the door and shoved it open. He ran down the stairs into the parking lot and looked for her. He wanted to grab her. There was no one. He fell to his knees and covered his face with his hands. Tears spilled down his cheeks. "I'm part of them. Can't do nothing about it."

The sounds of screaming sirens drew louder.

He forced himself up, first one knee and then the other. He started jogging away from the hotel and his stomach burned. He stopped, bent over, locked his hands on his knees and heaved the contents of his stomach. He shook his head. "Got to go back to the room and get that bag and raincoat outta there."

He didn't want to go through the same door that would lead him to the scene of the shooting. Circling the building he found another entrance in the rear and ran up a stairwell to the sixth floor, returning to his room shortly before 12:30 a.m. He put the raincoat in the box, placed the box in the bag, and headed for the street. "No checking out. Just get my ass outta here."

He took the elevator down to the lobby. The doors opened and the lobby was filled with hotel employees, guests, reporters and Kennedy supporters being interviewed by a variety of uniformed cops and plainclothes officers. Beauford took a deep breath and pushed the button marked six. The doors slowly closed.

"They ain't gonna let anybody outta here." The floors marked on the elevator flashed by when it hit him. "I gotta get rid of this stuff." He hit the button marked four, the elevator stopped, and the doors opened. Beauford took a step out of the elevator, holding the doors open with one hand. There was no one in sight and a waste can was just outside the elevator door. He jammed the bag and its contents into the can, stepped back into the elevator, went up to the sixth floor, returning to his room to clear his mind. *I can't stay here. Cops will be goin' room to room. They come here it's trouble. The room is under that Arab name and all I got is my ID. I gotta see if I can get outta here.* Beauford returned to the elevator, pushed the button for the lobby and headed down.

The doors opened and the same confused scene prevailed. The air was thick and heavy, drenched with sorrow. There were men shaking their heads in disbelief and women crying and moaning. The murmur of interrogations reverberated through the lobby. Three huge LAPD patrolmen and a man in a brown suit guarded the front door. Beauford wound his way through the maze of people. Beads of perspiration were on his forehead. The huge cops blocked the door. "Excuse me, officers, can I leave?"

"You been interviewed yet?"

He stood there contemplating which lie to tell. Yes, I have or no I haven't. My name's Muhammad Hasan or I'm Beauford Richmond.

"You been talked to yet?" the cop asked again.

He looked up into the brown penetrating eyes of the policeman. "No, no one's talked to me yet."

"Give your name to the FBI agent." The cop nodded in the direction of the man in the brown suit. "They'll call you as soon as someone is free to talk to you. You can wait over there." He pointed to an area of the lobby where numerous chairs from banquet rooms had been placed. People were sitting on folding chairs, lobby furniture, and the carpet.

He walked over to the young agent.

"Name please?" The agent asked.

"Beauford Tisdale ah.... Richmond."

"Address?"

"Ah, Tisdale my middle name." *They check for warrants, I'm fucked.* "Richmond is the last name. Maybe you oughtta erase that." He said, pointing at the name Tisdale written on the agent's list."

"We'll keep it straight. Go sit down over there until someone calls you."

"Okay, you sure that won't confuse nobody?"

"Mr. Tisdale, I mean Richmond, go sit down. Don't worry about it. When you hear your name go to the agent that's calling you for an interview."

Beauford nodded and sat down on the carpet in the corner of the room. One by one, people were called. He closed his eyes and tried to calm down, hoping that this trip wasn't going to end with his arrest for the murder of Napier's wife. His collar was saturated and his shirt stuck to his back. It was nearing 2:00 a.m.

"Beauford Tisdale Richmond," a tall slender agent in a pale gray suit called out.

Beauford stood and waved his arm.

"Over here." He pulled out his credentials. "I'm Special Agent Cowens, FBI. Sit down."

"Jus' so you got your records straight, Tisdale's my middle name. Richmond is the last name. Maybe you want to take that off so it don't get screwed up."

"No problem. Do you have identification?"

Beauford handed him the driver's license Reichardt had given him.

"This your current address?"

"Yes, sir."

"What brought you from Chicago?"

"I came to see Senator Kennedy." He lowered his head. "You know if he's gonna be all right?"

"We can only hope. You staying in the hotel?"

"No, I jus' came for the day. Was going back to the airport to try and catch the next plane home."

"Kind of expensive flying out for one day. What kind of work do you do?"

"I work for the city. Kind of a handyman."

"You make that much money you can be flying around like this?"

"I been doing some extra work for my boss and he gimme cash for the trip. You know on account of the extra work. He knows I really like the Senator. You know us city workers are heavy Democrats."

"You don't sound like you're from Chicago."

"I's from Mississippi. Moved to Chicago. But I still talk like a southern boy."

"Who's your boss?"

"Man, I don't wanta get him in any trouble. Can't we jus' leave it at this?"

"I have to get all the pertinent information, Richmond, and then you can go."

Beauford paused, "Helmut Reichardt. He's the Ward Committeeman. Office is at Marquette and California. He's an important Democrat."

"Did you see the Senator get shot?"

"No, I's too far away. I heard the shots. I...I," He stroked his forehead with his fingers. "I knew it was trouble. It's jus' bad times."

"You ever hear of Sirhan Sirhan?"

"No, who's that?"

"Don't matter. You see a short, dark-skinned Arabian man anywhere tonight?"

"No. Don't recall seeing anyone like that."

"You see anything unusual? Anything that didn't seem right?"

Beauford looked down, curled his lips, and shook his head.

"Alright, you think of anything you call the FBI in Chicago. It's also possible that agents from the Chicago office may contact you at a later date if there's any follow-up questions. Give me your address and telephone number and then you can go."

He gave the agent the information and left the hotel. He stood under the canopy. The street was filled with squad cars and other official-looking vehicles. He felt his stomach tumbling. His only safety net was going deeper into himself. Further away from those he knew. There were too many secrets. He thought, *if they check on Tisdale or end up talking to Reichardt, I'm a dead man.*

# CHAPTER FIFTEEN

## June 5, 1968

It was still a few hours before the sun would pierce the dark sky. A heavy layer of clouds obscured the moon and the damp heavy Mississippi summer air made FBI Special Agent Ray Ericson wished he was back home in Minnesota. If he were there he might be getting up at this time in the morning to go fishing on a cool lake. He wiped the perspiration off his brow, brushing his blond hair back. He took off his black horn-rim glasses and cleaned the lenses with his tie.

Ericson had been with the Bureau for ten years and was starting his second year of a temporary six-month assignment in Mississippi. He had seen enough freedom fighters, kluckers, burned churches, and hanged Negroes to last his career. He was ready to go home.

The Bureau had sent him a new partner. Someone he would have to mentor. He was one of those new breed of agents, well schooled and a Negro. One of the first Negro agents from the Academy. He wondered how much more time this would add to his temporary assignment and whether Clarence Daniels could hack it.

Ericson had heard about Daniels. He was born and raised in Atlanta, starting halfback at Florida A & M, law school at Emory, and finished in the top 10 percent of his FBI class. He knew the bureau needed a few Negro agents so it wouldn't appear as white as the Klan. But, the rumors gave him the impression that Daniels wasn't going to be anyone's token.

In a small opening surrounded by a cluster of oaks and elms east of highway 49 north of Ruleville, they waited for one of Ericson's informants in a bureau car, a beige-four-door Ford.

"I don't know if I have to say this or not." Ericson stirred in the driver's seat, "so don't take offense. It's something we need to discuss." He put a Salem between his lips, flicked his lighter with one hand and rested the other on the steering wheel. A gray cloud of smoke hovered in the car.

Daniels waved his hand, dispersing the smoke. His hands were large and thick. "I know what you're going to say, but go ahead."

"I don't know how this snitch will take to you. He's a Klanner. Hasn't been involved in any violent stuff but he's still one of the boys."

"You're from Minnesota and before that you were assigned to Fargo. So I'm guessing that I'm the first Negro that you've sat next to, talked to, and probably shook hands with. I'm used to being the first, Ray. It'll work out."

Ericson sucked on his Salem and blew the smoke out the window. The still air was interrupted by the sound of a truck coming up the dirt road. A pickup stopped where the dirt road met the opening to the woods. Ericson flashed his headlights twice and flicked his smoke out the window.

The pickup truck flashed back, doused its lights, slowly pulled into the opening, and parked next to an ancient live oak. A man got out of the truck and hurried into the back seat of the bureau car.

Ericson turned in his seat and watched the man's eyes glance at him, dart to Daniels, and shoot back to him.

"Who's he?" The man asked.

Daniels twisted in his seat facing the man.

"That's FBI Special Agent Clarence Daniels. My new partner." Ericson said.

"I don't know if I can do this. I'm risking my life talking to you guys for a measly couple bucks. That's bad enough. These guys find out I'm talking to a negra FBI agent they'll lynch me and my family."

"I'm sorry, sir; I didn't catch your name." Daniels' voice was deep, sounded like it came from a pulpit.

"Uriah, Uriah Beckwith."

"You mind if I call you Uriah?" Daniels asked.

Beckwith nodded.

"Good, I'm from Atlanta, Uriah. I know what the South is like. And I appreciate your courage for standing up for what's right."

"Yeah, okay," Uriah shrugged.

Ericson looked straight ahead with a smirk across his face. "So, what's going on with the Klan?"

"LeGrand told us yesterday not to talk to anybody because we don't know who might be talkin' to you guys. He said especially don't talk to Jimmy Napier."

"Why's that?"

"LeGrand thinks Jimmy might be talkin' to you guys cause he's pissed off at everybody. Jimmy's family been with the Klan from the beginning. A couple months back that one nig...ah, colored, that they was gonna kill, told everybody that he was fuckin' Jimmy's daughter. Jimmy went crazy. I was there. Jimmy chained the nigra up to his pickup. Was goin' to drag him 'til there was nothin' left. He puts the truck in gear jus' as the mayor comes by, says to let 'em go. The mayor gave Jimmy a ride home to try to calm him down. Later, me and Albert went to Jimmy's house to drop off his truck. Jimmy comes out saying that Tisdale, that's the colored guy, killed his wife and kidnapped his daughter. We ain't never seen that guy since."

"You think Napier killed him?" Daniels asked.

Beckwith shook his head. "Na, if he killed him he'd be braggin' about it."

"What do you think happened to Tisdale?"

"I don't know. But, I think the mayor knows. But he don't talk to us rednecks. He said something about some important man that night. A few days before that he said the man was looking for a shooter."

"Was that before King's assassination?" Daniels asked.

Beckwith paused, "Ah, maybe a month, maybe more. I don't rightly know the exact date."

Daniels nodded. "Who's this important man and why'd he want a shooter?"

"Don't know the answer to either question. But when the mayor asked about a shooter Jimmy told him that he might know one. They left together. Don't know what happened. I mean, if Jimmy ever got a shooter."

"You said Jimmy's pissed at all you guys. You think he'd talk to us?" Ericson asked.

"Nope. Never. He's pissed at the world. You'd have to have something big on him. Something that might be a threat to his little boy. That's all he's got left. Maybe then he might talk. But, I doubt it."

Ericson pulled a soft pack of Salems out of his shirt pocket. Popped one out and slipped it between his lips. "If you talked to him about bombing a church, do you think he might be interested?"

"Oh, yeah. He hates the whole world. Especially niggers..." His eyes darted in Daniels' direction. "I mean colored. On account of Tisdale killin' his wife and messin' with his daughter. So if it came to bombing a church, I'd have to hold 'em back."

Ericson flipped his lighter open and lit his cigarette. "You get a chance, you talk to him about that, and get back to me." He reached in his pants pocket, pulled out five $10 bills, and handed Beckwith the cash. "Here's fifty bucks. Talk to Napier and see if he's interested. If he is, call me."

Beckwith stuffed the cash in his jeans and hopped out of the car.

Ericson nodded his head. "We catch this boy Napier with his hands dirty, maybe he'll talk about this shooter. Then maybe I can go home."

\*\*\*

Nathleen Richmond returned to their apartment with Marlee after walking William to the school bus. She turned on the TV and sat down with her daughter and a cup of coffee.

"Here's the latest update on Senator Kennedy. Shortly after midnight in Los Angeles the Senator was shot three times by an individual identified as Sirhan Sirhan. Kennedy was taken to Good Samaritan Hospital and has been in surgery. A prognosis hasn't been announced. The alleged shooter is under arrest. Now we'll cut to a tape of the Senator's speech just before he was shot."

Nathleen stood, stepped toward the black and white TV. She didn't want to hear about any more violence. A TV camera panned the crowd at Kennedy's speech. She reached for the dial.

"Look momma, there's daddy." Marlee pointed at the television.

Nathleen froze. There was her husband standing thirty feet in front of the Senator. She became oblivious to the senator's words. "What's he doing there?"

*\*\**

It was 5:00 p.m. when Beauford walked in the front door of their apartment. His white shirt and blue pants were wrinkled. He was tired after two days without much sleep.

Marlee rose from in front of the TV and rushed to him, "Daddy, Daddy," folding her arms around his knees.

William came out of his room and hugged him waist high.

For a moment his downward spiral stopped. But his shame was deep-seated, something lurking below the surface, affecting every facet of his life from now on.

Nathleen stepped into the living room from the kitchen, a blue bandana tied behind her head and a yellow apron covered her clothes. "How was your trip?"

He patted the kids on their heads then pushed them away. "Okay."

"What did you say you were going to Los Angeles for?"

"Deliver some important papers to some lawyers. Had to be original documents." He walked past her toward the kitchen.

She followed him. "What did you do after you delivered those papers?"

Beauford exhaled. "What's with all the questions? It was just work and I'm tired." He pulled out a chair at the Formica table and plopped down.

"What did you do after you delivered those papers?"

He leaned back into the chair and rested his arms on the table. "Can I have something to eat? I'm tired and hungry."

Nathleen went to the stove and ladled macaroni and cheese onto a plate. She turned away from the stove and slid the plate across the table. "The kids already ate."

He grabbed the plate, dragged it closer, lifted a forkful to his mouth and chewed.

She sat at the table across from Beauford. "You gonna tell me or what?"

"Just waited in the lawyer's office 'til they said it was okay to go back to the hotel. Went for a walk. Watched some TV."

She cocked her head. "I saw you on TV this morning. The news had a tape of Bobby Kennedy before he was shot. You were there. You forget about that?"

He lifted another forkful and put it in his mouth.

She cocked her head. "Didn't you hear me?"

Beauford finished chewing. "You're wrong. Wasn't me."

Nathleen sat down, put her elbow on the table and rested her chin in her palm. "Beau, it was you. Why you lyin' to me?"

His eyes narrowed. "Don't you ever say that to me. All I been through tryin' to do the best for my family." He pushed the food across the plate with the fork.

She lowered her arm to the table and sat erect. "I saw you. Why can't you tell me why you were there?"

He jerked up, knocking his chair over. "I told you I wasn't there! So you keep your mouth shut and don't be blabbing such foolishness to nobody."

The children ran into the kitchen. Marlee cried, "Don't yell at my momma." William stood behind his mother, his hand on her shoulder.

Beauford threw his fork down. "I'm going out for a drink. Be back later. Don't wait up for me."

***

It was 7:00 Sunday morning, June 9. He raised his head from the pillow and kicked his feet off the sofa onto the floor. Beauford and Nathleen had not talked or shared their bed since he left the kitchen table. He walked into the kitchen, grabbed his jeans and shirt off of a chair, dressed, and left the apartment. Two blocks down Cicero Avenue he crossed the street to a greasy-spoon diner. Dropped a quarter into a newspaper box, picked up the *Sunday Sun-Times*, tucked it under his arm, and entered the diner.

Three early morning Sunday patrons sat in a booth near the door putting the finishing touches on a Saturday night out. They sipped on beers in brown paper bags, waiting for their breakfast order. A long narrow aisle separated the booths from the counter. The waitress was Rubenesque, in a black uniform two sizes too small, leaning against the counter. Beauford walked past her to the last booth. She followed him holding a pot of coffee.

He turned his coffee cup on the table right side up, pushed it to the edge of the table, nodded, and unfolded the newspaper. His eyes fixed on the front page as the waitress filled his cup. Staring up at him was a photograph of Robert F. Kennedy and the headline, RAY IS CAPTURED, BRITISH ARREST DR. KING SUSPECT.

Beauford spun out of the booth, knocking over his cup. It clattered to the floor. Coffee splattered onto the waitress and the floor.

"Ow! Watch it, idiot." The waitress grabbed Beauford's napkin and wiped the hot coffee off her arm and chest.

He pushed her aside, grabbed the newspaper, and barreled to the pay phone just inside the door. Picked up the receiver, put a dime in, and punched in four numbers.

The waitress came up behind him, "You gotta lot of nerve burning me with hot coffee cause you in such a hurry to use the phone. Get outta here."

He pushed her away, "Leave me alone." And punched in the last three numbers.

The burly short-order cook came from the kitchen, meat cleaver in hand. "You better getch you ass outta here before I havta cut you, boy."

Beauford's eyes glanced down at the meat cleaver. "Lem'me jus make this call. I be gone in a minute."

The voice on the other end of the phone said, "Yeah."

"It's me—"

The cook grabbed the phone out of Beauford's hand and slammed it onto the hook. "Get the fuck outta here."

Beauford dropped the newspaper and the pages scattered across the floor. He ran out of the diner heading for the ward office with one thought racing through his mind: *What if Ray talks?*

\*\*\*

Jimmy Napier gazed through his front window on Sunday morning and watched the 1963 red Ford pickup rumble up the dirt road that separated his barren fields. He hadn't had any visitors since the night Linda Joy was killed. He took a swig of his beer, turned, and looked at Junior curled up in a chair asleep in his T-shirt and jockey shorts. He shuffled to the screen door, pushed it open, and stepped onto the porch to wait for his visitor as the door slammed shut behind him.

The pickup stopped in front of the farmhouse and Uriah Beckwith stepped out. "Hey, Jimmy, thought I'd stop by and see how you doin'."

"How I doin'? You didn't seem too concerned about how I was doin' at the Dixie Lounge."

"I jus' wanted to get you offa the mayor. You coulda killed him. I didn't know Albert was gonna go nuts and start swinging." He walked to the front of the porch, hooked his thumbs in his belt, and looked into Napier's bloodshot eyes. "Sorry about that, Jimmy."

"Well, you know it's all that old fool's fault. If he woulda let me take care of Tisdale that night, none of this shit woulda happened."

"Yeah, you're right. That woulda be fine with me."

Napier took a swig from his bottle. "You wanna beer?"

"Sounds good to me."

"Sit down." Napier pointed to the rocking chair with a spindle backrest. "I'll be right back with a couple of cold ones." He went into the house.

Uriah sat down. Junior shoved the screen door open and came onto the porch. The barefoot boy climbed into the other rocker and stared at Uriah.

Napier kicked the screen door open, holding two long-neck bottles in each hand. "Thought I'd bring a few spares. Get outta that chair, boy, and let your daddy sit down."

Uriah reached over and mussed Junior's red hair. "How you doin', boy?"

He jerked his head away, pursed his lips and glared at Uriah. His little knuckles whitened as they squeezed the arms of the rocker.

Napier pointed one hand at Junior. "I said get your ass outta my chair."

Junior jumped out of the chair and ran into the house.

Uriah grabbed two bottles from Napier. "Thanks, Jimmy. So how you and the kid getting along, considering everything?"

Napier sat in the rocker. "After all the fuckin' years my daddy and his daddy bein' in the Klan, hangin' niggers, keepin' them away from our women and children. I expected my Klan brothers to be behind me. Then all of sudden some uppity-ups tells the mayor to let that nigger go. And we don't even know who these people are that are givin' the orders. We jus' go right ahead and do what they say."

"Yeah, it ain't right." Uriah took a gulp of his beer. "Use to be we made our own minds about what's right for us. Now outsiders tryin' to tell us what to do. Too many people gettin' soft around here. Fuck'em! We need to get back to doin' things the way we use to. We be alright. You hear they arrested the guy for shootin' King?"

"You're shitting me!" Napier shook his head. "That's too bad."

"Yeah, heard it on the radio coming over here. They arrested that white boy in England. Wonder how the hell he got out of the country."

"You can bet on one thing. This country's so fucked up they gonna fry that man's white ass for killin' that nigger," Napier said.

Napier took a long swig of his beer and thought about getting revenge on the mayor. *So cousin James Earl did it. This little secret could be worth some money.* "We should do something to honor that boy before they kill him."

"Yeah, need to go burn a nigger church, a house, maybe lynch a few in honor of that man." Uriah said.

Napier clinked his bottle against Uriah's. "Now you're talkin'. The sooner the better. I'll call you tonight and we'll set it up."

"Yeah, we gotta do this to honor that man," Uriah said.

*** 

Kathleen Pape answered the phone, "Hello."

"Kathleen. It's Tom Sakich. How're you?"

"I'm sorry, I can hardly hear you with all that traffic noise in the background."

Sakich raised his voice. "I'm on a pay phone outside. It's Tom."

"It's good to hear your voice. Been a long time."

"You know how it is. Sorry, we haven't been in touch."

"Yes, me too, Tom. Is Chrissie doing any better?"

"I'm afraid not. She has good days and bad days, but she's about the same. I just finished breakfast and I'm heading over to mass. I was wondering if I could talk to Ed?"

"I'll let him know you're on the phone. He's in his study with the Sunday paper. You know how you men are with the Sunday paper. I think it's some kind of male ritual. You take care of yourself now. I'll get Ed. Bye, Tom."

A few seconds later Sakich heard, "Interesting reading in today's papers. You see the UPI story regarding Sirhan's statements to the police?"

Sakich laughed. "He has no recollection of planning or committing the crime. Sounds just like what James said. What about the arrest in London…"

"James who, honey?" Kathleen Pape asked.

Pape paused, "Oh, I didn't know you were still on the phone. He's an acquaintance of Tom and mine. I'll tell you more about it later. After Tom and I are done."

"Okay. Well, good-bye, Tom. It was nice talking to you," she said and there was a click on the line.

"Sorry, I didn't know she was still on the line." Sakich said.

"I didn't either. Anyway, based on Sirhan's statements and his nationality, there's no doubt this was what Eckhaus set up."

"You think there's any risk if this guy in London talks?" Sakich asked.

"We've had no contact with him. The only one he's seen is the mayor."

"And the guy that delivered the money," Sakich said

"The mayor told me that guy has an outstanding murder warrant against him. He's not going to talk."

"What about the mayor?" Sakich asked.

"Don't worry about him. Let's not talk about it on the phone." The line went dead.

\*\*\*

Sunday morning, Beauford Richmond arrived at the ward office from the diner. He let himself in and saw Reichardt's empty desk.

"I'm in the back," a voice shouted.

Beauford walked to the backroom and saw Reichardt standing next to a tall black safe. "Thought I recognized your voice. What happened? Somebody didn't like you using their phone."

"You see the newspaper? They arrested the guy that shot King."

"I heard. Could be a problem we might have to take care of." Reichardt took a Colt .45 semi automatic pistol and a silencer out of the safe. "Right, Beauford?"

Beauford's eyes focused on the pistol. "You do whatever you have to. But, it ain't gonna involve me no more."

"Is that any way to show your appreciation? I got your daughter back for you, a place for your family to live, a good job, and a new name. And all you've done for me is run a couple of errands."

Beauford swallowed, arms at his sides, closing and opening his fist. He mumbled. "Yeah, so you could—"

"Neither you or I knew what was going to happen."

"I can't take this shit anymore. I'm through."

Reichardt screwed the silencer onto the pistol. "Yeah, you're through. Because you're the only link to Ray." He jerked the semi-auto up chest high.

Beauford lunged forward, getting one hand on the pistol pushing it upward. Pfft, a round went into the ceiling. With his other hand he grasped Reichardt's throat.

Reichardt pulled off another silent round into the ceiling. His eyes bulged and he struggled to breathe, collapsing to his knees.

Beauford leaned all his weight into Reichardt and he fell backwards onto the floor. Beauford straddled the man. His victim gasped for air. The pistol dropped from his hand thudding to the floor.

Beauford locked both hands around the man's throat, squeezing tighter.

He felt Reichardt's fingers trying to peal his hands off his throat. Reichardt gasped for air twice. Hoarse sounds. His strength weakening, fingers loosening. Slowly his hands dropped to the floor. His chest motionless.

Beauford took a deep breath, dropped his hands from the man's throat and stood. He looked at the pistol lying nearby and glanced into the safe. There were four stacks of twenties, each an inch high, each wrapped with rubber bands.

He gazed back at the pistol and picked it up. "This one is for you fucking white boys. You taught me how to play your game." He raised the pistol and squeezed the trigger. Pfft.

Reichardt's head bounced off the floor and landed with a thud. Blood oozed from the hole in the middle of his forehead and gray matter splattered across the floor underneath him.

Beauford grabbed the cash and two bank bags from the safe. Slipped the cash into one bag and tucked it under his shirt. In the second bag he dropped the pistol and silencer after wiping them down. He wiped Reichardt's throat with the rag in case he left any fingerprints. Stepping back he checked his clothing; no blood, no rips, everything looked good.

Beauford went to the front door. There was little traffic this early on a Sunday morning. He unlocked the door, stepped out, and let the door close. He took the bag holding the pistol and crashed into the glass portion of the door near the deadbolt lock and stuffed the bag in his belt. *Make it look like somebody broke in and robbed the place.*

Beauford trotted across the street into Marquette Park. It was a quiet cool summer morning. He felt a chill from the sweat evaporating off his shirt. The sun glistened across the still surface of the lagoon. Birds flew overhead. There was no one in sight. He took out the bag containing the pistol and heaved it into the lagoon. It splashed and the ripples slowed until the surface was motionless once again.

*** 

At 9:00 a.m. on Sunday a black Oldsmobile 98 parked next to the no-parking sign in front of the ward office. The chauffer pushed his door open, hustled to the rear door, grabbed the handle, and pulled it open. A shiny black shoe with the laces untied stretched out from the back seat followed a by second shoe.

"Vinnie, can you tie my shoe laces, please? It's getting too hard for this old man to bend over," Alderman Heidler said.

Vinnie squatted onto his haunches and tied the laces.

"Vinnie, your hair's getting a little thin on top."

Vinnie patted the top of his head. "Alderman, it feels like it's all there to me." Then he brushed a few black strands off the shoulder of his blue Banlon shirt and stood. He extended his arms, grabbed the alderman's hands and pulled him out of the car.

The alderman wore his usual black suit and black tie. "I'll just be a few minutes. Going to get some cash from Helmut. You wait in the car. Keep the air conditioner on. It's steamy out here."

Heidler dragged his handkerchief across his forehead and lumbered to the door. His black cane clicked on the sidewalk. He lifted his key chain, selected the key from one of many, and pushed it into the dead bolt lock. Before he could turn the key the door creaked open. His eyes shot to the broken glass behind the burglar bars on the door and the shards of glass on the floor.

He turned toward the car and waved his arm. "Vinnie, get your ass over here."

Vinnie exploded out of the car. "Whatsa matter?"

The alderman lifted his cane gesturing at the door. "The glass is broken and the door isn't locked. Go in there and see if everything's all right."

Vinnie pressed his forefinger to his chest. "Me?"

"Who else am I talking to?"

He took two steps into the office and looked from side to side, the bits of glass chinking under the soles of his black loafers. "Helmut?"

The alderman placed the tip of his cane in middle of Vinnie's back and pushed. "Get in there."

Vinnie looked over his shoulder at the alderman. "What if some nigger's in there with a gun?"

"It's safe, go ahead," Heidler whispered and flicked his hand in the direction of the back of the office.

Vinnie crept to Helmut's desk in the center of the room. "Hello, Helmut, you here?"

The alderman stood in the doorway and waved his hand at him. "Go. Go in the back."

Vinnie took a deep breath, slinked around the desk, and froze. "I see his legs. He's down on the floor." He took a quick step backwards, colliding into the desk, then spun around, and rushed to the alderman.

"Helmut, are you okay?" The alderman shouted.

There was no answer.

He shoved Vinnie toward the back room. "Go check him out. Maybe he's sick."

Vinnie sucked on his lower lip and blundered to the doorway of the back room. "Jesus Christ! Jesus Christ! There's a bullet hole in his head."

The alderman moved as fast as he could, his cane tapping, *clickety-click*, on the wood floor until he stopped behind Vinnie.

His eyes shot to the open safe. "Motherfucking. It's gone. All my money's gone."

Heidler stepped over Helmut's body, placed his hand deep into the safe and dragged his hand from side to side over the shoulder high shelf where his cash was usually stashed. Zoning forms and permits flew into the air, floating onto the floor, landing on Helmut's body and in the blood surrounding it.

"He's shot in the head," Vinnie repeated.

The alderman grabbed Vinnie's shoulder and pushed him down. "Check the lower shelves, see if my cash is in there."

Vinnie landed on his hands and knees. "Aaargh. You pushed me into his blood. It's all over my hands and my pants." He shook his fingers and the blood splattered to the floor.

"Do you see my money? He pushed his cane against Vinnie's back. "Look in there, will ya."

"Nothin' but dust and paper and shit. I don't see any money."

"Damn it! Clean your hands and go upstairs and check Helmut's apartment."

"Why don't we call the cops?"

"Go!"

Vinnie ran up the stairs in the rear of the room and was back down in seconds. "The door to the apartment is locked."

"Wait out front. Don't let anyone in, or tell anybody anything. I gotta call somebody."

Alderman Heidler watched Vinnie run outside, close the door, and stand guard. The alderman tramped to Helmut's desk, laid his cane on top of it, and sat down. He pulled out a black address book from inside his coat pocket and ran his finger down the pages until he found the number he wanted. He dialed the home telephone number of the Commander of the Eighth District of the Chicago Police Department.

"Commander O'Hearn." The voice was brusque.

"Tommie, it's Carl Heidler. I've got a problem."

"I was just on my way to mass. Can't this wait?"

"No. My ward office was broken into, some asshole stole my cash, and my committeeman's dead."

"Cash is always a problem. My condolences. I'll send two of my best over. Two that understand about cash. How much?"

"Twenty grand."

"I'll make it a priority. My men will be there ASAP."

\*\*\*

At 9:20 a.m. two squads, lights flashing, and an unmarked car skidded to a halt at the ward office. Two patrolmen ushered Vinnie into the alderman's car and then strung yellow crime scene tape from a wooden horse west of the entrance, wrapped it around the no parking sign, and tied it to a lamppost on the east side.

The other two patrolmen kicked in the door to Reichardt's apartment but found nothing indicating any intrusion.

Detectives Jacobazzi and O'Donohue stood in front of Reichardt's desk facing a seated Alderman Heidler. Jacobazzi looked more like a mob hit man than a cop. A slender man wearing mirrored aviator sunglasses. His black hair slicked back and down his neck. A black knit shirt clung to his chest, a charcoal gray sport coat hung over his left arm, and a nickel-plated .38 Magnum with a pearl handle was seated in a leather holster on his right hip.

O'Donohue was the alter ego of Jacobazzi. A lumbering giant wearing a five-shot .38 chief's special in a holster clipped inside his pants. He wore a white shirt, blue tie, and navy slacks, all purchased from Sears.

Heidler leaned back in the chair and it squeaked under his weight. He pointed at the detectives. "You guys got to find the fucker who did this. Probably some nigger. We're getting more of them in my ward. It ain't like it use to be. Teach him a lesson that he'll never forget."

Jacobazzi braced his hand on his magnum. "Don't worry alderman. We'll get the word out to our snitches and that boy will be begging for mercy."

"You got anybody you think might have done this?" O'Donohue asked.

"Can't think of anyone that would be so stupid." He shook his head. "I mean anybody that would actually know me and take my money."

O'Donohue pulled out a handkerchief and wiped his brow. "What about somebody that works here. They might know about the money."

"Only two, Reichardt and this black guy. Richards or Richmond. Something like that."

"How long have you known this black guy?" Jacobazzi asked.

"He's only been here a couple of months. From what Reichardt said, a real hard worker. Came up here from Mississippi."

"You have any identifiers on him? We'll do a check on him, see if he's got any priors." Jacobazzi laughed. "The nigger's probably good for this."

"I'm going to have to go through the papers and find his personnel file. Leave your cards and I'll get you the information as soon as I find it."

The detectives dropped their cards on the desk.

***

At 9:30 a.m. Beauford drove past the ward office. He saw two squad cars with red and blue lights flashing, and an unmarked car parked surrounding an Oldsmobile. Yellow crime scene tape was stretched across the front of the building.

He parked a block north of the office and watched as a paddy wagon double-parked next to the squad cars. Two uniformed officers strolled out of the wagon, pulling a gurney with a body bag on it, and entered the office.

Four uniformed officers hovered around the front door. A few minutes later they watched as a body bag containing Helmut Reichardt was dropped into the meat wagon.

*I'm gonna go to the office. Make it look like Reichardt was expecting me. Like I got no idea what happened.* Beauford parked on Richmond, pulled the bank bag with the cash out of his waistband, and stuffed it underneath the driver's seat. Sweat dripped down his neck and he could feel his damp T-shirt clinging to his back.

He got out of the truck, locked the door and walked down Marquette Road nervously flexing his fingers, thinking about how just a few hours ago they squeezed the life out of Reichardt. The thick summer air made it harder to breathe as his lungs quickly expanded and contracted.

Beauford walked up to the police officers. "Is the alderman all right? I see his car..."

"Who're you and what're you doing here?" a husky patrolman with a hooked nose asked.

"I'm supposed to meet Mr. Reichardt here. He had some overtime work for me to do today." Beauford pulled out his city ID card from his jeans. The muscles in the back of his neck tightened and his hand twitched as he gave the cop his ID. Feigning ignorance, he asked, "What happened?"

"Never you mind. You just stick around, the detectives will want to talk to you." The cop jotted down Beauford's name and address in a spiral notebook and gave the ID back.

Beauford took a deep breath and sat on the fender of the squad car. One of the patrolmen tilted his head and wrinkled his face. The message was obvious. Beauford jumped off, wiped the fender with the tail of his T-shirt, and leaned against the lamppost, looking away from the cops.

Jacobazzi marched out of the ward office and O'Donohue ambled behind him. Their suit coats swung over their shoulders and badges hung from their shirt pockets. They approached the patrolmen and exchanged whispers, turning their heads and glancing at Beauford.

The shorter detective turned and swaggered over to Beauford like a man who aspired to be important, the chrome color of his pistol and the pearl grip shining in the sun. His forehead glistened with beads of perspiration and his shirt's underarms dark from sweat as the temperature reached 90. "I'm Detective Jacobazzi. This is Detective O'Donohue," he said, pointing his thumb over his shoulder. "So what da you know about what went on here?"

"Nothin'. Nothin'." He shook his head and stepped away from the lamppost. "Jus' got here. Nobody told me nothin'."

O'Donohue stepped forward. "Who'd you come to see?"

"Mr. Reichardt, I work for him. He told me to come over Sunday morning and he'd have some overtime for me."

O'Donohue crossed his arms. "And what work were you going to do?"

Beauford shifted his weight from one foot to the other, wondering if he made a mistake and should have stayed away from the office. "I never know what I'm gonna do 'til Mr. Reichardt gives me my work orders."

Jacobazzi put one hand on the lamppost and leaned toward Beauford. "You ain't getting any more work orders from Reichardt."

"Whaddya mean?" Beauford furrowed his brow.

"He's no longer an employee of the city. He just left the office in a body bag," Jacobazzi said.

"Mr. Reichardt is dead? I can't believe it. I didn't even know he was sick."

O'Donohue laughed. "Ain't sick, somebody hurt him in the worst way."

"Everybody in Marquette Park liked him. Who would do anything like that? Old ladies used to bring him stuffed cabbage."

"You ever go in the back room?"

Beauford shook his head. "No sir, I never go past Mr. Reichardt's desk. I stand right in front of it, he gives me my work orders, and I go out and do what needs to be done."

"When's the last time you saw Reichardt?" Jacobazzi asked.

"Friday morning. Came into the office, got my jobs and left."

"If you hadn't seen him since Friday how'd you know to come in for work on a Sunday morning?" O'Donohue cocked his head.

Beauford licked his lips. "I ah, he called me Saturday afternoon. Told me to come in this morning."

O'Donohue nodded. "All right, you give your name and address to the patrolman and you can go."

"He already took my name."

"Go home," O'Donohue said.

Beauford exhaled. He had muddled through, what could have been a mistake.

Jacobazzi handed him his business card. "You hear about anything that has to do with this case, you call me. Oh, yeah. One more thing. You know if there was any cash in the safe?"

"In the back room? Told you ain't never been back there. Didn't know there was a safe." Beauford tugged at the collar of his T-shirt. "I'm just a clean up man. Only thing I need is stacked up in the corner. My bucket and mop, broom and shovel, and paintin' stuff."

Jacobazzi grabbed Beauford's T-shirt at the chest and yanked him close. "I got to tell you, right now, I like you for this. So if you did it, tell me now and I can make it easy on you. But if I have to do this the hard way, and I will, you're goin' to regret it, boy."

Beauford turned and saw the alderman walking out of the storefront. He waved at him. "Alderman Heidler."

The Alderman stopped, and leaned on his cane. His forehead wrinkled as he nodded at Beauford. "Everything all right, detective?"

Jacobazzi's fingers sprung open letting go of Beauford's T-shirt. "Just making sure he understands what's in his best interest."

"It's me, Alderman, Beauford Richmond. Yous remember? I painted your garage."

"Oh, yeah." He nodded.

"Just wanted to tell you how sorry I am about Mr. Reichardt being shot."

"Yes, this is a real tragedy...for the community. He did so much for the people in Marquette Park."

Vinnie scurried around, opened the door and Heidler stepped into the back of the Olds. Vinnie rushed back to the driver's seat. One of the squads moved out of the way and the Olds sped off.

Jacobazzi tapped Beauford on the shoulder.

He turned and they were eye to eye.

He took off his sunglasses and squinted at Beauford. "One more thing. How'd you know Reichardt was shot? I didn't tell you."

"Oh, ah, the patrolman told me he was killed. I jus' figured that somebody shot him."

"If I find out you're holding out on me. You'll be sorry. You ever been arrested?"

"No, never."

"I'm gonna check you out. You lying to me, you got any priors, and I'll be coming to slap the cuffs on you."

Beauford chewed on his lower lip. He wondered when the detective checked his name if he would find that there wasn't a Beauford Richmond.

# CHAPTER SIXTEEN

Sunday night, June 9, Special Agents Ericson and Daniels sat at Uriah Beckwith's kitchen table waiting to tape Napier's phone call. "When did you say your family would be back?" Ericson pulled his Salems out, lit one and tossed the pack to Uriah.

He tapped the pack and slid a smoke between his lips. "They ain't coming back 'til Tuesday sometime." He leaned over and Ericson lit his cigarette. Beckwith sat back in his chair and examined the microphone taped to the mouthpiece of his phone. "You sure this will tape the call?"

"Never failed before. How about you, Daniels?"

Daniels stood next to the refrigerator, away from the cigarette smoke filling the kitchen. "Nope, never seen that happen."

Beckwith looked at him, "How long you been an agent?"

"Not too long."

"Here's the plan. When Napier calls, you tell him you can do the burn tomorrow. I'll have four more cars out here, plus me and Daniels. We'll have a tape and a transmitter that you can wear so we can hear what you guys are talking about. When you're on the road, every once in awhile, talk about where you are or say something about a landmark. Like an old red barn or a truck on the side of the road."

"I gotta wear that stuff?"

"It's for your own protection. But you don't have anything to worry about. You've known this guy for a long time. He won't suspect anything and that way we know where you are."

"You gonna lose us?"

"No, it's just a safety precaution. It's 8:00. What time do you think he'll call?" Daniels asked.

"Who knows? Probably late. He gets drunk early and sleeps a good part of the day." Uriah leaned back in his chair, took a drag on his smoke, and pointed at the refrigerator. "You want a beer, Daniels? There's a bunch in there."

"No, thanks."

"How about some sweet tea?" Uriah laughed and paused, staring at the cigarette between his fingers and arched his eyebrows. "You hear that?"

The three men sat silently, listening. The sound of a truck engine grew louder.

"Look out the front window. See whose coming," Daniels said.

Beckwith ran to the front of his house. "Shit, it's Jimmy."

"Come back here," Ericson shouted as he ripped the microphone off the receiver and stabbed it and the tape recorder into his suit coat pocket.

Beckwith tripped, knocking over a lamp in his panic to get to the kitchen. The light bulb shattered, leaving him in the dark. He got up and stumbled into the kitchen. The truck pulled up to the front of the house, the engine became silent, and the truck door slammed. There was a banging on the front door.

Ericson grabbed Beckwith by the shirt collar. "You get rid of him. Tell him you can't do it tonight." He pushed him toward the front door.

Beckwith felt his way through the dark into the living room.

The agents listened.

"Shit man, didn't you pay your electric bill?"

Beckwith saw Napier's silhouette on the opposite side of the screen door. "I was takin' a nap. Thought you were gonna call."

Napier opened the door and stepped inside. "It's such a beautiful night. All the stars out, I thought I'd mix up a few cocktails and go for a ride."

"Cocktails?" Sweat beaded on Beckwith's forehead. He couldn't let Napier walk any further into the house with the agents fifteen feet away in the kitchen. He quick-stepped to Napier, put his hand on his shoulder, turning him around and directing him back to the screen door.

"Yeah, the kind you ain't gonna drink. Molotov cocktails." He laughed and slapped Uriah's shoulder. "Come on, Junior's waitin'. It'll be his first church burnin'."

"You takin' the boy?"

"Yeah, you gotta start 'em young so they learn."

"What church you wanna burn?"

Napier smiled. His small yellow teeth were visible through his smirk. "It don't make no matter. Start early we might find one with some niggers in it. Have ourselves a little Bar B Q."

"I can't tonight. I ah, got something I gotta do."

"This mornin' you were all worked up about honoring James Earl Ray after his arrest. What you gotta do that's more important than that?"

"I ah, ah."

Napier's jaw tightened. "You chicken shit. That's what you are."

"No, I want to honor the man. Jus' that ah, my wife, she's sick and—."

"Jesus Christ, come on Uriah. Put your old lady to bed with a shot of Jack and she'll feel better in the mornin'."

"She real sick."

"Where is she?" Napier took a step into the house. "I'll take care of her. I'll tell her what we're doin'. She'll be proud of you. She'll want you to go."

Beckwith stepped in front of Napier. "No, I can't leave her cause…"

Napier turned around and put his hand on the screen door. "Well, fuck it, then. Me and Junior do it without you."

"Wait a minute. Let me go talk to her and see how she feels." Beckwith turned and took a step toward the kitchen.

"Hurry up. Junior's in the truck waitin' on us. He's lookin' forward to doin' this." Napier shoved the screen door open, it whacked against the wall and slammed shut as he marched toward his truck.

Beckwith ran into the kitchen. "I can't stop him. You heard him—he's goin' with me or without me."

Ericson holstered his colt revolver. "You have any idea where he's going?"

"No."

Daniels pulled down the knot on his tie. "Where's the closest Negro church?"

Beads of sweat dripped down Beckwith's forehead. "How the hell would I know?"

"All right, you go with him. But whatever you do, don't let him bomb any church," Ericson said.

Beckwith spread his palms out. "How the hell do I stop him?"

"You got a gun?" Ericson asked.

Beckwith's brow furrowed. "Yeah."

"Get it."

He yanked open a drawer of the kitchen cabinet and pulled out an old Smith & Wesson five-shot revolver. "You want me to kill him?"

"Do what you have to do," Ericson said. "You better go join him in the truck. Wait any longer, it's not going to look right. One last question. Is his kid old enough to cause any problems?"

"The kid's about eight, maybe nine. I better go." He stuffed the pistol in the waistband of his jeans and pulled his blue denim shirt out, covering it.

***

Beckwith hopped into Napier's truck. Junior sat in the middle. Between Beckwith's legs was a cardboard box loaded with six gin bottles full of gas stuffed with rag wicks.

"You wanna smoke?" Napier asked.

Beckwith's eyes opened wide. "Whatta you crazy?"

"Relax, I was jus kiddin'. I put some tar in with the gas. It'll make the fire stick to whatever it hits." Napier laughed.

"Where we goin?" Beckwith asked, the revolver stuffed under his shirt pinched the flabby skin around his waist.

"Huntin'."

***

"I can't believe that idiot brings along an eight-year old when he's planning on killing people," Daniels said.

"Yeah. Let's go." They ran out the back door and hopped into their car. "We lose him and we're fucked. You'll be the first

Negro agent transferred to North Dakota and when I'm permanently assigned to Mississippi. My wife will divorce me."

Ericson started the Ford, but left the headlights off. They weaved down the dirt road from Beckwith's house to Route 8, heading west, the taillights of Napier's Dodge getting smaller.

"You better speed up. He's getting too far ahead," Daniels said.

"We're the only two vehicles on the road. I get too close and we're burned," Ericson said.

"Not anymore, there's a car coming toward us. It's flashing its lights. You better turn ours on until it passes," Daniels said.

"Fuck, it's a clear night with a full moon. I turn on the headlights and we'll get burned."

"Shit, that car that just went past us is a sheriff's car." Daniels turned in his seat looking back. "Damn, it's turning around and the emergency lights are flashing."

"I'm going to pull to the side and badge him."

"You lose Napier and we're fucked. And God knows what might happen if there's people in the church. I can't sit here risking that a church full of my people are about to be killed."

"You're going to have to." Ericson pulled the Ford onto the gravel shoulder. "The worst-case scenario is we lose him and Beckwith does the right thing."

"Can't trust Beckwith to do that."

"We may not have a choice." Ericson said, as he glanced in the sideview mirror. A lanky deputy sheriff in a crisp uniform moseyed up to Ericson's window.

"Gentlemen, you ought to know better than to be driving at night with your headlights off."

Ericson pulled out his credentials and flashed his badge. "Sorry, deputy. We're on official business trying to get to an appointment in Cleveland tonight that we're already late for. I guess in our rush we didn't notice. Turn them on as soon as we're back on the road."

The deputy leaned on Ericson's door and noticed Daniels. "You a G-man too? Ain't ever seen a darkee G-man and I seen enough of you guys the last few years."

Daniels pulled out his credentials, pointed them at the deputy but kept his eyes down the road.

The man shook his head. "Well, I wouldn't have believed it, if I hadn't seen it myself."

A half-mile down the road the brake lights on Napier's pickup flooded the road as the truck stopped. A flashlight beam from the passenger side illuminated a sign on the side of the road. The brake lights eased, then the taillights went off and the pickup turned up the road, disappearing from sight.

"All right, you boys turn on those headlights and be careful." The deputy waved Ericson and Daniels on and drifted away from the Ford.

Ericson turned the headlights on, stepped on the accelerator and pulled onto the road. He glanced in the rearview mirror and saw the cruiser head in the opposite direction.

Ericson stopped at the turnoff and Daniels read the sign. "Macedonia Baptist Church of God."

"I can see the lights from the church. I'll get out and run up there." Daniels said.

Ericson pulled onto the dirt road and doused his headlights. "Be careful."

"Careful? There could be a whole church full of people." Daniels bolted from the car.

*** 

Napier pulled his truck behind some scrub bushes. He leaned over, opened the glove compartment, grabbed a revolver, and tucked it in his belt. "Junior, you come with me." He grabbed his son's hand. "Uriah, bring the box."

"You sure you wanna bring the boy out there?"

"You bet."

They crept the next hundred yards through thickets of brush and shadows of tall elms. The tension, the damp night air, and the exertion soaked Beckwith's shirt with sweat. He kept several steps behind Napier, looking back for any sign of the FBI. He saw no one.

Napier lurked through the last stand of trees and stood tall and proud thirty feet away from the side of the church. A small collection of beat up old cars and pickup trucks were parked next to the paint-peeled frame building. Light radiated from kerosene lamps through the windows flashing across the hard clay and patches of grass.

Napier turned and waved to Beckwith. "Why you waiting behind? Git up here. Me and Junior will take three bottles for the front door. That oughtta be enough to trap 'em inside. You use the rest on this side with the windows in case any of 'em try to climb out. He took the box from Beckwith. "Well, you gonna take them three outta there or what?"

Beckwith took the three bottles out of the box. Napier held the box against his hip, grabbed Junior's hand, and headed to the front of the church. Beckwith twisted around looking for some sign that Ericson or Daniels was there. There was none. He marched to the side of the church, turned his back toward Napier, and pulled the pistol out.

Napier stood fifteen feet away from the front door, set the box down and lined up the three bottles in front of him. "Watch this, Junior." He picked up the first bottle and held it upside down. The gas soaked the rag wick while the lyrics of Amazing Grace floated from the church. He pulled a lighter out of his shirt pocket and struck the flint wheel. The flame wavered slowly in the light evening breeze.

Beckwith spun around, raised the pistol and jerked the trigger. *Click, click, click.* He flicked his wrist to open the cylinder. *It's empty.*

Napier touched the flame to the wick and it ignited into a blaze. He leaned back to throw the bottle.

"FBI," Daniels shouted. "Drop it, Napier!"

Napier turned into the night looking for the source of the voice. He yanked his pistol out of his waistband and pulled off a volley of shots that whizzed over Daniels' head.

Daniels fired back, hitting Napier in his throwing shoulder. The flaming bottle fell to the ground, crashing on the other bottles. The tar laden gasoline exploded, sticking to Napier like leeches, igniting him into a fireball. He leaped into the air as if trying to lift himself above the flames. Falling hard to the ground he attempted to brush the flames off with his hands. Red, yellow, and orange encased his body making a flaming silhouette in the darkness. He scuffled in the dirt struggling toward the church, trying to complete his mission. Screaming, he fell to the ground three feet from the entrance. The stench of burning flesh rose from his charred body.

Junior lurched toward his father.

Daniels dashed out of the darkness, picking the boy off the ground inches from his father's fiery body. He held Junior in his arms.

Junior twisted and turned. He beat on Daniel's chest, trying to free himself, trying to go to his father.

Beckwith disappeared into the night.

Parishioners ran from the church, aghast at the sight before them.

Tears ran down Junior's face. "You nigger FBI," he screamed. "You killed my daddy!"

\*\*\*

On June 10, 1968, James Earl Ray was arraigned in London's Bow Street Magistrates Court, charged with possession of an illegal firearm and a false passport. He fought extradition and was ordered held in the Wandsworth Prison, the largest prison in South London, built in 1851. The main buildings were like five spokes in a wheel surrounded by tall stone walls.

\*\*\*

Reichardt was buried on June thirteen, a cool Thursday morning. A long procession of cars was headed by a Chicago Police Department squad car with red-and-blue lights flashing. It proceeded from the Zolniak's Funeral Home on Pulaski down to Marquette, east past the tall shady elms of Marquette Park on the south and the ward office on the north, and south on California to 69$^{th}$ Street, stopping in front of the Nativity of the Blessed Virgin Church.

Two yellow brick steeples bordered each side of the church reaching high into the blue sky. The copper-colored casket was rolled from the black Cadillac hearse and the pallbearers carried it through the center set of large black steel double doors and up the aisle to the altar. The pews were filled with all the heavyweights from city and county government. Father Katauskas celebrated a requiem funeral mass and then Reichardt's body was taken to Evergreen Cemetery at 87$^{th}$ and Kedzie for burial. After the casket was lowered into the grave it was business as usual for the power brokers—backslapping, hand shaking, and deal making.

Beauford attended the entire ceremony. As the people left the gravesite, he approached Alderman Heidler. "Sir, it's me, Richmond."

Heidler nodded and took a step past him. "I have to go. I have a meeting with the mayor."

Beauford tapped him on the back. "There's something kind of important. I was hopin' that maybe we could meet in the next couple days. I got something to show you."

Heidler cocked his head and continued walking toward his car. "What is it?"

Beauford stepped in beside him, careful not to walk faster than the old man. "I need to show you. Don't have it here."

"Richmond, I'm really busy." He shook his head. "Especially after what happened. I've got lots of things to do to get everything back in working order."

"This'll only take a few minutes."

"I told you I don't have the time." He turned and took a step away.

Beauford swallowed, stepped forward and grabbed the alderman's sleeve.

The alderman shook his arm knocking Beauford's hand off. "Don't you ever grab me again," and took another step forward.

"I promise you sir that you won't be sorry giving me two minutes of your time."

Heidler stopped in his tracks, exhaled but didn't turn around to face Beauford. "If it's so important tell me now!"

"Can't, it's something I have to show you and give—"

"All right, I've got to stop by the office tomorrow anyway, 8:30 sharp, don't be late." Heidler stepped forward jabbing his cane into the ground, heading toward his car. "I'm only going to be there for ten minutes. I'm not going to wait for you. If you're not there, I'm gone."

Beauford beat Vinnie to the rear door of the Olds and opened it for the alderman. "No, sir. I'll be there right on time, even early. You'll see."

***

That same day in Ruleville, a hot sun was beating on the few mourners of Jimmy Napier. Albert, the Mayor, Uriah, Junior, and a few Kluckers watched as the pine box casket of Jimmy Napier was lowered into the grave next to his wife's.

Agents Ericson and Daniels watched through binoculars from behind a tree line a quarter mile away.

Junior had stood in almost the same place two months earlier and watched his mother buried, but now he was numb to the fact that he was alone in the world. Junior's mind was permanently imprinted with the vision of the flames devouring his father and the black FBI agent that was responsible for the incineration. His lips were pursed and he white knuckled fist tight against his thighs.

Uriah held Junior's hand as they approached the mayor. "You gotta help find a place for the boy to live."

Junior jerked his hand out of Uriah's grip.

LeGrand looked down at Junior; "I don't know what we can do. Jimmy drank the farm away. It's in hock to the bank. And this boy is gonna be as much of a nuisance as his old man was." He thought, *I need to send him some place so we don't havta bother with the last of the Napier men any more. Maybe we can send him to Chicago. They took the nigger.*

***

Junior was deaf to their conversation. The words his father had said at his mother's burial played in his mind, 'If I don't kill that nigger, Beauford Tisdale, and his son before I die, you'll promise to do that for the honor of your mother and sister.' And the picture of his father's smoldering body was a vision he could not erase. *I'll get even. I promise, Daddy.*

***

Beauford arrived at the ward office at 7:30 Friday morning and waited for the alderman. At 8:30 the black Olds 98 pulled up to the curb. Vinnie beat Beauford to the rear door of the car and helped the alderman out. Beauford rushed to the ward office door and opened it for the alderman.

"I didn't know you had a key."

They stepped into the office and Beauford locked the door, stranding Vinnie outside. "Mr. Reichardt trusted me. He knew I'd do whatever he wanted, when he wanted it."

"If you say. What did you want to show me?"

Beauford wanted to be out of Vinnie's sight. "Let's go to Mr. Reichardt's desk." Beauford followed the alderman to the desk, pulled the bank bag out from under his shirt and dumped the contents. Four bundles of cash tumbled across the top of the desk.

Heidler's eyes opened wide and he smiled. He grabbed the bank bag from Beauford, leaned over and scooped the cash back into one of the bundles. "How'd you get this?"

Beauford had rehearsed his story. "I don't want nothin' that don't belong to me. I came here early that day cause Mr. Reichardt told me to, said he had work for me. The door wasn't locked and the glass was broken. I was scared.

"Came in to see if Mr. Reichardt was okay and I heard the back door slam shut. Found him shot and the safe open. Who ever did this must of run out the back door when they heard me come in. They dropped your money when they were hurrying out. I locked the door so they couldn't come back in, picked up the money and got my ass out of there. Didn't know if they might be waiting around to shoot me next. Went to my truck and drove away. Thought I'd come back later to give you the cash. I never was gonna keep the money.

"When I came back the police was here and I didn't want to say anything about the money. Then that one cop says he likes me for shootin' Mr. Reichardt. I got scared. Where I come from, a policeman thinks you did something, you goin' to jail. So I didn't want to hang around and talk to you then. Figured I'd tell you when we were alone."

"You don't know anything about how Reichardt got shot?"

"Nope. First I knew of it was when I saw him."

Heidler lifted the bank bag. "You're a smart man, Beauford. I can always use a man like you." He tossed the bag from one hand to the other. "Let's keep this our secret."

He pulled out five $20's from the bag and handed them to Beauford. "Here's your reward for keeping my cash safe."

"Alderman Heidler, I can do a lot more for you than paintin' your garage and stuff like that."

Heidler raised his eyebrows. "Like what?"

"This ward is changin' fast. More and more of the people living here are Negroes. If you had a black ward committeeman it would really help to get the vote out for you. More of your Negro voters are opening businesses here too. They'd probably like to have one of their own collecting campaign contributions for you. They'd feel closer to you."

"You're a fast learner, Richmond, and you're ambitious. That can be good and that can be bad. You learn when to use your ambition to help me and when to be quiet, you can go far. Just like you did this time. You can be my man here. Let me know what's going on, and I'll take care of you."

Beauford gestured at the bank bag. "You know you can trust me. You name me ward committeeman. I can do a lot for you. Do anything you need done. Handle things like that bag for you."

"Richmond, I like you. We think alike. First, we need to wait a couple of weeks to mourn Reichardt. During that time you fill his shoes around here. If everything works out, you'll be the new committeeman. Go home. I'll be in touch." Heidler watched Beauford leave. The alderman was happy, his largesse had been returned and he was confident he could rely on Beauford in the future.

Heidler pulled a card out of his pocket, picked up the phone, and dialed.

"Homicide, Jacobazzi."

"Detective, it's Alderman Heidler. I want you to call off the dogs."

"What? You want me to stop the investigation?"

"Yeah, a good Samaritan got my money returned to me."

"What about Reichardt? Don't you want his killer caught?"

"If you catch him, fine. But you don't have to beat the bushes."

"I think that nigger Richmond did it."

Heidler cleared his throat. "What makes you say that?"

"I did a background check. See if he had any priors."

"He have any arrests?"

"Just the opposite. It's like he never existed. No Mississippi driver's license, no arrest, no birth records. He must of changed his name. Don't you want to know why?"

"I'm good at sizing up people. That's what I do every day. That boy wouldn't harm anyone. I wouldn't worry about him. I'm sure you have a lot of other cases you can be working on and if I hear anything, I'll let you know. Thanks for everything you've done." Heidler hung up the phone. He thought, *Just maintain the status quo and things will be good. Hell, he may even be better than with Reichardt, the way things are changing.*

# CHAPTER SEVENTEEN

On Friday afternoon, June 21, 1968, Eckhaus entered the Nashville Holiday Inn lobby and saw Tom Sakich seated in the lounge holding a glass filled with ice and an amber liquid. Edward Pape was browsing magazines in the hotel gift shop.

He stopped at the front desk. "I'm Charles Egan. I have a reservation."

The black female clerk paged through a file box. "Yes sir. We have you booked for one night. Will you be staying longer?"

"No." He dropped the cash for the room on the counter.

She counted the bills, handed him the key, and pointed to the left. "Room 214, the elevators are around the corner. Take it to the second floor and exit to the right."

Saying nothing Eckhaus took the key and disappeared around the corner. There were two men in suits waiting for the elevator. One carried a briefcase and the other a two-suiter. He waited for them to board, waved them on, and then took the stairway. He paused on the landing for the second floor, listening for the elevator ping or conversations indicating that there might be someone who might see him.

He heard nothing and opened the door a crack. No one was in the hallway. He stepped out, charged to the room, and let himself in.

Eckhaus draped his blue suit coat over the chair at the table near the window. He rolled up the sleeves of his white shirt to his elbows, sat down and looked out at the roiling black and gray clouds. Pape and Sakich wouldn't come up to the room until he called the concierge and left a message.

He pulled a pack of Camels out of his shirt pocket and tapped it twice against his hand until a cigarette popped out. Brought the pack to his mouth and slid one between his lips. He flicked his lighter and watched the tip glow red as he inhaled. He took a deep drag, let the smoke settle in his lungs, and blew a ring into the air. He laid the smoke in a glass ashtray on the table, reached into his suit coat pocket, pulled out latex gloves and began his search of all the usual places for bugs.

Ten minutes later he plopped down in the same chair, grabbed the remnant of his cigarette and crushed the butt in the ashtray. There was a lot on the FBI agent's mind. From the day of James Earl Ray's arrest in London, June 8, 1968, and to his upcoming extradition hearing scheduled for June 27, a mounting tension grew among Sakich, Pape, and Eckhaus as if they knew their house of cards was about to fall.

Eckhaus knew their strengths and weakness. Sakich wanted to charge on. Every day that he visualized his daughter, Chrissie, the injustices he had suffered burned into him, and he sought the revenge that had caused him a deepening depression, sleep deprivation, and the attempt to bury his anguish with liquor. He was their source for the cash that they needed to fund their mission, but he was also a weak link.

Pape had withdrawn into his position, Attorney General for Mississippi. He spent most of his waking hours at the capital, burying his mind in his work, not returning Eckhaus' calls for days at a time. Anything to maintain a state of denial rather than face the fear that Ray's arrest could lead to their downfall and destroy the legacy that was his father's dream.

Eckhaus was the professional without any personal loss to burden his emotions. He had to take over and review all the contingencies. How could he make sure they would not be detected? What loose ends had to be removed and then what would be their next step?

He laughed at the thought that his own FBI had unwittingly removed one loose end with the shooting death of Jimmy Napier—one of the few witnesses who could link them to James

Earl Ray through Mayor LeGrand. This left two people that had contact with Ray—Beauford Tisdale Richmond and Mayor LeGrand.

He analyzed the liabilities presented by them versus the risk of eliminating them. Richmond's only other contacts had been with Reichardt, who had been killed in an apparent robbery. Tisdale was living under the Richmond alias to avoid a murder warrant in Mississippi. It was unlikely he would become a problem, and why would he want to disclose his own involvement in the assassinations of King and Kennedy? Besides, Ray didn't know who the black guy was who delivered the cash to him and his identity was unknown to the people in Los Angeles.

Eckhaus grabbed the phone, called the concierge and asked him to page Mr. Wilson and tell him the meeting was set. He pulled off the gloves, slipped them back in his coat pocket and sat at the table. In ten minutes Pape came into the room with a *Newsweek* magazine twisted in his hand and sat across from Eckhaus. Five minutes later Sakich came, his cheeks flushed, his hand embracing a glass only half-filled.

Eckhaus looked at Sakich. If it weren't for the man's cash he would have gotten rid of him early on. Sakich's nose was lined with thin red veins. His hands were trembling. The ice in his drink clinked against the glass. "How many drinks did you have on the plane?"

"Who's countin'?" He laughed, sat on the bed, leaned against the headboard, and crossed his legs. "This is pretty cushy. Mind if I get a hooker up here after we're done?"

"Let's get serious. At some point in time Ray will be extradited. We've got to figure out where we go from there?"

The magazine coiled tighter in Pape's hands. "What do you think?"

"When Ray is returned to Memphis, we need to get someone in to talk to him. Find out where his head is at."

Sakich crossed one leg over the other. "Like how?"

"Knowing what I know, the political pressure, and the evidence there's no chance in hell he'd ever be acquitted. The rifle he bought was found at the entrance to a store down the street from the boarding house and it has his prints on it. The witnesses at the boarding house identified photos of him. There are many questions. Is he going to be a standup guy? Will he plead guilty if he knows he'll get a life sentence instead of the electric chair? And the bottom line is he going to talk to save his ass?"

"What's the problem? He gets in the local hoosegow, we pay a big black buck convict fifty bucks to filet him with a shiv." Sakich slid his hand forward as if slicing it into someone's gut. "Who would suspect anything? Somebody's goin' to do it anyway."

Eckhaus shook his head. "After Lee Harvey Oswald, security is going to be really tight. Ray will be locked up in solitary confinement and any visitor will be talking to him through bullet-proof glass."

Pape slapped the magazine in the palm of his hand. "So how do we get someone in to see him and who is it going to be? Obviously, it can't be one of us." He chewed on his lower lip, braced his elbows on his knees, gazing at the floor.

"It's got to be someone he knows and someone we can trust," Eckhaus said.

Silence filled the room.

Eckhaus slipped another Camel between his lips, stroked his lighter and lit the smoke. The sizzle of the burning paper broke the quiet.

Pape looked up, glanced at Sakich and then turned to Eckhaus. "There's only one person that meets that criteria, Mayor LeGrand. He's the one that got us Ray through Jimmy Napier. I'm sure you know Napier was killed by one of your agents while he was attempting to firebomb a church."

"We always get our man," Eckhaus smirked.

"Then why can't you get Ray?" Sakich said.

Eckhaus felt Sakich's eyes drilling into him. "Don't be an ass. With Napier gone we've got one potential witness against us removed and that also insulates the mayor to some extent. The only one that knows about the mayor besides us is Ray." He tapped his fingers on the table. "Edward, you contact the mayor. Press him hard if you have to. Tell him to tell Ray that we can guarantee life instead of the chair. Whet his appetite. Tell Ray if he escapes we'll get him new identification, plastic surgery, and enough money so he can disappear. Tell him what he wants to hear."

Sakich shook his head. "What if the mayor tells us to go fuck ourselves?"

Pape's knuckles grew whiter as his grip on the magazine tightened. "I don't think he will—"

"Come on, the mayor would have to be a fool to front himself." Sakich drained his drink. "He'll know some Fed will be on him the second he's done talkin' to Ray. Mr. FBI over there says we should always have a plan B," Sakich said smirking.

Eckhaus crushed his cigarette in the ashtray. "For once you're making sense. I can arrange to be the one that debriefs the mayor after he leaves the prison. There's no way the prosecutors will let anyone visit Ray without an appointment. I'll be getting copies of all visitors' request and logs as part of our investigation. I'll know when he's going. There won't have to be any communication between us."

Sakich chewed on the ice from his drink. "And what if Ray says, 'fuck no, I ain't seeing the mayor,' or even worse, 'the mayor is the asshole that got me involved in this?'"

Rain started tapping the window. The drumming became louder and louder.

Eckhaus felt their eyes fix on him. He leaned back in his chair. "If that's the case, our only alternative then is to get rid of anyone who had contact with James Earl Ray. With Napier gone that leaves only two, the mayor and that black guy." Eckhaus crushed his smoke in the ashtray.

Pape nodded. Beads of perspiration rolled down the back of his neck. "I'm reluctant to send anyone in to see Ray. There's a high risk involved in getting that close."

"There's a risk involved in not letting Ray think that someone on the outside won't let his ass fry in the electric chair. That he can get a life sentence if he pleads guilty. And if by some chance he escapes there will be money waiting for him and a life somewhere." Eckhaus laughed. "Even if that's all bullshit."

Pape chewed on his lower lip. "What if the mayor doesn't want to do it?"

"He will. I'm sure he'll understand the significance of what I just told you. Hell, he can even help Ray make up some kind of cover story," Eckhaus said.

Sakich kicked his legs over the side of the bed. "He can do the JFK conspiracy thing. You know the mob or the CIA was behind it. There's always some university professor that will take a story like that and run with it."

Pape nodded. "I'll talk to him about it." He stood, slid the magazine under his arm, and buttoned his suit coat. "Is that it for today?"

"We've got to get this covered before we move on," Eckhaus said.

"All right, I'll be on my way then," Pape said.

"Me too." Sakich grabbed his glass and took it with him.

\*\*\*

On July 19 Ray waived extradition. Shortly after midnight he was handed over to American authorities at London's Wandsworth prison and flown nonstop in an Air Force jet to Millington Naval Air Force Station where he landed at 3:48 a.m.

Federal authorities turned Ray over to Sheriff William N. Morris at the airfield. Ray was fitted with a bulletproof vest and transported in an armored van escorted by a dozen police cars and motorcycles for the twenty-mile trip from the airbase to the Shelby County Jail in Memphis.

When Ray's convoy reached the back of the jail, sheriff's deputies armed with shotguns were guarding the entrance. The other sides of the building were ringed by deputy sheriffs and highway patrolmen armed with automatic weapons. A county bus blocked the entrance prohibiting a view of Ray. He entered the jail at 4:29 a.m.

His prison cell was a 30-foot-by-10-foot, sixteen-bunk tank that was cleared and made into a personal dormitory for him. The windows were covered with steel plates making it impossible for him to be killed by sniper fire. Inside the tank a private cell was made for him. Because the windows were covered, the tank was air conditioned and he had his own bathroom. Police officers rotated around the clock on shifts making sure he didn't escape and wasn't harmed. A telephone was at the policemen's desk in case of emergency. Cameras kept Ray under twenty-four hour surveillance and the feed went to two monitors.

A bomb dump about six feet square made of sand bags was in Ray's tank in case an explosive device was smuggled in. The telephone company was ordered to seal underground tunnels that carried phone cables to the jail.

On July 22, 1968, Ray pled not guilty to the first-degree murder charge of killing Martin Luther King.

\*\*\*

A few days later, Edward Pape drove a gray four-door Chevrolet, owned by the state, from Jackson thirty miles north to the Sharkey Delta National Forest, a halfway point between Jackson and Ruleville. He took a dirt road along the bayou. The water moved so slowly it almost stood still. Golden strips of sunlight pierced through the willows and gum trees and the moss hung from the cypress into the water. A light wind ruffled their branches.

He took the road to a place where he used to fish with his father. It was easy to find but far enough out of the way for solitude.

Pape stepped out of the car, went to the trunk, and pulled out his fishing gear. He slipped into waders, took his rod, reel, and creel and waded through reeds, hyacinths, and a layer of algae that floated in the shallows until he was knee deep in the water. On his third cast he heard the rumble of an engine getting louder. A white Lincoln Town Car pulled up behind his car and Mayor LeGrand jumped out.

"So this is that secret waterhole you been bragging about all these years."

Pape lowered his sunglasses from the brim of his baseball cap to cover his eyes. He waved at Mayor LeGrand. "Get your gear and drop your line in. I guarantee that by the time we're leaving you'll have more green trout than you can eat in a week."

The mayor popped his trunk and put on his gear. He opened a tin of Red Man and slipped some loose strands between his cheek and gum. He put on his fishing hat covering his bald spot, walked through the ankle-high grass, and waded into the water, stopping about twenty feet downstream of Pape.

The smell of decaying wood, dead vegetation, and algae saturated the heavy air.

He put on a lure, cast his line out, and listened to it splash in the water. "Edward, this is the best idea you've had in ages. We need to get away from all that shit in Memphis."

"Would you believe the last time I was out here was with my daddy? I wasn't even in law school yet. That's how long it's been. Hard to believe. Time doesn't wait on us, Mayor."

The mayor reeled in his line and cast it out again. "Couldn't believe that son of bitch pled not guilty."

"His attorneys are just trying to get more money and notoriety from his case by stretching it out. Trying to keep their names in the headlines and on TV."

"I wasn't surprised when you asked me to go talk to that old boy. But, I was happy when you agreed with me that it could be dangerous."

"Ray ever says anything about you. You do like I told you—deny, deny, deny. There's nobody that can put you two together," Pape said.

"Hey, I think I see something feeding by those hyacinths. See those bubbles over there?" The Mayor pointed twenty yards downstream.

"There's no sense in fronting one of us when we've been so careful." Pape's line went taut and the tip of his rod jerked into the water. "I got one."

"You let him spit that hook you owe me five bucks." LeGrand laughed.

"Then you owe me five. Cause he's all mine. Easiest money I made in a long time." As he reeled in the fish it jumped two feet into the air. "Look at that boy. So pretty and shiny." He shifted his rod under his arm, grabbed the fish, pulled out the hook, and dropped him into his creel. "Now, I hope you followed my instructions and didn't tell anybody you were coming here. This is the best spot in the state."

LeGrand reeled in his empty line again. "Didn't tell a soul where I was going or what I was doin'."

"Good. You want to try the lure I caught this guy with? I've got an extra. It worked for this old boy." He waded toward the mayor, the water rippling around his legs, as LeGrand cast out his line again.

"Sure, give me one of those." LeGrand was reeling in his line when he got a hit. "He's taking my line out. This will make your catch look like bait."

Pape stood behind LeGrand listening to the whirl of the line coming off the mayor's reel. Beads of sweat broke on his forehead. He looked around. No one was in sight. He shifted his rod into his left hand, reached into his waders with his right, and pulled out a blackjack, eight inches of braided black leather with a loop at one end and a lead ball at the other.

He slipped his hand through the loop and raised his arm over his head. With all his strength he crashed the lead weight into the back of the mayor's head. The man's legs quivered. The rod fell from his hands. He crashed face down into the water. A cloud of silt surrounded his body and came to the surface.

Pape raised his leg and buried one foot into the middle of the mayor's back holding him under water. LeGrand's hat floated to the surface. Pape could see the welt on the mayor's bald spot. There was no laceration. It would look like he stepped on a slippery rock, fell and hit his head.

A few bubbles escaped from the mayor's mouth and came to the surface. His hair flowed with the current, drifting back and forth. A few minutes later Pape lifted his foot. The body slowly rotated around. The mayor faced him. His body began a slow trip downstream.

"Sorry Mayor. You were a good old boy." The words seized in his throat. "It was just too risky."

***

Eckhaus felt comfortable to meet, ready to start once more. Whatever stories Ray might tell would stop at the dead bodies of two men, Napier and the mayor, and a third, the black guy, whose identity Ray didn't know and now lived under an assumed name. The trance Sirhan's Arab associates had put under had worked. He had no recollection of murdering Bobby Kennedy. They were in the clear. It was time for Eckhaus to call another meeting.

This meeting was on a Friday afternoon in mid-August at the Ramada Inn in Nashville. The room and airplane reservations were booked under aliases. Sakich and Eckhaus sat at a round table near the window and Pape sat on the opposite side of a dresser close to the door.

"I wanted to meet so we could maintain our momentum," Eckhaus said, more relaxed than at their previous meeting. "We lost some of our personnel but I'm sure that they can be adequately replaced. From a positive perspective, losing the people we did eliminates our exposure. I think the first thing on our agenda, before we pick our next target, is to find replacements for those losses. We need to explore any possible candidates for new personnel."

Sakich nodded. "It won't be a problem. The Nazis and the Klan. They're fired up. We can have our pick of hundreds."

Eckhaus shook his head. "It's not that simple. We've got to make sure that these people are competent. People we can trust. Because they will be the layer of security that will insulate us." He looked at Pape. "Don't you have anything to say?"

Pape had his arms folded across his chest. He stood, then leaned against the dresser. "Yes, I have something to say. I received a call from the Chairman of the Republican National Committee a few days ago. To make a long story short, the Republican candidate for Governor of Mississippi has recently been diagnosed with cancer and will have to withdraw from the race. With the election just three months away they need someone to run who has name recognition. They said that they would support my candidacy. In the memory of my son and to fulfill my father's dream, I've accepted." Pape laughed. "The irony is, they said with the advances Mississippi has made in civil rights, and if I have two successful terms, there might be a place for me on the national ticket eight years down the road."

Eckhaus leaned back in his chair. His brow furrowed over his eyes. "I don't like trying to read between the lines. Exactly what're you telling us?"

"What I'm telling you is that I can't be involved in this anymore, it represents too great a risk against fulfilling the legacy my father sought for our family."

Sakich jumped out of his chair and charged Pape, grabbing his lapels, shaking him. "You motherfucker! This was all your idea and now you're backing out for your family's glory. To make a name in the history books. You son of a bitch. What about my girl? She might as well be dead. She lies there day and night, her life wasting away."

Pape grabbed Sakich's hands and jerked them off his coat. "I'm sorry, Tom. This never crossed my mind." He shook his head. "After I got the call I thought about this for a long time. I know I can't do both. Doing this is a way for me to achieve the goals my father had for my son and our family. I have to do this for Michael."

Sakich turned to face Eckhaus. His fist tightened at his side, knuckles white and he screamed, "You can't let him."

Eckhaus leaned forward. "Edward, they killed your son and now you're just going to walk away. You did this to avenge your son's murder. I would think that you would want to stay with us. Especially the way Michael was butchered."

"This is something I have to do. It's an opportunity that will never come again. It would be impossible for me to focus on both. One gets in the way of the other and I could never forgive myself if I didn't pursue this chance to fill the shoes that my father saw Michael walking in."

Eckhaus cleared his throat. "You realize there are certain risks you assume, when you become involved in something like this? I told you in the beginning that I will not be compromised."

Pape ran his hand through his hair and stared into Eckhaus' eyes. "You won't be compromised. The only people that know about your involvement are in this room."

Eckhaus shrugged. "That's two more than I feel comfortable with."

Pape nodded. "I still support what you're doing. I just can't risk being a part of it. You trusted us from the beginning. Why should that change?"

"Because when you break the chain it weakens." Eckhaus pointed at Sakich. "Look at him, he can't go a day without a drink."

Sakich shook his head. "You asshole, you don't have to worry about me. He's the son of bitch that taped you."

Eckhaus' eyes shot from Sakich to Pape.

Pape shook his head. "He's been washing antidepressants down with scotch. He's so drugged up he doesn't know what he's talking about."

"Bullshit, he told me he was going to tape you for insurance. Did it when you came down for Michael's funeral. Played it back to me later that night." Sakich crossed his arms over his chest. "Heard all about that nigger that was lynched for killing your old lady."

Eckhaus' face turned crimson. "That right?"

Sakich's tongue curled around his lips. "Yeah."

"I need to talk to Edward about this, Tom. Why don't you head home?"

"Think I will." He ran his sleeve across his mouth, turned and quickstepped toward the door. He stopped and glared at Pape. "You son of a bitch. How could you do this? It was the only reason I had to live and you've ripped it from me for your own glory. And I bit on all your bullshit."

Eckhaus rose from his chair. "Tom, leave."

Sakich's hand trembled as he grabbed the doorknob, twisted it, and opened the door.

Pape's eyes followed Sakich, he glanced at Eckhaus and then bolted for the door.

Eckhaus rushed Pape as Sakich slipped into the hallway.

Pape's right hand caught the edge of the door as Eckhaus' forearm cracked Pape in the back of his neck. His head crashed against the door and his hand was smashed between the door and the frame.

"Ah shit, you broke my hand," Pape screamed.

Eckhaus twisted Pape's left arm behind his back and spun him away from the door. He kicked it closed and ran Pape onto the bed, stomach down. He jabbed his right knee into the middle of Pape's back, reached down and pulled a five-shot .38 out of an ankle holster.

"What're you going to do, kill me?" Pape said.

Eckhaus gritted his teeth. "That's crossed my mind."

Pape's voice was muffled in the bed. "You can't believe that drunk. I promise you there's no tape." He twisted from side to side and Eckhaus put all his weight into Pape's back.

"You're a lying motherfucker." He pressed the pistol's barrel against Pape's temple.

Pape turned his head sideways and gasped for air. "I swear over Michael's grave there's no tape."

"How'd Sakich know about my mother?"

"I told him what you said the night of Michael's funeral. There's no tape!"

Eckhaus pulled the pistol's hammer back. "You hear that click. You know you don't have much longer when you hear that."

"You got to believe me. Listen to me. Please listen, even if I had a tape what good would it do me. It would only implicate me as well as anyone else. I'd be fucking myself."

Eckhaus pressed the barrel tighter against Pape's temple, denting the skin. "At this stage of the game I have to ask myself if I'm better off with you or with out you."

"You'll be killing me for nothing. Because there isn't a tape. You kill me then you've got to cover it up."

"This isn't going to look like a murder." Eckhaus grabbed a pillow, placed over it over Pape's head and buried the barrel of the pistol in it. He leaned down near the top of the pillow, close to

SINS OF THE FATHER | 205

Pape's ear. "This is my drop gun. I put one bullet into your head. It'll look like a suicide. Goodbye, Mr. Governor."

"Wait, wait, the tape is in the safe in my study."

"You fucking asshole. I ought to kill you for lying."

"I'm sorry. I lied because I didn't know what to say. It was a knee-jerk reaction."

Eckhaus threw the pillow to the floor. "And you're not lying now?"

"No, I promise you."

"How many copies are there?"

"I never made a copy. I figured the more tapes there were the greater the chance of the wrong hands getting it. I only needed one for insurance against you setting me up. I didn't know then if I could trust you. That was the only reason. In case you were setting me up."

"Fine, Mr. Governor to be. You can have your fucking family legacy. But first we're going for an airplane ride. That tape is mine." Eckhaus pressed the trigger and eased the hammer down.

Three hours later they landed in Jackson and took a rental car to Pape's antebellum home. It was a silent ride that was looking like a train wreck to Pape. He unlocked the door and stepped into the two-story foyer. "Hello, Honey. Are you home?"

There was no answer and that worried Pape.

"Let's get on with it," Eckhaus said.

"It's in the safe behind my desk in the study." He slide open the panel doors and stepped into the room heading toward his desk.

Eckhaus followed, locking the doors behind him.

"It's built into the cabinet behind my desk, floor level."

"This is what I want you to do. Open the cabinet door, then the safe and step back from the safe. Do you understand? Do not reach into that damn safe. If you do the next thing you hear will be a round going off."

Pape walked behind his desk, knelt down and opened the cabinet door. The next thing he heard was the sound of steel coming out of leather. He looked over his shoulder and saw Eckhaus holding a snub nose .38. "Take it easy, James. I'm not going to do anything stupid. I hope you don't."

"Do what I tell you and you'll be just fine."

Pape spun the dial to the right, then left and right again. He grabbed the handle, pushed down, it clicked and he pulled the door open.

"Back away, do it now."

Pape backed away and stood.

"Sit down in one of the chairs in front of your desk."

Pape followed his instructions. Eckhaus went behind the desk and knelt down. He peered into the safe. "What do we have here? A civil war era pistol. A nice Colt semi auto."

He pulled them out of the safe and laid them on the carpet. He opened the cylinder on the revolver and then pulled the magazine out of the semi auto. "Both loaded, must have crossed your mind to grab one of these. Good thing you follow instructions."

He glanced in again. "Looks like you've got some cash in here. A little mad money. Why would the gov have a stash of cash? I'd advise you not to answer that question on the grounds it might incriminate you." Eckhaus laughed.

"Where's the tape?"

"It's on the shelf in a manila envelope."

"I see it." He reached in, pulled out the envelope, sat in Pape's chair and faced him. Eckhaus tore open the envelope and shook it over the desk. A cassette tape bounced on the desk. He glanced at the tape and lowered the snub nose onto his lap—grips in his right hand and cylinder in his left.

"You've got what you wanted."

Eckhaus flicked the cylinder open, held the pistol up, and looked at the primers of five shells. "I guess its decision time." He flicked it closed.

There was a knock on the door. "Honey, are you busy?"

Pape looked over his shoulder. "I've got a surprise. Guess who was in town and stopped by to visit?"

The doors jarred as she tried to open them. "Unlock the doors so I see who's with you."

"One second, Honey." Pape smiled, rose from the chair, walked back to the doors, unlocked them and slid them open.

"Well, I'll be, Jim Eckhaus. What a nice surprise." She bounced into the room wearing a light blue jacket and matching skirt and saw Eckhaus rising from her husband's chair. She met him in front of the desk, gave him a hug and a kiss on the cheek. "What brings you into town?"

"I had some work down here on a case. Finished up early and I thought I'd surprise Ed with a visit."

"Can you stay a few days?"

"Unfortunately, I've got to catch a plane." He scooped up the tape and held it between his thumb and forefinger. "Got some important evidence I've got to take back to Chicago right away." He shook Pape's hand. "I'll be talking to you." He returned the kiss Pape's wife had given him. "Good seeing you both."

\*\*\*

Sakich flew back to Chicago and was home by 7:45 that evening. He telephoned the call-girl service where he had become a regular client and arranged to have a hooker dropped off.

"We have a new girl we think you'd like. A young one."

"Good, bring her right away. Too much shit in my life. I need something good to happen. Give you an extra hundred if she's here in an hour." He cradled the phone and mumbled. "Don't want to be alone."

Sakich sat in the living room filled with long shadows from the low sun filtering through the curtains. A bottle of Chivas Regal in one hand and a glass full of ice in the other. He filled the glass, sipped the scotch, and repeated this ritual again and again. The sun sank and Sakich sat in total darkness. Thoughts of many years ago ran through his mind, of his wife, and their new baby. In his mind's eye he saw them walking in the neighborhood. His perfect family, their new baby in one arm, and his beautiful wife holding his hand. Chrissie's baptism. Her first communion in her little white dress...

There was a light tapping on the door.

"The door's open," He said.

A shadowy figure stepped into the dark house and closed the door.

He heard the sound of a raincoat falling to the floor. Sakich spread his legs and pulled down his zipper. "Come here, baby." He heard the sound of light footsteps on the carpet, felt her forearms on his thighs, her fingers on him like she was praying and her lips enfolded him. "Oh yeah. You're good. I gotta turn the light on and watch you."

He set the bottle and glass on the end table, reached for the lamp, and turned it on. "Oh, my God. Get away. Get off." He jumped up and fastened his pants. He reached into his pocket, pulled out $300 and held it out. "Take this and leave, please leave."

"I'm sorry, did I do something wrong?" The slender blonde stood there in black lace bra and panties, and thigh-highs. "I don't want to get in trouble. I need the money bad. I can't afford to get fired."

Sakich fell back into his chair and started crying. Guilt that he survived and that his wife was dead and daughter incapacitated seeped to the surface. "You look like Chrissie. My little girl…" He gasped for air. "My poor daughter."

She knelt in front of him. "I'm sorry."

"She's as good as dead."

She leaned back on her haunches. "Do you want me to finish?"

"No!" He leaned forward, his elbows resting on his thighs, hands holding his head. "Take the money and go. Just get out of here. I've got things that I have to do."

She clutched the $300. "Thanks, mister. I'm sorry about your daughter." She slipped on her raincoat and left.

Sakich picked up the glass. He looked at the scotch, swallowed most of it, and threw the glass against the wall. "It's going to be all over tonight." He stood up, walked into the bedroom, and pulled open his dresser drawer. Fumbling through his underwear he pulled out a box, set it on the dresser, and opened the top. Sakich lifted out a Smith & Wesson 9 mm. Grabbed a handful of shells and loaded 14 rounds into the extended magazine and slammed it into the pistol. He slipped it in his waistband and put on a charcoal gray sport coat to cover the weapon.

Sakich left the house and drove his Cadillac to the near north side. He would show Pape. He wasn't stopping. He would conduct his own war and he would fight to the end. It was almost 9:00 p.m. when he parked the car in the circular drive in front of the sanitarium.

There was only a skeleton crew working on a late Friday night. The security guard at the door greeted him. "Hello, Mr. Sakich, ah, visiting hours ended at eight."

Sakich swallowed. "You don't mind if I visit my daughter tonight? I have to see her." He handed him a $100 bill.

"Ain't gonna hurt nothin', I guess. Have a good night, Mr. Sakich."

He headed to her room and carefully opened the door as if there was some chance he might wake her. He stepped into the room, closed the door behind him, and stood there watching her. "My little angel, you look so peaceful," he whispered as a tear rolled down his cheek. He walked to her bedside and gently stroked her golden hair.

"It was nice of you to visit me tonight. You certainly surprised your daddy. You naughty girl. You know Daddy's not always going to be around to protect you."

His hand stroked her cheek. "Your skin is so soft. Daddy's going to be leaving in a little while. He's got to chase down those bad people that hurt you and made Mommy so upset. Goodbye, honey."

He slipped the pillow out from under Chrissie's head, placed it over her face, and held it down with all his strength. He closed his eyes and struggled with the thought of killing his own child, wondering if this death was painful for her and vowed to feel as much pain as he had caused.

When he finished he lifted the pillow and watched her motionless chest. He leaned over and kissed her forehead. He fluffed the pillow, carefully lifted her head, and slid it underneath. He pulled the cover up, tucked her in, and the words choked out of him. "I couldn't watch you suffer anymore. I love you."

He walked down the empty hallway, heels clicking on the shiny floor. The guard opened the door for him. "Good night, Mr. Sakich. Nice of you to visit your daughter this time of night. I'm sure it means a lot to her."

Sakich nodded his head and went to his car. He rolled down all the windows and drove up Rush Street. The sidewalks were swarming with sweaty people on a warm summer night. Laughter and rowdy conversations floated through the air. Neon signs from the restaurants, bars, and strip joints flashing in reds, blues, and greens. Hawkers luring the men that passed. "No cover. Only a three-drink minimum. See the beautiful naked ladies."

He turned west on Division and saw and heard more of the same. With each block the colorful neon signs diminished, the street became darker, and the level of sound became quieter. Then he came into the presence of the tall concrete bunkers that were Cabrini Greens.

Sakich turned north on Larabee. Three old black men sat on milk crates passing around a bottle wrapped in a brown paper bag. He cruised the street at fifteen miles an hour.

A young black boy wearing a tight T-shirt stood on the curb. Behind him two young black girls twirled a jump rope and two more double dutched and sang out as they skipped rope, *"I was standing on the corner doing no harm."*

The boy tapped the side of his nose with his forefinger. He had cocaine to sell.

Sakich pulled to the curb and put the car in park.

*"And along came a policeman and took me by the arm."*

The boy leaned inside the passenger-door window resting his elbows on the door. "Got some good toot. Dime bags. Six bags for fifty. Get six bags man, the bitches will be crawling all over you."

*"He took me around the corner and rang a little bell."*

Sakich took a deep breath and leaned toward the boy. He reached under his sport coat, grasped the semi auto with his right hand and grabbed the boy's T-shirt with his other hand yanking him into the car. The boy hovered on the car door. Sakich pressed the 9-mm against the boy's forehead.

His eyes bulged out. "Mister, what you want? You can have all I got, money and dope." The boy's hands flailed about.

*"Along came a police car and took me to my cell."*

Sakich squeezed the trigger, the hammer drifted back, his hand trembling.

The boy closed his eyes. His face grimaced.

The blast reverberated in the car. The boy's head bounced against the ceiling of the car and his body hung on the door. Blood and gray matter splattered the interior.

The girls dropped their rope, screamed and ran.

Sakich's ears throbbed with pain. He let go of the boy, gripped the steering wheel, and stepped on the accelerator. The boy's body hung on the door as the car swerved and smashed into a street sign. Sakich cracked his head on the steering wheel. The capillaries in his forehead burst and blood flowed onto his face.

Hysterical people raced from the gunshot. Others ran to the accident. A man in a postal uniform opened the car door to help Sakich.

Sakich wiped his sleeve across his face. His eyes widened. He slammed the semi auto across the man's face and then jerked three rounds into his chest.

Sakich shifted into reverse and hit the gas. The engine died. He wobbled out of the Cadillac over the man's body, toward the high-rise housing projects pointing the pistol and shooting blindly, *bang, bang, bang*. Blood ran down his face.

Screaming tenants ran into the buildings or away from the mad man.

Sirens shrieked in the background, getting louder with each passing second.

Three squads came to a screeching halt surrounding his car. Their lights whirled and splashed red and white across the asphalt and on the faces of bystanders that were rushing from the projects toward the street.

Paramedics leaned over the boy and the postal worker. "They're gone."

The patrolmen left their cars, chasing the sounds of the gunshots.

Sakich saw two young girls and a teenage boy running toward a building. He fired at them, *bang, bang*. They opened the door and it crashed shut behind them.

He charged after them, rushing through the door and heard their footfalls going up the steel stairs. He rushed to the stairwell, pointing the pistol up at the shadows reflected on the walls by the cage enclosed light bulb, jerking the trigger three more times. The report stung his ears.

A door crashed shut two floors above. He raced up the stairs. His head pounding, heart racing. He turned, looked up at landing ahead of him. There was a burly man with a revolver pointed down at him. Five yards separated them.

Shots rang out. The muzzle flashes from both guns lit the narrow stairway. Bullets whizzed past each other's head and ricocheted off cement-block walls. Sakich kept jerking the trigger, *bang, bang, click, click*.

He felt a burning sensation in his chest. Colors turned to dark and gray shadows. The pain felt good, like it was pain he was stealing away from Chrissie. He grasped the hand rail. Fell to his knees, then onto his stomach. A pool of blood built a moat around his body. He gasped for a last breath of air.

# PART TWO

## CHAPTER EIGHTEEN

### February 1979

The death of Chicago's Mayor, Richard J. Daley, in 1976 stunned the city. The democratic machine rushed to appoint a replacement so business could go on as normal. Michael Bilandic was hand-picked by the powers-that-be as the new mayor. Unfortunately for Bilandic, those powers were not as mighty as Mother Nature. Six weeks before the mayoral democratic primary in 1979 twenty inches of snow fell during a thirty-hour period and this was on top of a ten-inch base of snow that had been compacted into ice. The streets were blocked by cars, trucks, and buses that had been vacated and buried under the snow and the "L" was frozen.

Jane Byrne was running a fierce campaign against Bilandic. The city was in gridlock and the voters were irate over its inability to remove snow from the streets. The Democratic machine was feeling the pressure. They had to deliver big time to show they still controlled city politics. The aldermen could use the strength of one-sided victories as clout over a mayoral candidate whose allegiance to the old Democratic organization was in question. It was two weeks before the election and precinct captains were feeling the heat. City workers were being pushed to get out the vote for the aldermen.

Carl Heidler had his people going door-to-door every night urging his constituents to get out and vote for him on February 27. No matter how cold it was, or how much it snowed, no one stayed in the ward office. Beauford Richmond, the ward committeeman for the last ten years, covered the impoverished east side of the ward, the black side, tromping through snow, knocking on the doors of would-be voters.

He promised to meet whatever needs were voiced. Get the snow off the street so I can park...Pick up the garbage that had been in the alleys for weeks...Get my kid a job with the city...Have my boy's drug case dropped...And how much will you give me?

***

On election day, Richmond, bundled in a large black parka, stood outside the polling place long before the sun emerged over Lake Michigan. At 5:00 a.m. the temperature was in the high teens and the wind was out of the north. There still remained twelve inches of snow on the ground and where the sidewalks had been cleared three-foot drifts were piled on the parkways.

At 9:00 a.m., it started to drizzle and continued for most of the day. Richmond was able to get a green plastic garbage bag from one of Heidler's constituents, ripping holes for his head and arms.

He cut slits in the sides of the garbage bag so each hand could be buried deep into the pockets of his parka, enabling him to wrap his fingers around the booty that waited for Heidler's constituents.

As voters approached the polling place Beauford strolled toward the door, palmed them $5, and said, "Alderman Heidler thanks you for voting." During the 1975 election the southsiders cost him $2 a vote, but the snow raised the price of everything.

By 3:00 p.m., the rain stopped and he was able to lose the garbage bag. At 7:00 p.m., the polling places closed and his pockets had been emptied of three thousand dollars, but the vote had been brought in. Jane Byrne won the democratic mayoral primary, but the machine had been successful. Alderman Heidler had defeated some unknown opponent by a landslide. Most of the other alderman had similar results. Beauford went to his home away from home.

He arrived at the high rise apartment of his mistress at 47$^{th}$ and Martin Luther King Drive. He had met Sheila Ubegu, a Nigerian with black satin skin, at a Democratic fundraiser. She had that ability to raise funds for whatever purpose she needed. He was able to get her on the city "welfare" roles. A no-show job buried deep in the city budget.

Sheila greeted Beauford at the door holding a bottle of champagne and wearing a red flimsy negligee.

"Honey, you gonna havta warm me up before I feel like sip'in some cold champagne."

"You come in and take your clothes off, Beau. I'll get you a hot bath and we can sip the bubbly together in the tub."

Richmond watched her long legs and the silhouette of her body through the red silk as she strolled out of the living room. He dropped his parka onto the white carpet and kicked off his soaked shoes. He laid his pager on a glass end table, stepped out of his wool slacks, and was left standing in his long underwear and a black sweater. He smiled and rubbed his palms together.

***

William Richmond, Beauford's son, was in his last semester at the University of Illinois Circle Campus in Chicago. He had struggled in the early years of school, making the difficult transition from the one-room shanty schoolhouse in Ruleville to the prison-like fortresses of Chicago inner-city schools. Metal detectors and security guards were at the entrances and bars on the windows. Nathleen had helped as much as she could and had obtained tutors from local community organizations to help William and Marlee. They had persevered and the long uphill climb had been successful with William about to graduate with honors in the prelaw curriculum. Marlee was doing just as well at Maria High School, an all-girl school, just east of Marquette Park.

William left the library late that night and arrived at his home on the east side of the fifteenth ward. Alderman Heidler had helped Beauford Richmond purchase the massive bungalow on the corner of Paulina and 71$^{st}$ Street with a loan that had very friendly terms from an owner of a trucking company that had several million dollars in city contracts. William parked his 1968 Chevy Nova on the driveway that had been plowed by city workers and walked down the cleared sidewalk to the front of the house. As he approached the corner, the porch light flashed on and he saw the silhouettes of two men in trench coats walking down the stairs. He nodded at the men as he crossed their path and climbed the stairs two at a time entering the house.

"Who were those guys?" he asked his mother as he hung his navy-blue down-filled coat in the closet and walked into the living room.

"Two FBI men," she said.

William eyes opened wide with anticipation. "Were they here about my application?"

"No, they weren't. But, you got a letter in the mail from the FBI today." She pulled the envelope out of her apron and handed it to her son.

He clutched it and looked up to the heavens, "Please God. Let it be. Let it be." He tore the envelope open and quickly unfolded the letter. "I don't believe it!" He shook both fists towards the sky. "Yes! Yes! They want me at the academy June 4th." He danced, spinning in a circle.

"I'm so proud of you." Nathleen said and hugged her son.

"Mom, what did those agents want?"

She stepped back and tilted her head, "They wanted to talk to your father about Alderman Heidler."

"Interesting, a lot of aldermen have bit the dust. I wouldn't want to be in his shoes."

"Right now I'm more concerned about you. What happens after you finish at the academy?"

"Let me read it to you. 'The class will be completed September 21st. At graduation the students are advised of their field office assignments. You will be expected to report to your respective field offices on October 1, 1979. During the time period after graduation and before reporting to your assigned office you will be expected to report to the office closest to your residence.'"

Her shoulders drooped and her eyes looked to the floor, "You mean you might not come back to Chicago?"

William stepped forward and put his arms around his mother. "Mom, they said there's a good chance I'll be assigned here because this is one of the largest offices. But, they can't guarantee it."

She took a step back and exhaled. "William, I'm sure you know that...." Nathleen's eyes looked down at her slippers and then struggled back up to her son. "Your father and I haven't been close for a long time…I'm filing for a divorce."

William paused and reluctantly nodded. "I know. Whatever happened to him? He changed after we moved up north. He just hasn't been here for us."

"I know this will be very hard on Marlee and…it would help us if you were here. I know how much this job means to you. Just please try to do everything you can to be assigned to Chicago. We need you here with us."

He looked at the letter hanging from his fingertips. "Have you told Dad yet?"

"No. I was planning on telling him tonight. But, I'm not sure if he's coming home. I didn't want to tell him before the election. He was tied up every day. But now that it's over…."

William looked into her face. "Do you want me to be here when you tell him?"

Her eyes welled with tears. "Sometimes he gets so angry. I…I don't know what he might do."

"Let me know when you're going to tell him and I'll be here."

"Thank you." She stepped up to him and placed her arms around his shoulders. "You're a good son. You're growing up to be such a good man. I'm very proud of you."

"Mom, I don't want to take sides. If this is something that you have to do, I'll be here to help you through it." He curled his lower lip.

"I wish I knew how long this would take. This divorce thing. Then you could ask the FBI if you could start after it's all over."

"Oh." William nodded and his eyes shifted down. If Heidler is dirty, my father has to have something to do with it. The more time the FBI has, the more likely they'll find out. Then they'll never hire me.

\*\*\*

The pager chattered as it vibrated on the table in Sheila's apartment. "Shit. What could Heidler want now?" He picked up the pager and glanced at the display. It was Nathleen.

Beauford heard the water gushing into the bathtub. He turned and picked up the phone off the end table. "With this goddamn weather something probably happened to the house."

The red negligee fell over his face. Sheila's hands slipped under his sweater and caressed his nipples. He turned and looked at her standing naked. "Not now, the old lady paged me."

He watched Sheila swivel, storm into the bathroom, and slam the door. He called his wife.

"Hello."

"What do you want? Its election night and I still got stuff I gotta do for the alderman. Probably be sleepin' in the office tonight."

"Where're you now?"

"In the office."

"You must have just missed him."

"Who you talkin' about?"

"I've got his card here. Let me read it to you, Federal Bureau of Investigation Special Agent Clarence Daniels. He said he stopped by the office but you weren't there so he came to the house. He wants to talk to you about an investigation of Alderman Heidler."

"Shit. What kind of investigation?"

"Don't know. Don't care. But, I sure enjoyed telling you. You think he might want to look into your...affairs?" The line went dead.

"Sheila! Sheila!" He slipped on his slacks, barreled to the bathroom door and opened it. "I got to talk to the alderman. I might not be back tonight."

She was leaning over the sink putting mascara on her eye lashes. She swayed her hips and pointed her naked ass in his direction. "You gonna miss this. But, I'm glad you're going." She waved her hand at him. "Go," she said pouting.

"Listen, if the FBI come around you tell 'em you go to work everyday." He paused, "Na, don't tell 'em nothing. You page me right away and we'll get you an attorney."

"I just might answer whatever they ask me." She swiveled her hips from side to side in beat with her message.

Richmond made a quick step into the bathroom knocking his hip into Sheila's.

She spun and slipped backwards into the bathtub. The soapy water cascaded onto the floor. Her head dipped below the bubbles and her legs hanging over the side of the tub. She pushed herself up until her head was above the water, mascara ran down her face. She shook her head and gasped for air.

Beauford pointed his finger at her. "I said you don't tell 'em nothing! You understand?"

Her eyes widened and she nodded.

"I got to go. This is serious. I'll call you later." He glanced at his watch; it was after 9:00.

\*\*\*

Ten years ago Junior Napier had been placed in a foster family in Cicero, a suburb west of Chicago. Since that time he ran away from three foster homes, was arrested for theft at age ten, and assault at age thirteen. Last year, after his sixteenth birthday, he dropped out of high school. He found work clerking behind bulletproof glass at a gas station in a dingy industrial area near the Cicero/Chicago border at Central Avenue and Roosevelt Road. With his pay, he was able to find a one-bedroom furnished attic apartment in a bungalow not far from the gas station. He shared the flat with his girlfriend, Patty Ignolfo, and his best friend, Bruno Marchalski. Junior and Patty slept in the bedroom and Bruno on the couch.

Bruno was twenty, a massive oaf, with long brown shaggy hair hanging over his ears. He had worked with Patty on the third shift in a stamping factory a few blocks away, until he was laid off a couple months ago. He had salivated over Patty, watching her ass every time she bent over to pick up a piece of sheet metal and put it in a stamping machine. It was tearing him apart that Junior was making it with her. He would have been happy to settle for a hand job.

Patty ran away from her stepfather's home after years of emotional and physical abuse. Even though Junior was two years younger than she, she recognized in him an anger that would protect her from anyone's advances.

Junior, his hair cut down to short bristles, ran up the back stairs to the apartment and opened the door. Bruno was seated at the yellow Formica kitchen table, gripping a bottle of Bud.

Junior tossed his black leather jacket on the kitchen table. His jeans had a hole at the knee and the shoelaces in his boots were broken and spliced together. "Hey man, I got outta work at 6:00 so we could go to the Nazi meeting tonight in the city." He grabbed the beer bottle out of Bruno's hand, and took a swig.

"Getch your own," Bruno grabbed the long neck bottle and twisted it out of Junior's hand.

"Lighten up. Patty here?"

Bruno kicked his feet onto the table and it wobbled as he pointed his thumb over his shoulder. "She's in bed sleeping. Can't take that factory job. Too tough on her."

"Gonna see if she's up. We've got an hour before we have to go." Junior smiled, rubbed his cold hands together. "Get me some before we go." He quietly pushed the bedroom door open.

Bruno raised his middle finger, "Jagoff."

Junior closed the bedroom door behind him, crept through the dark room, and sat on the edge of the sagging mattress. He pulled back her blanket and slid his hand down her bare-sleek back.

"Is it that late already?" She sighed.

"No. Came home early so me and Bruno can go to the Nazi meeting down in Marquette Park."

Patty leaned over on her left forearm, twisted her torso toward him, and turned on the small lamp next to the bed. The dim light from the top of the lampshade threw a circle of light on the Nazi flag on the wall above the bed. The light from the bottom of the lampshade spilled onto her raven hair, over her breasts, and down her backside.

Junior leaned forward and gently slid his hand across her nipple, down her back to her rear. "I like this little swastika you got tattooed on your ass."

She smiled, "I did it for you. It's the baby to that big one over your tit."

Junior pulled his green sweatshirt over his head baring a swastika that covered his right breast and another tattoo over his left breast that read Blood & Honor & Klan. He raised his hand and rubbed his left breast. "I got this one for my daddy to make sure I'll never forget him."

"He would be so proud of you. I want to go to the meeting with you."

"Sure, but I thought we might have some fun before it's time to go."

Patty grabbed his belt and released the buckle. "We can do both."

Junior slid open the nightstand drawer and picked up two green pills laying in a piece of tinfoil. "How about a little speed?"

She nodded.

He slipped one in his mouth, grabbed a can of beer sitting on the nightstand, bought it to his lips and chugged down the pill.

Patty stuck her tongue out and wagged it.

He placed the green pill on it and handed her the beer. She washed it down, put the beer on the nightstand and yanked his pants down. "Hurry, get under the cover."

Thirty minutes later Junior walked out of the bedroom. The glare from the light fixture over the kitchen table hurt his eyes that were dilated from the drugs. He jabbed for the light switch dousing the light.

Patty followed, dressed in Nazi black, a turtleneck sweater, leather hip-length jacket, tight jeans, and storm-trooper boots.

"Why she comin'?" Bruno asked. Listening to the moans coming from the bedroom had stiffened his sex. He took in a long glance and then turned his head away.

"Hey, she ain't freeloading like you. So shut the fuck up 'til you get a job. Here's your keys." He tossed them to Bruno. "Go warm up the car. We'll be down in a couple of minutes."

Bruno hung his head, pulled his stocking cap over his bushy hair, threw on his Navy pea coat, and thudded down the stairs.

Patty pursed her lips, "Why do you let him stay?"

"He's a brother. My daddy told me that this world is all fucked up. But when you find brothers that are willing to fight the enemies of the white race you need to stick by them."

\*\*\*

On the third try, the engine of Bruno's 1959 Chevrolet Impala groaned, and oily smoke belched from the exhaust. Patty climbed into the front seat and Junior sat against the door. She opened his jacket and climbed under his arm to stay as far away as possible from Bruno and because the heater in the car didn't work.

They headed east on a barren Eisenhower Expressway. The sky was overcast and a mist hung in the air from the hours of rain that day. The windshield wipers skidded across the glass sporadically. They exited south on California Avenue and traveled through adjoining ghetto neighborhoods.

South of the expressway was a black ghetto that was splattered with fancy cars, dilapidated buildings, and drug houses. Between Polk and Arthington, two young black hoods stood near the curb in front of a three-story frame building. The front stairs sagged, and the windows were boarded, but its cracked sidewalks and barren parkway were cleared of snow so business would not be interrupted. The boys tapped their noses signaling they had dime bags to sell.

Bruno slowed the car as they approached the boys on the curb.

Junior rolled down the window. "You fuckin' niggers all should be shot. You the enemies of the white race."

Bruno stepped on the accelerator. "Are you fuckin' crazy! Tryin' to get us killed!" The car sputtered and the engine died.

One of the street pushers raised his hand, and pointed his finger at Junior. "Hey, you fuckin' skinhead get that shit bucket outta here."

Junior pulled a Colt Chief's Special .38 caliber snub-nose revolver out of his coat pocket and pointed it at the pusher. "Who you talkin' to, nigga?"

The pushers turned and ran down the side of the building.

Patty pulled his hand down. "Put that away. What if some cop sees you?"

"Don't sweat it."

Bruno slammed the gearshift into neutral and twisted the key. The starter whined.

A man, a head taller than the pushers, came out of the shadows of the building. He reached into his jacket, pulled out a nickel-plated .38, extended his arm, his hand palm down.

A blast came from the man's pistol and a yellow flash jumped from its muzzle. The rear-passenger window of the Chevy exploded. Shards of glass flew into the backseat.

Junior felt a rush. Everything moved in slow motion. He dove over Patty.

The Chevy's engine backfired.

The man heard the backfire, dove to the ground, and squeezed off another round. It ricocheted off the pavement bouncing under the Chevy's chassis.

The engine rumbled. Bruno jammed the gearshift into drive and punched the gas. The car skidded on its bald tires and fishtailed down the street. Junior and Patty were thrown back against their seat. Shots rang out from behind them.

Bruno jerked the steering wheel one way and then the other as he straightened the path of the car. They came to a stop at the red light two blocks down at Roosevelt Road.

Bruno stared straight ahead, teeth biting into his lower lip. His fingers wrapped tightly around the steering wheel.

Junior looked at Patty and they started laughing.

"What the fuck are you laughing at? Coulda got us killed." Bruno shook his head.

"Niggers can't shoot straight. See the way they hold their pistols. Some white guy probably taught 'em to shoot like that," Junior said and they all laughed.

Bruno took his hand off the wheel, folded three fingers, extended his forefinger, and lifted his thumb. "Where'd you get that?"

"Took it from the gas station. Belongs to the owner, old man Kazurek. I'll put it back tomorrow. He won't even know it was gone."

They headed south on California. It was quiet in the car. Junior's mind flashed back to a hot summer night in Mississippi more than ten years ago. *The black FBI agent pointing a pistol at his father. The explosion of the shots paining his ears. The muzzle flash. His old man's body igniting into flames. The stench of his father's burning flesh filling his nostrils.* He lowered his head, closed his eyes, and his gut tightened.

Between Roosevelt Road and Nineteenth Street on the west side was Douglas Park. It created a border between the black and the Hispanic ghettos. South of the park, black wrought-iron fences surrounded houses and cars were low riders. The area populated with taco stands, bodegas and Catholic churches.

"This would be a good place for some target practice. Get me a few wetbacks. They all illegals anyway," Junior said.

Patty put her hand on Junior's. "Let's keep your pistol in your pants." She giggled.

Bruno's eyes shifted up.

At 26th Street, an ancient four-story building with pillars in the front housed the Cook County Municipal Court. Because of the ever-growing case load a tall glass building had been constructed just south of the original courthouse a few years ago. Although they contrasted in architecture the justice rendered in either building was the same Cook County style. Slow, overworked, and corrupt. Behind those buildings, surrounded by 20-foot walls topped with razor wire and towers with armed guards, was the Cook County Municipal Jail.

"Good place to put all those niggers and wetbacks," Bruno said.

"Yeah, but it's full of them already," Junior noted.

They crossed over the sanitary canal and under the Stevenson Expressway into a white neighborhood and headed to Marquette Park. The tension in the car eased. They approached 71st Street and turned east. "Bruno, drop us off. We'll get seats while you park."

Bruno grunted and a few blocks down pulled to the side of the street in front of a converted storefront. The windows and door painted black. Junior and Patty left the car. A cloth sign was draped above the door that read Rockwell Hall.

"Who's Rockwell?" she asked.

"George Lincoln Rockwell. He was the leader of the American Nazi party."

They stood in the alcove behind several men waiting in line to get in. On each side of the door was a tall man with a buzz cut in a storm trooper uniform, a brown jacket with epaulets.

"He talking tonight?"

Junior paid one of the Nazis $2 for their tickets. "No." He shook his head. "He's dead. Frank Collin is speaking tonight. He's the local leader of the party. Let's go find some seats." He grabbed her hand and they entered the old storefront. To the left was a large coffee urn sitting on a card table. A line of men waited for coffee. Others stood holding onto paper cups, steam rising from the hot beverage and cigarettes hanging from their lips. The smell of stale coffee and cigarettes permeated the air. Junior and Patty walked halfway down the aisle and sat down in wooden folding chairs.

"Leave the seat on the aisle for Bruno. You can sit next to him and I'll sit by you," she said smiling.

"He likes you. Don't know why you don't like him."

She stuck out her tongue. "He's stupid and I don't like the way he looks at me, staring at my ass and my tits."

"I stare at 'em to." He raised his eyebrows.

She grabbed his hand, moved it onto her thigh, and slid it up and down. "I like it when you look at me."

There was a thud as Bruno fell into his chair.

Junior watched Patty glance at Bruno. A frown covered her face and then she folded her arms and looked straight ahead.

Others were straggling in, talking and fidgeting as they sat down, chairs rattling and cigarette smoke floating in the air.

A man in full Nazi regalia stepped to the podium. He was slender, mid thirties, dark hair and soft brown eyes. He wore a brown shirt with a dark tie. A black belt crossed from his right shoulder to his left hip. A swastika was on a band high on his left arm.

Behind him was a picture of Adolph Hitler, and on each side of it Nazi flags hung from the faded green wall, by gold braid. The flags were red with a black swastika in the center. Above the flags were signs with the initials NSPA-National Socialist Party of America. Sixty people sat in the chairs and forty more lined the walls.

The speaker looked down at the podium, then raised his head and gazed out over the crowd. The room became quiet.

"That's Frank Collin," Junior leaned over and whispered to Patty.

Collin's lips narrowed and right hand shot out over the crowd. "Sieg heil!" he shouted.

German marching music blasted from the speakers. The crowd stood. The chairs skidded back and their boots rumbled on the wood floor as they returned Collin's salute, "heil!"

Then in unison Collin and the crowd shot their hands out again and again and shouted. "Heil! Heil! Heil!"

Collin griped the podium. His eyes narrowed and his lips pressed together as he surveyed his followers that awaited his words. "Greetings white brother and sisters. Please be seated. We are gathered here to continue the fight for the survival of the Aryan race and social justice for the white working class."

The crowd jumped to its feet and cheered.

Collin raised his fists and shook them. "We are the revolutionaries. We must recognize that little progress has been made." Spit flew from his mouth as he shook his head. "We must be willing to sacrifice for our cause."

The crowd stomped their boots on the floor. Patty covered her ears.

He banged his fist on the podium. "This is a struggle for the very existence of our white nation of people and the war against the inferior races and faggots. You are the storm troopers of the American Nazi Party and a White American Republic."

Collin raised his arm. "Heil!"

Junior jumped to his feet. "Heil! Heil!"

Patty, Bruno and the others followed. "Heil! Heil!"

Sweat spun from Collin's forehead as he jerked his head from one side to the other. "You are the final saviors of a world gone mad." He raised his fists and shook it. "America for the Americans."

The music blasted. Men raised their fist and shouted, "America for the Americans."

Collin raised his hands palms open. The crowd quieted. He leaned forward and said just loudly enough to be heard. "You may have to take a gun in your hand so we can win this war of racial purification." And he stepped down from the podium.

The men and women applauded and shouted, "Hitler, Collin, Hitler, Collin."

By 9:15 Junior, Patty, and Bruno were leaving Rockwell Hall. Junior marched down the seventy-first street waving the pistol overhead, yelling, "heil!"

Patty and Bruno goose-stepped behind him and joined in, "Heil! Heil!" Their arms reaching for the moon.

They got in the car and Bruno made a U-turn on 71$^{st}$ Street, back to California and headed north. Patty cranked up the radio and *My Sharona* blasted from the speakers. The defroster blew only cold air and windows fogged as Junior and Patty shouted and sang along. Bruno tried to wipe the moisture off the inside of the windshield with his glove as he drove but it was a useless task and the windshield fogged as fast as he cleared it.

A car flew through the red light heading west on Marquette Road crossing in front of them. Bruno slammed on the brakes but the Chevy cracked into the other car's rear fender. The bumpers locked and the cars spun in a circle, crashing into a lamppost.

The driver of the other car cracked his head against the steering wheel. He sat there dazed, leaning over the wheel.

"Ah fuck," Bruno shouted.

Junior, Patty, and Bruno got out of the car and looked at the crumpled fender, red shards of taillight scattered on the street, and their bumper trapped under the bumper of the car they hit.

"A shiny new black Cadillac. You sure know how to pick 'em." Junior said.

"It ain't my fault. He went through a red light and with all your screaming and yellin' the damn windshield fogged up. I couldn't see nothin'."

"We better see if he's all right," Patty said.

"You mean if we stay or bolt," Junior corrected.

They walked over to the Cadillac and Junior opened the door. "Wouldn't you know, it's some nigger driving a new Cadillac." Junior pulled the .38 out of his pocket and stuck the barrel near the ear of the unconscious driver. "Gonna start this war for racial purification." He pulled the hammer back with his thumb. "Sieg heil, nigga."

Red and blue lights flashed across Junior's face from the other side of the Cadillac as a CPD squad car pulled up. He released the hammer and stashed the pistol in his coat pocket.

A black policeman got out of the squad and walked over to the threesome. "What happened here?"

Junior stood in front of the cop. His hands buried in the pockets of his leather coat. A finger wrapped around the trigger of the pistol while he contemplated the possibilities. "This guy blew the red light. Crossed right in front of us. My buddy tried to stop but we caught the backass of the Caddy." His breath clouded in the cold air.

The driver in the Cadillac moaned, shook his head and leaned back.

The cop walked around to the Cadillac's driver's door. "You okay, sir?"

The driver patted his forehead with his fingers and looked at his hand for any blood. "Yeah, just a bump."

"Do you want me to call an ambulance?" The cop asked.

"No, can we make this short? It's election night officer, I'm Beauford Richmond, the ward committeeman here and I'm supposed to be meetin' Alderman Heidler."

"Mr. Richmond, can I have your license and I'll get the other driver's and fill out the accident report." The cop headed back to the Chevy, got an ID front each person and pointed at Junior and Bruno. "You guys see if you can separate the cars."

Junior and Bruno stood on the front bumper of the Chevy, bouncing up and down and Patty dropped the transmission into reverse, backing the car away from the Cadillac.

He listed their names on the report, gave a copy to Bruno, and crunched over the icy pavement to Richmond. "Here's a copy of the report. Mr. Richmond, being you work for the alderman and such, I'm not going to issue you a ticket."

"Thanks officer. I can go then?"

"Yeah, go ahead. Have a good night."

Beauford glimpsed at the report, stuffed it behind the visor, shifted into gear, turned the steering wheel and stopped. He shook his head, stepped on the accelerator and then moved his foot back to the brake. He pulled the report down and unfolded it. Looking at the section listing the passengers he saw the name, James Napier, Junior. He twisted in his seat and his eyes locked on the boy leaning against the fender of the Chevy, slender with a skin head. He pushed the button lowering his window and waved at the cop, "Officer, officer."

The cop held up his hand to Junior and Bruno. "Hold on a second."

He walked over to Richmond and he glanced at the cop's nametag. "Sanders, can you ask that kid Napier where he's from."

Sanders pointed to the accident report. "It says right there. He lives in Cicero."

"No, I mean where's he from originally? Where he was born?"

"Sure, Mr. Richmond." Sanders walked back to the Chevy and returned in a few seconds. "He said Mississippi. Ruleville, Mississippi and proud of it. Can you believe that little punk?"

"Yeah. That's unreal." *He looks like Napier. Can't be?* He chewed on his lower lip.

"You want me to let them go or should I give 'em a ticket on principle?"

"I got all I need. Let 'em go." He shook his head. *Wonder what happened to his old man? Wonder if he's up here too?* "Wait, Sanders. You're right, on principle you give him a fucking ticket. Maybe that'll keep those skinheads outta my ward." *Wonder what happened to Celeste?*

Sanders leaned into the open window of Richmond's Cadillac. "Why don't you head on to your meeting. If you're here it might rattle them up when I give him the ticket." Beauford drove away as the cop headed over to Bruno's side of the car. Junior was on his haunches examining the crumpled fender on the driver's side of the Chevy.

The cop ripped the ticket out of his book, "Marchalski, I've got to hold on to your license. In the meantime you can drive on this ticket."

Junior jumped up. "What! What're you giving him a ticket for?" He pointed down the street at the departing Cadillac. "That nigga drove through the red light. Bruno didn't do nothing wrong."

Sanders shook his head. "You're wrong. I was down the street. I saw the Chevy go through the red light..."

Junior bounded toward Sanders bouncing against the cop's chest. Sanders shoved him. Junior flew backwards, slipped on the icy street, and tumbled to the pavement. The revolver flew out of his pocket, spinning across Marquette Road.

Sanders pulled out his .38 Magnum. "Don't move or I'll shoot."

Junior froze, lying on his back on the pavement, flashing red and blue lights ricocheting across his face.

Sanders spun towards the car. Pointed his pistol at Bruno. "All right. Everybody out of the car. Hands up. Get on the ground. Face down."

Patty and Bruno lay down on the black ice while Sanders picked up Junior's revolver and called for backup.

# CHAPTER NINETEEN

Beauford Richmond left the scene of the accident and drove to Alderman Heidler's house on St.Louis south of 74$^{th}$ Street in the west side of the ward. As he approached the street, he thought, *the Feds are probably watching the alderman's house. I better not park in front.* He parked east of St. Louis and ran through a snow-filled backyard to the alley behind Heidler's house. He looked up and down the alley. It was still and quiet. The haze from the lamppost accented the tire ruts in the snow. He crept across the alley, opened the chain-link gate and sneaked to the back door of Heidler's bungalow. It was nearly 10:00 when he knocked on the door.

Heidler opened the door wearing a red flannel bathrobe and holding a drink. A cigar hung from his mouth. "I know why you're here. Good idea coming through the back. Assholes are probably watching my house. They've been everywhere tonight. Come in." He closed the door behind Beauford and they walked through the kitchen down a hallway past the dining room and into the living room. The house was filled with dark mahogany antique furniture. He put a finger across his lips and gestured to Beauford to unzip his coat.

Beauford eyes narrowed and he took in a deep breath. The room smelled musty, like an old man. He pulled the zipper down.

Heidler stepped toward him reaching inside Beauford's coat, running his free hand across his chest and then around to his back searching for a tape recorder. "Sorry Beau, but I can't take a chance. I don't know who might have been offered a deal by those fucking FBI agents."

"Awh, boss you know I wouldn't do you like that. Came here to tell you they were at my house tonight. But, I wasn't home. Wanted to see me about you."

"Sit down." Heidler pointed to the sofa and he collapsed into one of two winged-backed arm chairs facing the sofa. They were upholstered in tufted-green velvet, the arms shiny. His shoulders rounded and head tilted down.

Beauford crossed the Oriental rug, took off his parka, laid it over the arm of the sofa, and sat down.

Heidler shook his head. "There must be a whole bunch of 'em out tonight. Most of the precinct captains been contacted. They been calling me all night. I'm too old and too tired to be going through this." He rotated the burning tip of his cigar in an ashtray on a table between the chairs. Saliva dripped from the splayed end as he dropped the stogie into the ashtray. He sighed, "I'll be seventy in a couple of months. Can't understand why they're wasting their time on me. The Feds been throwing aldermen in jail for years and now they're finally going after my ass. I get five or six years in the penitentiary and it'll be a life sentence. I don't want to die in jail." He lifted the glass to his lips, took a long swallow of scotch, and grabbed the cigar.

"Don't worry, Alderman. They won't get nothing on you."

Heidler drew on the cigar, its tip reddened and he blew a cloud of smoke toward the ceiling. "Thanks for the words of encouragement, but we both know there's a good chance they're going to take me down. After forty years there's just too much shit to hide." He took another swig of the scotch, emptying the glass. "You've been around for a long time, Beau. You know how we do business, been my right hand man since you saved that twenty grand for me. Get yourself a scotch and pour another for me." Heidler held out his empty glass.

"Sure, boss." Beauford stood, took the alderman's glass.

Heidler folded his hands on his protruding belly, the cigar pointing toward the ceiling, and rested his head on the back of the chair.

Beauford went to the ornate bar against the wall behind the high-back chairs. It was dark cherry wood, its top black granite. He looked at a Waterford decanter with an embedded silver label marked 'scotch' and a bottle of twenty-five year old Chivas Regal with a red bow tied around its neck. He reached for the decanter, and shifted his hand toward the Chivas. *A nice gift from an appreciative constituent*, he thought. The cap was loose, he gave it a quarter turn, placed it on the bar and poured two fingers of scotch into each glass and stepped to the side of the alderman's chair handing him the glass. Heidler took a strong pull of the scotch as Beauford sat on the sofa.

Beauford brought the glass to his lips.

Heidler coughed, then started choking and gagging. His glass tumbled to the carpet, the remnants of the amber liquid spilling in his lap, and his cigar rolled down his robe, red ashes sparking into the air.

"Alderman, you okay?"

Heidler brought his hands to his throat. His head bounced back and forth against the chair.

Beauford dropped his glass to the floor and jumped to Heidler's side. The alderman's breath smelled like bitter almonds.

Heidler's eyes bugged out.

Beauford grabbed the alderman's hands. "What can I do to help you?"

Heidler yanked Beauford's hands away, jerked at his robe and pulled at his undershirt gasping for air. His tongue jerked out from between his lips. The alderman groaned, his body became limp and his head fell forward, chin to chest, drool running from the corner of his mouth.

Beads of perspiration dripped down Beauford's forehead. He dragged his hand across his mouth and then felt for a pulse in the alderman's neck. "Nothing." He stumbled back muttering, "I better get my ass outta here." *What if the Feds are watching? They been all over the city asking questions about him, they see me come to his house, and then he's dead. I'm fucked.*

He grabbed his coat. "Gotta wipe my prints offa everything before I leave. Now think man, think. What did I touch?" He pulled out his handkerchief, picked up the glasses, wiped them and the bottle of Chivas. "Go out the way I came in case they're watching the front door. I guess you beat'em, Alderman. They ain't gonna put you away now."

Beauford slipped on his coat, charged toward the kitchen door when he smelled something burning. He sped back to the living room and saw the Oriental rug smoldering. He picked up the cigar and stomped on the rug, extinguishing the crimson embers, and crushed the cigar in the ashtray. "I better take this with me." He dropped the cigar into his coat pocket and hustled to the kitchen. He wrapped his handkerchief around the door knob, opened the door, and peered through the glass of the storm door. He didn't see a car in the alley or anyone lurking about. He pushed the door open and stepped onto the stoop, quietly closing the door behind him, and crept through the ankle-deep snow heading two blocks down the alley, and then over to Homan Avenue. He slouched down in his car, took a deep breath, and waited for his nerves to settle.

***

Beauford headed home, parked his car in the driveway next to William's. His head swiveling around, searching for Feds as he opened the chain link gate and let himself in the back door. A faint light shone down the hallway coming from the living room. He heard the voice of Johnny Carson on TV and saw the shadows of William and Nathleen seated in the dimly lit room.

He kicked off his wet shoes, tossed his jacket over a kitchen chair, and bustled down the hallway, through the dining room and into the living room. "If anyone should ask I've been home since 9:30."

Nathleen frowned. "Is that what we should tell the FBI?"

His eyes narrowed and he stared at her. "You know I'm damn tired. I just been through a tough election. I wish you would stop giving me shit." He glanced at William and back at Nathleen. "Just do what I say."

William stood from the chair next to his mother, the letter from the FBI in hand.

"The FBI ..." Beauford paused, *better not say anything about Heidler's death.* "They been all over the city tonight talking to people about Alderman Heidler. Ruining the reputation of a sick tired old man that has helped a lot of people."

"What do you mean?" William asked.

"I'm sure your mother told you that they were here looking for me about an investigation of the alderman. I talked to the alderman. He's worried sick about dying in jail."

"Don't blame the FBI. Those agents were just doing their job. Maybe the alderman was worried because he had a reason to be," William said.

Beauford took two steps toward William and jabbed his finger in his son's face. "You don't know nothing about life. About the things people have to do to survive. You don't realize everything Alderman Heidler did for this family. So don't be taking one side when you don't know all the facts. You got a bad case of misplaced loyalties."

William swiped at his father's hand. "Aldermen get indicted all the time in this city. Heidler's been in politics for decades. He's probably dirty."

"Oh yeah, is that how you feel about me, too? I bet you think because I work for him that I must be dirty too."

William raised his hand, waving the letter in his father's face. "The FBI hired me." He glanced at his mother. "They want me to start at the academy in June."

"Are you sure that's what you want to do with your life?"

William put his hands on his hips. "I thought you'd be proud of me. Why do you have to stand up for a dirty politician? He's more important to you than your family."

Nathleen stood. "You two stop it. Aren't things bad enough around here? You want Marlee to come down and see both of you fighting?"

"Listen boy, I'm your father, not your friend. So don't be expectin' me to be happy for ya because you think your gonna be a hotshot FBI man. I've been struggling for twenty years to feed my family, keep a roof over your heads, and keep everybody safe. You got it soft. You'll never have to do nothin' because everything's been given to you. You're twenty-two and still livin' at home with your momma."

William's eyes narrowed. "You're my father? Oh, I didn't realize that. You haven't been a father since we left Mississippi. I don't know who you are."

"You ungrateful son of a bitch. You wouldn't be here if it wasn't for everything I did for you." His eyes flashed to Nathleen and he waved his arm, "None of you would."

William shot back, "The only thing we wanted from you was to be here for us. Instead you're out chasing something or running from something."

"Don't you talk to me like that. You'll never know what's its like 'til you're out in the real world. 'Til you have to make hard decisions. You never had to do that cause I made them for you."

William waved his arms. "Yeah, like what? I'll never know cause that's the way you made it. You and all your secrets."

Beauford's eyes narrowed and stayed fixed on his son. But in his mind he went to that secret place and saw what was left of Martin Luther King's face, his right jaw blown away and Bobby Kennedy lying in a pool of blood. His lower lip trembled and his hands opened and closed into tight fists at his sides. He fought the urge to punch his son. It hurt so deep. He knew he had to leave. "No, that's just the way it is. Cause you haven't lived life 'til you have to make the hard decisions."

"You stay in your little world. Keeping to yourself. I'm getting on with my life. I won't be here much longer." William glanced at his mother. "And when I'm done with the academy I'll be getting a place of my own."

"Well good for you, momma's boy. I'm going back to the office. Spend the night there. Get some peace and quiet."

William turned and looked at his mother. "Momma, isn't there something you wanted to talk to him about?"

Her hands twisted her apron. "Not now. We'll talk later."

"Ain't no reason to talk about somethin' we both know is dead. I'll be back tomorrow to pick up my stuff." Beauford stormed back through the living room.

Marlee was standing on the stairway out of sight of her mother and William, her hand reaching out to her father. "Daddy, I love you. Please don't go."

Beauford fingers caressed her's. "I have to baby. I love you too. I'm gonna make you proud of your daddy. He bolted out of the house and spent the night in the apartment above the ward office.

\*\*\*

The next morning Junior was in the same building he passed the night before at 26th and California. But this time he was at his hearing in the Juvenile Justice Division in the Cook County Municipal Court building

Junior slouched in a chair at a wood table in front of the judge's raised bench. His legs splayed out. He traced his finger through gouged initials in the table and stared at the faded green walls.

Next to him was a man in his late twenties. He wore a cheap blue suit, was tall, bone skinny, with a large nose and dark wavy hair covering his ears. In front of him on the table sat two accordion folders bursting with case files.

At the table to their right sat a smartly dressed man, mid-thirties, with ten folders laid across the table front of him.

The door to the judge's chambers opened and the judge stepped out. His robe flowing behind him.

The bailiff stood. A black man built like a stack of bricks. "Hear ye, hear ye, the honorable Judge Bernard Sheldon presiding. All persons having business before the court come to order. All rise."

The judge strolled to his tall black leather chair. He wore black horn-rimmed glasses, was balding with a thin row of blonde hair running from one ear to the other.

The man seated next to Napier stood. "Your honor, Jacob Moskowitz with the Public Defender's office, appearing on behalf of James Napier, Junior." He grabbed Napier by the back of his shirt and jerked him up.

The man standing at the table to their right smiled. "Robert Zurek for the state."

Judge Sheldon removed his glasses and put the police report down. "Mr. Napier, you have been charged with some serious offenses. I see you'll be 17 this Sunday. You're very lucky that you haven't reached your 18$^{th}$ birthday, otherwise you'd be in felony court. You were living with a foster family?"

Junior swayed from one foot to the other. "Yeah. I couldn't stand them anymore. Dropped out of school so I could get a job and take care of myself."

The judge picked up another report and paged through it. "You've run away from several foster families. You haven't demonstrated the ability to take care of yourself. You stole a gun from your employer, carried it concealed on yourself, and attacked a police officer."

"He was a nigga cop, gave my buddy a ticket cause the other driver was a nigga. He's the one that drove through the red light, not my buddy."

The judge slid his glasses onto the top of his head. "In my courtroom we don't address people in that manner."

Moskowitz placed his hand on Junior's shoulder and pulled him toward him, "Shh."

Junior pushed him away. "Hey, Jew boy. Don't be shushing me."

The Judge frowned, "Didn't you hear what I just said?"

Junior waved his arm at the judge. "Jus' shows that my old man was right. The Jews and the niggas are taking over everything and nobody's willing to put a stop to it."

The judge clenched his teeth. "I'm going to give you a second chance. Let's see if you can refrain from making those types of remarks. Perhaps you'll heed my advice and have a more civil tongue."

"Yeah, I can do that." Junior nodded. "But fuck it. What's the use? You're gonna screw my ass to the wall anyway. That's the way you guys are. Talkin' real nice just to cover yourself."

"Have it your way, Napier. I mean Mr. Napier." The judge grabbed Junior's folder with both hands and slapped it down. "Obviously you have some serious problems. The prosecutor has told me that your employer has fired you for stealing his pistol. So you have no income with which to support yourself. Both of your parents are deceased. You have a prior juvenile record for theft and assault. You're a danger to the community and based on your record of running away from foster homes you are very likely to flee placement. Therefore, this court finds that there is a matter of immediate and urgent necessity, and it is in your best interest that you be placed in a secured shelter care facility until the court finds that such placement is no longer necessary. Do you understand what I just said?"

"You locking me up? I got a Jew judge, a Jew lawyer, and a nigga cop. Well fuck me. Just wait 'til I get out. I'll get your asses."

"Bailiff, will you take this boy into custody until he is assigned to a facility. Next case."

"Let go of me," Junior screamed, twisting and turning as the black bailiff handcuffed him and dragged him to the lockup behind the courtroom.

\*\*\*

Late that afternoon, Officer Sanders parked his squad car in front of the ward office. He entered the office and saw Beauford sitting comfortably at Helmut Reichardt's old desk. "Mr. Richmond, remember me from last night?"

"Sure, Officer Sanders." Beauford stood and shook his hand. "Call me, Beau. That's what all my friends call me. Sit down." He pointed to the chair in front of his desk. "What brings you here?"

"The name's Charlie. Just wanted to bring you up to date on last night. That kid Napier, a real SOB. Like I guessed he would, the kid went ape shit when I gave his buddy the ticket. He rushes me so I push him. He falls down and a pistol flies out of his pocket. So I arrest him on a weapons charge. Anyway, to make a long story short, I got a call from the state's attorney just before I went on the street this afternoon. The kid went nuts in juvy court so the judge is gonna send him to St. Charles."

"What's St. Charles?"

"That's a medium security facility for boys."

"Jeez, that's too bad." Beauford laughed. "How long will they keep him there?"

"Odds are 'til he's 18. About a year."

"That's a cause for a celebration. Alderman Heidler gave me a box of Cuban cigars that somebody gave him. You want some?"

"Yeah, thanks, Beau. I better get back on the street."

Beauford pulled the cigar box out of the desk drawer and handed it to Sanders. "Stop by anytime you're around. Charlie, is St. Louis Avenue in your beat?"

"Not exactly. But if you need I can check something out for you. Why?"

"Usually the alderman checks in with us to see if anything needs his attention. Haven't heard a word from him today. I called his house a couple of times and nobody answered. Could you head up there, make sure he's all right? He found out last night that the FBI is looking into him and he was really upset." Beauford wrote down the address and handed it to Sanders. *Showing a little concern for the alderman will make me look clean to any prying eyes. Makes life a little more comfortable for me.*

"Sure, no problem. Thanks for the stogies."

\*\*\*

Fifteen minutes later Beauford's phone rang. "Beau, it's Charlie. I got bad news. Heidler's dead. Must have been a heart attack or something. You want me to hold off callin' it in, in case you wanna come here and see for yourself."

"Poor old man. I guess he couldn't take the pressure of the Feds coming down on him. No, go ahead and do your normal thing. With the Feds messin' around I don't want to get in the middle of anything. Thanks for your help, Charlie."

***

The coroner's office determined that Alderman Heidler was poisoned and declared his death a suicide. A week after the alderman's funeral, Beauford's presence was requested by the FBI at the Dirksen federal building.

He approached the federal complex in the heart of downtown Chicago, the area known as the Loop because the elevated train circles it. Looking at the buildings named after the late Senator Everett Dirksen and Representative Thomas Klucinski, Richmond mused, *it seems like if the Feds don't catch you they name a building after you.* The tall matching structures were made of black steel and glass and hovered over an orange bird-like Chagal in the federal plaza.

Beauford straggled through the gray marbled lobby to the north bank of elevators. He stood in front of the elevator doors waiting for what seemed forever, licking his lips and cracking his knuckles. Finally, a door opened and he went up to the ninth floor. He stepped out into the hallway. On the east side was a set of heavy wooden doors with a keyless entry system over the doorknob and security cameras hanging from the ceiling. On the west side was the FBI lobby. Large bulletproof sheets of glass protected an innocent-looking blond receptionist probably not more than twenty years old. He approached the glass and spoke into a small microphone. "I'm Beauford Richmond. Agent Daniels wanted to talk to me."

"Please take a seat. I'll call him."

Agents entered and exited the doors on both sides of the lobby while Beauford waited for ten minutes. A tall muscular black man followed by a slender white agent, both dressed in blue suits, approached him. The black agent flashed his badge and credentials in Beauford's face. "I'm Clarence Daniels and this is Douglas

Wise. We're both special agents with the FBI, Mr. Richmond. Please follow me."

They went from the lobby into one of the nearby barren interview rooms. The room was not much larger than a prison cell and contained four gray metal chairs and a matching table with a tape recorder on top of it. They all sat down.

Beauford pointed to the tape recorder. "You gonna use that?"

"No. That's just there if we need it," Wise said.

"Mr. Richmond, we wanted to talk to you about the death of Alderman Heidler." Daniels said.

"Well, you guys know more about that than anybody else." Beauford pulled a toothpick out of his overcoat and put it in his mouth. "He died causa you guys."

Wise's eyes glanced at the ceiling. "What do you mean by that?"

"He was an old man. He ate too much, smoked, drank, and when he heard you guys was after him he couldn't take it no more. It stressed him out."

Daniels leaned forward and put his hands on the desk. "How do you know that?"

Beauford leaned back in his chair, rocking back and forth on its rear legs. "The night you guys were running all over the city asking questions about him. My wife paged me after you stopped by my house. I was worried about the old man so I called him. He was really upset that you guys had questions about him and you didn't come to him first. He told me he woulda talked to you guys. He was really upset that you were ruining his reputation for no reason."

"Where did you call him from?" Daniels asked.

"I don't remember exactly. That was election night and I was all over the ward. A pay phone somewhere."

"If he would have talked to us why do you think he committed suicide?" Wise said.

"I dunno. All these alderman you took down. To city workers a lot of the charges seem like they're trumped up. Not enough to put a man away for as long as you do. He was scared. Scared of dying a lonely old man in jail on some charges you guys dreamt up."

"So you don't think he was poisoned by somebody?" Daniels said.

"Nah, everybody loved Alderman Heidler. He was a sweet old man."

Beauford felt Daniel's eyes drilling into his. "You drink scotch, Mr. Richmond?"

"Sometimes. Why?"

"It was a good thing you didn't stop by the alderman's house on election night. A bottle of Chivas Regal that was on his bar was laced with cyanide. Kind of unusual that a man would poison a whole bottle of scotch. You'd think that if he was going to do himself in he'd just put it in the glass he was drinking from."

Beauford swallowed. One sip he would've been dead. "You're the experts. Why you asking me?"

Daniels sat back in his chair. "When was the last time you saw him?"

"Sometime during the morning on Election Day. On the street somewhere. Don't remember where exactly."

"You didn't go to his house that night?" Daniels stared.

Beauford paused and cleared his throat. "No. I already told ya."

Silence penetrated the air. Wise leaned forward. "Kind of strange, there were two glasses of scotch on the bar. They both had traces of cyanide, makes you think that that somebody was visiting the alderman that night."

"I told you I wasn't there. I told you everything I know. You done with me?" The skin on his forehead furrowed.

"Mr. Richmond, I'm going to prepare a report of our meeting here today summarizing our conversation. Once I put your testimony in writing that's it. If we find that you lied to us you can be charged with a felony, making a false statement to a federal agent. Is there anything you'd like to change before I put pen to paper?"

Beauford's eyes glanced to the floor. "No, what I told ya was to the best of my memory. If I remember anything different I'll be sure to call you up."

"Okay, you can go." Wise walked Beauford out of the office to the bank of elevators.

Beauford lunged into the elevator and watched Wise as the doors closed. He blew air out between his lips and cocked his head back. *Good thing I didn't take a sip of that scotch or they would of found me laying next to the alderman. Don't make no sense. If the alderman didn't commit suicide, who killed him?*

# CHAPTER TWENTY

At 6:30 a.m. the beige van, marked Illinois Department of Corrections, rolled down Lincoln Highway past empty cornfields and then alongside a twelve-foot-high chain-link fence topped with barbed wire, enclosing the 900-acre site of the Illinois Youth Center in St. Charles, the medium-security facility for young men. The Center was little more than a penitentiary for boys and its population consisted of juveniles who had committed adult crimes, and mentally and emotional ill boys who were a danger to themselves as well as others. In the institution the boys are referred to as youths.

The van pulled up to the entrance. A motor hummed and the gate clanged open. The driver pulled the van up twenty feet and the gate closed. The guard in the red brick security building walked up to the driver and verified the writs transferring James Napier, Junior, and five other juveniles to the center. The guard walked around the van, peering through the dusty windows counting heads. When he finished he waived to the officer in the security building. The interior chain link gate, topped with barbed wire, slid open and the van entered the grounds.

The vehicle bumped down a crushed-stone road and stopped at the reception center at the west end of the three-story brick school building. Three black youths with floppy afros, a slender Hispanic boy with a tear drop tattooed on his left cheek below his eye, a white boy with hair covering his ears, and Napier hopped out of the van. Their hands were cuffed in front and the handcuffs fastened to a three-inch high leather belt that secured the cuffs at their waist. They shuffled their feet along as much as the leg irons would allow as they scuffled into the reception center on the first floor.

Their cuffs and leg irons removed, Napier and the other new arrivals lined up in a narrow windowless room. They were ordered to strip off their street clothes and were hosed down by a guard to delouse the newcomers. Napier stood at the end of the line next to the other white boy.

A black guard with Jeri curls pulled a latex glove over his right hand and raised his index finger. "Okay, boys bend over and grab your knees. We can make this easy—or not."

Napier bent over, stared at the cold cement floor, glanced at the boy next to him and mumbled. "Another faggot spook getting his jollies off on us."

The guard's eyes ran across the boys. "I hear a comment?"

There was no response.

"Good, maybe we can do this easy then."

The guard side-stepped down the line, inserting his finger into each boy's cavity, searching for contraband. They had become numb to the exercise, one responding with fake groans of pleasure.

Napier heard the boy next to him grunt. Napier's gut tightened. He held his breath and clenched his teeth. *Got to keep cool. Get out of here as soon as I can. Got a promise to keep.* He felt a finger probing his cavity. Junior's fingernails dug into the flesh of his thighs. The indignity ended.

They were handed towels that were worn and ragged to wrap around their waists and marched into an adjoining room. There was a long table with steel folding legs, three empty chairs on one side and three black guards seated on the other side.

"Attention!" A tall white man with a crew cut stepped in front of them. There were epaulettes on his shoulders and a gold badge on his shirt pocket. He held a clip-board in his left hand. "I'm Lieutenant Potempa." He crossed his arms, holding the clip-board between his broad chest and arms and took a wide stance with his legs. "You do what I say and we'll get along just fine. Now this here is where you're going to be interviewed for the purpose of identifying marks, taking emergency contact information, and making a clinical and academic assessment. You cooperate with the officer sitting across from you because he's going to be the one evaluating you." Potempa waved his finger at Napier and the two boys behind him. "You three sit down."

Napier slipped into a metal folding chair at one end of the table. The white boy sat in the chair next to him and one of the black boys at the other end. The three remaining stood behind them.

The guard held Napier's writ and entry report in front of him. "Name and date of birth?"

Napier folded his arms across his chest and glared at the black man seated across from him. *Bet this nigger's granddaddy was a slave and now he's fuckin' evaluatin' me.*

The guard leaned back in his chair. "I said, name and date of birth? Ain't going to ax you again."

Junior closed his eyes and took a deep breath. *Ax me. They all talk like that.* He exhaled through his mouth. *Got to save my hate. Save it up for later.* He lowered his head, opened his eyes and focused on the shiny cement floor. "James Napier, Junior," he mumbled and gave the man his birth date.

He raised his head and saw the guard staring at his chest.

The guard's lips pursed. "Identifying marks? Description and location."

Junior knew there was nothing he could do about his tatts. He lowered his arms and pushed the right side of his chest out. 'Blood & Honor' were above his right tit and '& Klan' below it. He pointed with his right thumb and then to his left side where a swastika covered his breast. He stared into the guard's eyes.

The guard peered at him and leaned on his elbows toward Junior. "Notification in case of EMERGENCY."

Junior smelled liquor on the guard's hot breath. He wanted to get face to face, show him a little attitude. Instead, he exhaled trying to keep his cool. "Patty Ignolfo." Then he gave her address and telephone number.

"Education?"

"Two years high school."

The guard sat back in his chair. "Based on this interview you are judged academically and clinically fit." He pulled a pencil from behind his ear, checked three boxes.

Junior leaned forward and glanced at the check marks. Each box that was checked was under the column labeled "high."

The guard spun the paper around so Junior could read the categories. They read escape risk, level of aggression, and threat group orientation.

"SOB," Junior mouthed.

The guard smiled and slammed the sheet in the out box on the table. He leaned back into his chair, resting on the back two legs. "I got to read this to you. Then you mosey over there." The guard motioned with his chin. "And get the cardboard box against the wall behind you with your case file in it."

Napier looked over his shoulder and the guard picked up a sheet of paper off the table. It was covered in clear plastic, its surface scratched with a crack that ran from one corner to another. He read the contents. "The box contains all the personal items you will need—deodorant, toothpaste, toothbrush, soap, comb, shampoo, sheets, towels, bedspread, pillows and blanket. Your clothes including blue jumpsuits, a week's supply of underwear, socks, canvas shoes, pants and shirts, and a winter jacket. You're responsible for everything in your box. Don't lose, trade or give away anything because it will not be replaced if you don't have an article to turn in. Get your box, boy, and put your clothes on." He flicked his wrist and spun the paper onto the table. "Next."

Napier charged off the chair to the box, threw the towel in it, pulled on the underwear and socks. He stepped into the jumpsuit, zipping up the front covering his shivering body and slipped on his shoes. The two other boys followed. The next three sat down in front of the guards and went through the five-minute evaluation process. They were all marched down the hall for fingerprinting. After printing they washed their hands.

"Finish up and fall in on the yellow line," Potempa ordered.

Napier stood, leaning to the left. The boy next to him scratched his head, the third wiped the ink off his fingers on the pant leg of his jumpsuit, and the other three were wandering back from fingerprinting.

Potempa slammed the clipboard to the floor. It hit with the crack of a pistol. "When you're told to fall in you stand at attention!"

The boys stood tall on the yellow line.

"That's better. You." He pointed at Napier. Fall out, pick up my clipboard, give it to me and fall back in."

Napier moved like an obedient soldier.

Potempa took the clipboard and pointed with it. "You, you, and you, take the coats out of your box and put 'em on. Do it now."

The boys slipped on the ragged blue coats.

"Pick up your box. Right face!"

Napier and the boy behind him turned right. The third one turned left.

Potempa put his hands on his hips and shook his head. "Well, that's not too bad. Only one retard in this group."

The third boy turned around.

"We're going double time, single file through those doors ahead of you a hundred yards to your new home, the Lincoln Cottage. I'll be right behind you. Don't stop until you hear my command." Potempa put on a coat and baseball hat with a badge emblem on the front.

They marched as fast as they could, holding the cumbersome boxes against their chests with both hands, down a sidewalk past barren elms toward a single-story brick building. Their breaths fogged out of their noses and mouths.

"Halt!" Potempa shouted.

In front of them was a wooden sign that was nailed onto a two-by-four stabbed into the ground. It read, Lincoln Cottage, a circular brick building with three wings that jutted out like spokes in a wheel.

They faced a red steel door with a small square window in it. Potempa walked to the door, took a large metal key off his belt. It clanged, metal against metal, when he stabbed it into the lock and turned the key. He yanked the door open. The thick steel hinges creaked. "All right boys, I'm turning you over to your cottage officer, Mr. Newton. You follow the same rules that I gave you and you'll do all right by him."

A thick-girthed black man, about forty, stood inside the door. The short sleeves of his uniform shirt were wrapped tight around his heavy biceps. "Get in, get in, move, move, move!" The door slammed shut behind them and tumblers creaked as Potempa locked the door from the outside.

Inside were the reception area and the guard's control room. Newton pointed at the window in front of the control room and barked out, "Okay boys, that is my office. You need to talk to me, you knock on the window and speak through the holes drilled into the glass. You do not, and I repeat, you do not, ever enter through the door unless I tell you." He paused for emphasis and then pointed at the sign on the wall. "This is wing number one. It is the shower facility and recreation area with seating, a television, and a Ping-Pong table for your enjoyment." Then he motioned with both arms at the remaining wings. "These are wings number two and three. They are your residential wings. Each wing has fourteen living quarters meant for one boy. Unfortunately, most of you will have to share your room. The doors to the rooms open and close electronically from my office. They are opened at 6:00 a.m. so you can shower before breakfast and locked when lights go out at 10:00 p.m. Under no circumstances are you to enter a residential wing if you don't reside in it. Any questions?"

Newton looked around. "No. Good." He glanced at his clipboard. "Napier, Johnson, and Alvarez follow me. I'll take you to your assigned rooms. Be ready to march to the dining hall for breakfast in fifteen minutes."

Newton sauntered down wing three, leading each boy to his assigned room.

Napier was last. He stood in front of the red door to his new home. It had a narrow window for inspection purposes.

"You need to talk to me, you refer to me as Mr. Newton. This is your living quarters for as long as you'll be here. It's inspected every day, so keep it clean. If it doesn't pass inspection you lose privileges. Your roommate is Bruce Ogren. Everyone has showered already. At 7:30 the cottage marches to breakfast. You get twenty minutes to eat. Then you march to your classes. All of you boys from wing three go to the same classes. You will fall in and march together. Any questions?"

Napier stood silent.

"You do not talk when you're marching. You understand?"

"Yeah." Napier stood there holding in his outstretched arms his box of possessions for the undeterminable future.

"It's not 'yeah.' From now on it is 'yes, sir, Mr. Newton' or 'no, sir, Mr. Newton'."

"Yes, sir, Mr. Newton."

Newton nodded at him. "Get in and get settled." He glanced at his watch. "You've got twelve minutes."

Napier stepped into the cell and dropped the box on the top bunk. The wall opposite the door had a two-foot wide by four-foot tall inoperable window. On the wall opposite the bunk beds were a stainless steel sink, toilet, and shelf. He looked at the white boy with long shaggy hair, lying below. "How many niggas in this place?"

"Don't know exactly. Heard somebody say there's something like 330 of us in here. Probably more than half are black," the tall slender boy said.

"Shit, I don't fucking believe it." Napier shook his head and slammed the bottom of his fist against his bunk.

"You better settle down. Anything you do out of order and they write you up. You lose privileges."

"I don't give a fuck." He shook his head. His lips moved, but he just mouthed what he was thinking, *gotta keep my hate buried and my cool up.*

"You will. The more they write you up the longer you'll be locked up in this joint. So you better learn to give a fuck. Cause they can send you straight from here to Joliet when you reach age."

"It's cause of the niggas and Jews that I'm here and now I got to live with the spooks." Junior shook his head.

"Keep your voice down. There's spies all around that talk about ya to get in good with Newton."

A bell shrieked down the hall and the echo of shoes clattered in the hallway outside of their living quarters.

"Come on. We got to line up and march to the cafeteria."

Napier stood at the rear of the line in his wing. They were two across and twelve down. He did a quick head count, *thirteen blacks, two spicks, and nine whites. More black and tans than whites.* He pursed his lips and his face reddened.

He watched those ahead of him as they marched out of the cottage into the cold morning air. Everyone was wearing the institutional blue jumpsuit and coat. He shook his head and followed the commands.

"Forward march. Right! Right!" Into the cold air they went three hundred yards, past two more cottages to the front of the cafeteria. "Halt!"

They marked time in place, waiting for another group marching out to their classes. Junior moved his feet up and down in cadence with the others.

He couldn't believe this was going to be his life. For the rest of the day he ate breakfast, lunch, and dinner in silence at twenty-minute meals. Marched six times from one fifty-minute class to another, and then back to the Lincoln Cottage where he isolated himself in his quarters until the next morning when the routine started again.

At night he lay in bed and began his ritual, plotting the revenge he had promised his father and more. He slipped his arrest report from his case file, read the false tale that had put him here. He could feel the icy pavement on his back and see the black hole of the barrel of the cop's pistol pointed at his head. His breathing quickened.

Junior stared at the bunk above him, his mind flashed back to Mississippi. *Daddy, I know how bad you wanted to burn down that church and all them niggas inside. I seen that spook FBI man shoot you. He didn't give you a chance. They're cowards. Knocked you down into those fire bombs. You were brave. Tried to march right up to that church even though your flesh was burnin' right off. I'll never forget your screams and that awful smell—the kerosene and your skin. I was gonna save you. But that nigga that shot you grabbed me. Wouldn't let me go. But, don't you worry, I'll get him.* He folded his lips and wiped a tear from his eye.

He could see his father as clearly as if he were standing inside the red door of his cell. Except his old man was standing behind the church in Ruleville, looking down into Junior's mother's grave. His father knelt down beside him and put his hand on his shoulder. Junior could smell the whiskey on his father's breath, sweet and warm. "Boy, if I don't kill that nigger, Tisdale, you got to promise me on your mother's grave that you will. Him and his boy." The vision of his father faded away.

Junior opened and closed his fist and licked his lips. He turned over his arrest report and removed a stub of a pencil from his box. His fingers tightened around the pencil, his knuckles whitened and he traced over the names he had printed on the back side—Moskowitz, Sheldon, Sanders, Richmond, Daniels, Tisdale, Tisdale's boy. "Niggas and Jews," he mumbled. "Niggas and Jews." *Keep cool, bury the hate 'til I can use it.* The bell rang, the lights faded, and the room turned dark. His eyes closed but he would relive it all over again in his nightmares.

# CHAPTER TWENTY-ONE

Marlee Richmond leaned against the back wall of the City Council. In front of her were forty-nine aldermen watching her father at the dais with Mayor Byrne. He had snuck her out of school so she could be present when he was appointed interim alderman. She took a deep breath and smiled, loving that her dad arranged this, but aware that she couldn't tell her mother or William.

Marlee smoothed the lapels of the navy suit that she had picked out at a designer store on Oak Street with a fancy Italian name and glanced down at the matching leather pumps her father had bought her from Marshall Field's. Marlee was living her dream.

The words coming out of the mayor's mouth were white noise as Marlee's mind drifted to the night her father left the house. She had heard William and her father arguing and came down the stairs. Could feel the tension pressing against her chest and could hardly breathe. She remembered her father's fingers slipping through hers and heard him say, 'I love you,' and feel the lump in her throat. Wondered if she would ever see him again as she watched him escape through the back door of his own house. He said, 'I'll make you proud of me.'

That night she went to her room and filled her diary. *I'm afraid of what's happening to my family. I love my father but I have the feeling I won't be seeing much of him. He has changed so much. Why does William have to be so selfish and leave us for that job? Can't he see that we need to stay together? If we can stay together during this trouble I know that we'll be a stronger family than before. I'm going to do everything I can to keep us together. My Daddy needs me and I'm going to be there for him even if I have to hide it from Momma and William. Please, God, help me.*

Her eyes welled, she cleared them with a tissue and looked back at the dais.

"Ladies and gentlemen, it is my honor to introduce the new interim alderman of the fifteenth ward, Beauford Richmond." Mayor Byrne stepped back and Beauford took her place.

Everyone in the city council stood and applauded the new alderman. He now was a member of their brotherhood.

She watched her father raise his arms, acknowledging the ovation. She was proud of him. He wore a tailored navy pinstripe suit, a custom-made white shirt, a red silk tie, and $300 Johnson and Murphy shoes that she had helped him select. She had watched him open his wallet and pull out a handful of hundred-dollar bills to pay for everything. He continued nodding and raising his hands as if he had been to the podium many times before.

"Thank you, Mayor Byrne. I promise you, the members of city council, and most importantly, the people of the fifteenth ward that I will try to follow in the footsteps of Alderman Heidler and attend to their every need just like him." He backed away from the podium and the Mayor stepped up.

"Thank you, Alderman Richmond. I know like everyone else here that I have a lot of work to do. So I'm going back to my office to do what needs to be done to keep this city working. That's our motto, 'The city that works,' so let's keep it that way. Thank you." She stepped down and turned to exit the council room.

Beauford tugged at her sleeve. "Mrs. Mayor, my daughter is here and I was wondering if we could get a picture of you and her together? It would mean so much to her. She took the day off from school to watch my appointment and she really looks up to you."

"Of course. A little free advice, Beauford." She placed her hand on his arm. "A good politician never misses a photo op."

Beauford waved to Marlee and mouthed, "Come up, come up."

Marlee pointed at her chest with her finger and her lips shaped the word, "me?"

Beauford nodded.

A plain-clothes officer embraced her arm and led her past the sitting aldermen up to the dais.

"Your honor, this is my daughter, Marlee." A wide grin spread across Beauford's face.

The Mayor shook her hand. "Pleased to meet you. Alderman, you have a beautiful daughter."

Marlee had turned sixteen and the sitting aldermen were eyeing the attractive young woman she had become. She was blessed with Nathleen's pouty mouth and her mocha skin. "Mrs. Mayor, it's so special to meet you. All the girls at school are so proud of you. You're a role model for us, being the first woman mayor." A flash from a camera forced her to blink her eyes and her smile turned flat. *What if my mother or William sees the photograph?*

***

A few days later a charcoal-gray Mercedes Benz 450SL convertible pulled in front of the ward office. The driver, a tall olive-skinned man wearing a black leather jacket, charcoal-gray Armani slacks, and black leather Ferragamo shoes, got out of the car. He strode into the ward office, "Congratulations, Mr. Alderman." He stuck his hand out and shook Beauford's hand.

"Thanks, Mr. Ippolito."

He patted his black, slicked-down hair. "Got time for a ride? I want to show you my new Mercedes."

"Sure."

They left the office and Ippolito handed him the keys. "Here, you drive."

Beauford sat down into the soft black-leather seat. He started the engine and paused to listen to the almost silent motor.

"Ever drive a Mercedes before?"

"Never been in a Mercedes before." He pulled away from the curb, driving west on Marquette Road. "I can't believe the ride. It's like…like floating on air. I don't feel nothing."

"Beau, you know a lot of aldermen drive Mercedes. You ought to look into buying one for yourself." Ippolito's mind was like a machine that never stopped humming. It was constantly scheming and planning. Nothing was ever said without purpose or reason and his black eyes felt like they bore into you. "You're a man of position now. About time to move out of that old house of yours and get something a little bigger."

"I'm outta the house. Me and the wife split."

"Should I be sorry or happy for you?"

"Jus' wasn't happening anymore. She just doesn't understand what I've been..." He shook his head. "We lead different lives."

"Well, I guess it's best then. Where're you living now?"

Beauford didn't mention Sheila Ubegu's apartment. No need to mention his girlfriend, the ghost payroller. "Most of the time I stay in the apartment above the office. Ain't bad." Beauford turned north on Homan.

"Beau, I've got a couple of furnished rental condos near north. One of them is vacant. You can stay there. Use the office address as your official residence. But you don't have to live there. Give me a couple of days. I'll have the place cleaned and you can move right in."

"Thanks, Mr. Ippolito. Can I see how much pep the car has?"

"Go for it."

Beauford punched the accelerator and they jerked back in their seats. "This baby can move, Mr. Ippolito."

"Hey, don't mister me no more. The name's Dante. You're taking Heidler's place, so you're going to be on a first-name basis with lots of people. I'll have one of my boys drop off the keys for the condo and a parking pass at your office. In the meantime," he pulled out an envelope from his inside coat pocket, "used to give this to Heidler. From now on you'll be getting it. One of the boys from the Department of Transportation gets a piece of that. Heidler used to hold his share for him. The man from CDOT will come see you."

Beauford slowed down to twenty-five and turned east on 66th Street, cruising past brick bungalows and two-flats and stopped at California. "Sure. How much do I...." He paused not wanting to seem too greedy. "Does he get?"

"How you work out the split is up to you guys. That's not my concern. These city contracts are worth a lot of money to a lot of people. You're in the right place at the right time. I do a lot of city business in your ward, so you get a piece of the city contract. In the future, you need some work done in your ward, you keep me in mind. You got to handle this right. This stays with only the people that have to know. You don't tell any bitches, wives, drinking buddies, nobody. My people don't tolerate any weak links."

Beauford slid the envelope into his right pants pocket. He zipped down California and pulled in front of the ward office "You can count on me, Dante." He brushed his hand over his pants pocket to reassure himself that this was really happening.

Beauford felt the course of his life changing. The last ten years he was operating on sheer will, forcing himself to take each step, to get past each day. Now that meandering course seemed to be coming to an end. This arrival at a new place in his life helped him step away from the guilt of the past. It had brought potency to his life he had never felt before. He no longer felt the victim of corruption. He had power and his own piece of the action. It was now his turn. Heidler had been old and scared, a weak link. He had had to go.

"Like I said, the keys for the condo will be dropped off later today. Should be ready for you by the weekend." Ippolito got out of the car and walked around to the driver's side.

Beauford pushed open the driver's door, stepped onto the street, and handed Ippolito the keys. They shook hands. As the Mercedes pulled away, he noticed an open case of twenty-five year old Chivas Regal in the back seat. He rubbed his hand across his lips, swallowed, and thought about Alderman Heidler's cyanide-laced Chivas Regal.

Beauford headed to the backroom of the ward office and opened the safe. The irony hit him. Ten years ago, he stepped over Reichardt's dead body and took $20,000 in cash out of Heidler's safe. Returning that money to Heidler turned out to be the wisest thing he had ever done. All it really cost him was one dead Nazi. He looked at $3,000 in hundred-dollar bills that Ippolito had given him with the knowledge that more would be coming each month. Beauford now had his personal stash.

\*\*\*

In late April Junior was in the youth center's library. It was a makeshift room consisting of worn shelves holding a hundred dusty paperbacks and the *Chicago Sun-Times* and *Tribune* newspapers after they were handed down by the staff. Ogren was sitting at a table with a couple of other youths from another cottage. He looked at Napier and jerked his head motioning him to the table. Napier sat down at the chair next to him.

Ogren motioned across the table. "This is Frank Soder. He wants to talk to you. I'll see you later." Ogren closed *The Sun-Times* he was looking at, its pages creased and corners turned. He pushed it across the table and left.

Napier looked at the mass of humanity sitting in front of him. He was Junior's height but weighed one hundred pounds more. A swastika was tattooed on Soder's right ear lobe.

Soder grabbed the newspaper and flipped it over to the sports page. "They like it when we're readin' something. Makes 'em think we're expanding our minds." He turned over a page, keeping his eyes on the page and whispered. "Heard you ain't a friendly guy. You feeling more sociable today?"

Junior followed his lead, grabbed a book lying on the table and cracked it open. "I'm just tired of being fucked over. So I don't talk to nobody. Avoid trouble that way."

"Everybody needs somebody to talk to." Soder's jowls shook. "When you turn eighteen?"

"March, next year."

"That's a long time to put yourself in solitary."

Junior stared at the book, aimlessly flipped his finger through fifty pages. "Yeah. I just can't get over living with niggas." Junior clenched his teeth and his face turned red. "I get so pissed, one of those niggas looks at me the wrong way I'm gonna kill him."

"Junior, you got to chill."

"I know. I know. I'm doing the best I can." He closed the book.

"Listen, Man. When you reach age they got to release you or send you to Joliet. All depends on how the cottage guard, counselors, and teachers write you up. My old man comes to visit us as much as he can. You talk with him when he comes. He's got plans for guys like us. He's Frank Collin's number-two man. In the meantime you gotta calm down so you can get out. Then you can do all the things that need to be done." Soder turned the newspaper over and glanced at the front page.

Junior pushed the book away and dragged the newspaper toward him. He jabbed his forefinger down on the photo on the front page. "That's him. That's fuckin' him. That's the asshole that ran through the red light." He read the caption under the photo.

*Mayor Byrne appoints Beauford Richmond as interim alderman. New alderman and daughter meet mayor.* "No wonder my ass is in here. A nigga politician. You know they're gonna protect his ass."

\*\*\*

On June 4 William Richmond reported to the FBI Academy located on the United States Marine Corps base at Quantico, Virginia. For the next sixteen weeks he would be a NAT, a new agent trainee. The competition was fierce among the new agents. One of the principle motivating factors was that by finishing first in class, a new agent was given a pick of field office assignments. However, the source of William's motivation was an underlying resentment for having to live with a man who a decade ago ceased being his father. He was obsessed with the craving to understand what or who had stolen his father's psyche. It pushed William beyond anyone's expectations. He had to prove not only that he could survive on his own, but that he could succeed, and succeed beyond whatever his father's accomplishments might be.

At the academy William breezed through the legal exams. His attention was caught by the glamour of working drugs, organized crime, or the swat team. With that in mind, he pushed himself, working on his physical training, running and lifting weights.

William woke an hour early everyday at 5:45 and put on his FBI-issued T-shirt and shorts. On Monday, Wednesday, and Friday he ran the 5-kilometer path through the darkened woods as a thin band of orange-yellow light showed low over the horizon. The only sound to be heard on these lonely runs was the crunching of twigs beneath his running shoes and his heavy breathing. He felt the twitch of his muscles and the dampness of his sweat-soaked shirt. William saw his time drop from twenty-four minutes to twenty.

On Tuesdays, Thursdays, and Saturdays he was the first one to flip the switch in the weight room. The first workout of the week was chest and triceps, then back and biceps, and, on the last day, shoulders and legs. His pectorals burned as the weights clanged onto the bench and he dropped the dumbbells to the mat with a thud, his biceps stinging.

His proficiency with firearms, semi automatics, AK-47s, and Remington 870 shotguns, went from the bottom 10 percent to the top 10 percent by the end of his class.

In the early defensive-tactics classes, William took a beating from NATs that had tasted the experience of someone dying in their hands—NATs that had been in the Special Forces, the Marine Corps, and police departments. His body was sent flying through the air and bouncing across mats. His arms and legs twisted and handcuffs slammed down, bruising his wrists. But, by the end of the class, William was the gladiator that left many of his opponents sprawled on the mats.

Evenings consisted of staying up late into the night studying Department of Justice procedural manuals, preparing mock-case exercises, and icing down purple bruises and sore muscles. William could feel his momentum growing. He knew a place on the SWAT team in a field office was within his grasp. He saw his competition. They had a running start on him but he knew no one could outwork him. By the last week of training William had pushed himself to fourth in his class.

***

Beauford was adjusting to life on the near north side. He left Lawrys after a prime rib dinner and two glasses of scotch, courtesy of the maitre d', and strolled north on Michigan Avenue. The breeze off Lake Michigan freshened the night air. The lights from the Gold Coast stores and hotels illuminated the Magnificent Mile. He could feel the energy of the buzzing crowds enjoying the star-filled night. He passed the John Hancock building, turning east on Delaware, heading to his condo.

The black doorman dressed in his red top hat and matching knee-length jacket with gold buttons opened the front door. "Good evening, Mr. Alderman."

"Evening, Jones." Beauford entered the lobby, rubbing his stomach Jones hustled back and pushed the elevator button for him. Beauford nodded and palmed him a five-dollar bill, boarded it and got off at the third floor. He ambled down the blue oriental runner to the end of the hallway and entered the one-bedroom furnished unit. Beauford flipped on the tape player and collapsed into the overstuffed black-leather sofa, listening to Coltrane's saxophone fill the room. Picasso and Jackson Pollack lithographs decorated the walls. A gentle glow flowed from the dimmed recessed lights in the ceiling. He kicked off his shoes and unbuttoned his slacks and sighed, easing his belly over the waistline of his pants. "Ah, life is good." His eyes gradually closed and he drifted into sleep.

A ringing startled Beauford. He picked up the phone.

"Mr. Alderman. This is Jones. There's a Mr. Falcone says he's here to see you."

He shook his head. "I don't know no Falcone."

There was a silence on the phone as he heard Jones relay the message. Beauford overheard the man's response, "I'm from CDOT."

Beauford jumped to his feet, pulled his gut in and buttoned his slacks. "Jones, send him up."

A few moments later there was a knock on the door. Beauford barefooted to the door and opened it. Falcone was fiftyish, dressed in a gray silk suit. His green eyes were tucked away in the folds of his flesh. His gray hair flowed back from a rising forehead.

"I was just having a few drinks with Dante Ippolito. He suggested I drop by and see you." Falcone swaggered past Beauford into the condo. "Nice place. Dante's taking good care of you."

Beauford closed the door, returned to the sofa, and slipped his shoes on. "What can I do for you?"

"I think you've got something from Dante that belongs to me."

Beauford leaned back and crossed his legs. "Ain't got nothing here."

Falcone pulled out a Macanudo cigar from his inside coat pocket. He held it up, "Do you mind?"

"No, go ahead."

Falcone clipped off the end, dropped it into a Waterford ashtray, and pulled out a gold Dunhill lighter. He struck the lighter and rolled the tip of the cigar in the red and yellow flame. He placed it between his lips and pulled in his breath. The tip glowed red, and a puff of gray smoke floated to the ceiling. He pulled the cigar away from his mouth. "We need to make arrangements to get it to me—tomorrow night. I'll be back at eight. I need two from each month. That's from March, April, May and June."

"That don't leave much for me."

"You're new in the game, Alderman. Don't get greedy and you'll do very well. Besides it isn't all for me. There's pockets I got to take care of."

"Like who?"

Falcone jerked the cigar out of his mouth and pointed at Beauford's forehead like he was ready to brand him. "It's none of your fucking business. Just do as I say and you can do well. But if you keep that fucking attitude you can count on one thing. Problems. Do I have to go any further?"

Beauford looked down at the shiny oak floor. *Shit. I get a piece of something going and somebody got to crowd in on it.* "How much were you getting from Heidler? I bet he wasn't giving you two."

Falcone put the cigar between his lips and inhaled. His face was getting as red as the tip of the stogie. "Listen, boy. It don't matter what went on before because it's a new game with different players. You're serving your apprenticeship and getting a good piece of cash. So you better take your piece of the cake and be grateful. There'll be more for you later, after you have an opportunity to prove yourself."

Beauford paused, contemplating his words. "Dante said that the split is up to you and me."

"It is. And I just told what it is and why. Are you having a hard time hearing me? You keep this up and you're gonna end up drinking some of Heidler's scotch. You understand what I'm telling you?" The cigar bobbed up and down between his lips.

"Yeah, but—"

"There ain't no buts. I'll be back tomorrow night and you better have eight waiting for me or the ward will be looking for a new alderman. You understand?"

"But I don't have the cash. I bought a Mercedes. Ippolito told me I should."

"You son of a bitch. You knew that money wasn't yours. This is what you're doing tomorrow. You take the title to your Mercedes, go to a bank, get a loan, and cash the check. Make sure you get all 100's and bring the cash here. I'll be here tomorrow night like I said. You understand?"

Beauford nodded and Falcone moseyed his way back to Rush Street.

\*\*\*

In mid-September, two weeks before William's class would graduate, James McAlister, the Special Agent in Charge of the Chicago office, called Clarence Daniels into his office. "Close the door and sit down."

Daniels sat in one of the two maroon leather armchairs in front of the SAC's desk. The walls were decorated with framed headlines from major cases McAlister had been involved in over the last twenty-five years. Behind McAlister's chair were the stars and stripes and several photographs of McAlister with J. Edgar Hoover, President Johnson, President Ford and President Carter.

"We're getting five NATs from the Academy. They'll be reporting Monday, October 1'. I'd like you to give them an orientation to the office."

"Which five?"

McAlister looked at the roster of incoming agents, "Hill, Ilich, Richmond, Uhler, and Acevedo."

"Richmond? I thought that we agreed with his father being involved in local politics he should go to some other field office."

"I know we discussed that but I decided that I wanted him here. He did really well on his initial interview. I tried to trip him up myself but the kid wouldn't fluster. I think he's got the potential to be a good agent. He ranks fourth in his class now."

Daniels shook his head, "Jim, this is an accident waiting to happen. His father worked for Heidler." He held his thumb and forefinger and inch apart. "You know I was this far from indicting Heidler. Then somebody murders the old man. What if we find out that Richmond's father had something to do with Heidler's murder? They'll be looking to roll somebody's head for hiring the son of a guy that's involved with a dirty politician and might know something about his death. They care more about our image than they do about making cases."

"Do we have any evidence that indicates what you're suggesting may be true?"

Daniels shook his head. "No, not at this time. I just have a hunch about this. Are you sure you don't want to put Richmond somewhere else? Once he's here you'll have to go through a lot more to transfer him out."

"If there's an indication that his father is involved in any illegal activities or may become a subject of an investigation we'll recuse the kid from having anything to do with those cases."

"But Jim—"

"I've other considerations, too. Things that you don't have to be concerned with. Frankly, Clar, I've got to grab every black agent I can or I won't meet the guidelines for hiring minorities set by HQ. If I don't meet the quotas I'll get all sorts of shit. So I'm sorry if you don't like it. But this is the way it's going to be."

Daniels looked down, pursed his lips, and took a deep breath, *no one can ever accuse us of letting logic interfere with a bad decision.* He raised his eyes, "But—"

McAlister raised his hand. "I don't want to hear anything else about this. I don't need any more aggravation. One more thing and you can go. I'm transferring you from the political corruption squad to the civil rights squad. HQ wants us to put more man-hours there. I'm putting Richmond there too and I want you to work with him. Teach him the ropes and keep an eye on him."

Daniels' chest swelled with anger. He stood, charged to the door and turned facing McAlister. "I don't believe this. First you're bringing the kid here against my better judgment, then you're transferring me out of a squad that I helped get going, and now you want me to work with him? To be his partner?"

"I don't want to talk about this anymore."

"Well, I do!"

McAlister crossed his arms over his chest, leaned back, and exhaled.

Daniels' eyes narrowed. "I want you to make me two promises. If this kid gives even the appearance of impropriety, we fire him."

"That goes without saying."

"You have a sit-down with the two of us and tell him what you just told me, that he has to recuse himself from any investigation regarding city politics, and that I was transferred against my wishes because of him."

McAlister pushed himself away from his desk. "You really want to make this kid feel at home."

"If he's going to be my new partner I don't want to have to be the one telling him everything we just talked about. He should know everything up front but he should hear it from you, not me. It's only fair. This isn't the academy. This is the real world with all its politics and asinine reasons for why we do things the way we do."

"You know, sometimes I think you forget who the boss is. After your orientation with the NATS bring him in."

***

Mid-morning on Monday, October 1, Daniels headed to McAlister's office and William Richmond treaded behind him.

"If you don't mind me asking, why does the SAC want to talk to you and me and not the other new agents?" Richmond asked.

"You'll hear it from the boss's mouth. There are things you'll learn here that they can't teach you at Quantico." Daniels knocked on McAlister's open door.

"Come in, men." McAlister rose and shook William's hand. "Welcome aboard." He nodded at the chairs. "Sit down."

William sat in one of the chairs in front of the SAC's wooden desk. Daniels closed the door and sat in the chair next to William.

"William, I was just going through your training file. I wanted to personally congratulate you on your outstanding performance."

William nodded. "Thank you, sir."

"I see you listed your assignment preferences for the SWAT team, narcotics, and organized crime. I don't want to disappoint you, but normally these assignments go to more experienced agents. I'm sure that at some point in your career, if you continue this level of performance, you'll have the opportunity to work in these programs."

"Sure, I understand that I have to pay my dues. I just wanted you to know that I would really enjoy the challenge of those types of assignments." *Worked my ass off to get on the SWAT team and they'll probably sit me behind a computer somewhere. Bite my lip for now.* "But I'll be happy to start in any program where you feel I can make a contribution."

McAlister smiled and nodded at Daniels. "William, I'm going to assign you to the civil rights squad. You'll work with Clarence. I couldn't think of a more qualified agent for you to learn from."

William paused, "Thank you, I'm sure that I can learn a lot from Agent Daniels." *I'll be chasing around unemployed rednecks. Shit, I might as well be back in Mississippi.*

"There's one more thing I have to talk to you about. We have an unusual circumstance. Your father was closely associated with an alderman who was a subject of an investigation. I'm not implicating your father in any wrongdoing, but as a result of his relationship with the alderman we have to recuse you from any involvement in any investigation where your father may be a potential witness." Then the words slipped out, "witness or otherwise."

"Sure, I understand that." William nodded. *He's probably going to be indicted.*

"Purely in an effort to cover all the bases, I have to caution you that you are on a probationary status your first year. Any act that gives even the appearance of impropriety could result in your termination."

"Mr. McAlister, I assure you that I will not compromise the Bureau for my father or anyone else. My relationship with my father could only be described as, well, at best, distant. I would have no reason to respond to any favors he might ask of me."

"It's more than that. It's not a question of even not responding. If your father even makes an overture to you, you have to notify us."

William's eyes narrowed, "Of course." *What the hell, maybe he's not indicted; maybe they hired me to set him up.*

"All right, I think we have a complete understanding of where we all stand in this matter. Again, welcome aboard."

Daniels cleared his throat, "I think you forgot one thing."

McAlister stared at Daniels. "Daniels and I decided that it was best if we were totally open with you. Just so there are no misunderstandings. Daniels was the case agent on Heidler. I'm transferring him out of the public corruption squad against his wishes, so you can work with him."

William tensed his fingertips together. *That's great. A partner who's gonna be pissed at me because I messed him up.* "I don't want to affect someone else's career. It doesn't seem fair."

"Don't worry about that, William. Daniels is going to be good for you to work with. You'll learn a lot from him. Right Clar."

"If you say so. It's getting close to lunch. I've got some things to do. Are we done here?"

"I guess so," McAlister said.

"Okay, William, let's go." They walked out of the office and down the hallway. "I'll hook up with you later. Give you a list of things you'll need to start on. In the beginning it'll be a lot of background work, going through old files, computer databases, and things like that to gather intelligence. Real exciting things. I'll see you after lunch."

William stopped and watched Daniels walk away. He muttered, "Busted my ass for sixteen weeks for nothing. I got to get away from this guy."

## CHAPTER TWENTY-TWO

### November 1979

Kurt Soder strolled into the visitors' room of the Illinois Youth Center like General Patton entering a briefing. Ten of the fifteen wooden tables were occupied by boys and their visitors, mostly parents, brothers, and girlfriends, most of whom were pregnant. Their murmurs, laughter and crying filled the room. Their eyes turned to Soder and the room quieted. He was a tall man, mid forties, with thinning blonde hair combed straight back and a thick build, solid from shoulders to waist. He took off his aviator glasses and cleaned the yellow lenses on the sleeves of his khaki shirt, looking for his boys.

He was a few minutes early for their two o'clock appointed time. It wasn't every father that could claim to have two sons locked up at St. Charles. He had arranged for both of his sons to have identification numbers that ended in odd numbers so he could visit them on Sundays. Boys with even numbers had to take their visitors on Saturdays. Then he sat down at a table to wait for his boys, reading the messages of love, obscenity, and gang signs carved into the table top with ball point pens. Eyes turned away from him, whispers of conversations resumed, and he killed time carving a swastika into the table top.

The Soder brothers, Frank and Earl, entered the room cackling at each other until they saw their father. They rushed to him and he stood, reached across the table and smacked each of them in the shoulder.

Soder bent over, reached between his legs, grabbed the chair and sat down. "How's my boys doing?"

The boys grabbed their chairs, dragged them out from under the table, and plopped down. "We're doing great, dad." Frank, the older of the brothers nodded his head and his chin disappeared into the roll of fat that was his neck. He looked his father in the eye. "Couple of weeks and we're out of here."

"I know boys. No more coming to this shit hole. We'll all be free of this place. You guys can work at the gas station. Fuck school."

"Cool man," Earl said. He was a head shorter than his older brother and was a miniature version of his father. "Frank, I can help you work on that '56 Chevy, right Frank?"

"Yeah, I'll teach you. But you can't touch it if I'm not there."

"How's that other boy you were telling me about. What's his name, Jimmy or Junior?"

"Junior, Dad." Frank leaned across the table and whispered, "He's smart and he's pissed. He can't wait to get out of here and do some damage."

Earl smiled, and nodded in agreement.

"Does Junior have an odd number?" Soder asked.

"I dunno." Frank said.

"Earl, go talk to the boy and find out. If he does, bring Junior for a little conversation. I got to see if this guy has the right attitude."

"Dad, the guard won't let him out, cause you're not on his visitor's list," Earl said.

Soder winked at Earl. "Don't worry about the guard. I slip him a twenty every time I come out to see you boys."

Earl marched over to the sleepy guard. He had a few words with him, pointed his thumb over his shoulder at his dad and the guard waved him out the door.

Kurt Soder looked at his eldest son, cocked his head and said in a hushed tone, "Frank, you think this boy has the sense to do what he's told? We don't need some pissed off skinhead running around shooting niggers and kykes because he thinks he's been fucked by the world. Draws the wrong kind of attention. We need people with discipline."

"You talk to him. He'll listen to you, Dad. He gets out in March if he plays it smart. He's real mad, but he's keeping cool. You can visit him three or four times before he's released, talk some sense into him, he'll be even more mellow." Frank nodded, his jowls flapping. "Then he'll be ready to do whatever you want."

\*\*\*

Earl ran to Lincoln Cottage and hurried down the hallway to the last room. Junior was lying on the bed, bare-chested, reading a copy of *Mein Kampf* someone had put between the covers of *Catcher in the Rye*.

Earl smiled. "Hey, my old man is here. Want to talk to him?"

"I'm busy, Earl." He turned over on his side. In three months his slender biceps had developed tone and density. His deltoids bulged over his triceps. "The List" had motivated him to spend his free time in the in-house version of the Illinois Youth Center health club. Galvanized pipes stuck in coffee cans and old buckets filled with cement became barbells and dumbbells. His eyes returned to the book. "I'm trying to learn more about the way the world should be run." He underlined a passage he was reading.

"My old man is a smart guy." Earl's face saddened. "He ain't like me, Junior. He's one of the top Nazis here."

Junior laid the book down on his bed and stood. He slipped his shirt on and put his arm around Earl. "You're not dumb, Earl. You're one of us and we've got to stick together. Right?"

"Right, Junior." His eyes lightened and a smile crossed his face. "You really think I'm not dumb?"

"How could you be with an old man like your dad? Let's go see him."

\*\*\*

In ten minutes two contrasting figures walked through the doorway. Earl Soder's shirt hung over his waist and pant legs sagged over his shoes. Junior's shirt stretched tight across his chest and was tucked firmly into his slacks. They walked up to the table where Frank and his father were seated.

"This is my dad, Junior," Earl said.

Kurt Soder stood and firmly shook Junior's hand. "Sit down, son. My boys have been telling me a lot about you. They said you haven't had any visitors. I thought it might do you some good to talk to somebody from the outside."

Junior flipped a chair around and straddled it, resting his elbows on the back. "I could have visitors if I wanted. I told my girlfriend not to come. I don't want her seeing me living like this." He leaned forward. "I can't stand having niggas all around."

Kurt Soder nodded. "We're all on the same page. But, you can benefit even from a bad experience. It makes you stronger."

"Frank and Earl told me you're close with Frank Collin. I saw him talk at the Rockwell Building last February. That was the night I got in trouble."

"It's a small world, Junior. I was there that night. Wasn't that a great night? Man, it was powerful. The place was packed with young and old and you were a part of it. You belonged there."

Junior rocked back on the chair. "I want to be part of that, Mr. Soder."

"Call me, Kurt. The future of our organization is in the hands of people like you and my boys. Us senior people can help you. Tell you about the history, but we'll be relying on you young people to regain the power and bring justice back to the world."

Junior's face brightened and he leaned forward. "This is a war and I ain't gonna stand on the sidelines watching the niggas and kykes take the world over. We got to make things right."

Kurt Soder pointed his finger at Junior. "You're right, son. But, we've got to be smart about this. My advice is to be on your best behavior so you can get your ass out of this place as soon as you can. Don't let these monkeys get under your skin. That's what they want to do so they can fuck with you. Everyday we're growing stronger. More and more men and women seeing our perspective. But we have to be careful. We can't be running around wild destroying everything that's been accomplished. If we plan our growth, our actions, we'll once again become a world power."

"I'm sick of getting my ass kicked." Junior shook his head. "That's what happened to me. I'm in here cause of a nigga politician and kyke lawyers."

"I know you got fucked over big time and we can help you get revenge. But you have to be in touch with the big picture. If we do this right we can have our place in the world. We need to gain political influence. That can get us a lot further than violence for the sake of violence." Soder tilted his head and looked at Junior out of the corners of his eyes. "Now I'm not saying there won't be a time when violence will be the appropriate tool to use. We have to be careful before we go that route. But getting whatever weapons we need will never be a problem."

Junior had heard the words he needed to hear. Getting whatever weapons we need will never be a problem. "That makes a lot of sense to me, Kurt. You can count on me to do whatever you need." He would tell Soder whatever he wanted to hear if it would put him one step closer to wiping out "The List."

*\*\*\**

Over the next few weeks Daniels and William started putting the pieces of the puzzle together. But more than that was coming together. Their relationship was growing in mutual trust. Daniels saw the effort William was putting into the work even though he wasn't working on the kind of assignments he had hoped. And when Daniels looked deep enough, he saw in William the agent he had been ten years ago. A young black man attempting to prove himself on his own, in a white man's world, without losing his identity.

William had felt Daniels' attitude change. At some point in time, he didn't know exactly when, the initial resentment he felt from Daniels shifted to conditional support. And then the conditions evaporated. He knew Daniels would look out for him, let him grow and stumble if necessary, but be there to right him.

One of the first things they did was send a young white agent with a Marine Corps buzz cut to one of the Nazi meetings at the Rockwell Building. He joined the American Nazi Party and got on the mailing list. Within a few weeks they were receiving their own personal hate mail sent to an undercover address used as a mail drop.

They sat at William's battleship-gray desk in the bullpen on the ninth floor in the Dirksen Federal Building. One desk among fifty fit into ten rows of five for the two squads, the political corruption squad where Daniels was previously assigned and the civil rights squad where he was the acting supervisor. Daniels was able to overhear all the juicy stories from the ongoing cases of his old squad. Which alderman was going to be indicted next. Who was copping a plea and going to cooperate to knock down some bigger fish. And which old crony was going to get hammered with a big sentence because he was unwilling to flip. Chicago was a fertile area for an agent assigned to political corruption. But, so far it wasn't looking like a hotbed of big cases sitting out there to be plucked for civil rights violations.

Daniels looked at the Nazi literature and dropped it on William's desk. "Wonder how the skinheads would feel if they knew they were sending all this trash to a couple of black FBI agents."

"I think we ought to rent a couple of Nazi uniforms and show up at their next meeting. They might close up shop and then we could work on something significant."

"I agree. You go in. I'll monitor the meeting from the van." Daniels laughed. "You must be trying to piss off McAlister. He doesn't want to lose any of us boys." Daniels leaned forward and whispered, "He'd look bad to headquarters if the black head count went down a notch."

William smirked. "You're some mentor. I'm trying to think big and you're giving me reasons for not working."

"All right, hotshot. Here's some things you can do. Take the names of everyone mentioned in this literature like Collin, Soder, and the registrations on the license plates we picked up and run them through NCIC and check the indices to see if they're mentioned in any 302s. One more thing, do a title search on that Rockwell building. Let's find out who owns that place."

"More exciting work. You think we might ever go out and talk to anybody?"

Daniels smiled, "Yeah, sooner than we thought. I'll be free of the acting supervisor's job. McAlister just told me they've assigned a permanent supervisor. A guy from the national office. His name's Eckhaus."

"What's the word on him?"

"He's had some major assignments. Coordinated the King assassination investigation. He was in the special operations branch, worked on the undercover review committee, and handled relationships with foreign banks for undercover operations. He's got a couple of years to go before he can pull the plug. He should be all right."

"Sounds good."

Daniels stood and stretched his arms overhead. "I'm going to meet my wife for lunch. Let me know if you find anything interesting."

"I'll head over to the county building, do the title search, and grab a bite over there." William left the federal building and walked north on Dearborn. The November wind went right through his overcoat. He crossed the Civic Center Plaza past the bird-like Picasso to the large gray monstrosity, half of which was Chicago's City Hall and the other half the Cook County Building. It has always been a mystery how one half of the building cost substantially more to build than the other half. It was a metaphor for Chicago politics—the hidden cost of getting things done.

He headed downstairs to the Torrens and Plats Department. A ceiling full of fluorescent lights shone down on long rows of steel tables pushed together, each twelve-feet long and four-feet wide. Under each table were five shelves that contained three-foot by three-foot musty books with handwritten entries that recorded the history of Cook County's real estate transactions over the last one hundred years. The tops of the tables were polished to a shine from all the years the massive plat books had been slid across them. People poured over the books for a variety of reasons: some were county clerks recording transactions, others were lawyers' flunkies finding out who owned a property so they could sue the right party, or slum landlords looking for properties they could buy on the cheap from foreclosures or tax sales.

William found the book containing the transactions for the Rockwell building and slid it off the shelf onto the table. *Just one more moment of excitement as I bust the biggies*, he yawned. He flipped through several pages until he found the correct page based on the legal description and ran his finger down the page. "Here it is." He pulled a spiral notebook out of his inside suit coat pocket and jotted down the information. "Purchased April 18, 1968, by Bavarian Agri, N.V., no liens. What the hell is N.V.?"

He headed to the stairway up to the main floor and saw his father and another man standing face-to-face in a dark corner of the landing between the two flights of stairs. William drifted back behind the wall and watched. His father quickly reached inside his suit coat pocket, pulled out an envelope, and stuffed it in the other man's inside coat pocket. The other man's lips pursed and he grabbed one of Beauford's lapels and pulled him close, crushing the lapel in his hand. Words were exchanged in a hushed tone and the other man shook Beauford.

William watched. *Do I go up there and stop whatever's going on? Why should I? What do I understand about his life, his world?* But his father looked like he needed help. William rushed up the stairs taking two at a time, head down, pretending not to see his father and then stopped just before bumping into them, acting surprised, not knowing what to say.

Beauford's eyes jolted wide open and then he smiled. He looked back at the other man.

The other man released Beauford's lapel and brushed it. "Little piece of lint." He nodded at William.

"This is my son, William. He's a FBI agent," Beauford said. "William, this is Mr. Falcone. He's the Deputy Commissioner of the Department of Transportation. A very important man in city government."

Falcone nodded again at William. "Beauford, I have a meeting I have to run to. I'll talk to you later about those budget figures. Nice to have met you, William." He went up the stairs and disappeared into the crowd on the main floor.

"What was that about?" William asked.

"What are you talking about?"

"I saw you put something in his pocket and he didn't look too pleased."

"Oh that…that was the proposed budget for his department. These department heads think they run their own little empires. Sometimes we got to break the news to them that it ain't so."

"It looked a little more intense than a disagreement over a budget."

"Don't read more into it than there is. You make a habit of that and you can cause a lot of trouble. Everything isn't a massive conspiracy like they probably taught you in your FBI school." He took a step up the stairs and turned. "And everything isn't the business of the FBI." Beauford trotted up the stairs and melded into the crowd of people milling about City Hall.

William shook his head. *The line of bullshit never ends.* He headed back to the office, wondering if he had received a message from his father. His eyes looked like they were reaching out to him for just one second. A look he hadn't seen since Mississippi. He wasn't sure how to read his father, or even sure if there was a message. He decided to head back to the office and finish the rest of his exciting assignment. William had a list of fifteen local Nazis from the literature they had received in their post office box over the last two months and the license plate checks. He headed over to the computer terminal to run the NCIC checks. "Maybe the new guy will juice things up around here. I've never spent so much time doing so little."

The results of William's searches were less than inspiring. A few arrests for petty theft, disorderly conduct, and a couple of outstanding warrants for traffic offenses. He reached forward to shut off the computer and hesitated. "What the hell. See if any of my forefathers had problems with the law." His fingers stumbled across the keyboard as he typed 'Tisdale, FNU' for first name unknown and hit the enter button. He slid back in his chair, crossed his legs and yawned as the computer digested his request.

The screen listed forty-three hits with outstanding warrants. The left-hand column listing names, last name first, the second column the date of the warrant, next the issuing agency, and then the charge.

His eyes casually ran down the list. *Something to do to kill the boredom.* He leaned back in the chair, folded his hands behind his head and read the first names, Abraham, Adam, Albert, Ali, Alphonse, Anthony, Bailey, Barney, Beauford, Bobby, Brock, Carlton..."

He blinked his eyes and slid his chair up to the monitor. He ran his finger across the screen. Tisdale, Beauford, warrant issued April 1, 1968, from Sunflower County Sheriff, Indianola, Mississippi, for murder and kidnapping.

"That son of a bitch." William sat back in the chair, exhaled and rubbed his temples with his forefinger and thumb. That's why he forced us to leave Mississippi. That's why he changed our name. He put us through all this because he killed someone.

His mind drifted back to that day eleven years ago when he saw his Grampa hung. His father dragging him through Blackhawk Bayou rushing to leave, refusing to answer his question, "Why do they want to kill you so bad?" Now he knew the answer. The Klan killed Grampa for something his father did. He wondered who his father killed. William now understood his father more than he ever had. He was a son of a bitch.

Daniels stepped into the room, "Well, anything interesting?"

276 | LEE WILLIAMS

William hit the off button on the monitor. "Ah…just finished. Just routine petty charges. I printed them out." He ripped the paper off the printer. "You want to take a look at them?"

"Yeah, thanks." Daniels grabbed the printout and perused down the list.

William sat there wondering. Does this qualify as something I have to tell Daniels about? The name Tisdale means nothing to anybody.

Daniels waved the printout in front of William's face. "Hello. Are you there?"

"Yeah. How's the wife?"

"The usual. 'Do you have to be working so much? The kids need to spend more time with you. My mother's coming to visit for two weeks. Can't we afford a bigger house?' You ought to get a wife. It's good for your personal growth."

William leaned forward and looked at the blank monitor. If he had been hiding from that murder warrant all these years, what would that do to him?

"What about the title search?" Daniels said.

William looked down at the floor. I've got to find out who he killed.

Daniels tapped his shoulder. "Hey, I asked you a question. The title search?"

"Oh, sorry, came back to Bavarian Agri, N.V. What's the N.V. stand for? Never heard of that."

"That's unusual. That's a Netherlands Antilles corporation. That's one of those offshore islands where people hide their money."

"Hmm." William folded his arms across his chest. *I've got to go to Mississippi.*

## CHAPTER TWENTY-THREE

### November 22, 1979

William pushed himself away from the dark cherry wood dining-room table after devouring two servings of his mother's Thanksgiving dinner. "Mom, you're the best. If they had a cook like you at Quantico no one would ever leave for a field office."

Nathleen folded her hands in her lap and smiled. The light from the six candle shaped bulbs on the chandelier flickered across Marlee's face. Nathleen looked at her. "How about you, Honey, did you enjoy your meal? I made the dressing just the way you like it."

Marlee lowered her head and shifted her brown eyes to her lap. "May I be excused? I have to call one of my girlfriends about a homework assignment."

"Sure, Honey. You study so hard."

Marlee's chair skidded back, she stood and padded upstairs to her room.

Nathleen's mouth closed in a narrow tight line. Her face deep in thought. "She wanted me to invite her father. The holidays are going to be so hard for her."

William could barely control himself. The veins in his neck stood out like cords. He wanted to rush up the stairs, grab Marlee's shoulders, shake her and blurt out, "You don't know him. He's a murderer and a kidnapper." But he sat there stewing, holding his breath.

He needed to get up, to do something to freeze the anger that was building. "I'll clean up the table and do the dishes. You stay here, relax, watch TV, and I'll come join you when I'm done."

She placed her hands on the arms of the wooden chair and pushed herself up. "I'll join you. We'll get the dishes done and then we can both relax for awhile."

He needed to be alone, to simmer down. "No, no, no. You've done enough. You relax. I'll take care of this."

"Oh, alright."

Thirty minutes later, William joined his mother in the living room of the bungalow. The sofa and chairs were covered in plastic and faced a console TV. An old movie played showing the Thanksgiving parade from the 1930s. He brought two cups of coffee, set them on the coffee table and sat on the sofa next to his mother. An uncomfortable silence filled the air for a few minutes.

"William, I need to know, for Marlee's sake, if your father's in trouble with the FBI?"

"Mom, the only thing I can say is that if he was, I really couldn't talk about it. So you can take that as a positive." He glanced at the floor, *not in trouble with us yet, but the State of Mississippi is another story.*

She sighed. "I feel like you're holding something back. I don't really care about your father, but if he is in trouble I need to know so I can break it to Marlee. I don't want the first time she hears about it to be on the TV or read it in the papers. That would crush her."

William exhaled. "Mom, I can't. There's disclosure laws that prohibit me from giving anyone information about a case. I could be fired." He leaned forward, placed his hands over hers. "Just trust me that if something comes up I'll handle it in the best way I can."

Nathleen closed her hands into tight fists. "How can I protect your sister? If you ever know anything, you have to tell me so I can tell her."

William could feel his anger building again, the blood creeping in his veins.

Nathleen lowered her head. "So there is something. Oh, my God. Poor Marlee."

His hands slid off his mother's and he straightened up. "I told you there isn't." He rose from the sofa. "I have to get up early tomorrow, going out of town. I better go."

Nathleen raised her head and swallowed. "Where're you going?"

He figured telling half a lie was better than lying completely. "I'm going to Mississippi on a case."

"Are you going alone? Is it dangerous?"

"No, it's just routine stuff. I'll be meeting up with an agent down there."

Nathleen stood and took a step toward the kitchen. "I'll give you the leftovers. You can save money instead of eating at restaurants."

"I'll be back the beginning of next week. The turkey will keep better in your fridge than on the road. I'll have some when I get back." William hugged his mother. "Thanks for dinner, Mom. I'll call you when I get back."

"Be careful, William."

William returned to his partially furnished one-bedroom apartment on the east side of the 15<sup>th</sup> ward. His underwear and socks were still stored in cardboard boxes. Three new suits, one gray and two blue, hung in the closet, with ties for each suit on its respective hanger. The kitchen cabinets had packages of paper plates and plastic silverware and six glasses. A mattress lay on the bedroom floor, next to it a lamp and a stack of books—Baldwin's *Go Tell it on the Mountain* and *Another Country*, Ellison's *Invisible Man*, and Alex Haley's *Malcolm X.*

He fell into the one piece of furniture he had had the time to buy since returning from Quantico, a recliner that faced the TV. He picked up the phone from the floor and called Daniels' direct line in the office to leave a message on his answering machine. He figured that Daniels would probably be off Friday to have a long holiday weekend with his wife and kids, so he wouldn't get the message until Monday. "Clar, its William. Some personal business came up and I have to leave town for a few days. I should be back Monday or Tuesday at the latest. Put me on leave, or if you have to, leave without pay. Happy Thanksgiving. Thanks."

He prepared for an early departure before settling down in bed, slipped his 9 mm Glock into his holster, slid his FBI credentials into the inside pocket of his black leather jacket, grabbed a flight bag and packed it with extra clothes, a box of ammo and tried to sleep.

The buzzing alarm clock jolted William awake and he silenced it, knocking it over. He swung his legs over the side of the mattress and dragged his fingers over his face. *Do I really need to know if my father is a murderer?* He pursed his lips and exhaled. *I do.* He left the dead alarm clock on its back, grabbed a quick shower, jumped into his clothes and was on the street before the sun pierced the horizon. A white vapor exited his nostrils in the chilly air and a vision captivated him—the haunting image of his grandfather's trembling body, a rope tight around his neck, hanging from an oak tree in the woods surrounding Blackhawk Bayou. He grew surly thinking about it.

He headed south in the two-year-old Camaro he had bought, trading in the Nova his father had gotten him. He hoped this trip would give him a sense of who his father was and what had happened to him. The events of the past few days wandered through William's mind. His conversations with his father had diminished to almost nothing over the last eleven years. Now a chance encounter seemed to open a door for him to his father's world. But, it was a door he was reluctant to step through. What if his father was a murderer, a kidnaper, had changed the family's name to avoid being caught, and had been on the run since they left Mississippi?

That contradicted the man he had known as a child. How could he have changed so much? His father would come home from a long day working the fields and his tired face would light up at the sight of his children. Evenings, his father and grandfather sat in rocking chairs on the front porch, William on a rickety stool between them and his baby sister cuddled in a blanket in his father's arms. His father told them how their heritage was to work the earth, how good their lives were, and that their wealth lay in the closeness of their family. Grandpa smoked a corncob pipe and nodded along with William's father's stories.

When they left Mississippi, the man abruptly abandoned his family, first emotionally and then physically. He developed this edge. He became distracted, moved into a dark mood from which he never escaped. William hoped that this trip held the possibility of revealing something that he had been totally unaware of, something that would help him understand his father's life. From deep in the recesses of his mind his strongest motivation surfaced. He was his father's son and he feared that his father's tormented soul was his inheritance. He hoped that if he could rescue his father, he could free himself of his bequest.

***

A few hours after dusk, William pulled onto a gravel lot off of Route 8 a few miles east of Ruleville. The red neon sign blinked "unflower Resort," the S dead to the night. The beams from his headlights flashed across seven small frame cottages, one of which doubled as an office. He entered.

From behind a worn curtain a clerk appeared. His skin was leathery, face cobwebbed with lines, hair short, scruffy and gray. He had a two-day-old stubble on his face and leaned into a glass counter containing two boxes of Hav-A Tampa Cigars, a couple of bags of Big Chip Potato Chips, ten packs of Lucky Strikes and a handful of Nestle's chocolate bars barely visible through the smudged top. "Whadda you want boy?" He said, a dark sediment covered his teeth.

"I need a room for two, maybe three nights."

"Okay, you gotta pay cash in advance. We don't appreciate you people bolting out before the bill is paid."

William bit his lower lip and nodded, *the good old south.* "How much?"

The clerk pulled a tin of Redman from the pocket of his flannel shirt. His finger nails were dirty and cracked. He chomped off a piece of chaw, let it linger in his cheek before he started chewing and sucking. The tobacco smacked between his tongue and missing teeth. "Seventy-five bucks for three nights." Brown juice dripped out of the side of his mouth.

William shifted from one leg to the other. "The sign out front says $20 a night. Shouldn't that be $60?"

The clerk lifted a paper cup off the counter and spit into it. "We don't need your business that bad."

William pulled $300 in cash in fives, tens and twenties out of his pants pocket. Counted out $75 and threw it on the counter.

The old man snatched the cash and pocketed it, reached behind him and grabbed a key off of a wood rack. "Take the cottage at the end." The key skidded across the counter top.

William grabbed it and drove his car to the far end of the parking lot. The sky was cloudy, the rising moon barely visible. He grasped his bag, walked to the door, looked over both shoulders, unlocked it, and stepped into the one-room cabin. He hit the wall switch, turning on a lamp on the nightstand, locked the deadbolt and slid the chain in the door.

A musty smell filled the room, as if the windows had been closed for some time. A queen-sized bed with a swayed mattress was backed against the wall in the middle of the room. Facing the bed was a 13" black-and-white TV secured in a stand bolted to the floor. A teetering wooden chair was next to the nightstand and green carpeting worn to the backing in spots covered the floor. A door with peeling white paint led to the bathroom.

William opened the window a crack to let the fresh air in. He stripped down to his boxer shorts, slid his Glock under the pillow, and lay down. He spent the night tossing and turning in a fitful sleep, wondering what the next few days would hold for him and his father.

\*\*\*

The clerk watched William heading back to his car. "Boy gonna be nothing but trouble. Some spook dressed to the gills. Probably a local boy that went north, made a ton of money selling dope, and came back to flaunt it."

He saddled up to the phone, picked it up and dialed. "This is Clarkson at the Sunflower Resort. Tell the sheriff I got a young black boy that just checked in. All dressed in a leather coat, driving some fancy sports car. He looks like trouble to me. Paid cash in advance for three days."

\*\*\*

At 9:30 Saturday morning, Beauford's phone rang. He leaned across the bed and picked up the receiver. "Hello," he said in a raspy voice.

"Mr. Alderman, Mr. Falcone here to see you," Jones, the doorman, said.

Beauford heard the phone tussled away from Jones.

"Tell the doorman to buzz me up," Falcone ordered, "then we'll go for a walk."

There was a pause. "It okay, Mr. Alderman?"

"Yeah, let him up." Beauford hung up the phone, slid out of bed, and stepped into his pants. There was a loud knock on the door. "Be right there." He pulled on a sweater, slipped into his Ferragamos, lumbered to the foyer and opened the door.

Falcone barged in, his long black trench coat flowing behind him, pushed Beauford back, and slammed the door. "Don't say nothin'!" He spun Beauford around, crashed him against the wall and jammed one hand against the back of his neck. He kicked at Beauford's feet, "Spread'em!" With his other hand he patted him down, first his arms, then chest, and back, around his waist, and down his legs. "Get a jacket."

Beauford pointed to the camel hair overcoat lying on the sofa.

Falcone picked it up, checked the pockets, and squeezed his fingers down the coat, feeling for anything that felt like a tape recorder. He tossed the coat to Beauford. "Let's go for a walk." He opened the door and shoved Beauford out. "Don't talk till we get to Oak Street beach. I like the sound of the wind and waves."

Falcone locked his hand onto Beauford's elbow and they headed west on Delaware past the Drake Hotel, turned north on Michigan, navigating into the foot traffic heading to appointments or expensive shopping at stores on the Magnificent Mile. Falcone pushed him across Oak Street. They stopped on the cement walk at the beach. The sun tried cracking through the pewter sky. Whitecaps crashed into the beach and the wind bristled through Falcone's graying pompadour.

Falcone released Beauford's elbow and jabbed both hands into the alderman's chest, turning him so he peered into his eyes. "So what was that? Your fucking FBI son being there, coincidence or what?"

"I didn't know he was in the building. Just happened that way."

"I hope that's the truth. Because if you think him being a FBI agent makes any difference to anybody you got another thing coming. It's just going to be harder on you. Now everybody's got a reason not to trust you. But that's another matter. What the fuck happened to my money? You were good for a couple of months and now you're late again and holding back on me again. That envelope only had four G's. Shoulda been eight, asshole?"

Beauford put out his hands, palms up. "I was going to tell you, but then William came by."

"Tell me what?"

"I fucked up."

Falcone took a deep breath. "What the fuck did you do now?"

"I went to Hawthorne, played the ponies. I was hot, could do no wrong. I bet a grand to win the first race and won $2500. So I upped my bets. Won again. Put it on the daily double and trifecta. Turned cold. Cold as ice. I gave you all I had left, except a grand."

Falcone jammed his hands into the pockets of his coat and shook his head in disbelief. "You stupid son of a bitch." Spit flew from his mouth.

Beauford took a step back and wiped the spit off his cheek. His eyes broke away from Falcone's face and he focused on his thoughts, *Should of never held that money for Alderman Heidler. Gotta get out of this mess. Feel more alone than I ever did.*

"You come to my office tomorrow with the thousand you got. From now on you bring everything Ippolito gives you to me 'til you make up the four g's and two more for vig. Then you'll start getting your cut again." Falcone stepped back from Beauford. "And don't play any fucking games like talking to your boy about this stuff." He turned, kicked at a paper cup blowing by, and walked away.

\*\*\*

That same Saturday morning William awoke and sat on the edge of the bed. He rubbed the fog from his eyes, padded barefoot to the window, pushed it up, and gazed through the patched screen. Before him lay a green field of winter wheat. The sun shone brightly through a powder-blue sky. Memories of his boyhood in Mississippi flashed through his mind. His mother standing over a wood-burning stove, pouring a flapjack mix onto a skillet, bacon sizzling in a frying pan, and his father sitting at the kitchen table sipping steaming coffee. William could almost hear his mother. "Good morning, son. Go get Marlee and bring her in for breakfast. It's almost ready." His daydream faded and the harsh reality of why he was there came to mind. He had to find out if his father was a murderer.

He plodded into the bathroom and gazed into the scratched mirror, looking at his tired face. He was having second thoughts about this trip. If the truth turned out to be the worst possible scenario, what would he do then? He turned on the faucet, leaned over, and splashed water on his face. *What the hell, I'm here, I've got to give it at least one day and see if I come up with anything.* He stepped into the shower.

The water gushing out of the nozzle was cold, smelly well water. He refused to use the unwrapped bar of soap in the dish. William jumped out of the shower, pulled a frayed white towel hanging from a rod on the side of the sink and dried himself. He shaved, put on blue jeans, a black print shirt, slipped his Glock into a clip-on holster, and slid the holster inside the waistline of his jeans. William flung on his jacket, filled an extra magazine with ammo, put it in his pocket, slipped his credentials in the inside coat pocket and headed to his car.

He sped out of the parking lot toward Ruleville. He was 200 yards down Route 8 when a black four-door Ford Crown Vic pulled out from behind the motel office and followed him into town. William parked in front of Rolly's Diner in Ruleville's town square. Lush green Bermuda grass dressed the grounds. The Confederate flag waved from a flagpole surrounded by park benches shaded by tall oaks.

The diner was between the bank and the general store. Most of the customers that filled the counter seats and half of the booths were Rolly's regular morning white crowd, a few dressed in white shirts and ties who stopped in before going to their jobs at the bank or insurance company and others in open shirts, slacks or bib overalls. The aroma of fried eggs and sizzling bacon filled the air.

William picked up a copy of the *Enterprise Tocsin* newspaper from a stack of papers lying under a brick near the front door, tossed a quarter down on the stack, and entered the diner. On the left side was a long counter that faced the grill. An aisle separated the stools from six red booths that were flush against the wall on the right side. His eyes paused on the Confederate flag hung on the back wall.

He strolled past the counter and heard conversations about politics, soybean prices, and bass fishing boats. He sat down in a booth and paged through the newspaper, waiting for service. The cacophony fell silent. He looked up from the newspaper to see customers eyeing him. A waitress a few booths away glowered at him and looked away. "Could I have a cup of coffee and a menu?" He looked back into the paper.

William heard a car door slam and glanced up from the paper. He noticed the patrons turn toward the door watching the tall man with mirrored sunglasses in the freshly pressed uniform. He saw the deputy's head turn toward him. The man's shiny boots clicked on the tile floor as he walked to William's booth and slid into the seat across from him.

William folded the paper, eased it down and saw his reflection in the sunglasses of the lean black man. "Good morning," he glanced at the nameplate above the shirt pocket, "Deputy Jackson."

Jackson leaned forward and whispered in a deep voice. "You happen to notice that we're the only two black folk in here?"

"So?" William shrugged.

"I don't know where you from, boy. This might be 1979, but it's still the south. There might not be a sign that says 'Whites only' but if you want to get along while you're in this town you'd better watch where you eat and where you stay. Come with me." Jackson stood and strolled to the door.

William grabbed the paper and left the booth. The patrons turned from their meals and fixed their eyes on the two black men. William nodded to the customers and smiled.

Jackson opened the door and he and William exited. As the door closed he heard the silence in the diner turned into a buzz of conversations about the two men that who just left. Jackson ambled to the Camaro and leaned against the fender. William rested his elbow on the roof of his car. Jackson towered over him. "So what brings you here?"

"Some family business."

"You got family here?"

"Not now. Used to live here. Doing a little family history."

"You got ID?"

He thought about showing him his FBI credentials and decided against it. *He's black, but that doesn't mean I can trust him.* He pulled out his wallet and handed Jackson his driver's license.

"Richmond, William Richmond. I don't remember a Richmond family. What part of town did your folks live in?"

"Around Poverty Road by Blackhawk Bayou. My family had some land there a while ago."

"All right. From now on when you lookin' for a place to eat stay on the south side of town. You won't cause no ruckus down there." He reached in his shirt pocket removed his card. "You got any questions call me. Here's the office number. I figure I need to know how long I gotta be looking out for you. When you leaving?"

"Wednesday morning at the latest."

Jackson cocked his head. "Try to stay out of trouble." He stood up and tipped the brim of his hat. His long legs carried him across the street in a few strides.

William headed to the south side and had breakfast at a little shanty off the highway. It was fronted by a patched asphalt parking lot veined with green weeds, sided by a vacant store, and its customers were all black. After eating he drove south twenty miles to the office of the *Enterprise Tocsin* in Indianola.

The newspaper's office was located on Main Street among a block of brick-and-frame buildings bordered by the courthouse on the east end and the Indianola State Bank on the west. The courthouse was old and noble looking. A portico supported by six tall white columns fronted the entrance and the building and grounds were kept neat and trim by six black men wearing orange jumpsuits with the letters DOC stenciled across their backs.

William approached the newspaper's storefront office, a brown frame with green double doors separating matching windows. Two short columns supported an overhang and between the columns was a wooden sign scribed in black letters with the words *The Enterprise Tocsin.* He entered and walked to the counter that covered the width of the office. Behind the counter were two rows of three desks. On a Saturday morning only one desk was occupied.

A heavyset black woman, mid thirties, sat there, talking on the phone while admiring her long red fake fingernails. She cradled the phone, shimmied up to the counter, and rested her butt on a stool. Her dark-eyes moved up and down William. "Hmm, Honey, what can I do for you?"

He gave her his billboard smile. "I need to look through some of your old newspapers."

"No problem, like last week, last month, last year?"

William leaned forward and rested his elbows on the counter. "April 1968."

Her eyes blinked. "Lordy, Lordy. 1968! Ain't nobody ever asked for anything that old. Let me see what we got." The stool creaked as she stood and waddled back to an old white man sitting at a desk deep in the back corner of the office.

The man wore a well-starched white shirt and a blue-striped bow tie. She leaned toward his ear and spoke loudly. "That young man up there wants papers going back to April '68. We got 'em going back that far?"

He nodded, took off his wire rim glasses, wiped the lenses with a handkerchief from his pants pocket, and slipped the glasses back on his pencil-thin nose. He stood, skinny as a rail, spine badly curved, and shuffled to the counter. His beady eyes strained through the Coke-bottle glasses. "What dates in April?"

"I don't know exactly. I guess I should start at the beginning of April."

His eyes looked up to the ceiling. "The paper's a weekly, I believe that would have been the fourth. All right, follow me." He turned and his brown wingtips scuffled along the wood floor toward a back room. William walked through a gate in the middle of the front counter and followed him. "The old papers are bound together, six months in a book. You'll have to lift them off the shelves. Too damn heavy for me."

"No problem. How long have you been with the paper?"

"I don't know, a lifetime, maybe two. What do you want with these papers anyway? You were just a little boy back then." The old man entered the back room, which doubled as a storage and break area. The stale aroma of burnt coffee, office supplies, and dusty old newspapers filled the room.

"I'm doing research on my family, Mister...."

"Harling, L. C. Harling. Help yourself to some coffee if you'd like," he said, pointing at a percolator sitting on a card table. His hand was covered with liver spots. "The papers you're looking for are on those shelves behind the supplies. I wish I could tell you they were in some kind of order, but that would be a lie. You can use that step stool and bring the books down to the card table."

"Thanks, Mr. Harling."

Harling put his hand up to his ear. "I'm sorry, you say something?"

William spoke up. "Thanks, Mr. Harling."

Harling nodded and left the room. William moved the step stool next to the metal shelves and climbed up. Behind boxes of pens, pencils, adding machine tapes, steno pads and other office supplies he saw large binders bound in gray cloth the size of the newspaper, coated in dust, piled helter-skelter on top of each other. He moved the supplies to the side and started pulling out the books. They were in no chronological order. After removing several volumes and shoving others to the side he saw two volumes lying next to each other marked 1968 volume I and II. He grabbed them both, stepped down to the floor, and carried them to the card table.

William stepped back and looked at the dust covering his leather coat and jeans. He brushed it off, removed his jacket, pulled his shirt out to cover his pistol, and sat down at the table.

He opened volume I, paged to the first issue for April. The headline jumped at him, "Local Man's Wife Killed," and underneath in smaller type, "Daughter Kidnapped." He read the entire article.

> Beauford Tisdale, a black man, attacked and killed Linda Joy Napier and kidnapped her seventeen-year-old daughter Celeste at approximately 1:30 Tuesday morning at the Napier residence 10 miles north of Ruleville. James Napier, husband of the deceased and father of Celeste, attempted to fight off Tisdale but was knocked unconscious. Napier was not aware of any reason for Tisdale's attack. Tisdale has not been found and should be considered armed and dangerous....

William stared off to a place he couldn't see. His throat tightened and his stomach roiled. Having a name put next to the murder charge made it real. It took something out of him that he felt would never come back. He remembered when he found his grandfather. He leaned back in the chair, shook his head, and pictured that day in his mind's eye. *The man at the blue pickup truck saying, "He's going looking for old man Tisdale's son. He's next." Seeing his grandfather lynched. His father finding him, dragging him through the bayou back to their truck. That question his father wouldn't answer. "Why do they hate you enough to want to kill you, Daddy?"* Now he had an answer. His father was a murderer.

William read the story again and closed the binder. He sighed, slid down in the chair, and lowered his chin to his chest. Why did his father kill her? Was it in a fit of passion? Was he stealing something from her? Something besides her life? And what about the daughter, why would he kidnap her? Was she still alive or did he kill her too?

He wondered what he should do now. Go back to Chicago and tell his father he knew about the murder? Turn in his father? Could he reconcile his loyalty as a son against his obligations? He had to make a choice. He didn't know if it would haunt him—or set him free.

William sat up in the chair. His forehead wrinkled. Something didn't make sense. He was sure he found Grandpa's body on Sunday after coming home from church services. If the Napier woman was killed early Tuesday morning following that Sunday then the reason anyone would have for killing his father would have nothing to do with the Napier woman. Why would his father kill her? It couldn't be for revenge. Surely that Napier woman didn't kill Grandpa.

A knock on the door frame startled William. "Finding what you were looking for?" Harling asked.

"Yes. Yes, thank you, Mr. Harling." William pondered for a moment and then asked, "Sir, do you recall the murder of Linda Joy Napier from Ruleville back in '68?"

Harling brought his pipe to his mouth, flicked his lighter, and sucked on the pipe. Smoke lifted to the ceiling and the aroma of the sweet tobacco filled the room. "Strange things happened back then. If I recall correctly they never found the fellow that was suppose to be the killer. Never found Napier's daughter either. Some say they ran off together. Some say he killed her, too."

"Nobody knows what happened to the daughter?"

"Not that I know of. You could check with the sheriff. Maybe they got some leads they never went public with. But there aren't too many secrets in a small southern town. Why are you so interested in the murder? I thought you were doing a family tree." He puffed on the pipe.

"Ah, no reason. Headlines caught my eye." William heard the evasive words exit his mouth, watched the smoke from Harling's pipe twist toward the ceiling and disappeared into the air.

"If I recall correctly that Napier family had a streak of real bad luck. Couple of months after the wife was killed, the husband was shot by the FBI."

"What? When did that happen?"

Harling moved toward William and paged through the newspapers. He stopped at the front page of the April eleventh issue. "King Murdered." He took his pipe from his mouth. "Those were bad times." He continued paging through the papers, through May and into June and stopping at the issue for June thirteenth. The headline read, "Ray Arrested in England." "Ah, here it is."

Harling pointed to a story on the bottom of the page. "Local Man Killed by FBI."

"Thanks, Mr. Harling." William pulled the binder off the table, resting it on his lap, his way of letting the old man know he wanted some privacy.

"I guess I'll go back to my desk. Let me know if you have any more questions."

William's concentration was buried in the newspaper. "I'll be a son of a...." He continued reading.

> Ruleville native James Napier was shot and killed by an FBI agent while Napier was allegedly attempting to firebomb The Macedonia Baptist Church of God late Sunday night. Napier is survived by his seven-year-old son, James Junior....

William shook his head. "This is too much. My father killed the wife and kidnapped the daughter and an agent killed the husband. He got copies of the articles and mumbled as he left the newspaper's office, asking himself, "Where do I go from here?"

## CHAPTER TWENTY-FOUR

"Sunflower County Sheriff's office. Can I help you?" A woman with a piercing voice answered the phone.

"Is there someway I can get in touch with Deputy Jackson?" William asked.

"I just saw him a minute ago. Hang on." She shouted, "Darius, if you're in here you got a call."

Jackson walked into the radio room. "You call me?"

She handed the phone to him. "Deputy Jackson."

"Deputy, this is William Richmond. Remember, we met at Rollys this morning."

"Sure, I remember."

"Can I buy you lunch?"

"It's only been a couple of hours since I left you. You in trouble all ready?"

"No." William laughed. "I'm not in any trouble, just want to bounce a couple of things off of you."

"Where are you?"

"Maude's."

"The best barbecue pork in Ruleville. That's worth a couple of bounces. I'll be there in ten minutes."

William sat at a table next to the window, alternating staring at the menu and then at the parking lot waiting for Jackson. He wondered if the deputy could shed any light on the newspaper articles about his father. He watched Jackson parked his Crown Vic and enter the restaurant. It bustled with the activity of the lunchtime crowd. Waitresses scurrying about carried platters of ribs to their customers. The patrons' incessant chatter included what water hole the crappies were hitting in, whose kid got busted, and which white farmer was hiring help for the soybean harvest. A rotund woman with a face the color of milk chocolate came out of the kitchen wearing a blue bandanna do-rag and a large white apron covered with sauce stains. "Deputy Darius, I haven't seen you in a month of Tuesdays." She gave him a hug. "What finally bring you around?"

Jackson pointed at William sitting at a table for two near the front window.

"Oh, the quiet one," she said.

"Maude, can you bring us two of your pork specials and a pitcher of sweet tea?"

"Sure enough."

Jackson strolled from the front door and sat at William's table. "So what's going on?"

"I've got a situation I'm checking on from 1968. I was wondering if you might know anything about it?"

"Well two things. First, I'm from Greenville, didn't get here 'til 70. So I don't know much about what happened before that. Second, why should I? I do some snooping around for you just gonna get me in trouble. I got to live here long after you be gone."

William tapped his fork on the table. "What if it was official business?"

Jackson looked into William's eyes. "You a cop or something?"

William leaned forward. "FBI."

Jackson's eyes bulged. "Well I'll be. We finally made it to the big time."

"I'd like to keep that between the two of us."

Maude sauntered up to the table carrying a massive round tray. She slid two plates of barbecue pork, collards and okra in front of them. The rich spicy meaty aroma of the sauce filled the air. Next came a basket of hot rolls, a tub of butter, a pitcher of sweet tea, and two glasses brimming with ice, beads of moisture dripping down the sides. She smiled, waiting for a sign of recognition.

Jackson slid his arm around her sizable waist. "Thank you, honey. This is an acquaintance of mine from Chicago. William, this is Maude. Makes the best Q in Sunflower County."

William nodded. "Nice to meet you."

Maude curtsied and moseyed back to the kitchen.

Jackson dipped his fork into the pork and took a mouthful. "Hmm, I'm glad you called. I missed this place."

"Looks like they missed you." William said. "About 1968. Think you can help me?" He cut the edge of his fork into the tender meat.

Jackson whispered, "So what happened back in '68 that's got the attention of the FBI?"

William wanted to tell him the whole story, anyway the story as he speculated it was. But he found himself becoming a man of secrets, felt his father's traits churning in his soul. William hoped the awakening of these traits wasn't the hidden cost of discovering who his father really was. So, he only told Jackson enough bits and pieces so he could get what he wanted. "In April there was a murder of a woman, Linda Joy Napier, and in June her husband, while attempting to fire bomb a church, was killed by an FBI agent. I'd like you to get me copies of all the reports related to those two incidents. If there's any related incidents I'd also like copies of those reports."

Jackson wiped his chin with a napkin. "You know, this ain't no place where they do big time investigations. You'll be lucky to get a page on each situation."

"Whatever you can get me would help and I'd appreciate if you can keep this under your hat?"

"I'll try, but if somebody finds out I'm digging in ten-year-old files it'll get attention."

"See what you can do. One more thing, the Napier's daughter, Celeste, was kidnapped. See if there's any information about where she might be. I can only be here a few more days so I need this stuff as soon as possible. Can I call you later tonight?"

Jackson dropped his fork to his plate. "I thought I was just helping a brother. Didn't know I was getting involved in a federal investigation. I'll have to wait 'til the shift change. Call me around six. Won't be so many people around that might get nosy."

William smiled. A federal investigation? Not really, at least not yet. "I'll call you then." They finished their meal and went their separate ways.

William sat in his car listening to the hum of the motor. A sight came to him, his grandfather sitting in his rocking chair in the backyard of the house. He would climb onto the gentle man's lap and share his ice-cold lemonade. He felt safe and secure. They would say little but he was content. William's heart filled with warmth, his body relaxed, his breathing slowed. He decided to go see the old house.

Heading north past the Town Square and Rolly's to Route 8 and west out of Ruleville, William then turned onto Long Road. The closer he got to The Drew Ruleville Bridge the greater the weight William felt on his chest, the shallower and quicker his breathing became.

The bridge came into view. His throat constricted, stomach boiled, and beads of perspiration rose on his forehead. He drove onto the bridge. The wooden slats beneath the tires clapped. William's mind flashed down to the bayou. Eleven years ago from this spot in the bayou he heard the voices of men. He climbed out of the water and found his grandfather lynched by two white men. William looked at his hand on the steering wheel. It was trembling just like he did eleven years ago. He pushed down on the accelerator, the Camaro screamed off the bridge, dirt and gravel spit from the tires.

He turned onto Turner Road and the dogwoods and redbuds that were there eleven years ago were gone. Paralleling the road was a barbed-wire fence that locked in acres of sandy colored soybeans as far as the eye could see. William headed north a couple of miles intending to take Poverty Road to the dirt road that would lead to his family's old house. All he found left of Poverty Road was five feet of gravel that ended at a barbed wire fence. William pulled his car onto the remnants of Poverty Road. He opened the door, stood on the floorboard, and saw three combines on the horizon. The hum of the huge red monsters' grew louder as they neared. The machines slowly moved down the crop rows, giant teeth separating the plants, cutting them near the base, and then separating the plant from the bean. The plants went through the thresher and the resulting straw was spit out of the spreader onto the ground. From the top of the combine beans flew from the unloading tube into grain carts that followed. He watched the drivers. They were black men, and the men walking near the grain carts were black. A sense of justice came to him. At least his people were working the land that was once his father's.

He waved at the farmers, stepped off the floorboard, and walked around his car. A young light-skinned man in dusty overalls hopped off a grain cart and walked toward William.

"You must be lost, mista. What you doing back here?"

William leaned against a fence post. "My family used to own a piece of this land."

"Your family used to own land?" He pushed up the lid of his straw hat. "Why'd you ever leave?"

He felt ashamed he couldn't tell him what he hoped. "Because of the Klan. They killed my grandfather and framed my father on a murder charge. We had to run or my father would've spent his last days in Parchment waiting for the gas chamber." Instead he came up with, "Oh, my father wanted to head up north to the Promised Land for a job. We couldn't get by on ten acres. How long have you had the land?"

The man pulled a red bandanna from his overalls and wiped the sweat from his brow. "You dreaming if you think we own this land. Some company owns it. We just hired help."

"I thought that since you were working the fields that—"

"Na, ain't the case. Most land around here still owned by white folk and their company." He stuffed the bandanna in the pocket of his overalls.

William shook his head. "What company?"

"Don't remember exactly, some name that ain't too familiar."

William realized the land that had been his family's for one hundred years had been lost. He wondered if the land had been swindled from his father. His gut twitched with anger. Some son of a bitch had screwed his family.

He turned his back on the farmer, got in the Camaro and squealed into a U-turn on Turner Road, heading back to the county seat, back to Indianola. He had enough time to trace the ownership of his family's property and return to Ruleville by six to call Jackson.

\*\*\*

Junior leaned against the wall in the reception area of Lincoln Cottage. He picked up the telephone to make his one allowed monthly call. He read the sign on the wall as the phone rang several times. <u>Your phone call may be monitored and or recorded</u>.

"Hello," she answered in a winded voice.

"This is a collect call from the Illinois Youth Center. Do you accept the charges?" the operator said.

"Yes! Yes I do." Patty said.

"Hi, it's me."

"I was just coming home from the factory, heard the phone ringing, and ran up the stairs. I thought it might be you, didn't want to miss your call."

"Guess what?"

"You got your release date?"

"Tomorrow...Why are you crying? You should be happy."

She wiped the stained gray sleeve of her sweatshirt across her nose and sniffled. "I'm happy. I missed you. I haven't seen you since March. I can't believe you'll be home in a day. I want to pick you up when you get out."

"No. I told you I don't want you to see this...this place I have to live in...with all these...you know. Besides I already got a friend picking me up. He's the father of a couple of guys that were released earlier. Good guys, you know what I mean."

"Will you come straight home?"

"Just wait for me. I might spend a couple of hours with this guy. Then I'll come home and we'll celebrate. It'll be just like the old days. You and me and Bruno. Goin' out for beers."

There was silence on the phone. "Bruno don't live here no more."

"What? Since when?"

"Since a couple of weeks ago."

"He finally get an old lady of his own?" Junior heard Patty's breathing speed up.

"No."

"Don't tell me he got busted. I'm finally getting out and he's in the slammer. Shit!"

"No, Junior." There was a pause. He had to strain to hear her. "He attacked me."

There was nervous quiet. Junior said. "I don't believe—"

"What do you mean you don't believe it," she interrupted. "You think I let him?" You blaming me? You weren't here asshole. You don't know what happened. You're no better than he is."

He could feel the energy of her fury. "Just settle down. When I get out we can talk about this and get everything fixed up. He just touch you? I mean he didn't?"

"He raped me! He fucked me! You understand that? You think we can patch that up?" The connection broke.

Junior's face turned red and his temples throbbed. But he couldn't risk an outburst. It could set back his release for weeks or get him transferred to an adult institution. Junior eased the phone down on the cradle, closed his eyes, and muttered, "Motherfucker. One more asshole to add to the list."

***

By mid-afternoon William found himself back on Main Street in Indianola. He parked in front of the red brick courthouse. He entered through the glass double doors. The chancery clerk's office, which maintained the real estate records, was to his right. William entered the rectangular shaped office. On the walls were old photographs of the town and the county fathers. Six fluorescent light fixtures hung from the ceiling casting a soft glow. Two rows of three long counters held plat books and section books, which contained hand written entries of the real estate transactions in Sunflower County.

Behind a desk in the far corner snoozed a heavyset man in his thirties. He was leaning back in his chair, dusty boots resting on top of a wooden desk. The top of his head bald and shiny, brown unruly hair grew over his ears, and his jowls vibrated with each snore.

William approached him, "Excuse me." Then in a louder voice, "Excuse me."

The man shook his flabby cheeks and swung his boots off the desk and onto the floor with a bang. "What?" He wiped his hands across his bleary eyes. "Something happen?"

"I'd like to check some land records," William looked at his nametag on the Levi shirt, "Mr. Lundy."

"You can't startle a man like that if it ain't something important. About to give me a heart attack." Lundy scratched his hairy belly that protruded from the opening where a button was missing from his shirt.

"You're too well rested to get a heart attack. Can you show me where to check on property around Ruleville?"

Lundy stood up and stretched his hands over his head and yawned. "Yeah, sure. All these books contain the grantor/grantee index for the county. Most of the property records go back before the War Between the States. Where around Ruleville is the property located?"

"Northwest of town a couple of miles, near Blackhawk Bayou."

"Follow me." He waddled to the center counter in the back row and bent down, examining the township numbers on the spines of the plat books on the shelves below the counter tops. Lundy grabbed one with two hands, it was three times the size of a city telephone book in width, length, and depth, rested it against his belly as he pulled it from a lower shelf, turned and let it fall with a slam onto a table.

He grasped the red cloth cover, opened the book and looked at the map on the inside. "This looks like it'll cover the area you talking about. If you don't know the property number you'll have to go to the pages that list the township you think the property's in. Then check those white books, the section books over there, for the list of the grantors and grantees for the name of the owner or buyer you're looking for. The next three columns give you the date, nature of the transaction, and document number. Simple enough." He nodded his head. "I'll be at my desk if you have any questions."

William watched as Lundy ambled back to his desk, sat down, parked his boots on top of it, and closed his eyes. His fingers traced the map on the inside cover. "Township twenty-two, section four or five, north range four west. Looks like the old house should be in that area."

He paged through the section book, turning over dulled yellow pages until he found the section for township twenty-two. Washed out blue-black ink faded into the thick paper. The handwriting was from another century. Styled almost in calligraphy. William ran his finger down the grantee column. Entries from the late 1860s bore names that kindled his memory, Beverly, Cannon, Rule, and Tisdale. He continued down the same column for several pages and time unraveled into the next century. The land was passed from father to son, generation after generation until April 11, 1968. On that date each plot was conveyed to C. Virden and two weeks later to Bavarian Agri, N.V.

The name filtered through William's mind. Then it hit. That was the same corporation that owned the Nazi headquarters in Chicago. He looked at Lundy. "Excuse me. Excuse me."

Lundy turned his head in William's direction. "What do you want now?"

"How do I get addresses for the people that purchased these properties?"

"Jot down the document numbers and I'll look 'em up on the microfiche for you." He dropped his feet to the floor and muttered, "I might as well, ain't gonna get no peace 'til you leave."

William wrote down the numbers and gave them to him. Lundy disappeared into a back room, returned a few minutes later, and handed him the addresses. "Here, Virden lives in Greenville and the only thing on this company came back to a bunch of lawyers in Jackson. Anything else you want or are you going now?"

"No, I'm going. Thanks. Thanks a lot." *Won't get anything from lawyers. I'll pay Virden a visit.*

# CHAPTER TWENTY-FIVE

## Saturday, November 24, 1979

Junior stood on the Illinois Youth Center's asphalt parking lot waiting for his ride. Next to him was a cardboard box containing most of his worldly possessions. He hardly noticed the crisp late November sun. His psyche was torn between his sense of relief that he was out of that place and the vibrating anger that had built up within him. He had had to eat with them, sleep with them, and breathe the same air. He felt like he needed a squeegee to scrape off their scent. His only solace was to seek revenge against those that had put him there and to honor the promise he had made to his father. That time was rapidly approaching.

A black Buick Electra 225 pulled into the parking lot and gracefully came to a stop at his side. An electric motor hummed and the passenger window glided down. "Hop in, son," Kurt Soder said.

Junior looked through the open window at the glistening black leather upholstery. It would be the first time in months he would be sitting on something other than steel or plastic. He opened the door, got in the car, and settled into the soft leather.

Soder smiled. "Welcome back to the free world." He took a pack of Lucky Strikes out of his shirt pocket, flicked his wrist, and a cigarette jutted out a half-inch from the pack.

Junior slid the smoke between his lips and pushed in the lighter in the dash. Ten silent seconds later the lighter popped out, he put it to the cigarette, and drew on it. He felt his head spin as the nicotine filled his lungs.

Soder grabbed the back of Junior's neck and shook him, "You're out boy, scream, yell, give 'em the finger, celebrate."

"Let's get the fuck out of here." He pulled himself up and sat on the passenger door, looking across the roof of the Buick as it pulled out of the parking lot onto Route 38, "Fuck you, assholes." He raised his middle finger as they passed the guard in front of the entrance. Junior dropped back inside the car, kicked off his shoes, slouched down and rested his feet on the dash. "You were right, had to get that out of my system. Felt good." He laughed

Soder laughed with him, "Where to now boy. You want to get laid. I know a place we can go to—"

"Nah, my old lady will take care of me when I get home." He interlaced his fingers behind his head and stretched back, hoping Patty wouldn't be so pissed off since Bruno raped her that she wouldn't let him near her. It wasn't his fault what happened and he was going to right the wrong. "I got some business to take care of, some promises I made to my old man…and to me."

"Sure I know what you mean. I got you a coming out present." Soder pushed a narrow black box across the seat toward Junior.

He sat up, grabbed it, and threw off the lid. "This for me?" He couldn't recall the last time someone had given him a gift. Junior admired the blade. An ivory pommel sat on top of a black enamel handle. Inset in the pommel was a silver badge. The badge depicted a German helmet superimposed over a swastika and below the helmet the letters 'N.S.S.F.B.St.' were engraved. Underneath the nickel plated cross guard of the dagger was a stainless steel double-edged blade. The sun glistened off the edges of the blade. "What do the letters stand for?"

"National Socialist German Organization of the Stahlhelm. That dagger, the Germans called it a Nahkampfmesser, it was made in the 1920's. The Stahlhelm was a pro-Nazi semi-official police force. That's why I gave it to you. I see you as a policeman for us, Junior. Someone willing to not only define our vision of the American way of life, but someone also willing to enforce that vision."

Junior lifted the dagger out of the box and touched the point of the blade against the tip of his index finger. Three drops of blood oozed from his finger onto the edge of the blade. He watched the fluid drip down the cold steel. He turned the dagger so the red liquid floated across the spine of the blade and turned it again watching the blood drift back to the other side making a Z pattern. All the time thinking about whose flesh this dagger would penetrate. Those on his list and probably a few others whose names he didn't know yet. "Yeah, policeman for the Nazis. I like that."

"Got one more thing for you." Soder handed him a leather sheath with two straps running across it. "It's a wrist sheath, strap it on your forearm, and you carry the dagger under your sleeve. You come up on the asshole from behind, cover his mouth with your left hand, and in your right hand you got the dagger. Jerk their face to the left and jab the blade into the jugular. In twelve seconds the shit's dead. Dead quiet and you feel their death in your hands as their body goes limp. It's not cold and impersonal like shooting someone. It has a certain dignity to it."

"Yeah, but some people don't deserve dignity."

Soder nodded, "That's true, very true." He pulled a paper bag out from under his seat. "If you have someone in mind that doesn't deserve dignity you might try this."

Junior placed the dagger back in its box and reached into the bag and pulled out a Colt 9 mm semi automatic.

"It's an expensive piece. Serial numbers have been removed. It's clean and ready to roll."

He cradled the pistol in his hands, stroking the barrel with his thumb. It was like his dreams had come true. "I have a lot of things that I need to do. One of them deserves dignity. The others don't matter." He stashed the pistol in his waistband and pulled out his light blue shirt covering the pistol. Junior rolled up his left sleeve, fastened the sheath to his forearm, and slid in the dagger. He looked at Soder as he pulled down his sleeve, "Finally, after all this time, I'm out and I have everything I need."

\*\*\*

Junior spent the day with Soder's sons drinking beer in the back of the Soder's gas station on Kedzie near Marquette Park. Frank sat on a chair behind a small wooden desk and Earl on the corner of the desk. Junior sat on a cot pushed against the wall. He held a can of beer in one hand and the other hand petted a German Shepard puppy curled up between his legs. He drained his beer and threw the empty toward a waste paper basket besides the desk. It clanged off the crushed cans that overflowed the top and bounced across the floor. "Alright, I've had enough of you guys. Take me to see my broad. She should have been home from the factory a couple of hours ago." He grabbed his crotch and laughed.

Frank drove, Earl sat in the front passenger seat, and Junior sat in the back sipping on a beer. They rode through the city to the attic apartment on the eastside of Cicero. Ink blue clouds covered the moon and stars. The street lights shone down on the Buick as it pulled to the curb on the block full of brick bungalows and frame cottages.

"You a little horny, Junior? You got the big one waiting for her or did you get any of those pygmies to go down on you in St. Charles?" Frank broke into a heavy laughter and slammed the steering wheel with his fist.

Earl popped open a beer, guzzled half of it, and belched. He turned and looked at Junior in the back seat. "You want some of my beer?"

"Bunch of fucking comedians. I'll call you guys in a couple days." Junior barged out of the car, so focused on Patty he left the box with his clothes and case files in the back seat.

Frank lowered his window. "Hey, mind if we come up and watch. I can give you a few pointers."

Junior gave him the finger and the Buick squealed away as an empty beer can flew from the car bouncing across the sidewalk. His head spun with his alcohol drenched brain and he stumbled from one side of the gangway to the other. The back door was locked so he searched his pockets for his old key, tried to jam it into the dead bolt lock but it didn't fit. "Shit." He jabbed the top button of the two doorbells. The lower one was for the landlady. He wanted Patty at the door not the toothless hermit, old-lady Penarski. He shifted from foot to foot and stabbed the button again and again. Finally, he heard the upstairs door slam and the sound of foot steps padding down the stairs from the attic flat.

The door opened a crack and Patty peered at him, a red deep v-neck blouse hung loosely over her breast revealing the lace of a black bra. Her red lips parted. "Where you been? I left work after lunch, thought you'd be home." She turned and headed upstairs.

Junior followed closely behind, "I told you I'd be with my buddies for a while." He looked at her jeans tight around her buttocks and stroked it.

She reached back and slapped his hand away. "Stop it!"

They entered the flat and stood in the kitchen next to the yellow Formica table with chrome legs. Junior put his arms around her, pulled her to him, and forced his lips onto hers. She twisted her head away. "I can smell the beer on you. Don't touch me. I don't feel like it."

He grabbed her jaw turning her face to him and thrust his tongue into her mouth. Patty fought him, beating her fist against his chest.

"Come on, baby. I ain't had any in a long while."

Patty took a step back. "Me either. Any that I wanted." She pushed him away and walked to the other side of the kitchen table. "You think you can spend your first day out getting drunk with your asshole buddies, then come home and get laid? Forget it."

Junior realized this approach wasn't working. "I'm sorry, baby. I didn't have no choice. I tried to get home earlier but it was their car." He drifted around the table toward Patty.

"Don't come any closer. I've had enough of you low lifes."

Junior felt his anger rising but hid it. He had learned while he was in St. Charles the usefulness of burying his rage. "Come on, you know I love you." Junior took another step toward her. His breathing quickened, chest expanding and contracting. He placed a hand on her shoulder. "I'm not Bruno...."

She smacked his hand off. "How could you even mention his name? Get out of here."

"This is my home." He grabbed her shoulders, "Why're you treating me like this? I need you." He pushed her against the wall and tore her blouse open kissing her breast.

She rounded her shoulders trying to protect herself, folding her arms over her breasts and twisting from one side to the other.

"Don't fight me, baby. You know you're mine." Junior pushed her down onto her knees.

Her hands slid down his waist over the 9 mm to his hips. "You got a gun."

He yanked the pistol out of his waist and held it at his side. "Unzip my pants. Come on, just blow me, Patty. We don't have to fuck. Not 'til I take care of Bruno. I'll make him sorry he ever touched you."

Her chin trembled. Silent tears rolled down her cheeks.

"Come on, Patty. Show me you love me."

She froze and looked at the dirty gray tile floor.

"Patty." He grabbed her raven hair, jerked her head up, and looked down into her brown eyes. "I never had to hurt you. Don't make us start like this."

Patty turned her head and looked at the blue steel pistol.

He pulled his zipper down, lowered his jeans to his hips and forced himself into her mouth. He jerked her head back and forth by her hair. "Come-on baby, get in to it." His hips thrusting against her face.

She whimpered, saliva sliding down her chin.

He couldn't hide his anger anymore, "Did you cry for Bruno too?" He pictured Bruno's hulking body over hers. Patty thrashing her hands against Bruno's chest. Bruno groaning as he came and rolled off of her.

Junior jerked her head faster and faster, his hips flailing against her face, tears avalanching from Patty's eyes. But nothing happened. Junior soused with beer remained limp and his buried rage exploded. "See what you done to me." Spittle flying from his mouth. He shoved her to the floor, pulled up his jeans, and stashed the 9 mm in his waistband. He rushed out, the door banging behind him.

*** 

It was 5:30 when William pulled into Ruleville. He had to wait a half-hour before reaching out for Jackson so he stopped at a package goods store down the block from Maude's and picked up a cold six pack of Jax. He regretfully headed back to the Sunflower Inn and parked in front of the office. Clarkson was staring at him from behind the counter.

He opened the door of the Camaro and barged into the office. The same scraggy face confronted him as the day before.

"You checking out? Just so you know, you don't get no refunds on prepaid rent."

William shook his head and smiled. "Well, I guess I'll stay the whole three days then. It's nice to know that you want me around."

Clarkson picked up the paper cup from the counter and spit his chewing tobacco into it.

"You have any telephone books for Greenville and Jackson?"

He pointed a bent finger to a stack of frayed telephone books piled knee high to the right of the door. "Whatever we got is over there."

William walked to the books and started pulling them out. He found a 1977 book for Greenville and a 1975 for Jackson. "These will do."

The old man crossed his arms over his chest and smirked, "In case you didn't notice there's no phones in the rooms and the pay phone outside doesn't work."

William ignored him, flipping through the pages in the Greenville book until he found the page listing eight Virdens and tore it out.

Clarkson waved his arms. "Hey! What ya doing? Don't be ripping that book apart. What if somebody else needs to look somethin' up? You people ain't got no consideration for other folks."

William opened the Jackson telephone book and ripped out the page with the law firm's listing. "Can I use your office phone? I only need to make one call." He folded the pages from the phone books and placed them in his shirt pocket.

Clarkson wiped his sleeve across his mouth. "Who you calling?"

"Deputy Jackson." William said.

He squinted and stared at William. "Why you calling him?"

William flipped open his credential case and flashed his badge in Clarkson's face. "That's why."

Clarkson reeled back from the counter and paused. His chin jutted up and nostrils flared. "Make no difference. Yeah, you can use the phone—for five bucks." He reached behind him, grabbed the phone, and banged it on the counter. "And don't forget to wipe it off when you're done."

William pocketed his credentials and tossed a five-dollar bill on the counter. "I bet you broke the pay phone so you could pad your wallet." He dialed the number.

"Sunflower County Sheriff."

"Can I speak with Deputy Jackson?"

"Hold on. I've got to forward you to another number."

William paced back and forth in front of the counter; phone pressed to his ear, hoping that Jackson had found some bit of evidence or maybe a witness that might exculpate his father. But he realized there was a chance that just the opposite could happen. He could prove up the case against his father and then he would have a decision to make.

"Jackson."

"It's me, Richmond. Any luck?"

"Can't find a damn thing. This place is a mess. Broken storage boxes lying on the floor, files and papers all over. I'm covered in dust, dead bugs, and mouse shit."

William sighed, "Maybe if I came and helped you look—"

"Forget it. Somebody finds out there's a FBI agent, especially a black one, going through these files I'll be back picking cotton like when I was a boy. I'll give it another hour and let you know how I'm doing."

"All right. The telephone situation here isn't the best." He glanced at Clarkson. "Can you stop by?"

"If you're sure this is worth the aggravation I'll go through everything that's left. But it'll be late by time I finish. I'll meet you at Maude's tomorrow around nine. You can buy me breakfast for doing your dirty work."

"It could be real helpful if you find something. I appreciate your help." William hung up the phone and marched out of the office refusing to dignify Clarkson's existence with even a glance. He drove to his unit, crashed into bed, popped open a can of Jax, and took a long draw. He unfolded the pages from the Greenville telephone book and compared the addresses against the one from the Sunflower County Chancery Clerk's office. He slapped the sheet of paper. "A match, that's where I'm heading after meeting Jackson tomorrow." He drank two more cans of Jax, went out for dinner and fell asleep watching the black and white TV.

\*\*\*

Junior walked down Roosevelt Road heading to Dick's Joint, the local biker/skinhead bar, assuming it was still there after the eight months he spent at St. Charles, and if it was Bruno would be there. The November wind pierced his light jacket and newspapers tumbled across the pavement. Streetlights cast a yellow haze into the night, glistening on the moist streets. Headlights from passing cars spilled their lights on him.

It had been a rough night, rejected by Patty and then his manhood failing with the thought of his former best buddy doing her lurking in his mind. He patted his forearm and felt the dagger under his sleeve. It pushed the rejection and failure to the back of his mind and made him think about what he had to do.

As Junior approached the end of the block he could hear the harsh music coming from Dick's Joint on the corner. The bar was an old storefront. Too many bodies had been tossed through the windows so they had been replaced with sheets of plywood that had been painted black.

Junior got to the door and looked down the side street. Two Harley's were parked on the sidewalk and Bruno's Chevy was sitting at the curb. The smell of stale beer and smoke hit him as he opened the door.

A black enamel bar ran the length of the room. Its surface was sticky, gouged with initials, swastikas, and a bullet hole here and there. The only light came from red twinkling beer signs, green and gold flashing from the jukebox, and a Hamm's beer lamp shade that hung over the pool table in the center of the room. Its faded green felt spotted with stains from initiating women into the bar's biker club. The jukebox against the back wall blasted Black Sabbath. The owner, Dick Yost, was standing behind the bar. He had salt and pepper hair, closely cropped, and wore a black Harley tee shirt. He had wide square hands and was missing the upper half of his little finger on his right hand.

In front of the bar were two skinheads dressed in black leather, and Bruno.

Bruno turned and leaned against the bar. His brown eyes narrowed and fear crept into them. He grabbed his beer bottle by the neck and lowered it to his side.

Yost looked over the shoulders of the two skinheads. "Hey, Junior. When you'd get out?"

Junior gave a quick glance to Bruno. He took in a deep breath and slowly exhaled. *Chill, man. Chill.* He forced a smile. "Bruno, Dick, how the fuck are you guys?" Junior walked up to Bruno and punched him in the shoulder. "Man, I just got out this afternoon. Made this my first stop."

Bruno brought the beer up to his mouth, took a slug, and smiled. He introduced Junior to the two skinheads, Dwight and Walter. They wore sleeveless T-shirts. Their heavy arms littered with the faded blue ink of jail tats.

Bruno grabbed Junior's arm and pulled him over to the bar. "Give this man whatever he wants. It's on me." He reached into his pocket and laid two twenties on the bar.

"Put your money away, Bruno. This is on the house." Yost said. He set up five shot glasses, filled them with whiskey, and set a bottle of beer behind each glass. "Welcome home, Junior."

They raised the shot glasses.

"To Junior," Bruno said.

"The free man," Yost added.

Their hands rose up into the air, the shot glasses clinked together and they downed the amber liquid.

The night went on with Junior telling them about life in St. Charles, and Bruno and Yost getting Junior up to date with current events. What fags they rolled and whose heads they had cracked open. At 11:00 p.m. Dwight and Walter put on their leathers and left. They were going to their motorcycle gang's club for the rest of the night.

Bruno and Junior strutted to the pool table.

Junior told Bruno stories that made him laugh, disarming him. "Those niggas were so dumb. One of them had to keep his laces tied because he didn't know how to make a knot. Went by his room one day and he's sleeping with his shoes on." Bruno laughed and poured down a shot. Junior nursed his.

There was no mention of Patty until Yost shouted out, "Where's your broad, Junior?"

Bruno drew back the cue stick ready to sink the eight ball for a win and stopped.

Junior stood on the opposite side of the table. He watched Bruno's gaze follow along the top of the cue stick and rise to focus on him. Junior gripped his cue stick with both hands and fought the urge to bust it over Bruno's head, grabbing the shot glass on the edge of the pool table and draining it. The whiskey burned down his throat and boiled his stomach. "I haven't talked to the bitch in months." He looked at Bruno for his reaction.

Bruno smiled and struck the cue ball. It sliced off the eight ball sliding into the side pocket. The eight ball harmlessly bounced off the cushion.

"You dumb fuck. You scratched and lost again." Junior laughed.

Bruno tried a quick response, but his thick tongue and floating head only allowed spit to run down his chin. He collapsed onto the pool table, face flat against the felt, cue stick bouncing on the floor.

"You better go home before you puke all over the table." He slid Bruno's arm over his shoulder, lifted him off the table and pushed him in the direction of the door. Bruno zigzagged the twenty feet from the pool table to the door. He took one step out the door and collapsed on the sidewalk.

"Take care, Junior. Great to have you back, man," Yost waved.

"Great to be back. I'm just going down the street. Spending the night with a broad a buddy fixed me up with. I'll put Bruno in his car. He can drive home when he sobers up." Junior stepped out the door. The cold night air revived him. Bruno was on his haunches.

"I don't feel so good." Bruno wiped clammy sweat off his brow.

"Give me the keys. I'll drive you home."

"Junior, I don't live there no more. I got a basement apartment on 55$^{th}$ court and 20th Place. By the El parking lot." He held the keys up and Junior grabbed them. Bruno jerked forward, his mouth filling with the contents of his stomach and puked on the sidewalk.

Junior hooked an arm under Bruno and lugged him to the Chevy. He yanked leather gloves out of his coat pocket and put them on, opened the door and dropped Bruno into the passenger seat. Bruno leaned against the door, face smashed against the cold window, eyes sealed shut.

Instead of heading toward Bruno's apartment he went in the opposite direction, north on Central Avenue under the Eisenhower Expressway into Chicago's Westside ghetto, a land of boarded-up graffiti-covered buildings. Junior imagined the cop's version of what they would find, *a drunk drives blindly into the wrong neighborhood, tries to sleep it off, looks like one of those things.*

Junior turned west on Jackson into Columbus Park, driving past the lagoon into a secluded area surrounded by barren trees. The wind blowing through the branches created shadows that danced through the interior of the car. He crawled over the seat, not wanting to risk the dome light going on, and sat behind Bruno. A six pack of Budweiser was in the backseat. Junior opened one and poured it over Bruno's head.

Bruno turned his head side to side. "Where…where're we?"

Junior slipped the dagger out of its sheath. He leaned forward, reached over the seat and covered Bruno's mouth with his left hand.

Bruno muffled out. "What're you doin'?"

Junior moved closer, next to Bruno's ear. "Treating you with dignity. Not like you treated me."

"Didn't do nothin' to you."

"I'm locked up and you fucked Patty. You call that nothing."

"That's a lie."

"Patty told me. Wasn't no lie. You don't fuck your friends. Especially your friend's lady." He put the tip of the dagger against Bruno's neck and pressed breaking the skin. A thin line of blood oozed down his neck. Junior's adrenaline began to pump and for the first time in a long time he knew what it was like to be in control. Then his anger was tempered by fear or doubt, couldn't figure out what it was. Junior's hand trembled, then his lip. He bit down on his lip. He began doubting his purpose. Bruno was a brother, a warrior for the white race.

"I don't want to die, Junior," Bruno cried. "She wanted it and I couldn't help myself..."

Junior's grip lightened and then the vision of Bruno thrusting into Patty came to him. He heard her cries and groans. He jerked Bruno's head back and plunged the dagger deep into his neck. Bruno arched back and his hands flailed about his neck. He gripped Bruno's chin, yanked back, the dagger making a horizontal cut across the neck. Bruno squirmed and twisted. Blood spit out of his jugular soaking his clothes and the car seat. Bruno gurgled out a few unintelligible grunts. Then his body stilled and in twelve seconds he was dead.

Junior wiped the blade off on the back of the seat, leaned over it, and grabbed the two twenties out of Bruno's pants pocket. *Make it look like some gemoke robbed him.* He kicked out the rear window and squirmed out of the car. His gloves were slick with blood, he dropped to his knees and wiped them off in the fallen leaves. He crept through the woods, tossed the gloves in the lagoon and headed back to Cicero, to safer grounds.

\*\*\*

Sunday morning William parked next to Jackson's Crown Vic in front of Maude's and strode into the restaurant. Maude was hovering over Jackson like a teenage girl with a high school crush. He couldn't see the two of them together. Jackson was like a sapling, tall and lanky, and Maude was one fireplug high and two wide. But those thoughts were just a brief diversion when he noticed a manila folder on the table in front of Jackson.

He swung into the seat across from Jackson ignoring Maude. "You found something?"

Jackson ripped off his mirrored sunglasses, held his hands out, palms up. "Where's your manners, boy? Say good morning to the lady."

He glanced up at her, "Sorry, good morning, Maude." His eyes shifted to Jackson. "Can I see that?"

Jackson slipped his sunglasses back on and shook his head. "I hope all you Yankees don't have manners like yours. Order your breakfast so this lady can get back to work."

He pushed aside the menu Maude offered. "I'll have whatever he's having." His eyes glued to Jackson's. "Can I see it now?"

"Don't get your hopes up, not much in here." Jackson pushed the file across the table.

William opened it and read a copy of James Napier's complaint filed against Beauford Tisdale for the murder of Linda Joy Napier and the kidnapping of Celeste Napier.

> The nigger had a knife at my daughter's throat and pushed her mother, Linda Joy, down the stairs. She died from the fall. Must of broke her neck. I fought with that nigger, Tisdale, but he hit me in the head with the butt of his knife. When I come to, the nigger and my daughter's gone. Don't know why he did this. Use to pay him good money for working my farm.

William flipped the page over to the next copy summarizing the shooting of James Napier.

> FBI agent Clarence Daniels said he shot Napier after...

He stopped reading and dropped the report to the table. In all the war stories Daniels had told him he never once mentioned killing anyone. He rubbed the back of his neck with his hand. William felt betrayed. Was their relationship just a pretense of trust and friendship? If so, it might be even worse than the relationship he had with his father. There was no pretense there.

"Something wrong?" Jackson asked.

William picked up the report and finished reading it.

> ...Napier shot at him. It should be noted that Napier was standing out in the open with his little son, Junior, nearby. The agent was hiding behind some trees.

"Did you read these?" William asked.

"Sure, you mean about that Agent Daniels that killed Napier. Sounds like the cracker got what he deserved. So what's the problem?"

"You're right." William nodded, "no problem. Down here I'm surprised Daniels wasn't arrested."

"You talk like you know him."

"He's my part...he's in the Chicago office, where I'm assigned."

"You know about him killin' that guy?"

William shrugged.

"Some guys are quiet about stuff like that. They never really get over it, even if it was a righteous shoot. Why do you need all this stuff?"

"It's one of those things that I really can't talk about, grand jury secrecy."

"I sort of figured that. Anyway, there was one more thing that I found."

Maude's arms jiggled as she slid two plates of grits and white gravy, a plate full of biscuits, and two cups of piping hot coffee onto the table. "Enjoy gentlemen," she said, eyes glued to Jackson.

Jackson blew her a kiss. "Thank you, Honey," and mixed his grits into the white gravy.

William took a sip of his coffee, slid the plate away from him, and leaned back into his chair. "I'm not very hungry. You want mine?"

"Don't mind if I do." He grabbed William's plate and scooped the grits and gravy onto his plate. "You looked disappointed. Sorry, I didn't find anything that could help whatever you're trying to do." He dropped a biscuit into the gravy, cut off a corner with his fork, and put it in his mouth. "Hmm. Woman can cook. Only trouble if I hooked up with her I'd end up being twice as big as she is." He slipped a photo out of his shirt pocket and spun it across the table to William.

"Who's this?"

"Celeste Napier. Only thing I could find on her. Since she was allegedly kidnapped and missing somebody threw a photo of her in the file in case a body was found. No information on her whereabouts." He took another piece of biscuit, swirled it in the gravy, and let it linger in his mouth. "Yes sir, that woman can cook."

\*\*\*

William started the fifty-mile trip from Ruleville to Greenville heading west on Route 8, south on interstate 61 through the small towns of O'Reilly, Shaw, Helm, and Heads. Each town looked like the other, black and impoverished, shotgun houses with tin roofs and dilapidated trailers that groaned in the wind. Between the towns were old pickup trucks parked in front of one room shanties built on cypress stumps and the remains of harvested cotton fields, woody one-foot tall branches with intermittent puffs of cotton hanging from them, and signs on trees that read Jesus Saves. Not much had changed in Mississippi in eleven years. From interstate 82 it was a ten-mile drive west to the river town of Greenville. He tried to imagine how this guy Virden fit into the land deal. He didn't recall the name from his childhood. But it sounded white and he didn't know too many white people back then.

William went to the address in the telephone book that matched the one the clerk from the chancery office had given him for Virden. He pulled up to the corner of Broadway and Main and saw the house. An immaculate two-story white frame with a mansard roof. The building ran deep into the backyard. The front entrance was covered by a brief portico supported by two ten foot white columns. Attached to the eastside was a screened-in porch. Fine trimmed shrubbery and bushes graced the yard and a five-foot high black wrought iron fence gave the appearance of protecting the inhabitants.

He parked his car in front of the house and approached the front door. A brass knocker on it was inscribed Virden. William rapped it against the door. A few seconds later a woman in her sixties with silver blue hair wearing a plum shirtwaist dress tightly cinched around a slender waist opened the door.

"May I help you?" Her voice pure southern and her skin was as unblemished as milk.

"I'd like to speak to Mr. C. Virden please."

"There's no one here by that name."

"I got this address for him from the county records. Do you know if he had resided here in the past?"

"My father, Clive Virden, built this house. But he died twenty years ago. You must be looking for another Mr. Virden." She started to close the door.

"Wait. Did your father have a brother or a son that might have used this address? It must be the right address or it wouldn't be in the real estate records."

"No. My father and I were both only children. Now, if you don't mind I have business I need to attend to."

William pulled out his badge. "Ma'am, I don't mean to be obstinate but I need to talk to this person. It can't be your father if he died twenty years ago. That would be in the late 1950s. I need to talk to this person about a 1968 real estate transaction."

She looked at the badge. "Federal Bureau of Investigation, well, I suppose you better come in." A ten-year old girl, skin the color of a penny with tightly curled brown hair, peered around the lady and stared at the badge. "Missy, why don't you go upstairs and play." The little girl skipped up the curved stairway to the second floor. The lady stepped aside and held the door as William stepped into the foyer under a tear drop chandelier. He followed her into the parlor. She walked with the grace of an actress crossing the stage.

"I'm Special Agent William Richmond. You're Ms. Virden?"

"Yes, that's correct, Olivia Virden. Please sit down. May I offer you some tea or coffee?"

"No thanks, I'll pass on the beverage." William sat in one of the two gold armchairs across from a white sofa that Ms. Virden sat in. Separating them was a white French provincial coffee table.

Gold curtains ran from ceiling to floor. The papered walls were pale blue with a pattern of fleur-de-lis. "Cute little girl."

She crossed her legs and pulled the dress over her knees. "Yes, she's adorable. What is it you want with this person, C. Virden?"

William cocked his head. "It's about a real estate transaction."

Her blue eyes glanced down as she stroked her black leather pump. "What kind of real estate transaction?"

William tilted his head. *She's too coy.* "So do you know a C. Virden besides your father?"

"Let me explain something to you. You see, I've been very fortunate. I inherited this house from my father and my former husband was a very affluent man. He was the mayor of Ruleville. He gave me a very generous settlement when we went our separate ways. Bless his soul. So, I thought if there was only someway I could thank God for all the wonderful things that have blessed my life. I turned my home into a safe haven for young ladies that have been less fortunate than me. Gave them a place they can call home, where they know they'll be safe. So, over the years I have taken in many girls. I try to expose them to some of the advantages I've had in my life: education, music, and manners that a proper lady should have. Give them a little sophistication. So hopefully they will be able to return to society and lead their lives in a decent manner."

"That's very kind of you." William tapped his fingers on the arm of his chair. *Daniels says never interrupt them once they start talking and keep them talking.* "How many have you helped?"

"I don't count them. It's not like I'm trying to reserve a place in heaven."

"You're really very kind. I mean you're literally saving these girls lifes. Can I have a list of their names?"

"I'm sorry I can't do that. It's my policy. Some of these poor girls have had relationships with terribly violent men. For their safety I can't risk that their names might become public knowledge and something horrible might happen here. It could endanger everyone that lives with me. I would never forgive myself." She shook her head, pearl necklace swinging from side to side.

William sighed and looked down at the oriental carpet. "Let me ask you a general question that would not require you to identify anyone. Do you have any knowledge of any real estate transaction any of your girls may have been involved in during 1968 regarding property on the outskirts of Ruleville?"

"Honestly, no, I can't say that I do. Why don't you leave your business card and perhaps I can get in touch with some of them and see if they have any recollection of such a transaction."

"How about your husband? If he was the mayor of Ruleville he may know about it."

"The poor soul. I'm afraid after we divorced his life just crumbled. Married some young floozy that just wanted his money." She raised her hand, waved it, and rested it over her other hand in her lap. "He died in a fishing accident. Slipped on a rock, hit his head and drowned."

"Oh, I'm sorry." *Damn it. Striking out on all fronts,* he thought. "What was your husband's name?

"Josephus LeGrand, I took back my maiden name after we divorced."

*Looks like a dead end. Get out of here before she goes on and on* "I have to return to Chicago in a few days so I guess the best thing to do is to give you my card. Just in case you hear from any of your girls. I'll write down the telephone number of Deputy Jackson from the Sunflower County Sheriff's office. If they can't reach me they can call him and he can relay the message to me." William handed her his business card.

"All right, I'll do my best to get in touch with them." She rose from her chair and straightened her dress.

"Do any of the girls live around here? I could always contact them while I'm here and save you the trouble."

"No, once they get their lifes in order they generally move away from the bad experiences that brought them here."

"Do they stay in touch?"

"I get a postcard or telephone call now and then. I'm happy that they're beginning their new lives and hope that I helped them a little bit." She patted the bun of hair on the back of her head.

"One last question. Do you have any living with you now?"

"No, I'm little to old now. I haven't had a new girl in years."

They walked to the foyer and the lady opened the door. He turned to leave when he heard footsteps coming down the stairs. William looked over his shoulder and saw the little girl holding the hand of a slender woman with white skin and a smattering of freckles across her cheeks. Her red hair was in a shoulder length ponytail and her eyes were green. She wore horn-rim glasses, a white blouse, straight leg jeans and black pumps. Around her neck was a gold chain with a small cross.

"Can you watch Missy tonight? I've got to go to the computer lab to finish my home work," the redhead said.

William's eyes opened wide. It was her. The girl in the photo, Celeste Napier.

## CHAPTER TWENTY-SIX

William took a step off the front stoop of Ms. Virden's house mumbling, "I've got to get Celeste Napier away from Virden. It's the only way I'll have a chance to talk to her." *The old lady's probably peering through the curtains,* he thought as got he into the Camaro, pulled away from her home, sped around the block, and parked west of the house on Main. From that position he could see the front door and the backyard. He looked at his watch; it was 11:15 am. He would wait it out.

Seven hours later darkness settled in as horns of freighters at the docks a mile west hooted, sounding their departure. There was no activity at the house except for a light, in what he believed was the kitchen. It had been on 45 minutes before the room went dark. He hoped that would mean that Celeste was going out to stretch her legs, buy some groceries, or whatever just so she would get away from the house and he could talk to her away from the protective Olivia Virden.

Fifteen minutes later the front door opened and Celeste stepped out carrying a brown tote bag, its strap taut. She wore black slacks and her red wavy hair bounced on the shoulders of her green double-breasted jacket with each step. She walked east on Main toward him and stopped at Broadway standing under the Greenville Transit System sign. William had no choice. This was his best opportunity—maybe his only one. Hopefully, Olivia

Virden wasn't looking out the window and the redhead wouldn't run back to the house.

He pulled the Camaro up to the transit sign and stepped out of the car. "Excuse me, Miss. You probably remember me. I'm William Richmond, the FBI agent that was at your house earlier today." He slipped his black leather badge case out from his inside jacket pocket, flipped it open and showed her his credentials.

She canted her head and looked at him with wary eyes. "I remember."

"I came back into town. I have an appointment with a witness on another case in about a half-hour." He lied, wanting to make this meeting look like pure happenstance. "And I saw you and wondered if I could have a few minutes of your time."

"Sorry, but I don't have time. I'm waiting for a bus so I can get to the computer lab. I've got two hours reserved and it's not easy to get time." She looked at her watch.

"I'd be happy to drive you there. I can ask you a few questions on the way so I can close this file and you don't have to wait for the bus."

She took a deep breath and looked at her watch again. "I guess that would work out for both of us. I really don't care for riding in those buses anyway and lugging these books around is a pain." She stepped into the Camaro, brushed her hair off the shoulders of her jacket and dropped her tote bag to the floor with a thud.

William hopped in the driver's seat. "What school are you going to?"

"Mississippi Delta Community College, just head north on Broadway and take a right on Union."

*Break the ice*, William thought. "What're you taking?"

"Computer programming and I suggest you start asking your questions because we'll be there in a little while."

"Ah, okay. In 1968 there were several pieces of property around Ruleville that were transferred from various people to a C. Virden and a few weeks later transferred to a company by the name Bavarian Agri, N.V. Are you familiar with these transactions?"

"I don't know. Like Ms. Virden told you. We girls that stay with her take an assumed name to protect us from the foolishness we got ourselves involved in. Ms. Virden allowed me to use her name. C. Virden's me, Celeste Napier. I'll tell you everything I know about whatever you ask me. I've seen enough in my years in

Mississippi—seen my little brother running around in a white sheet when he was six years old. Don't even know where he is now."

"That's too bad." *Sounds like Ms. Virden talked to her after I left.* "Were you involved in any real estate transaction?"

"Sort of, it's a long story. I'll give you the short version. My father kicked me out of the house. He was a drunk and an abusive SOB. He dropped me off at the Ruleville bus station late one night and I took the first bus out. It stopped in Greenville about 2:00 in the morning. I was tired and took a room at the first hotel I saw."

William nodded.

"The next day I ran into Ms. Virden's former husband, Mayor LeGrand, in the hotel. He was meeting some man on business. He insisted that I tell him what I was doing in there. He knew what my father was like and felt sorry for me. The mayor took me to Ms. Virden's place and I've been there ever since. Thank God, if it wasn't for her I can't imagine where I'd be."

"And when did you get involved in these land deals?"

"A few days later the mayor stopped by Ms. Virden's. He told me how ashamed he was of what my father did to me. He said that he figured that I didn't have much money and out of concern for me he could pay me for some land deals that he and some investors were making. All I had to do was sign some papers. He told me it was all legal and for signing the papers I'd get $400 cash on the spot. So I did it."

"Did you know who the sellers or buyers of the properties were?"

"I didn't look at anything. I just signed where he told me to sign and took the money. I was eighteen, scared as hell, and all alone." She pointed at Union Street. "Turn right here."

William turned. "Is it much further?"

"No, just about six blocks."

"Before you get out of the car I've got something I'd like to show you if you don't mind. I'll have to get it out of my bag in the back seat."

She pointed as they approached the school. A single-story cement block building. "Pull into the parking lot on this side right here. The computer lab is near this entrance."

William shifted the car into park and lifted his brown leather portfolio out of the back seat. He paged through the items in it and pulled out a copy of the *Enterprise Tocsin* article about the murder of her mother, Linda Joy Napier, and handed it to her. "I hope this doesn't upset you but, I really need to know everything you can tell me about your mother's death."

She looked at the caption heading the article and handed it back to him. "I don't need to read it. I lived through it."

William paused. His heart raced. "You mean it's true."

"Poor Beauford," she shook her head. "I'm sure it was a case of Mississippi justice. They strung him up someplace." She looked at William hard, brow furrowed and green eyes narrowed. "Do you know if he's alive?"

William didn't answer. Possibilities ran through his mind. He had just proved that his father wasn't guilty of kidnapping but had he found the witness that proved him guilty of murder? If he told her he's alive was she going to push the murder case?

Her face reddened. "Well, is he? Is he alive? Can't you say something?"

*Tell her anything just to pacify her for now.* "I'm tracking down some leads that might result in something but I can't tell you just yet. Not until I'm finished."

"When will that be?"

"I don't know. I'm trying to track him down and if I do I'll have to arrest him on the outstanding warrant from your mother's case. I can't tell you because if he disappeared it wouldn't look good. Like you tipped him off."

"You don't understand." She shook her head. "Beauford didn't kill my mother. I heard my father and mother arguing about...about me. He was rushing up the stairs to my room and he must have pushed her. I heard her tumble down the stairs and groan. Your father was never there that night. My father was a mad fool and a drunk. Then he told the Klan that Beauford did it. When I said Mississippi justice, that's what I meant. That's why I thought they hung him. Then when I heard that my father was killed by that FBI agent it didn't make any difference what they did to Beauford then because my father got what he deserved."

"But it did. My father...I mean Beauford?" William stopped, frozen by his misspoken words.

Celeste fell back in her seat. "Your father's Beauford. But you said your name's Richmond. What's going on?"

∗∗∗

On Monday morning the new Supervisory Special Agent, James Eckhaus, arrived in the office for his first day of work at six-thirty. He liked to be the first one in the office to create an image of the work ethic he expected from the agents in his squad. The reality was Eckhaus couldn't sleep. Spinal arthritis woke him in the predawn hours every morning after a fitful night. Eckhaus' daily ritual in the morning darkness was a long hot bath to loosen aching joints while waiting for the four Vicodin he washed down with a shot of Jack Daniels to kick in. He had not aged well. Crew cut hair had turned thin and gray. Bags under the eyes told people he had put in his time and a once slender waist now hung over his belt. Eyeglasses that should have been worn stayed in his inside coat pocket. Eckhaus' ego wouldn't let him appear to have any weaknesses and the man had the same expectations of anyone that worked for him.

His office was stark. On the left corner of his desk were a black telephone and two packs of Camels. On the right side was a large glass ashtray Eckhaus brought from Washington. He had crushed out a cigarette every twenty minutes. Five-quarter-inch stubs lay buried in a pile of ashes and smoke curled up from a cigarette burning on the side of the ashtray. Next to it was a yellow legal tablet and a TV remote. The top page of the tablet was filled with illegible scribble and resting on the tablet was a ballpoint pen with blue ink. The only color he used. A small television sat on the credenza against the wall opposite his desk. He kept the volume on mute unless there was a news flash. The walls were minus the usual photos, headlines, and awards that decorated the offices of most old-timers. He didn't want to remember his yesterdays. Eckhaus just wanted to make it through another day and in two years get out, unscathed.

The first order of his command was an unannounced squad meeting at eight that morning, whether all the agents were in or not. Eckhaus leaned on Daniels to gather the troops and Daniels and nine other agents were in Eckhaus' office at the appointed time. Three agents, including William Richmond, weren't.

"Daniels, where's my missing agents?" Eckhaus barked, the aroma of stale tobacco on his breath.

"I raised Rodriquez and Allen on the radio. They were on surveillance. Both of them are on their way in. Richmond left a message on my answering machine last Friday. He requested leave and expects to be back in the office Thursday morning."

Eckhaus leaned on one arm of his chair and then the other, shifting his weight, trying to ease his discomfort and feeling the need for more Vicodin and another shot of Jack Daniels. "Where the hell is he?" Eckhaus coughed, covered his mouth with his hand as he hacked up phlegm, swallowed it, and shook his head. "You should check your answering machine everyday. Doesn't matter if you're on leave or if it's a holiday."

Daniels took a deep breath, eyes narrowed, shoulders tensed. He gave Eckhaus an icy stare. "I don't know where he is. Said he had to leave town on personal business. I called his apartment and no one answered."

Eckhaus picked up the burning cigarette laying on the ashtray, tapped a quarter inch of hanging ash onto the pile and took a deep pull, letting the aggravation he felt by the lack of Daniels and Richmond's allegiance dissipate. "First day his new SSA is in and he takes leave. He's probably fucking some bimbo he picked up. His request for leave is denied. He's on leave without pay." His eyes gazed across the agents in his office, watching to see if there was any reaction to his order. Eckhaus was daring any one of them to challenge him. It would give him one more opportunity to flex his authority. "I don't know how things were run in this squad before I got here, but from now on all leave has to be approved by me in advance. In this job we have to be able to respond to any and all contingencies. We can't have agents taking off on a moment's notice. Any questions about that?"

Some of the agents shook their heads and others shrugged. The meeting continued for another hour with Eckhaus glancing at his notes on the legal tablet while he laid down his interpretations of FBI procedures and policies. "All right, unless there are any questions you can all leave." He pointed at Daniels. "Except you and the last one out close the door." Eckhaus laughed under his breath as he watched the agents herd out of the office. He contemplated with joy the bitch session they were going to have about their new boss.

"I want you to keep calling Richmond until you get in touch with him and tell him to get his ass in here." Eckhaus said, the cigarette butt between his lips wobbled up and down.

Daniels stood in front of Eckhaus' desk. "He's a reliable kid. He wouldn't just blow off a couple of days."

"I appreciate your loyalty to him, Clarence, he being a young black kid and all. But, I don't make separate rules for anyone. Even if McAlister made him your flunky. We've got to lay down the law, if necessary make an example out of him, or we'll have agents running around doing whatever they please."

Daniels' brow furrowed. He leaned forward resting his palms on the front of Eckhaus' desk. "He's not my flunky and I'm not yours. I'm not going to spend my day calling him. If he had to go on leave, I'm sure he had a good reason and he'll be back as soon as he can."

"I see." Eckhaus pulled the cigarette butt out of his mouth, brought the pack to his lips, slid one between his lips, and lit it with the stub of the Camel he had been smoking. "Whatever, let me know if you hear from him." He crushed the butt in the ashtray. His yellow fingers took the cigarette out of his mouth and he gestured in the direction of the door signaling their meeting was over and thought, *don't get mad, get even.*

## CHAPTER TWENTY-SEVEN

William left Celeste with the promise he would get back to her soon and explain why he was asking questions about his father and why his name was no longer Tisdale. But, first he had to return to Chicago to have his father answer the questions he had for him. He drove through the night arriving at his apartment on Monday, beating the sunrise by a couple of hours. He collapsed into bed not sure what he should do. Contact his father? He didn't even know where he lived. The only place he could find him was the ward office or city hall. What would he tell him? Guess what, Dad. That old murder charge you never told us about. I've got the evidence to prove you're innocent.

After a fitful few hours' sleep he awoke a little after 9:30 and noticed the message light blinking on his answering machine. He figured it was Daniels from a few a days ago and dialed his office number without brothering to listen to the messages.

"FBI, Special Agent Daniels."

"It's me."

Daniels whispered, "Just got out of a squad meeting and your new supervisor is pissed. Where the hell have you been? I've left messages for you and just about beat down the door of your apartment."

"I'm sorry. Can we meet someplace? I need your help."

"Are you in trouble?"

"No. I don't think so. Will you meet me?"
"When and where?"
"The Planetarium parking lot in an hour."

\*\*\*

Junior spent Saturday night and all day Sunday in a flophouse above a strip joint on Cicero Avenue. His companion was a twenty-dollar hooker who was twice his age who he picked up after her last performance on the stage. He woke up mid morning on Monday to the sounds of a squeaking mattress penetrating the thin red walls that separated his room from the next. Sticking out of the ragged cover was a platinum blond head of hair the texture of straw.

His head pounded from the liquor, but his ego was soaring. He had succeeded in marking one name off his list. He had moved in a direction he had been thinking of for a long time. Taking control had made all the difference. His sexual prowess had been restored. There was a feeling of momentum, euphoria, almost a giddiness that was propelling him forward. He couldn't wait to move on to his next prey.

Junior sat on the edge of the bed, at his feet were his pants, shirt, and jacket lying in a heap on top of his shoes. Next to them an empty half-pint of Jim Beam and several empty tinfoil condom packets. His eyes caught the crusted blood on the end of his jacket sleeves. It was like awakening from a dream and wondering if it really happened. Did he really kill Bruno? He felt no guilt. It was something that needed to be done and he did it. Now he had to get rid of the blood-stained jacket.

He reached under the sagging bed, retrieved his pistol and dagger and gently stood to keep the mattress springs from creaking. He lashed the dagger's sheath to his left forearm, put on his pants and shirt, stashed his pistol in his waistband and crept out of the room into the hallway, leaving the snoring hooker behind. There he finished dressing, rushed down the stairs and leapt over an old man sleeping in the stairway. The stench of urine reeked from the man's tattered clothes.

Junior hurried down the block hopped a CTA bus on Cicero Avenue and set out for Marquette Park.

\*\*\*

Daniels pulled into the planetarium parking lot and saw William sitting on the fender of his Camaro. He got out of a blue four-door Plymouth. The biting wind off Lake Michigan blew the collar of his trench coat against his cheek and he pushed it off his face. "What's going on?"

William shoved his hands into the pockets of his black leather jacket, headed for the 12<sup>th</sup> Street beach and Daniels followed. Pale gray clouds blew like smoke across the sky and curling waves crashed onto the beach.

"Where you been?"

"Mississippi." William paused and his brow wrinkled. "I went down there because I found that there were outstanding warrants on my father for murder and kidnapping."

Daniels shook his head. "Can't be. They would've come up during your background investigation. Immediate family members are always checked for arrest records."

"Richmond isn't my family's real name." William knew he was letting out a secret and he didn't know what the consequences would be. He could feel his pulse pounding in his neck. "It's Tisdale."

Daniels' brow furrowed. "What?"

William told Daniels everything—how his grandfather was lynched and he overheard the men that hanged him threatening to kill his father next. His father finding him and ignoring the question, 'Why they wanted to kill him?'

That his father rushed the family to Memphis and returned to the bayou that night to bury his father. While he was gone another group of white men kidnapped William's sister. When his father returned he was bruised and muddied. They left for Chicago and stopped by an office in Marquette Park. A man there gave his family an apartment and his father a job. The next day his father went out of town and returned the following day. Later that day he left and returned with Marlee and it was around that time that he changed their name.

"He changed your name to avoid being arrested?" Daniels said.

"He didn't do it." William went on to explain how he found Celeste Napier and she said that it was her father that killed her mother and he told the Klan it was Beauford that killed her. She didn't come forward at that time because she thought his father was lynched by the Klan and a few months' later her father, James Napier, was killed by an FBI agent.

William stopped and looked into Daniel's eyes. "How come you never told me you shot someone?"

Daniels did a double take. They walked in silence for thirty feet. The wind whipped the waves against the beach. Daniels stopped and gazed out at the lake.

William turned and faced him. "The sheriff gave me a report that states you killed James Napier. You told me a thousand war stories. How come you never told me about that?"

"All the training and macho bull shit they give you at Quantico. They make it sound like there's lot of glory in shooting someone. But when you've done it, when you've taken a life, you never forget it."

"But an asshole like James Napier. He was about to fire bomb a church, kill a lot of innocent people."

"I know it was a good shoot. But it's not something I like to talk about. I can still see Napier's son. I shot his father just as he was going to throw a Molotov cocktail. He dropped it and it fell onto a couple he had at his feet. They exploded. He went up in flames and staggered toward the church. His kid couldn't have been more than six. He ran toward his father, fell down, and scuffled toward him, crying. I scooped him up inches from his father. Flames are jumping from Napier's body. He's on his knees screaming. We're breathing in the stench of his burning skin. The kid's beating on my chest screaming 'Let me go. You killed my daddy.' Does that sound like a story you'd like to tell?"

William rubbed the back of his neck. "I understand. It sounds bad."

"Not many people know about that and that's the way I want to keep it. Anything else come up in Mississippi that I should know about?"

William told him that his father's land in Mississippi was owned by the same foreign corporation that owned the Nazi building in Chicago. Celeste told him that the mayor of Ruleville, this guy LeGrand, paid her $400 to sign the real estate papers. She signed them under an alias she was using while she was hiding from her father. It was C. Virden, LeGrand's wife's maiden name. Celeste was staying with her. He died several years ago. She didn't know anything about the transaction.

"Why'd you do all this? Seems like your father has left all of you behind."

"Last week, when I was doing those title searches at city hall, I'm coming up the stairs and I see my father giving an envelope to some Italian-looking guy. The guy looks like he's ready to tear my father's head off. So I run up the stairs acting like I hadn't noticed them and bump into him. My father had this look on his face like...like he was relieved to see me, like he was reaching out to me, wanted to talk to me. I don't know." He shrugged. "Maybe it was me and not him."

Daniels nodded. "You needed to find out why he left. To get an answer to something that's been eating at you."

William closed his eyes and pulled his lips inward. It was hard for him to admit that maybe he was dealing with his needs and not his father's. Or maybe it wasn't a need but a fear. A fear of what, he wasn't sure. That sent an emotion resonating in his chest that he couldn't identify. A fear that had some truth to it. "Maybe that's it."

"Who was the guy he was talking to?"

"I don't remember. Some guy from the department of transportation."

They faced each other. Daniels put his hand on William's shoulder. "If you want me to talk to your mother or father or just tag along with you I can do that." Daniels dropped his hand from William's shoulder and stuffed it in his pocket. "In the meantime, you've got a problem with Eckhaus. He was really pissed that you weren't in today. Put you on leave without pay. What're you going to tell him?"

"I can't tell him the truth. If the Bureau finds out that Richmond isn't my real name I'll get canned." William looked at Daniels and then felt his eyes break away from his partner's. He realized that by confiding in Daniels he had just put him in the trick bag.

Daniels glanced at the waves crashing on the beach. "So?'

"I don't know what I'm going to say. Lie, I guess," William said.

"I don't think that's a good idea. You try to cover up your name change, I can guarantee you it will surface and you'll get canned for the cover-up. With the murder of your grandfather by the Klan it wasn't unreasonable for your father to change your name. I think you should tell Eckhaus everything you just told me."

\*\*\*

Junior stepped off the CTA bus at Kedzie and Marquette Road and waited for it to head down the street. After it passed, Soder's gas station came into view, a faded yellow building lined with tin tiles, six pumps and two bays. A sign above the bays read Kurt's Gas & Auto Repair—Full Service Station. Earl was standing at the pumps in greasy coveralls gassing up a 1972 green Dodge, and Frank was smoking a cigarette behind the counter.

Earl looked confused, wiped his hand across his chest, and waved.

Junior crossed the street and gave him their typical greeting, a punch to the shoulder.

Earl frowned and rubbed his shoulder. His other hand holding the gas nozzle. "Hey, man. What ya doin' back here?"

"I left that bitch's place. Don't need her crap. You guys got the box I left in the car with my clothes and things?"

"My old man put it in the back room. I think he's in there now."

Junior walked into the front of the station, grabbed a candy bar from a rack near the door, unwrapped it, and took a bite. Frank's nose was buried in a *Penthouse* magazine he held close to his face as he shoved a handful of potato chips into his mouth. Separating Junior and Frank was a glass counter containing boxes of cigars and in front of it stacks of newspapers. Behind him were racks filled with cartons of cigarettes. "Frank, you're concentrating so hard you're gonna blow a fuse."

He held up a centerfold and smiled. "She's mine. All mine." He looked outside and back at Junior. "Where'd you come from?"

"Had it out with Patty. Took the bus down." He pointed at the centerfold. "Her tits are nicer than that broad's."

"Yeah, well I guess you didn't get laid." Frank laughed.

"Fuck you." He took another bite. "Where's your old man?"

"In the back room." Frank bent his arm pointing his thumb over his shoulder.

Junior walked around the counter facing a door covered with a poster of a blonde in a string bikini straddling a Harley and knocked.

"Yeah?"

"Kurt, it's me, Junior."

"Come on in, son."

Junior pushed the door open and saw Soder reclining on a cot against the back wall. Next to the head of the cot was a small wood-veneer desk covered with bills and an adding machine, its tape rolling over the paperwork. The aroma of burnt coffee came from a coffeepot sitting on a hot plate on a black two-drawer file cabinet at the other end of the cot. Next to the file cabinet was a refrigerator about the same height and on top of it was a 13-inch black-and-white TV with rabbit ear antennae covered with tin foil. On the floor next to the cot was Junior's box. Soder was reading Junior's arrest report. He flipped the page over.

"What's all these names?"

Junior closed the door, grabbed the report out of Soder's hands, and stuffed it in the pocket of his jeans. "Nothing. That's just for me. Nobody else's business."

Soder swung his legs around, put his feet on the floor, and sat on the cot. "Junior, why don't you sit down?" He glanced at the cot.

Junior took a deep breath. He felt like the secret he carried with his father had been violated. Resentment festered within him. He wanted to tell him to fuck off and walk away. But this was the man who had counseled him without judging him, without breaking his trust. The man who had given him the tools he needed to do the list. Junior sat on the cot next to Kurt.

Soder was smooth. "I know you've a got a lot to be angry about. Things you want to do. You know I support you in that. Let me help you."

Junior felt like a burden was lifted because he had someone who was willing to help him. There was a lot to do, almost overwhelming. He didn't know where or how to start. Just a little help would make it easier to get the job done and then he didn't care what happened. "I ain't got no job, no place to stay."

"You can stay here if you like, Junior. You got a bed, a hot plate, a little fridge and TV. You'd be all set. No one knows you'd be staying here so nobody would know where to look for you. If you get my drift?"

He looked around the room that was smaller than the cell where he had spent the last eight months. But it looked good to him. He wouldn't feel exposed like he did at St. Charles. It was a place where he could hide from the rest of the world, do what he had to do, and return for shelter. "You'd let me stay here?"

"You want to make a little cash on the side, you could pump gas or whatever." Soder reached into his pocket and pulled out a roll of cash. He pulled off five twenty-dollar bills and stuffed them in Junior's shirt pocket. "Here's a little advance. Maybe you can walk down the street and get some new clothes." Soder noticed the blood on his sleeve. "Your old stuff is...old."

"Thanks, Kurt. No one's ever me given things before, not like you."

"I'm glad I can help you and I'm willing to help you in anyway I can." He held out his hand. "Let me see that list."

Junior reached into his pants pocket, pulled out the wrinkled sheet of paper and placed it in Soder's hand.

"You want to tell me about this then we can figure out how I can help you?"

"When I was a kid this nigga," Junior pointed to Tisdale's name on the paper, "broke into our house. He killed my mother and kidnapped my sister. I ain't never heard from her since. He probably killed her too. When we put my mama in the ground my daddy made me promise that if he didn't kill Tisdale and his son before he died, that I would kill 'em in honor of my mother."

"Your momma was killed by that nigger? What about these others?"

"These two niggers, Richmond and Sanders. It's because of them that I had to go to St. Charles. The accident that we got into was Richmond's fault and the cop gives a ticket to my—buddy. Turns out that Richmond is an alderman and that's the reason the spook cop gave us the ticket. Then the cop starts pushing us around. I wasn't going to take any shit from that spade."

"What about these two Jew boys, Judge Shelton and Moskowitz?"

"That's the judge and public defender on my case. That was a royal setup from the beginning. They had to be in with Richmond."

"And this one, FBI agent Daniels."

Junior took his wallet out, removed a folded yellowed copy of the report from the Sunflower Sheriff's office and handed it to Soder. "A Klansman gave this to me before they sent me up here. The motherfucker killed my old man."

Soder unfolded the report and shook his head in disbelief. "FBI agent, that could be tough. And this last one, Bruno?"

"He's done."

\*\*\*

William returned to his apartment to catch up on his sleep and try to make a decision with a clear head. Then he could figure out what to tell Eckhaus and how to deal with his father. As he lay in the darkness of his room he realized he needed to talk to his father alone. Having someone else along would only make his father suspicious, especially if that person was Daniels. Besides, this had to be personal if there was a chance of reducing the distance between him and his father. This meeting could impact what he would tell Eckhaus about why he was gone.

Dusk came over the city as he left his apartment and drove in the damp cold of the late November night to his father's ward office on Marquette Road. He slowed as he approached the office. There was a red Mustang convertible parked in front. The inside was dark except for the light from a desk lamp. He noticed two people, his father sitting at a desk and a second person standing in the shadows in front of the desk. He parked the car a quarter-block away and walked to the office, stopped next to the door and peered around the corner through the glass. His father sat shaking his head and pointing a finger at a young dark-skinned woman. She had her hands defiantly on her hips, then raised them gesturing in a heated, unintelligible conversation. William backed away from the door and returned to his car. *I need to talk to him alone. Give them fifteen minutes. If she's not out by then I'm going in.*

Fifteen minutes later William parked in front of the ward office, behind the red convertible and saw the two combatants still going at it. "Screw it. I'm going in." He jammed the gearshift into park and got out of the car. His unzipped black leather jacket as he entered the office. Inside the walls were covered with posters of Mayors Daley and Byrne, and former Alderman Heidler, but mostly of his father, Alderman Beauford Richmond. His father was seated at his desk with the Stars and Stripes on one side and the city flag on the other. He looked like the self-appointed king of the fifteenth ward sitting there in his navy blue designer double-breasted suit and red silk tie.

Beauford stopped in mid sentence—his eyes locking on William. "What do you want?"

"Who's that?" the lady asked. The valley between her ample breasts revealed by the deep vee in her charcoal gray sweater.

"That's my son." He glanced at her. "My son, the FBI agent." His eyes shifted back to William.

"I need to talk to you," William said.

\*\*\*

Beauford pondered who he would rather talk to and the answer was neither. He was tired of arguing with his mistress, Sheila the ghost payroller, about why he couldn't give her a raise for a job she never had to go to and wondered if William was here for professional reasons. There certainly weren't any personal reasons. But if he could get rid of William, he was sure he could get Sheila off her high horse, head back to her place, and get laid. "We're having an important conversation. Can't it wait?"

"No, it can't. This has been put off for eleven years."

Beauford took a deep breath. "Sheila, honey, could we finish talking about this later?"

Without responding she turned and picked up a fox fur coat lying on the desk behind her. She bent over revealing painted on black leather pants and charged out. The sound of her stiletto heels clicking on the floor faded away. The office door slammed shut, she ran to the convertible and fishtailed away.

Beauford smiled, laughed it off like it was nothing, and to him it was nothing. His work was not a job but a game—the game of Chicago politics where the only thing that mattered was cash and power. If you had one, you probably had the other, and life was fine. And everyone you associated with was in the same game, with the same rules. So you respected each other's privacy because you knew that everyone had secrets and because of that, it was easier for Beauford to blend his deepest and darkest secrets into this chapter of his life—except for those long nights when those dreams from earlier chapters came back to haunt him. The crack of the shot fired from the smoking rifle barrel so close he could almost touch it. King collapsing on the terrace of the Motel Lorraine. It would play over and over again. The sweat would roll down his head and neck soaking his pillow. Sometimes he wished that white man, Ray, had pulled the trigger on him in the hallway of the boarding house. If it wasn't King, the picture in his dream changed to Los Angeles. The shots fired and the senator falling to the ground. He gave chase to the lady in the polka dot dress, running and running, gasping for air, his fingers reaching out, almost having her within his grasp, but never catching her. The only thing he caught up with was a bottle of Jack Daniels. When he awoke in the wee hours of the morning, the booze brought him back to the darkness of night where his mind blacked out and he could sleep. But even this new life wasn't everything he thought it would be. The cash was gone as fast as it came and then there was Falcone. Beauford was determined not to end up like Heidler.

Now there was a new potential threat to his existence. Someone who wanted to go back eleven years to what? Beauford had taken a giant leap away from all that with the promise that he would never return, and anyone who would threaten his existence would be crushed. The only trouble was he didn't know that person might be his son. But what could William know about the old chapters? Beauford thumped his fingers on his desk. A diamond ring on his little finger sparkled under the light from the desk lamp. "So what is it you want?"

William pulled a chair from a neighboring desk and slid it in front of his father's desk. He wasn't going to stand in front of him like a loyal subject waiting for permission to sit down. He took off his black leather jacket, placed it over the back of the chair and sat. "I was in Mississippi the last couple of days."

The finger thumping continued. "So?"

"Can you stop that?" William gestured toward his father's hand, attempting to gain some sense of control.

Beauford folded his hands behind his head and leaned back in his chair. "Sorry, didn't know it bothered you. So, why'd you go to Mississippi?"

"Last week, after I ran into you at city hall. I was doing background checks on some people, had some time to kill. I ran the old family name, our real name, and you came up with a couple of warrants, one murder, one kidnapping. So maybe 'why we left?' is a better question than why I went down there?" William said, trying to gain the upper hand by being the one asking the questions.

"Are you here to arrest me?"

"No."

"Isn't that your job? Shouldn't you if you're really going to be an FBI agent?"

"Why do you have to play your games? Why can't you be straight with me and tell me what happened?"

Beauford smiled. "What do I tell you? Just enough to give you the minimum, to satisfy your curiosity. Or should I tell you the whole story? One that no one would believe." He laughed and kicked his feet onto the desk. "I dare you—go ahead and arrest me. I'm not afraid. Those charges could never be proved."

"So, you knew about the warrants. Is that why you ran out of Mississippi?"

"Not I, we. In case you don't remember."

William took a deep breath, sighed, and rubbed the back of his neck. "In case you don't remember it wasn't exactly 'we.' You never told me why those men that lynched Grandpa wanted to kill you. Why those men took Marlee? What did you do to get her back? Tell me why that happened! Tell me everything!"

Beauford slid his feet off the desk, onto the floor, and laughed. "No, I don't think so."

"The house our family lived in for generations was burned down and the land is owned by some foreign corporation," William said.

Beauford took a cigar out of his coat pocket and rolled it between his thumb and forefinger. "Ancient history, got to learn to live in the here and now."

William looked to the floor and slowly raised his head. "When I saw you last week in city hall, I got the feeling that you wanted to change things. The look on your face. There was something about it. I thought that if I could find that something...I know we lost time together that we can't get back...but it doesn't have to be the way it is."

"My son, the big hero comes to the rescue."

William's eyes welled with tears. His emotions ranged from anger to contempt. He didn't understand his father. He had come to bring them closer and his father was mocking him. His throat tightened and he choked on the words. "Can't you just talk to me?"

Beauford looked into his son's eyes and could see that over the years what he had done to him, had stolen something from him that could never be replaced, leaving a permanent mark. He thought about what their lives would have been like if this nightmare had never happened. If he had just walked away from

Celeste Napier these abhorrent memories wouldn't exist. Beauford believed his father would be alive, or at least would have had a peaceful death, not one with a rope around his neck. His son wouldn't have that image of his grandfather in his mind. They would still be in that cabin, without any possessions of substance, except for each other. His life had become a wreck—his marriage, his relationship with his children and even his relationship with himself. He didn't even know who he was anymore, or if he could find himself—even just a shadow or a piece of who he once was would be more than who he was now. He had made a statement with his life. A statement that denied everything that was once important to him.

Beauford took a deep breath and exhaled. He felt weary. The price of living with his secrets was tearing him down. He wondered what might happen if he didn't hold back. "I didn't kill nobody. I didn't kidnap no one." He thought saying that, telling William would ease the burden. But it didn't, the weight just got heavier because the other secrets crept up one space closer to the surface and even more threatening.

William brushed his sleeve across his eyes. "I know. I talked to Celeste Napier."

Beauford's heart shuddered. The events of eleven years ago felt too close. He felt like it was midnight and Jimmy Napier had just ripped that photograph into pieces and threw it into the bayou. Like Napier tripped him and he was sucking in that stagnant water, dragged up the bank where death waited impatiently for him. That was the only part of his feelings that had a sense of comfort.

"She told me you didn't kill her mother and you didn't kidnap her. She heard her mother tumble down the stairs. Saw her father at the top of the staircase and she said that you weren't there."

"She have anything else to say?" Beauford looked William squarely in the eye and paused. He waited to see if there was one piece of information that might seem like nothing to anyone else but that might have some significance to him, or to someone else who knew more, who knew the secrets.

"No, like what?"

Beauford clicked into his mode of one-upmanship. The one he learned in the game played in Chicago politics, feeding his ego by topping his adversary. "You can tell her that her scrawny red-neck little brother is here in Chicago."

## CHAPTER TWENTY-EIGHT

Four-thirty Tuesday morning Eckhaus rolled out of bed onto his hands and knees. The pain spiraled up his spine like a flaming arrow. He grimaced and reached out for the nightstand, grabbing it with one hand and then the other and pushing himself up onto his feet. He reached for the bottle of Vicodin, shook out three white 500-milligram tablets and slammed them into his mouth. With his quivering hand he grasped a half-filled glass of Jack Daniels. The amber liquid danced from side to side as he brought the shaking glass to his lips and washed down his relief.

He lumbered out of the bedroom, stumbled down the hallway to the bathroom, giving the light switch a glancing blow. The glare from the fixture above the mirror blinded him until his eyes adjusted and his reflection bared the deep lines in his cheeks and the crow's feet in the corners of his eyes. This day started just as painful as any other but there was one thing that gave him something to look forward to: he was going to make this day a living hell for somebody—William Richmond.

He filled the tub with hot water and soaked for an hour, shaving in the tub. Then he dressed in his navy sport coat and gray slacks, white shirt and blue tie with red stripes, and black shoes and overcoat. He slipped a .38 Chief's Special into his clip-on holster, caught a cab from his apartment and headed to the Klucinski

Building. He bought a large cup of black coffee and three donuts from the Dunkin Donuts across the street from the federal building.

At 6:30 he took the elevator up to the ninth floor and stepped into the lobby of the FBI. A rookie agent sat at the reception desk reading the *Sun-Times* waiting for the clerks to arrive at eight. Eckhaus made a mental note of the agent's casual attitude, punched in the combination on the door, and headed down the dimly lit hallway.

Eckhaus had a hitch in his walk as he headed into his office, flicked on the light, and closed the door. He tossed his overcoat on the coat rack at the door, sat down and adjusted the .38 on his hip. He spread his donuts and coffee in front of him while he reviewed his notes on the legal pad he had used for his squad meeting in preparation for Richmond. Eckhaus slipped a Camel out of a pack, tapped the smoke twice on his desk, packing the tobacco, placed it between his lips and lit it. He drew on the cigarette, the paper crisping as the ash grew hotter. The smoke filtered through his lungs. The nicotine settled his nerves. He swiveled to his right, opened a four-drawer gray file cabinet, pulled out Richmond's personnel file and tossed it on his desk.

He punched the button on the remote turning on the TV. The white noise offered a soothing hum as Eckhaus perused the file. A video of Ronald Reagan filled the screen. Eckhaus grabbed the remote and raised the volume. The announcer said, "Last night, Ronald Reagan announced he was a candidate for the Republican nomination for President."

Eckhaus shook his head, "That's all we need a fucking actor running this country."

The announcer continued, "Governor Reagan hasn't named any prospective vice presidential running mates yet, but an anonymous source has suggested that the leading candidates are former CIA Director George Bush and former President Gerald Ford."

"At least if the old cowboy doesn't last through his term we'd have someone with experience." He started paging through Richmond's file. "My missing agent. You're going to have a very interesting career. Probably a very short one." He laughed.

The announcer went on, "One dark horse vice presidential candidate has been mentioned, the Governor of Mississippi, Edward Pape. Now a word from our political commentator, Joe

Versico. Joe, what do you see as the ramifications of Governor Reagan's announcement?"

Eckhaus crushed his smoke in the ashtray. *Pape, you son of a bitch. All the shit you put me through and then for the sake of your family legacy you crapped out on me.*

"Thank you, Tom. As the political wars start to ignite for the upcoming campaigns, this announcement is a big one. A big one because it's likely to unite the Republican Party as they haven't been united for decades. Governor Reagan is the strongest candidate the Republican Party could have mustered. He already has a multi million-dollar campaign war chest from his victorious races in California and this announcement will open the flood gates for contributions from major Republican supporters who want to be the first to get their foot in the door of the White House. And this is Joe Versico from Washington, D.C."

*Million-dollar war chest, what a waste of fucking money.* Eckhaus stretched for the remote and silenced the television. Pain shot up his spine and ripped up his neck. He dropped the remote and leaned forward onto his desk, grimacing. He reached down and pulled open the desk drawer, grabbing a brown plastic bottle. Struggling, he twisted off the top, dropped the container onto his blotter, and two 750 milligram tablets spilled out. Eckhaus grabbed them and threw the pills down his throat followed by a gulp of coffee. "I can't take two more fucking years working like this. The pain's only going to get worse."

He wrapped his fingers around his neck and massaged it, *After all I've been through, the "G" should put me on disability. I've done everything the Bureau could ask of one man. SACS line up fat corporate jobs—security director, trouble shooter, consultant.* He saw himself lying in the surf on some beach in Antigua or St. Martin, could smell the salt water, feel the ocean breeze and taste a Jack on the rocks. That would ease his pain. *See what I can get out of the government.* His brow furrowed. Then he smiled, *Pape, governor of Mississippi. He must have a war chest of his own. I'll sell him his legacy.*

\*\*\*

William stepped into the elevators in the federal building and glanced at his watch, 7:45 a.m. He shook his head, there was no way he could tell Eckhaus the truth. He'd probably fire him on the spot. Like Daniels said, 'first year probationary status, you could be terminated without cause, lying about your name would give Eckhaus ample reason.' The old 'visiting a sick relative excuse' would have to do and the best he could hope for was a letter of reprimand for not getting the leave approved, and possibly a few days off, added to Eckhaus' abuse.

William stepped out of the elevator, punched the combination on the keypad, entered the office area, and ventured to his squad's bullpen. The agents' desks were lined up five rows deep and four across. Desks were assigned by seniority, so naturally the more experienced agents sat near the windows overlooking Dearborn Street and the newer agents' desks paralleled the aisle farthest from the windows and in direct view from Eckhaus' door.

Eleven agents were already in this morning, some standing, some at their desks. A few had smirks on their faces, while others choose to display little emotion. William figured that they thought sometime in the future they might be in his shoes. He dropped his trench coat over the back of his chair.

He turned and faced his supervisor's office. The door opened and Eckhaus stood there. He felt his supervisor's eyes grilling him. Smoke curled from a cigarette hanging from the man's mouth and steam rose from a cup of coffee in his right hand. Eckhaus jerked his head, motioning for William to enter his office, turned his back on him and stepped into his office.

William took a deep breath, *my ass is grass*. One step inside Eckhaus' office and he was hit by the stench of stale cigarette butts followed by the command, "Close the door." He complied and stood in front of his supervisor's desk. No invitation to sit was offered. At that moment, he knew Daniels was right, he would tell Eckhaus everything—that his father changed his name and about those trips he made after they moved to Chicago.

\*\*\*

Eckhaus sat down, crushed his Camel in the ashtray and tapped his pen on the legal pad leaving a trail of dots. He realized that his priorities had changed from Richmond to Pape. *I can't waste more than a few minutes on you, boy.*

He stared into William's eyes. "There's no place in this organization for a lone wolf who wants to come and go as he pleases." He slid a cigarette out of a pack on his desk and slipped it in his mouth, grabbed his lighter with the FBI emblem, brushed his thumb across the striker wheel, brought it to his cigarette, and inhaled. The tip glowed red and the smoke curled to the ceiling. "I've got very important things to do and you're not one of them— right now. I don't even want to hear whatever bullshit story you concocted to cover the time you were gone. If I did, I might feel obligated to check it out and I don't feel like creating more work for myself."

William nodded.

"But you're not getting off easy. I'm going to document you. In case you don't understand what that means, its one slip-up and you're gone. Every morning you'll give Daniels a list of what you'll be doing that day and the following morning a list of what you accomplished from the previous day's list. The following Monday you give me the complete list from the prior week. From now on, whenever you plan on taking any kind of leave, you'll clear it through me in writing at least three days in advance. You're on probation. I don't need to document you to get rid of you. It would just make it easier. Is that clear?"

"Yes, sir."

"Any part of that you don't understand?"

"No, sir."

"Leave and close the door behind you." Eckhaus laid his cigarette on the ashtray and pulled out his Rolodex from the desk drawer.

William did an about-face, walked halfway to the door and turned around. "But, sir, what I was going to tell you is really important."

"You think I don't have things to do that might be more important to me or the bureau than what you have say?"

William swallowed. "I'm sure you do sir, but this is important too."

"I'll tell you what. When I finish the things that I have prioritized I'll contact you and then you can tell me your tale. Until then," he pointed to the door, "this meetings over." Eckhaus watched William turn around, walk to the door, open it and leave. He heard the door close and the click of the bolt as he fingered through the cards in the rolodex stopping at the B's. He picked up the phone and dialed a number he had called many times when he was in the special operations branch at headquarters.

"Barclay's Bank, may I help you?" the receptionist said, with a prim and proper English accent.

"Connect me with Mr. Stamley."

"One moment please."

Eckhaus leaned back in his chair. He rotated the burning tip of his cigarette in the ashtray and fantasized about how perfectly this would work. Offshore bank account, money goes in, money goes out, wash it through a couple more accounts and it's as clean as could be. Antigua would be beautiful.

"Reginald Stamley, security director."

"Reg, it's James Eckhaus, FBI. How's everything in Bermuda?"

"Fine, old chap, and in Washington, D.C.?"

"I'm not in D.C. anymore, been transferred to Chicago. I've got my own squad now. But I still have some of my old responsibilities, overseeing some of the undercover operations."

"Just like my days at Scotland Yard. They think if you can do one job fine, you can do two even better," Stamley said.

"I see you've been there, done that. Anyway, I know it's getting close to lunch there and I don't want to be responsible for you being late for whatever Agnes is making because you're talking to me. Could you activate an undercover account for me? If everything goes right we should be sending a couple of hundred thousand through it and then off to another account. You can contact me directly here in Chicago. I'll be handling the case from here. No need for you to contact Washington."

"Hold on, my good man and I'll give you an account number and name. Let's see, account number 86-4343. That account is under the name of Garrison Consulting Services, Limited. How many years to go before you join me in retirement, James?"

"I've got a couple of years before I'm eligible. I still get a kick out of the job, so I might hang around." It seemed like the appropriate thing to say. Giving the image of pushing the envelope to the end and no one would have any reason to doubt his integrity.

"Don't hang around too long. There's a whole big world out there."

"Don't' worry about me, Reg. One day I might be your neighbor. Usual procedure on this, give me a call when the money comes in." He gave Stamley his Chicago number.

"You've got it. Till next time, James."

Eckhaus didn't hang up the phone, instead he pressed the switch hook. *Why not? One more call and my day's work is over.* He lifted his finger, dialed directory assistance, got his number and placed the call.

"Mississippi State Capitol building, may I help you?" The drawl smothered the words.

"Connect me with the governor's office."

"One second please."

See if he appreciates my offer to help him fulfill his legacy. Eckhaus laughed.

"Governor Pape's office."

"I'd like to speak to the governor."

"He's in a meeting right now. If you'd like to leave your name and number and the nature of your call someone will call you back."

"I suggest you interrupt his meeting. I think he would be very interested in talking to me."

"I'm sorry sir, I can't do that."

"Yes you can, and you will. This call is in regards to the murder of his son eleven years ago."

"I'll try sir. What was your name again?"

*No way do you get my name.* "Cabrini, Cabrini Green." *He'll know what that means.*

"Please hold and I'll forward your call."

Eckhaus held the phone to his ear. He knew he was falling victim to the bureaucratic runaround and disdained it.

"Mr. Green," a youthful sounding voice said. "This is Malcolm McFarland, Assistant to the Governor. Can I help you sir?"

Eckhaus knew there was one thing that would put Pape on the phone. "Look, McFarland, I know Ed Pape from eleven years ago. I investigated his son's murder. I need to speak to the Governor now!"

"Yes, sir. Hold on, sir. I'll have to check with someone."

In seconds Eckhaus heard the voice that was as smooth as a Kentucky sipping whiskey. "James, you got new information?"

Eckhaus smirked. "Something has come up that we need to talk about, in person. Any chance you might be in Chicago in the near future?"

"Is it about Michael?"

*If that's what he wants to hear I'll bait the hook.* "Related to that."

Pape paused. "I'm meeting with the Republican National Committee this weekend in Chicago. I'll be staying at the Hilton downtown. But, they have me booked solid all weekend and I'm catching a redeye back late Sunday."

"I'll be at your hotel Friday night at eleven. Make sure you're there." Eckhaus hung up the phone.

*** 

William sat at his desk and took a deep breath. He had tried to tell Eckhaus but was stopped. The supervisor made the meeting into almost a nonevent—except for the fact he was one step away from being fired. He thought about the things he had to do: get back to work on the Nazis here in Chicago, make a list for Eckhaus and a list for himself. The first thing was to call Jackson and ask him to get a statement from Celeste so his father's warrants could be revoked and the most pressing thing, talk to his father again. William could feel there was something his father wanted to tell him or could tell him, and didn't understand why his father refused. Why did he have to guard himself against his son of all people?

Jackson took his call and agreed to do whatever was necessary to get a murder warrant off a black man. He'd talk to Celeste in the next few days and call him back with the results.

*** 

Kurt Soder and Junior sat in the black Buick Electra in the parking garage on 26th street facing the Cook County Criminal Courts Building on California Avenue. Between California Avenue and the garage was a grassy parkway with barren trees.

This was the first time Junior had seen the courthouse from the front. A grimy gray structure seven stories high. Lawyers in suits, policemen in uniforms, and witnesses and defendants dressed in everything from mink coats to sweatshirts and patched jeans stood outside smoking cigarettes, drinking coffee from Styrofoam cups and eating sweet rolls purchased from concession trucks parked in front of the courthouse. Some of the men and women lingered in front of the revolving doors waiting until the last minute before their court calls, wondering whether they would return home or get locked up. To the north of the building was a parking lot surrounded by a tall chain-link fence and a security booth at the entrance on California Avenue. The cop manning the booth waved-in Cadillacs and Lincolns driven by middle-age white men.

"See that parking lot, Junior." Soder pointed. "That's got to be where judges park. Every guy pulling in there is driving a car the size of a boat. You wait in the car, I'll go to the courtroom and get a good look at the judge and that attorney Moskowitz."

"I want to go in there with you."

"I know. But we can't take the chance one of them might recognize you. We'll come back this afternoon and follow one of them home. We'll move slow but sure. Then we can start making more serious plans."

Kurt got out of the car and headed to the entrance. He walked through the crowd of people lingering outside the doors and into the art deco vestibule. A cacophony of sounds hit him. The murmuring of a hundred conversations, the jangling of handcuffs, the squeaking wheels of trial carts containing guns, dope, rape kits, and police reports being wheeled by assistant states attorneys heading to courtrooms. At each elevator a computer printout was pinned to a bulletin board listing the court calls alphabetically by defendant, case number, judge's name, and courtroom number.

Kurt stood among the throng of people. He smelled the sweet scent of cologne and looked to his right. Standing there was a man in a sequined green and gold wide brim hat, matching jacket, pants and platform shoes. From the other side came a salty sweaty stench. The man's cheeks were sunken. He had holes in the knees of his soiled pants and a damp spot at his crotch.

Everyone was looking at the printout on the bulletin board for their case, or their son's case, or somebody's case. When Kurt got close enough, he ran his finger down the page, finding a case assigned to Judge Shelton. "Courtroom 219." He stepped into the first elevator door that opened and pushed the button for the second floor. The elevator filled, surrounding him with black and brown ghetto gangsters, homeless people, suits, and uniformed policemen.

The elevator came to an abrupt halt and the doors screeched open. He stepped out with a cluster of others onto the ancient marble floor and saw more of the same milling about. At the end of both sides of the hallway were signs listing the courtrooms. He glanced left, saw the sign for 219, and headed there.

In the hallway were lawyers on the make for clients who would sign over their bail money as their legal fee. Gangbangers hanging around to intimidate witnesses or sign a homeboy who was in lockup. Victims showing up for their fifth or maybe tenth court call.

Kurt approached the courtroom, two large wooden doors, beat and scraped by decades of justice. He pushed the doors open, stepped into the aisle that was flanked by ten rows of pews on each side and picked a seat in the last row on the left. Prosecutors and defense attorneys verbally jostled with each other from two tables in front of the judge's elevated bench. To the right was the jury box and in front of it a lectern. The court clerk assembled docket sheets and files as the pews slowly filled with families and friends of the defendants and victims.

A door opened behind the bench and the judge strode in from his chambers, his black robe flowing behind him, and the bailiff declared, "All rise."

Kurt stood with the rest of the courtroom inhabitants.

"The Municipal Court of Cook County is now in session. The honorable Judge Shelton presiding. All be seated." The scuffling of shoes on the floor and the banging of briefcases on the pews echoed across the room as everyone sat.

He watched the robed man closely. Mid forty's, short-thinning blonde hair turning silver at the temples, average height, horn-rimmed glasses, and cheeks in the early stages of jowls. Kurt thought about the judge's reputation, *more of a social worker than a lawman. Especially when it came to niggers and spics. He was a good target.*

Three prosecutors and various defense attorneys approached the lectern when their cases were called, as did the public defender assigned to the courtroom, Jacob Moskowitz. He carried a cardboard box full of case files. Soder figured he was the kind of young man who still lived with his mother. He was in his late twenties, medium height, bone skinny, short black wavy hair combed forward, wire-rim-coke bottle glasses and a cheap blue suit. He looked like an easy mark.

Kurt watched for about twenty minutes. He wanted to see their mannerisms, the way they walked and talked. All things that would help identify them later. He thought, *the judge and the public defender are cut from the same cloth, both of them Jews.* Then quietly he slid out of his pew and returned to Junior.

\*\*\*

Mid afternoon Soder and Junior returned to the Criminal Courts building driving a 1974 Chevy that an elderly Lithuanian widow had dropped off for an oil change at the gas station. They found an open meter and parked the car half a block south of the courthouse. Soder went to Shelton's courtroom and waited outside the door for court to recess for the day. By 2:30 the court's business was done.

Junior sat in the driver's seat of the Chevy with his arms crossed over his chest, feeling the dagger sheathed to his forearm through the black leather coat he had bought with the cash Soder had given him. He uncrossed his arms and slid his hand over the 9 mm on his hip. "Exploratory trip, bullshit. I'm ready to do this now."

Junior had been mindlessly tapping his foot to the beat of a succession of songs on the radio when he heard someone running toward the car. He looked over his shoulder and saw Soder hustling down the street.

Soder grabbed the door handle, opened the door, and hopped into the car. "He just left the courtroom. Head up to toward the guard's house and grab a parking spot up there so we can get a good look."

Junior started the car and crept north up California looking for a parking spot as he got closer to the judge's parking lot. "Shit! Ain't no spots."

"Just sit here, double-park for as long as you can. Keep your eyes peeled on the cars coming out. See if we spot him."

It was a replay of the morning, only in reverse. Cadillacs and Lincolns coming out of the parking lot, but with a lot more enthusiasm on the faces of the drivers than when they came in this morning.

"That's him! In the white Caddy," Soder said, resisting the urge to lift his hand and point. "Damn it. He's turning south."

They watched the Cadillac go past them in the opposite direction. Junior glanced in the side-view mirror and saw an opening in the traffic. He punched the accelerator and squealed into a U-turn, falling in two cars behind the judge.

"What the fuck are you doing? We're right in front of the courthouse, cops all over the place, and in a car that's not registered to either of us. Damn it, Junior."

"Sorry, Kurt. Didn't want to lose him."

Soder was red faced. "Use your head. If we got stopped and you got a ticket there'd be a record putting us here. You can't be so careless."

The judge made the traffic light at 31$^{st}$ Street, making a left-hand turn and Junior sped up screeching through the turn and running through a yellow light.

"Pull over!" Soder shouted. "Pull over now!"

Junior jerked the car to the curb. "Come on, Kurt—"

Soder grabbed Junior's arms, twisted him so they faced one another and felt the dagger. Then rushed his hand to the boy's hip and felt the grips of the 9 mm. "You planning something I didn't know about? Get out of the car."

Junior stepped out of the car. Angry blood rushed through his veins. He reached for the hilt of the dagger, wanted to zip the blade across Kurt's throat, get back into the car, and take care of the Judge.

Kurt slid over to the driver's side and rolled the window down. "Cool down. Take a deep breath."

Junior's chest rose and fell with each quick breath. He stared at Kurt and then looked down the street for the Cadillac. It was nowhere to be seen. He kicked the Chevy's door. "Damn it."

"Listen to me."

"The car's gone, Kurt."

"You gonna listen to me?"

He exhaled and lowered his head. "Yeah."

"Get in." Soder pointed to the passenger seat.

Junior ran around the car and got in.

Soder pulled away from the curb. "You realize what would happen if a cop stopped you? You don't have a driver's license. He pats you down and you've got a hot pistol and a dagger. You wouldn't be back at St. Charles. Your ass would be in Joliet and you'd be some nigger's bitch."

"Kurt...." He folded his arms across his chest. "I just want to get these people."

"What do you see at the red light up ahead?" Soder pulled over to the curb, not wanting to get too close to the judge's car.

Junior's eyes glistened with anticipation. "The Cadillac."

"You'll listen to me from now on?" The red light changed to green, the Cadillac went on, and Soder pulled away from the curb.

Junior looked toward his feet. "Yeah. Yeah."

They followed the Cadillac to the Stevenson Expressway, then north on the Dan Ryan to the Kennedy and then the Edens Expressway where the judge exited eastbound on Touhy. They went past tailored lawns and tall oaks. Women wearing designer coats walked French poodles with fancy haircuts and pink bows. Two young boys with yarmulkes ran along the sidewalk tossing a football back and forth.

"See those boys over there with the funny hats on. That's how you know we're in Jew town," Soder said. "These Jews are all lawyers and accountants. They steal more money with a pencil than all the crooks with guns. Then they go walking around praising all sorts of programs for niggers and spics trying to make themselves look good."

A block ahead of them the Cadillac's turn signal blinked and it pulled into the driveway of a white brick ranch home with an attached one-car garage in the upper middle-class suburb of Lincolnwood. Soder pulled over, they watched the judge get out of his car, carrying a briefcase and walk to the front door. The door opened, a portly brunette greeted him with a peck on the cheek, and a white dust mop of a dog ran around his feet yelping and jumping up to his knees. The dog and the judge entered the house and the door closed.

Kurt and Junior stayed down the block for twenty minutes, then drove to a deli where they had coffee and sandwiches, and came back a half-hour later. The Cadillac was still in the driveway. Kurt pulled a pen out of his pocket. "Write down the address and license plate. We'll visit him another time."

"Why not now?" Junior asked, fondling the grip of his 9 mm.

Soder glanced at Junior, saw his hand at his side. "It's too soon for that. We're going back to the Rockwell building. I got to see if you can shoot."

***

Beauford sat on the overstuffed burgundy leather sofa in his condo. On top of the glass coffee table in front of him was a bottle of Jack Daniels he had opened that evening. It was now one-third empty. Next to it was a glass filled with ice and honey-colored booze. The noise of the traffic from the street below echoed between the canyons of the tall buildings as rush hour and dusk arrived together. Last night's conversation with his son went through his mind and with every sip of whiskey his past became more vivid and dreadful.

Beauford remembered his father's dream, the one passed on to him. The family's land would go from father to son. At one time Beauford believed he would watch his grandchildren grow up on the same land, in the same house. Now the land was gone, the house long ago destroyed, and his relationship with his son had been nonexistent for over a decade.

He wanted the courage to tell William why all this happened. But he wasn't sure he had it within him. Could he trust William and talk to him, tell him everything and hope for his understanding and forgiveness.

He brought the glass to his lips and took a gulp. The ice clinked as he set the glass back on the table. He was so tired of this life. His worthless existence. He felt it in his soul, the insubstantial nature of his character. His palms were sweaty and tears rolled down his cheeks. His hands shook.

He leaned back into the sofa cushion with a sob. He reached to the end table and picked up the telephone. The numbers were blurred and he thumbed the O.

"Can you connect me to the FBI? Thanks…Hello, I need to talk to my son, William Richmond, he's an agent, thank you…He's not in the office…Can I have his home phone? But I'm his father…Okay, I understand." He left his telephone number, cradled the phone, took another sip from his glass, and laid his head back.

***

William was parked west of Kedzie on 71st Street. He and three other agents were surveilling the Rockwell Building to gain additional intelligence on the Nazi party.

"Unit 1174 from base."

He was startled to hear his radio number called but then happy to have some stimulation for what had been a boring surveillance, with the only activity being a janitor sweeping the front steps. He picked up the mic and keyed it. " Go base."

"Can you drop a dime on us over a land line?"

"10-4. 1118 from 1174."

"I heard the transmission, 1174. You might as well 10-7 now. Nothing's happening here."

"Thanks 1118."

"Standby 1174. There's a black Buick just pulled in front of the building with two occupants, male, whites. Why don't you drive by the car and get a look at these guys. See if it's anybody we know about."

"10-4." William pulled the gray Plymouth away from the curb and approached Kedzie, slowing down to get a good look at the two men in the Buick. "The driver is Soder. The passenger is a young guy, late teens, early twenties, red hair, wearing a black leather coat. I'll go make my call now. 10-4."

"Yeah, go ahead, if there's any activity we'll be transmitting."

William headed up Kedzie to a Michael's Restaurant across the street from Soder's gas station. William ordered a cup of coffee, walked to the pay phone in the entryway, and dialed the base station.

"FBI, base station." The dispatcher said.

"This is Richmond, you wanted me to call in."

"The receptionist took a call for you. She said the caller claimed to be your father and he wanted to talk to you. She advised him that you were in the field." He gave him the telephone number.

William jotted it down. "Thanks."

The dispatcher added. "Just to let you know it sounded kind of fishy. He asked for your home number. Wouldn't your old man have that? She said the caller sounded like he had belted down a few."

William ignored the dispatcher's question. "Thanks again." He held down the switch hook and tossed a couple of coins into the phone.

*** 

Soder pulled up to the Rockwell Building and gave Junior a key ring. He looked to the street and watched a young black man drive past him, seemingly focused on him. "The gold key is for the front door. My office is behind the stage. The silver key is for my office. Between the desk and the wall there's some targets in a box. Grab six, we'll do some shooting tonight." Soder smiled. "Not the kind you wanted to do, but we better see how good you are first."

Junior got out of the Buick and ran up the stairs. A sense of excitement overcame him at the prospect of shooting the pistol. It made him feel that he was that much closer to keeping his promise. He pictured his father when they watched his mother's body lowered into the earth and her coffin covered with shovelfuls of dirt. The look on his old man's face that was hard for him to understand back then and still was today, a look that he now thought of as combination of grief and guilt.

Junior opened the door and ran through the auditorium to Soder's office. Struggling in the dark with the keys, finally getting it into the dead-bolt lock and pushed the door open. He reached inside and flicked a switch, lighting the office. Directly in front of him was a wooden desk flush against the black paneled wall. A German flag hung on the wall above the desk. To the right of the desk were two black four-drawer filing cabinets with stacks of Nazi literature on top. To the left, in the narrow space between the desk and the wall, was a cardboard box slightly taller than the desk and almost as wide. The top was open. Junior grabbed several sheets and pulled them out, laying them on top of the desk. He smiled at the targets of black men with large Afros and menacing faces. Took the pistol out of his waist and pointed it at the target. "Here's one for you, Tisdale, for killing my momma. Right between your fucking eyes."

He put the pistol back in his waist, rolled up the targets, and ran back to the car. "Let's go." Junior paused, gathering the courage to say what he needed to say. "Kurt, thanks for your help. Sorry about earlier."

"You've had it tough, son. Tougher than I ever thought. I'm glad I can help you." Soder grabbed the back of Junior's neck and jostled him. "Let's stop at the gas station. I've got ammo there."

\*\*\*

The coins clanged down into the bank of the phone and William pushed the buttons. The phone rang several times and he was about to hang up when he heard, "Yeah."

"Dad? It's William. Did you call me?"

There was a long pause.

"Dad?"

"Yeah."

"You alright?" William looked through the window and saw the Buick pull into the gas station. One of the FBI cars pulled around the corner and parked not far from the restaurant. The red-haired guy got out of the passenger side, entered the station, and returned to the car in a few minutes.

"You wanted to talk," Beauford said.

William shook his head. "Right now?"

"Yeah. Why don't you come to my place, you've never been here."

"Dad, we're right in the middle of something—"

Beauford interrupted. "William, I need to talk to you now...now or, I don't know how much longer I can hold on."

"Where're you?"

Beauford gave him the address on East Delaware.

"What're you doing there? That's not in your ward." He shook his head. "Never mind, I'll get there as soon as can." William hung up the phone and hustled to his "G" car. "Shit." He got on the two-way. "1118 from 1174."

"Go. 1174 we're heading north on Kedzie approaching Archer."

"Something just came up. I've got to head to the north side if it's alright with you."

"Ah, sure 1174. Check back in if you're available later. Over."

"God damn it." William threw the mic on the passenger seat and headed to his father's place. *All I need is for Eckhaus to find out I dropped out of a surveillance. He'll fire my ass.*

\*\*\*

Soder and Junior entered Karl's Guns and Surplus on Archer. The walls were filled with military rifles and any weapon that passed the slimmest legal test. Glass counters filled with revolvers and semiautomatic pistols formed a square around the small interior of the store. Mannequins dressed in battle fatigues were suspended from the ceiling.

Karl Weidlich sat on a stool in the rear, cash register in front of him, door to the range behind him. Thick forearms stuck out from the rolled up sleeves of his Army shirt. A faded blue tattoo of a dagger with a drop of blood dripping from its point started at the top of his right forearm and ended at his wrist. Short blond hair slicked back with Brylcreme glistened under the fluorescent lights.

"Karl, how're you doing?" Soder shook his meaty hand.

He smiled and nodded at Junior. "Great Kurt. Who's your boy?"

"He works for me at the station. Wanted to give him a little pistol training in case some gemoke tries to rob the place."

"You can never be too careful. Go ahead, the range is empty."

Soder pulled a ten spot out of his pocket, placed it on the counter. He stepped to the left of the counter and opened a green steel door. Inside were eight booths separated by steel panels with a hinged platform. Junior handed him the pistol. He laid it and a box of 9 mm ammo on the platform, removed the magazine, loaded eight rounds from the box and slapped it back into the pistol.

"You ever shoot a semi auto before?"

Junior shook his head.

Soder stepped into the booth, hung a target and cranked the wheel on the panel on the right side sending the target seven yards down range. "Put on your ear protection." They both grabbed headgear and put them on. He grabbed the pistol and faced down range. "Let me show you how its done. Grip the pistol firmly in your right hand, wrap the fingers on you left hand around your fingers on the pistol. Keep your arms extended, wrist firm and gently squeeze the trigger and aim for center mass—the kill zone."

There was a loud bang. Junior jumped. Cordite filled their nostrils. Light shown through a circular hole dead center in the target.

Soder rested the semi auto on the platform. "Now you try it."

Junior smiled, stepped into the booth and grabbed the pistol. He pointed it down range and jerked the trigger four times— *bam, bam, bam, bam.*

Soder shoved his open palm against the back of Junior's head and shouted, "No, no, no. Put the pistol down and take off you ear protection."

Junior followed his orders.

"I told you squeeze the trigger not jerk it. Do it gently like you caressing a tit. Look at the target. There's still only one hole. You didn't even hit the paper, let alone the target."

"Okay, okay." Junior turned facing the target, put on the headgear and gripped the pistol. He squeezed the remaining three rounds one at a time and put the empty gun down.

"Well, that nigger would've killed you about three times and you still didn't put a hole in him." Soder shook his head. "Keep on practicing. I'm gonna buy some more ammo. I can see we'll be here for a while."

Junior fired another eight rounds before putting one on the paper and one in the leg of the silhouette target. Over the next hour he fired over a hundred rounds. The floor was covered with empty shell casings. His pattern of shots on the target became smaller and shifted to the center.

"How am I doing," Junior asked.

"A hell of a lot better than when we came in."

Kurt put up the last clean target and sent it down range.

"Watch me, I got three rounds left." Junior's pressure on the trigger slowly increased. The pistol steady in his hand. He fired the first round. There was a bullet hole between the eyes. Did it again, leaving a hole in the mouth and the final shot hit the kill zone—a hole in the heart.

# CHAPTER TWENTY-NINE

Thirty minutes later William was cruising up Michigan Avenue and turned at the John Hancock building onto Delaware Place wondering what his father was doing in the Gold Coast. The high-rises and in-vogue restaurants were a far cry from the bungalows and three-flats of Marquette Park. He pulled the Plymouth into the Hancock public parking garage and spiraled up the ramp parking the faded blue "G" car between a black Mercedes and a forest-green Jaguar. He ran across the street and the doorman in a red coat with gold epaulettes opened the door.

He followed William into the vestibule. Large Chinese vases flanked each side of the entrance. Art deco wall sconces cast soft tones onto the bronze wallpaper. The black-marble floor glistened from that day's waxing. The doorman stepped behind a walnut console. He looked at the young black man in the black leather jacket and khaki pants. "Who would you like to see?"

"Beauford Richmond."

"And you are?"

"His son."

"One moment." The doorman picked up the intercom phone and rang 3-C. "Hello, Alderman. This is Jones. Fine, and you, sir…A young gentleman here says he's your son…Yes, sir." Jones nodded at the etched-glass security door and pushed the button on the console releasing the lock.

"Thanks," William said, entering the foyer. Gold latticed elevator doors separated, he stepped inside, and pushed the button for the third floor. The doors opened and he stepped into the hallway onto an oriental carpet of blue hues and followed the sign directing him to units A-C. He passed the same wallpaper and sconces that had decorated the vestibule and came to a solid-oak door with a gold C mounted on it. William pushed the doorbell button.

Moments later he heard the deadbolt lock turn and the door opened. His father stood there, the smell of whiskey reeking from his pores. He was in his stocking feet, navy-blue suit pants held up by maroon suspenders, and a white shirttail hanging down along one hip. His eyelids were heavy. Eyes glassed over. William was shocked by his father's girth. The night before his body had been camouflaged by a tailor-made double-breasted suit. Now he looked like a man on the downhill side of the darkest moment of his life.

Beauford stood in the foyer of his condo, one hand against the wall to support himself. "Come on in." He staggered down the hall, bracing each step with a hand against the wall, and plopped onto the sofa. He took a deep breath and leaned his head back against the overstuffed cushion.

William entered the living room and saw the leather furniture and glass-top coffee and end tables. He threw his jacket onto the sofa, baring the brown leather holster holding the 9 mm semi auto Glock on his hip. Canvassing the room, his eyes caught the walnut entertainment center filled with the latest in electronic gear. The sound of Miles Davis emanated from tall speakers. Van Gogh and Picasso posters hung on the walls. A soft glow emanated from recessed lights. The oak floor was covered with a black area rug. William sat down next to him, looked at the half-empty bottle of Jack Daniels and the Manhattan glass filled with melting ice cubes on the coffee table. He slid the bottle to the side. There was a heavy tension in the air. "What's going on?"

Beauford was silent, trying to gather up his courage. He leaned forward and wailed. "If it wasn't for Marlee and you and your mother, I would of let them kill me." He held his head in his hands, elbows on his knees, trying to control his shaking body.

William realized that his father was in pain, though he wasn't sure what caused it. *Something that happened long ago or the pangs of liquor wasting away his mind.*

\*\*\*

Beauford felt like his entire body was roiling; his soul revolting against the denigration it had suffered through the lies, killings, corruption and the cost to him of the relationships and love that he had cast aside. He had to set it straight but was chained by denial of his past. There was a whirling in his ears. Sweat spewed out of his pores. A low guttural noise exorcised from the depths of his soul. His guts twisted, turned and heaved, and the contents gushed past his lips shooting across the room.

\*\*\*

William fell back into the sofa shocked at the eerie sounds, frightened by the sight of his father's curse-like sickness, and repelled by the rank odor of the vomit. He lunged forward grabbing his father as the man coughed and the remainder of the vomit hung from his chin, dripping onto his shirt.

William ran into the bathroom and turned the cold water on in the black marble sink. He grasped the edges of the sink, wondering what demon had possessed his father. Looking into the mirror he saw the reflection of the matching Jacuzzi and shower stall behind him and towels monogrammed with the letter I. What was his father doing here and whose place was this? He grabbed the towels, threw one in the sink, wrung it out, and returned to the living room. He wiped his father's face and shirt with the wet towel, noticing the deep furrows in his forehead and the creases around his eyes. William wondered what tension, what experiences, could have generated those lines. He patted him dry with the second towel. "Do you want me to call the paramedics?"

"No. No," Beauford gasped. "Just stay here with me, please. I need to lie down."

William stood. "I'm here as long as you need me." He took the towels, cleaned up the vomit on the coffee table and rug, and threw them into the Jacuzzi.

Beauford lay on the sofa and closed his eyes.

William returned and sat on the edge of the sofa. He didn't know if this was the right time to push his father to talk, but his old man had called him to open up. "Dad, who was going to kill you?"

"What?"

"Before you got sick you said if it wasn't for Mom, Marlee, and me, you would've let them kill you. Who would have killed you?"

"That was the booze talkin'. Nobody—"

"Bullshit!" William's anger flared. His father was reverting to his old ways, like the games he played last night. "You said on the phone that you didn't know if you could hold on. What did you mean?"

***

Beauford wished he had never called William. He wanted to put this all behind him. Now he was being confronted with his inadequacies by his son. A tear rolled down his cheek and he closed his eyes. It was time to give it up. He had exhausted his defenses. Now he had to release himself and not pretend that he would be healed by what he was going to say. He wasn't a hero. There was no credit to be taken. He owned his own shame and anger and this had nothing to do with William, except that William had become one of his victims. At least his son would know what he had been through, assuming he would believe him. "Go into my bedroom. In the top drawer of the dresser, under my socks is a zip-lock plastic bag. Bring it here."

William returned and handed the bag to his father. He pulled the bag open and an old airline ticket and a matchbook spilled onto the coffee table.

William sat there, eyebrows slanted down, lips partially separated. "What's this stuff?"

"You should take these papers to your lab or whatever you call it and have them check it. See what they can find on these papers."

"I need to tell them what they're looking for and why. And 'why' is the question that's in my mind, too." William took a pen out of his shirt pocket and used it to push the matchbook and ticket around to get a better look at them. "This airline ticket is from 1968. If this is evidence of any crime the statute of limitations has expired—unless it's a capital crime. You have to tell me more. The name on this ticket is Muhammad Hasan. Who's that?"

"For one day, that was me." Beauford went on starting with the night at Blackhawk Bayou when the Klan gave him the choice of where he could die. "I shoved it up their asses and told them I wanted to die in Napier's barn where I fucked his daughter. Celeste came on to me. Said she was going to claim rape if I didn't. Napier was hitching me up behind his pickup when Mayor LeGrand showed up. He stopped Napier. I didn't know why. LeGrand told me to go back to Memphis, pick up my family and go to Chicago. Gave me a business card of a man in Chicago who would get a place for us to stay and a job for me. But, LeGrand didn't tell me that they took Marlee and I wasn't gonna get her back until I made a delivery for the man in Chicago."

William leaned forward. "What did you have to deliver?"

Beauford picked up the glass from the coffee table, sipped the water from the melted ice and set the glass down. "The guy I met in Chicago was Helmut Reichardt, the ward committeeman. He gave me a brown paper bag and a couple of little books. They were passports. Reichardt told me there was a room for me in a boarding house in Memphis, wait there for someone to pick up the bag, and as soon as that was done I could come back to Chicago. He told me when I returned we'd get Marlee back." Beauford took a deep breath.

William nodded. "Evidently everything went all right. I remember Marlee was back with us right away."

"Got to Memphis and almost got into an accident. I slammed on the brakes and the bag rolled to the floor and a bunch of cash fell out. Went to the boarding house and later a white guy comes for the money and passports. I lay down to take a nap before I started home and there's commotion in the parking lot behind the boarding house that wakes me up. I looked out the window. I see Dr. King and the next thing..." He paused and choked on the words. "...I heard a shot and Dr. King collapses."

William sat there, a look of disbelief on his face.

"The man I gave the money to was Ray." His own statement crushed him. Saying it out loud made it impossible to deny his actions and the consequences.

"Are you sure? You only saw him for a few seconds. You were all worked up after what you'd been through, it was probably somebody else. This probably had nothing to do with King's assassination. I mean, it was investigated thoroughly. How could... ?"

"It was him," Beauford blurted out. He felt the muscles in the back of his neck tighten and heaviness in his chest. He took a deep breath, trying to slow the pounding beat of his heart. "I know it was him because I thought he was going to kill me. After the shot was fired I grabbed my things and ran out of the room. Ray was in the hallway, with the rifle. He looked at me and then ran down the stairs."

William exhaled. "Jesus."

"The next day we got Marlee back and then Reichardt told me about the warrants in Mississippi. That's when I changed our name."

"You know I've got to report this."

"Why? The killer's in jail. You got the man."

"But if all this is true there was a far-reaching conspiracy, not just the act of one assassin."

Beauford wiped his hand over his lips. "Isn't there some way you can check things out first? See if some of these people are in your files and maybe there's a reason for how this worked out...I don't know. It scares me to talk about this. To live through it again."

"I don't know. Let me think. There's a guy I trust. He's been like a father to me." William looked up and saw the pain on Beauford's face. "I'm sorry, but you know what I mean. Let me try to get in touch with him and I'll get back to you." William started to stand.

"Don't go." He put his hand on William's arm and then leaned forward resting his forearms on his knees. "There's more. A couple of days later Reichardt sent me on another trip. This one was to Toronto to deliver an envelope to Ray. It must have been the rest of his money."

\*\*\*

"Jesus." William couldn't understand his own emotions. He felt a bizarre giddiness. He was sure it wasn't from his father's openness. There was a selfish side to this feeling. He felt important. He had something big in the palm of his hands. If he could corroborate his father's statements he would break the biggest case ever, and maybe, just maybe the biggest cover-up ever. He would keep this to himself, not even tell Daniels. Then he would show Eckhaus how good he was.

"The airline ticket and matchbook, what do they have to do with all this?"

\*\*\*

Beauford looked at William. There was a change in his son's posture, the tone of his voice. He sat aloof, the look of an official posture. Care had departed from William's voice and he was searching for information like a heat-seeking missile.

Beauford sat back, creating a distance between them, trying to size up this change in William. He had gone this far; there was no sense in stopping—or was there? The trust that William was seeking from him didn't seem reciprocal at this moment. But this was his son he was talking to, the one who wanted to change the way things were. Maybe he wasn't reading the boy right. Maybe what his son was offering scared him. He sighed, and with apprehension went on. "It was a couple of months later...."

Beauford paused as the nausea came back to his stomach and he dry heaved. He reached out for William's hand and nodded. "I'm okay. I got to get this out." He paused. "Reichardt told me he wanted me to go on a trip to California. I told him I wasn't going to be a part of another murder. I wasn't going to take no gun or money. He said it was nothing like that. I just had to deliver a dress. He gave me that airline ticket and matchbook with the Arab name written in it that the hotel reservation was under." Beauford leaned forward and took a deep breath.

William pushed on, "What happened then?"

The question hit Beauford as if an icicle was thrust into his chest. It was cold, pointed, and penetrating. He looked down at the floor. "Next day I flew to LA, went to the hotel and waited. Some woman came to the door and barged into the room. She undressed right in front of me and put on the dress—a fancy thing with polka dots. Then she charged out of the room."

"That's it?"

"No, you were too young then, that's why you don't remember."

"Don't remember what?"

"After she left I thought I'd go for a walk, maybe get a drink. I went down the elevator and it stopped on two. I heard somebody speaking, people cheering, whistling, and clapping. I got off to see what's going on and go into this meeting room that's stuffed with hundreds of people waving signs. There's red, white, and blue banners hanging from the walls. I couldn't even see who's up there speaking and hardly heard what the guy is saying. I worked my way through the crowd, getting closer to the front. They were cheering for Bobby Kennedy."

"Don't tell me."

Beauford nodded. "That was the night."

"But just because you were sent there doesn't mean your trip was related to the assassination."

"That's not the end. I worked my way closer to Kennedy and he finished his speech. It was like I just floated with the crowd that wanted to be with him. I wasn't too far away, I heard shots, and people shouting, 'The senator's shot! Get the SOB!' There was all sorts of commotion. People jumped on the shooter and I looked across the crowd and saw the lady with the polka-dot dress. She's smiling, 'til she saw me. Then she took off and I'm fighting through the crowd trying to get her. She ran out a back door into the parking lot and disappears. I remember her shouting, as she ran pass a cleaning lady, 'We shot the senator!'"

"No one will believe this."

"There's proof I was there. I tried to sneak out but the cops and FBI were all over. Some FBI agent interviewed me and I was so nervous I told him my name was Beauford Tisdale Richmond. I was so afraid that they would check the records and see those warrants for me. But nothing ever happened. I told your mother I had to go to deliver some original papers for city business. When I got home she had seen a news clip of Kennedy's speech that night, and saw me on it. I told her that was impossible cause I wasn't there, but she knew it was me. I couldn't live with it anymore, all this shit on my mind. Couldn't sleep, sweating away the nights 'til I drank enough so I couldn't remember anything."

"That was the last assassination. How come they stopped?"

"I don't know. Not for sure anyway. Maybe cause I killed Reichardt."

## CHAPTER THIRTY

There were egos in the Bureau that needed to be fed with their own self-importance. These people would stab anyone in the back who attacked the results of their investigations or secretly run with rumors that would disprove the results of someone else's case. Allegations that the assassinations of Reverend King and Senator Kennedy were conspiracies could become the most significant cases in Bureau history. Unknown to William, there was one person who would squash this story if he knew about it. That was the man he worked for.

Wednesday morning, William sat at his desk in the FBI office deaf to the ringing of phones, cacophony of conversations, and shuffling of people. He stared at a yellow legal pad in front of him contemplating what his father had told him last night. On one hand it seemed like a distant dream, or more appropriately a nightmare or a figment of his imagination. But on the other hand William was beginning to realize it was a prize.

William thought it preposterous that his father was involved in two of the most infamous crimes of the century. Just as preposterous was a rookie agent barely out of Quantico trying to figure out what to do next in a case of this magnitude. The young agent's ego was feeding on the institutional climate of the Bureau and he wanted to hold on to the investigation himself. Once he approached Eckhaus he would lose all control of any investigation that would result. He wouldn't let some rookie work this case. William could justify keeping it under his hat for at least a few days while he attempted to corroborate what his father told him. After all, his old man was drunk on half a bottle of whiskey last night. He centered a pad in front of him and jotted down some notes.

1. Check indices re BTR interview in LA 1968. Verify he was in LA.
2. Call Jackson-check on Mayor LeGrand, date of death, does it jive with King's assassination? Obtain any reports. Anything suspicious about death?
3. Check with Chicago PD re report on Reichardt's shooting. Self defense-any ramifications to BTR
4. Send Holiday Inn matchbook and ticket to lab. Get around Eckhaus' approval?
5. Long shot-check with Holiday Inn in Knoxville for week before RFK shooting for rooms booked and paid for in cash. Name?

He tapped the pen against the pad, filling the upper right corner with a circle of blue dots. *What else? What else? There must be something I'm not thinking of. Another long shot.*

6. Check LA hotel for registration under the name of Muhammad Hasan.

The phone rang and William jumped in his chair. "FBI, Special Agent Richmond."

"It's me, Jackson. Gotta hold of your lady last night."

"Thanks for getting right on that. How'd it turn out?"

"Good. Good, she gave me a statement. Ought to be good enough to clear Tisdale. You didn't tell me he was your daddy. If he's you daddy why's your name Richmond?"

Eckhaus walked up to William's desk, grabbed the legal pad, and thumped its edge against the palm of his hand.

"One second," William covered the mouthpiece, his eyes following the legal pad, watching each time it hit Eckhaus' meaty palm. Hoping that he wouldn't stop to read his list. "Yes, sir."

"You going to be long?"

"No, sir." William's heart beat so hard he thought Eckhaus would hear it.

"We're having a debriefing on last night's surveillance in five minutes. It would be nice if you could join us."

Debriefing last night's surveillance. The words hit him like a heavyweight punch. Did Eckhaus know he skipped out? William didn't want to make a habit of residing in his supervisor's doghouse. He hoped that Eckhaus had alienated the other agents in the squad enough that they would prefer to be silent rather than front him off. "Yes, sir. I'll be done in a minute."

Eckhaus dropped the pad on the desk with a thud and returned to his office.

William grabbed the pad and turned it over. He decided to ignore Jackson's inquiry about his father. Hopefully, the subject wouldn't come up again. On a personal level he was glad to get his father's record clear but the rest of the information hung over him like a dark cloud. Professionally, the information his father gave him sparked his ambition. If only it wasn't his father who was involved in the assassinations it would be so much easier. But he wasn't ready to talk about it yet. "Sorry, Jackson. My boss had a couple of questions for me."

"We all gotta answer to somebody. Anyways, what you want me to do with this lady's statement?"

"Mail a copy to me and get the original to a judge to get the charges dropped."

"Being your daddy and all you want me to fax it? Get it to you faster."

"No! Just mail it." That's all he needed was somebody picking it up at the fax machine. "That'll be fine."

"Calm down. You people up north got to learn not to take things so seriously."

"Sorry. I owe you. If I can ever be of help to you call me."

"There was one thing that your young lady brought up that I didn't put in her statement. Kind of unrelated matter."

"What's that?"

"Well, I don't know how much credence you wanna put in this. She said that night that LeGrand found her in that flophouse, he was meeting with a guy she thinks was James Earl Ray."

William flipped over the pad and jotted down the new information. "Jackson, can you do me another favor?"

"Boy, you gonna have to put me on your payroll. What is it?"

"Can you get me whatever you have on LeGrand's death? Investigative reports, autopsy, whatever you can find."

"And you want this when?"

"The usual, ASAP, thanks again."

"One thing before I go. The lady wants you to call her ASAP."

"Yeah, I plan to. Talk to you later." William hung up the phone and scribbled another item to his list.

    7.  Check indices on LeGrand; see if there's any connection to JER.

He slid the pad into his center desk drawer, locked it, and was the last one to join the meeting. Everything went smoothly except for the evil eye Eckhaus gave him as he peered over his glasses.

***

Junior slipped on black leather gloves and drove the beige 1975 Volkswagen Beetle that had been dropped off at Soder's for a tune-up out of the station. It wasn't for a test drive. He had learned a lot from his one-day crash course on surveillance with Soder and felt he could do it on his own. At 2:30 he pulled the VW into the parking garage and parked against the west wall on the third floor facing the courthouse. He used old camouflaged binoculars Soder had at the gas station to watch the people leaving the building.

Junior's imagination went to work. The binocular became a scope on a sniper's rifle. He fixed the crosshairs on the people leaving the courthouse and annihilated them one after another with perfect shots between the eyes or directly into the heart. After an hour of shooting imaginary targets boredom began to set in. He should have checked to see if Moskowitz had worked today. What if it was some Jew holiday? He pictured him praying at temple, "Please let me be a rich man." Junior started to curse himself. It was late Friday afternoon and if he had stayed at Soder's they would be in one of the repair bays cracking open a case of cold Old Style getting ready for the weekend and here he was waiting on some kyke that might not even be here.

By five the garage was nearly empty. Junior was rocking back and forth slamming himself into the back of the driver's seat listening to the car radio. His impatience gnawing at him.

A solitary figure left the courthouse carrying an overloaded, worn leather satchel in one hand and several legal size folders in the other.

Junior peered through the binoculars. "Your momma would be so proud. You working so hard." He cranked the key and the engine stuttered, slowly trying to turn over. "Shit." He turned the radio off and tried again. The engine groaned and the result was the same. Junior banged his fist against the steering wheel. "Mother fucker."

He got out of the car and ran to the stairwell in the southwest corner of the garage. It was dark and he took two stairs at a time, rushing down tumbling onto the second floor landing. He knelt on all fours, chest expanding and contracting. He just wanted to follow Moskowitz to his car and he was fucking that up. If he could just find out which car was Moskowitz's it wouldn't be a lost night.

Junior heard the ground floor door scrape against the cement as it shut. He stood, his knee aching, and leaned against the cold concrete wall. He rubbed his knee, felt the tear in his pants, and the wetness of his own blood. His heart was pounding in his eardrums. The sound of footfalls on the steps below getting louder as the man's leather shoes dragged against the steel stairs.

\*\*\*

Moskowitz felt like he was in over his head. He had eighty cases in his inventory. Three trials scheduled to start next week. In two of the cases, he hadn't interviewed the defendants yet and he had first seen the discovery material on these cases this afternoon. His clients were two gangbanger dope dealers and a rapist. He laughed, correct that, alleged dope dealers and rapist. Judge Shelton had given him three continuances on the rapist; he couldn't dare ask for a fourth.

He had another lost weekend to look forward to. Researching cases, reviewing investigative reports, spending a good portion of his Saturday and Sunday in Cook County Jail talking to clients that thought being in jail was a badge of honor. He pictured himself running through the ghetto looking for witnesses who were at best a fifty-fifty chance of showing up in court. All this for $16,000 a year.

He longed for the days when he was a law student and worked for spending money in his grandfather's shoe repair store in Skokie. At that time the Law held such high ideals for him. Now the Law was a burden and he didn't know if he was up to it.

His broomstick arms ached from the weight of his satchel filled with law books and case files. Moskowitz was weary from the overwhelming nature of Cook County justice. He had lost cases to lying cops and legal tricks he thought he should have won, won cases he should have lost, and was afraid to ask why.

\*\*\*

Junior stepped forward leaning over the metal railing watching him. The man stopped halfway up the stairs, rested the heavy satchel on the floor, and shook his tired hand. He switched the folders to the other hand, picked up the satchel, and continued up the stairs. Junior leaned against the wall in the corner of the landing.

His impulse for blood was taking over. His taste for revenge for the time he spent in jail and the murder of his mother and father dominated his emotions. Beads of sweat rolled down his forehead, stinging his eyes. His knee throbbed. The sound of the footfalls became louder. His reality was reduced to this moment. The man turned facing the last landing, five stairs from Junior.

Junior reached up the sleeve of his leather coat, grabbing the handle of the dagger. He watched the dark shadow move closer, one step at a time. Junior unleashed the dagger from its sheath and lunged into the man as he reached the top step. He grabbed the man's shoulder, pulling him close and pushing the dagger into the man's gut.

\*\*\*

Moskowitz felt an icy spear penetrate his abdomen and then the heat of pain rushed through his body. He felt transfixed in the headlights of death, losing control of everything, his satchel and files. His fingers grasped for them and closed on nothing. He needed them for....The pain erased the reason in his mind. He leaned into the man in front of him. *What's happening?* Twice more he felt the spear and grasped for the source of his pain. His vision turning from light to blackness. He fell to his knees, hands feeling his abdomen, finding a deep crevice, trying to keep his guts inside his body. Blood gushed out, oozing over his hands, down his pants. *I'll be awake in a little while. It'll be okay.* He was losing it. Felt wobbly, pushed, tumbled back. *Why me? I'm just...trying to do the law.* He fell to the landing below his last breath going as he longed for his grandfather's shoe repair store.

\*\*\*

The man fell into Junior. The satchel and files falling, papers cascading and floating down the well between the stairs. Junior pulled the dagger out and lunged it into his victim again and again. The man fell to his knees holding onto his attacker. Junior pushed him back and watched Moskowitz roll to the landing below as the last breaths of life escaped his body.

He jumped down to the landing and rifled through Moskowitz's pockets finding a set of car keys and his wallet. "You son of a bitch. You owe me for the time I was locked up." He opened the wallet and removed twenty-two dollars. "Cheap bastard. What is this? The allowance you got from Momma." He dropped the wallet and stashed the cash in his pocket. Junior held the blade up and watched Moskowitz's blood drip to the floor. He smiled, dragged the blade against his victim's navy blue trench coat, and ran up to the third floor. The only cars still there were the VW, a ten-year old midnight blue Buick Park Lane, and a Ford. He glanced at the keys again. "GM keys. The Buick must be a hand me down from his old man." Junior ran to the VW, gave the steering wheel, dashboard, and door handles a quick wipe down with a rag from the back seat, grabbed the binoculars and headed to the Buick. He slid into the seat, started the car, and noticed something sitting on the dashboard. It was Moskowitz's yarmulke. Junior lowered the window and threw it onto the garage floor. "Here Jew boy, you probably need this for a rightful burial." He drove the Buick out of the parking lot and headed to Cicero to catch a few brews.

\*\*\*

On Friday the FBI office started emptying out by three in the afternoon. By early evening a skeleton crew was left. At six William took his briefcase and headed to the file room. The after hours would be a good time to check the indices for Josephus LeGrand, Muhammad Hasan, and Beauford Tisdale.

The file clerk, Cindy, was munching on a Snickers as she stacked a group of file jackets two feet high on her desk to be filed. She was in her fifties, petite for a mother of four, and had been in the file room for fifteen years.

"Hi Cindy, I've a ton of paperwork to do. Why don't you take your dinner break? I can do my work here, just as well as at my desk." William said.

"I usually don't go 'til eight."

"I've got enough work to last me for two days. Go ahead, take some extra time if you need it."

"If you don't mind. I did want to do some shopping at Fields." She grabbed her purse and coat.

"Take extra time if you need it. I'll be here." Good place to hide from anyone left in the office.

William sat down, opened his briefcase, laid the request to the forensic lab on the desk and scribbled Eckhaus' illegible signature to the transmittal requesting an expedite fingerprint analysis on the matchbook and airline ticket. He would drop it in the Friday evening express mail on his way out. He wanted to know as much as possible before he had to hand over the investigation. There was a self-centeredness that was growing in him. Didn't he deserve some of the credit for unearthing the conspiracy? He wanted to be more than the typical grunt rookie agent running errands for senior agents. He had busted his butt in Quantico and where had it gotten him? On some squad that was doing little more that chasing ghosts from World War II. He had stumbled onto something significant and was intent on working it as far as he could, to the end, he hoped and what if the end found there was a cover-up in the original investigation? Even better.

He found no references to James Earl Ray in the LeGrand dossier. He did get hits verifying that a room at the Ambassador Hotel had been registered to a Muhammad Hasan the night of Senator Kennedy's assassination and that a Beauford Richmond had been interviewed that night at the hotel. William closed the file and waited for the night clerk to return. Corroborating his father's story gave him a queasy feeling. Hearing the story was one thing. Now that he was proving that his father was involved in the assassinations of King and Kennedy, the story became a bitter pill to swallow.

Cindy returned at 7:30 and he headed to his sparsely furnished apartment to make the phone call he dreaded. He had the feeling that Celeste was going to be one pain in the ass but she was the one who would be responsible for having the charges against his father dropped. As long as she didn't come to Chicago it shouldn't be too hard to deal with her. He just wasn't sure of his reasoning, if it was better for her or him. But he couldn't just shut her off because even though she didn't know it, she might be useful to him in the conspiracy investigation. After what she had been through she deserved at least a phone call. Maybe he could convince her she would be better off not seeing his father. He punched the numbers into the phone.

"Hello."

"Celeste, it's me, William."

"What took you so long to call?"

"It's only been a couple of days…"

"I'm entitled to know what's going on."

William paused. What makes her think she's so entitled?

"I made reservations to fly to Chicago Monday."

"Why do you want to come here?"

"I want to see Beauford."

"I don't understand."

"Do I need a reason?"

"It makes no sense to me—"

"I want my daughter to meet her father."

There was a long silence on the phone.

"What…Why didn't you say something about this before?"

"The girl you saw on the staircase with me at Mrs. Virden's. That's Missy. That's your step sister."

"He's not the man you knew in Mississippi. He left our family a long time ago. Divorced my mother. I think you should reconsider. It might be more painful for the child than—"

"I don't care what you think. He's my child's father and she has a right to meet him. We'll be on Delta flight 73. Lands at Midway at 4:00 p.m. I'll expect you there to pick us up." The phone went silent.

\*\*\*

Eckhaus watched Bill Kurtis and Walter Jacobson sign off of WBBM's 10:00 p.m. news, left the office and hailed a cab at the south side of the federal building on Jackson. He stepped into the back seat. *Great a fucking towel head. Probably doesn't know where the Hilton is.* "You know where the Hilton is?"

"Yes, sir. Take you directly there."

Eckhaus looked forward to parking himself in a bar, having a shot and a beer to ease his aching back, and review the story he had created for Pape.

The cabby hit the meter, headed east on Jackson and turned south on Michigan Avenue past Grant Park. The traffic was heavy with Friday night partiers. The cab wove through traffic and was in front of the Hilton in less than ten minutes. He gave the cabby four dollars for a three dollar fare as the doorman, dressed in red, opened the cab door. He stepped out of the cab and looked up at the building.

It covered the entire block of 700 south Michigan Avenue. A bulky twenty-seven story building constructed over fifty years ago. It had been the home to many meetings in smoke filled rooms that had decided the fates of politicians.

Eckhaus walked under the giant canopy that extended from the building to the curb. Another red-coated doorman opened a gold door and Eckhaus entered the foyer. Curving staircases on each side led to ballrooms. Forty feet above him the ceiling was bordered in gold filigree and in the center was a painting of winged angels flying through white and blue clouds. He moved from the plush red carpet to the black marble floor of the main hallway. A sign on the wall gave directions: one arrow pointing right for hotel registration and another pointing left to Flanigan's Pub. Eckhaus turned left.

He walked into Flanagan's. A square shaped bar filled the center of the room. The most likable element of the bar to Eckhaus was its emptiness. The least likable was the Irish music that rang painfully in his ears.

Two men sat at one end of the bar, both with red hair turning gray, in cheap navy blue suits. One of them had red jowls and a matching veined nose. The other had pale white Chicago winter skin stretched tight across his bony face. The knots on their respective red and gray ties were pulled down to somewhere between shnockered and passed out. On the bar in front of them were train schedules, two steins of Guinness Stout, and change from a twenty. Commuters debating which strategy would work best for them. Leave now to catch the next train, go home to a nagging wife and screaming kids, or have another pint. They ordered up.

A forty plus year old barmaid with straw colored hair that was several times removed from her natural color waited on them. She leaned into the bar showing her stuff in a low cut frilly short sleeve blouse that was made for a woman that was twenty pounds lighter and fifteen years younger.

Eckhaus sat at the far end of the bar away from the threesome. He looked through the windows on the Michigan Avenue side and watched a cop chase a homeless man away from the hotel.

The barmaid jerked her head in Eckhaus' direction, removed her jiggling arms from the bar and sauntered down to him. "What do you want, Hon?"

"Give me a shot of Jack and a draught."

"Why don't you come down to the other end of the bar and join the party? I'll give you your order on the house. The manager's gone. We'll have a good time."

"No thanks. I'll have mine here." He laid a five on the bar.

She shrugged. "Suit yourself."

Eckhaus tapped his finger on the bar. "Drinks please."

She grabbed the cash, stuffed it in her bra, and got his drinks.

Eckhaus sipped the whiskey. He felt a burst of heat in his throat and relaxed as the warmth slid down to his stomach. The pain in his back dulled and he reviewed the high points of the script he had gone over several times in the office today. If he had to he'd appeal to Pape's desire to fulfill the legacy that was to be his dead son's, to his thirst to satisfy his aging father's ambition, and that he could be the man his father had hoped he would be all along. He would tell Pape he inadvertently found out about a threat to his lofty goals.

Eckhaus looked at the photographs of Ireland, Irish people, and their family crests that decorated the walls. "Bunch of ragtags. That's why they drink so much." He grabbed the stein and jerked back a slug. He glanced at his watch, it was time to head upstairs and secure his future. He pushed the stein away, embraced the shot glass, and knocked down the remaining whiskey. The glass clinked as he lowered it to the bar. He looked into the empty glass and laughed to himself as he thought of all the shots Pape would be paying for with the Republican Party's contribution to his retirement fund.

Eckhaus left the bar without a glance at his fellow patrons, headed to hotel registration, and got Pape's suite number. He took the elevator to the twenty-third floor and walked down the hallway. Eckhaus stared at the suite number on the door, reached into his inside coat pocket and turned on the mini cassette tape recorder. A tape would give him something to use even if Pape wouldn't fall for his scam. Certainly there would be at least a couple of good admissions that would get a large sum of money out of him. And if he did go for the scam and later changed his mind, the tape would be the cement that would hold the deal together. Eckhaus knocked on the door. Moments later he heard the chain slip off its clasp, the dead bolt turn, and the door opened.

"Hello, James." His voice had the finesse of a modern day Rhett Butler. Pape was as slender as he had been ten years ago. His hair was still the same, but now with a dash more of silver at the temples that made him look like a vice-presidential candidate. He wore a navy-blue pullover sweater, black slacks and loafers with tassels, and held a martini glass filled to the rim. He extended his other hand. "You're looking good."

Eckhaus stood there in the wrinkled brown suit that he had been wearing since six that morning, trench coat hanging over his arm. "Your eyes aren't what they use to be." He walked past Pape's extended hand into the suite. In front of him was the foyer, twice as long as it was wide, art deco wall sconces softly lit the Rembrandt replicas on the walls. Eckhaus followed Pape across the deep blues of an oriental carpet into the dining area with sitting rooms on both sides of a dining room table that sat eight. Above the dining room table was a tear drop chandelier. The light from it spread across the ceiling, creating shadows that looked like washed out leaves. Beyond the table were windows overlooking Grant Park and Lake Michigan. They walked toward the windows four armchairs surrounded a French provincial coffee table. A matching liquor cabinet was against the wall.

Pape held up his drink. "Martini, can I get you one?"

Eckhaus sat in one of the armchairs. "I prefer whiskey. Jack Daniels, if you have it."

"The suites are well stocked." Pape went to the liquor cabinet, poured the whiskey three fingers deep in an old-fashion glass, and gave it to Eckhaus.

Eckhaus took in the suite. "Quite a room. Who's picking up the tab?"

"Courtesy of the Republican National Committee. They're a gracious host."

That was just what Eckhaus wanted to hear. The purse strings were open.

Pape swirled the vodka with his finger. "So what is it that brings us together after all this time."

"There may be a problem. One that might interfere with your vice-presidential candidacy."

Pape's forehead furrowed. "How's that?"

"I heard through the grapevine that an attorney contacted headquarters. He has a client who claims to have information that would reveal that King's assassination was a conspiracy."

Pape laughed, sat in the chair opposite Eckhaus, and parked his feet on top of the coffee table between them. "Oh, come on, James. After all this time and the thorough investigation you conducted, who would believe such an allegation? He's just another conspiracy theorist and just like all the others he'll be shot down because no one will believe him. And you'll be there to protect us."

"I'm not in the loop. They might consult me, but by that time this would be a snowball rolling downhill." He took a sip of the whiskey. "From what I heard the attorney had a letter hand carried to the Director, for his eyes only, with a few specific pieces of evidence or testimony. The attorney is asking for $200,000 in cash up front for his client and a complete new identity if the Director decides to go forward. A total new make over, not the witness protection program, and the Director is seriously considering this request." He took another sip, exhaled, and pawed across the five o'clock shadow on his face.

"After all this time, I'm so close and now this has to happen." Pape loudly exhaled. "What can we do? If even a rumor of this gets out I'm ruined. The RNC will turn their back and run away like I've got the plague." He ran his fingers through his hair. "My father is eighty-one. This would put him in his grave. Who could it be? LeGrand knew me and the only link to both of us was Sakich. But they're both dead."

"That's why I called you. I thought I could help. The only thing I heard is that it's a woman." Eckhaus pulled out his Camels, put the pack to his lips, and slipped one out. He dragged his thumb over the striker wheel of his lighter, moved the flame to his smoke, and inhaled. "By any chance you didn't whisper in some shagger's ear in a moment of passion?"

"Don't be ridiculous." Pape stood, paced back and forth in front of the windows. The headlights of the cars on Lake Shore Drive pierced the ink black night. A beam from the lighthouse on the breakwater outside of Navy Pier circled into sight, disappeared for five seconds, then came back into view. Pape spun and threw his glass against the wall shattering it into pieces. "Who the hell could she be?"

"Who knows? If Sakich or LeGrand were trying to get in some broad's pants and wanted to impress her. At a time like that, a guy's dick takes over he'll say anything." Eckhaus took a long drag on his smoke.

"If it was LeGrand, could be one of his wives. The second one, he wouldn't have to tell her that to get in her pants. Just toss her his credit card. His first wife. She got a good piece of money from him. But she came from good stock, sophisticated lady, wouldn't want to listen to anything like this." Pape wiped the perspiration off his forehead with his sleeve. "If he was fucking some broad on the side how can we find out about her?"

Eckhaus liked the way this was going so far. He hadn't had to make any of his bullshit appeals to Pape about fulfilling his dead son's legacy or his old man's ambitions. "It's a long shot trying to guess who she might be. But if we find out through the Bureau or otherwise, we need to have a plan for how we're going to handle this."

"I can't have this go public. God damn it, it'll ruin me. If it did come out, how could I prove a negative, that I wasn't involved? This has to be stopped before your Director gets a statement from her. If he has a statement he can move on it, even if she's gone."

Eckhaus glanced at the nude painting of a rubenesque woman hanging above the liquor cabinet. "That leaves two options. Buy her out or get rid of her."

"There's no guarantee if we give her the money that she won't come back for more or decide to talk later."

"I agree. But it's risky for me to put my nose where it doesn't belong."

"Can't you volunteer? It would be logical since you oversaw the first investigation. Don't forget, you've something to be concerned about too."

"If you want me to handle this, I need you to help me."

"How's that?"

"My health is going." He leaned back and grimaced. "My back is killing me. I can't do the job myself. I'm going to have to hire somebody. It'll cost money. I'm trying to get out early on disability and that's not going to help my pension. I need some money to take care of myself."

"How much?"

Eckhaus wanted to shoot for the bank but there was no sense in getting greedy. He'd have his pension, some cash he had banked, and he didn't need a lot to live off of. "$200,000, the same as the girl is asking for. For that I can get the job done, subsidize my pension, and you become vice-president."

"Where am I going to get $200,000?"

"How about your Republican friends? They've got millions in campaign funds. Must be costing a fortune to put you up here for the weekend. You could probably get a couple of hundred thousand from them for a local fundraiser, no questions asked. I'm sure a winning ticket is worth $200,000 to them and the vice presidency is worth it to you." Eckhaus took a drag on his cigarette and exhaled the smoke through his nose. "We don't have a lot of time."

"I could do that. How do I get the money to you?"

Eckhaus didn't want to look too well prepared. That could take away from his credibility. "I'll line something up. In the meantime you see if you can think of any candidates who might be our lady and I'll see what I can find out on my end." He gulped down the rest of his whiskey and they walked to the door.

Eckhaus grabbed the doorknob. "How should I get in touch with you if something comes up?"

Pape handed him his business card. "My pager number is on here. Put in 1968 after your number I'll know it's you. Easy number for both of us to remember."

Eckhaus took a step into the hallway.

"Wait." Pape grabbed Eckhaus' forearm. "That land we got in Mississippi. LeGrand paid that girl some cash to be a nominee on the transaction. What's her name? Shit. The daughter of the guy that led us to Ray."

"Those were your guys. I didn't know those people."

"Napier. That's the guy's name. I can't think of the daughter's name. But you should be able to find her."

"What's Napier first name and where's he live?"

"It's Jimmy. But he's dead. An FBI agent shot him while he was bombing a black church. He was from Ruleville. It's got to be in your files, so it shouldn't be too hard to trace her down. He trusted her enough to have her act as a nominee on the land deal, he must have had something going on with her."

Eckhaus was smiling inside. If he had to get rid of some redneck broad to collect 200 G's it would not be a problem. "I'll check her out. Get back to you."

# CHAPTER THIRTY-ONE

Junior drove the Buick through Friday night traffic, parking a half block away from, Dick's Place, in Cicero. He pushed open the door and looked at the black shadow of Moskowitz's blood staining his shirt. He zipped up his jacket concealing the splotch and headed to the bar. Apprehension inched through him. He wondered how he would be greeted after Bruno's murder. No one knew he was the killer but he was sure some suspected him. Some would be scared of him, others would respect him for having the balls to ice somebody. The apprehension turned into pride. He was riding high from that sense of satisfaction a man gets from completing something that was extremely important to him and in his eyes doing it well. It was time for him to celebrate.

He stepped into the bar and the aroma of stale beer hit. The beer signs flashed greens and reds through the smoky haze. The bar was jammed with bikers and skinheads dressed in leather and tattoos. There wasn't anything close to conversations because shouting was the only way to be heard over the heavy metal blasting from the jukebox.

Junior leaned on the end of the bar closest to the door. He saw Dick Yost setting a handful of longneck bottles on the bar for a group of skinheads. His eyes caught Yost's. Within minutes, he would know if he had to flee or if the bar was his sanctuary.

Yost nodded at his customers, pocketed a ten spot, and opened two more beers. Junior braced his hands on the end of the bar, ready to push himself away. The barkeep marched toward him, placed the beers on the bar, put his hand around Junior's neck, and pulled him close. "Patty told me what happened. You're safe here, Bud." He released Junior, and nodded at a redhead leaning against the pool table being entertained by three bikers.

Junior caught a glance of her through the crowd of bikers. She was wearing a low-cut black leather vest revealing a deep valley between her breasts and matching leather pants that hung low on her hips. Red hair swept down to her shoulders.

Yost pushed Junior in her direction. Beer in hand, he meandered through the maze of bikers, and circled round the table getting glimpses of her but never getting a solid look at her face. There was a familiarity about her. The way her head jerked back when she laughed. But he didn't know a redhead. He stepped behind the three bulky men dressed in leather who had her cornered. One of them turned, "You want somethin'?"

The redhead's eyes caught Junior. She burst through the bikers and placed her lips onto his. He felt her tongue penetrating his mouth.

"What the fuck's this, baby." A hand reached out grabbing her arm. The faded blue tattoo of barbed wire flexed on his bicep. "I bought you two beers. Where do you think you're going?"

She glared at him. "Get away from me, asshole." She yanked her arm away. She grabbed Junior and dragged him to the back of the bar and into the ladies' room.

A blonde with bony cheeks and dark circles under her eyes stared at them. She pressed a thin finger to one nostril and tooted white powder from a long nail on her pinky finger.

The brunette next to her added a ten-dollar bill to a roll of cash and stuffed it into her jean pocket. "You two want some nose candy?" She said as she checked her black eye shadow in a cracked mirror that hung on the gray wall scribbled with swastikas.

The redhead sniped at them, "Get your asses out of here."

The blonde wiped her nose with the back of her hand and sniffled while the brunette smiled and looked at Junior.

"You're either in a lot of trouble or you're going to be a lucky man." The brunette pushed the blond towards the door and sauntered out of the bathroom.

The redhead stepped up to Junior, only a breath away from him. "You like my hair? I did it for you after I heard about Bruno. I wanted to have your fire."

Junior set his beer on the tarnished sink. "Patty, didn't know it was you 'til I got a good look at your face." He put his fingers through her hair. "I like it, it's hot."

"Baby, I'm sorry about the other night. I missed you, wanted to be with you, and you were with those guys." Patty stood on her toes, pressed her lips against his, and slid her tongue over Junior's. She stopped, shoved him against the door, reached over his shoulder and clicked the lock. Her face grew hard. She popped the four snaps of her vest letting it fall to the floor. Patty grasped Junior's head and brought his mouth to her nipples. Giggling as he sucked, groaning as he bit. "You're hurting me, do it harder." She pushed his head up. "I was mad at you but I knew that you'd prove you loved me." Patty's crimson lips perked at the corners of her mouth and she went down to her knees. Big brown eyes looked up at him. "If I hurt you or caused you pain the other night, I'm sorry. But I'm gonna suck that hurt out of you right now." She took him in her mouth and he smiled.

Junior leaned back against the door and watched Patty's head jerking back and forth, her breasts bouncing up and down. He felt heat rushing through his body, his breathing hastening, and he knew he had no control of this. He gushed into Patty's mouth and grasped her head. She stopped and looked up at Junior.

This moment was the affirmation that everything he had done the last few days was right. With each person he crossed off his list he was gaining strength. Killing Bruno and Moskowitz avenged those that harmed him. Taking care of Shelton would do the same. He felt a sense of impatience, anxiety set in. He wanted to wreak vengeance on those responsible for the death of his father and mother. Junior remembered that birthday present from his father, the Klan meeting. He was enforcing God's laws and didn't want to stop. He couldn't stop. He needed to go on. He wanted to bring justice to God's world, to his world.

Junior grabbed Patty's arms and pulled her up. He slid his hand between her legs and stroked her loins. "I've got something I have to do tonight. When I finish I'll stop by."

"I'll be waiting for you. Be careful."

Junior returned to Moskowitz's Buick. He glided his gloved hand across the fender of the car. "Your gonna be my gas chamber

on wheels, baby. We gonna make this a special day for the Jews."
He squealed out of the parking spot heading to the Eisenhower and
north on the Kennedy Expressway, returning to Lincolnwood.

***

Judge Shelton and his wife had returned from their usual
Friday night deli where they had supper and settled in for their
typical night of TV viewing in the paneled den overlooking the
backyard. The couple lay back in their matching Naugahyde
recliners. Elise in a pink chenille robe with matching slippers and
Bernie in striped boxer shorts and a T-shirt stretched around an
emerging spare tire. The white dust mop jumped from one lap to
the other when one of them stopped petting her.

Elise folded *The Enquirer,* setting it on the arm of her
recliner and stroked Fluff asleep on her lap. "Bernie, honey, could
you go to the fridge and get me a piece of the leftover coconut
crème pie? I don't want to wake Fluff."

He stuffed the newspaper in the side pocket on his recliner,
gave the dog a look of disdain, and exhaled loudly. "Just once I'd
like to finish the paper without an interruption." The announcer's
face covered the TV screen. "Just when the news goes on too." The
foot rest of his recliner slammed down. He jumped to his stocking
feet and huffed to the kitchen.

Elise pointed the remote at the TV and lowered the volume.
"I don't know why you don't wear that nice silk bathrobe and the
leather slippers my mother bought you for Chanukah."

The judge muttered under his breath. "You're getting your
pie, I don't need to hear about your mother." He raised his voice.
"I'm not making another trip until I'm done reading the paper and
watching the news, so if you want something to drink tell me now."

"You better reheat the coffee for me then."

"Jesus." He shook his head.

"Did you say something honey?"

"It'll be a few minutes."

***

Junior drove the Buick down the judge's street, cruising
slowly past the white-brick ranch house, spotting the Cadillac in
the driveway. He realized what good fortune it was that the VW's

battery went dead—Moskowitz's Buick blended into the neighborhood better than the bug.

Shelton's house was the fifth from the corner. Junior figured he was better off parking on one of the streets paralleling the judge's house. He drove to the corner, headed east and went up the next street, parking behind a deli on Peterson. He felt the dagger on his forearm and the 9 mm on his hip. He had shown too much dignity. It was time to give these people what they deserved.

Junior stepped out of the car and took a deep breath of the fresh night air. He zipped up his leather jacket, covering Moskowitz' blood on his shirt, and walked down the quiet street watching his shadow grow and shrink to nothing as he passed from one streetlight to the next. Glancing into the lighted houses he saw mothers and fathers playing with their sons and daughters. He wondered what it was like to be one of those kids. Would his family had been like that if they'd had the chance? Celeste came to mind. He hadn't thought of her in a long time. The way their father treated her. Why did he do that? He added her into his equation because she was one of his losses too. "Who knows what that nigger did to her." His anger was stoked.

He was five houses from the corner. A beige-brick raised ranch with a door in front and another on the side bordered by the driveway. The house looked dark and the garage was closed. No cars were parked in front. He walked to the side door and faked ringing the doorbell. Waited a few moments and walked to the backyard.

*** 

The Judge walked into the den balancing a cup of coffee on a saucer and a piece of pie and a fork on a plate, placing them on a TV tray next to his wife's recliner. "Here." He walked to the glass sliding patio doors and peered into the backyard.

"Don't stand there in your underwear." She put a forkful of pie into her mouth and slurped some coffee. "What if the neighbors are watching?"

"Eat your heart out, Mrs. McGillicutty." He laughed. "What's the matter, don't you remember *The Honeymooners*?" He slid the glass door open. "It's a beautiful night," and pulled the screen door closed. "Might as well get some fresh air in here. It'll be a long winter."

"Bernie, I'm cold." Another forkful of pie passed her lips.

"Why don't you go watch your program in the bedroom and I can finish the paper and get some fresh air."

"We hardly spend any time together and when we do…" she lumbered forward, sliding one side of her butt and then the other, using every bit of energy she could muster getting to the edge of the recliner as the remaining half of the pie slipped off the plate to the floor. "See what you made me do? You want to be alone, you can just clean up the pie too." She marched through the kitchen carrying Fluff and *The Enquirer* to the bedroom, slammed the door, and cranked the volume up on the TV.

"Thank, God. Peace and quiet." He fell back into his recliner, popped open a beer he had smuggled in, and returned to the newspaper.

***

Junior stared at the back of the judge's house from behind the bushes that separated Shelton's backyard from the neighbors. He heard the faint noise of the television through the screen door and watched the judge's wife leave. Junior saw the piece of coconut crème pie on the floor, and the backs of two recliners. One appeared empty and the other one he saw a newspaper supported by a chubby hand on one side and on the other side a hand grasping a beer can and the paper.

Junior slipped between the bushes, creeping past a birdbath, onto the flagstone patio, and up to the screen door. He grasped the handle of the sliding screen and gave it a light push. It moved. Slowly he slid it open and stepped inside. "Hello, Judge."

The newspaper came crackling down. "What the hell…"

"Remember me? You, Moskowitz, and the two niggers set me up."

"I don't have the slightest idea what you're—"

"Shedup. Tonight me and my friend are doing the talkin'." Junior pulled the 9 mm out of his waistband.

Shelton waved his hands in front of him. "Listen, son. I honestly don't remember what happened. But if something went wrong I'm sure we can rectify it. Justice—"

"Didn't you hear me?" He stepped up and waved the pistol in front of the judge's face. "Shedup, you bag of shit. You don't know a thing about justice. I'll show you justice."

Perspiration ran down the judge's face and the underarms of his T-shirt darkened. "You don't want to do this son—"

Junior pressed the barrel of the 9 mm against the judge's lips. "Open your fucking mouth." He jammed the barrel into the Judge's mouth. "Only way I'll get you to shedup." He thumbed the hammer back. It clicked into place.

The judge's hands trembled and his teeth rattled against the ink-blue steel.

Shelton focused on the barrel of the pistol, the hand holding it, and the hammer ready to fall. He tasted the hard steel. There were words being uttered that he didn't comprehend. His eyes were stinging from perspiration that dripped off his brow. The judge sucked in air, chest heaving, and air gushing out of his nose and mouth. His teeth clicked on the steel. He was going to die. He felt a warm liquid rushing down his legs.

Junior's nose wrinkled and he inhaled. "I smell piss." He threw the paper off Shelton's lap and laughed. "You pissed in your undies. That's good enough for me. Just wanted to see you cry. But you pissed in your shorts like the faggot you are. Ain't much of a man behind that black robe. Ain't that so?"

The judge nodded.

Junior pulled the pistol out of the judge's mouth. "Gotta clean your spit off before I go." He dragged the barrel across Shelton's T-shirt and then pressed the barrel into the judge's chest like he was screwing it into his heart.

The judge's shoulders rounded, chest heaved, and he gasped for air. His eyes stared at the hammer of the pistol. He gripped the arms of the recliner, knuckles turning white.

Junior dropped the pistol to his side. "Relax man. Can't you take a joke? You better have your old lady powder your ass and change your diaper." Junior laughed as he walked between the recliners to the screen door. The judge turned his head following Junior. He stopped at the door and looked over his shoulder at the judge. "One more thing, Jew boy. Here's some justice for you. Serious justice." He raised the pistol. The judge raised his hands in front of his face. Junior fired one shot, resonating in the room.

The judge's body jumped like a puppet that was jerked by his strings. Then settled into the recliner, one arm twitched. The bullet penetrated his right palm, hitting below the right eye.

Junior stepped out the screen door. The TV broadcast from the other room became louder. As he retraced his steps cutting through the bushes he heard a woman's scream and the yelping of the dog from the Shelton's house. He laughed—like a hyena when he finds a carcass in the middle of the night. Junior bounded down the neighbor's driveway, up the street to the deli, and jumped into the Buick.

The piercing shrill of sirens become louder as he pulled away from the deli heading to the expressway and back to the west side. Junior dropped the Buick off in Columbus Park, close to the same place he had left Bruno. "Make it look like some nigger killed Moskowitz, like it's a racial thing, and that's okay cause it was." He hustled out of Columbus Park, under the Central Avenue viaduct that separated the ghetto from Cicero, and to Patty's apartment spending the night there, finishing what she had started earlier at Dick's Place.

\*\*\*

Six thirty Saturday morning Eckhaus entered the FBI offices just like he did on weekdays—except he was on a mission today. He had to run through the indices to find out what he could about the Napiers. Although the 302s, investigative reports, would be filed in the originating field office, he could find summaries of the reports accessed through the agencies computers.

He made a query of the system under "Napier, James," and came up with numerous hits. "Not an uncommon name." He keyed down the list to hits from 1968. "Here's one June 9, 1968. Should be my man." Eckhaus called up the summary. "Shot by Special Agent Clarence Daniels during attempted bombing of black church. Alleged member of KKK." Eckhaus shook his head. "Clarence, didn't know you were a hero." He input Napier's FBI number to see if he was mentioned in any other files. "Here's something interesting. Beauford Tisdale, male, black. Wanted on outstanding warrant for allegedly killing Napier's wife and kidnapping his daughter Celeste. This guy had it worse than Pape or Sakich. No wonder he was bombing churches." He lit a smoke and queried Celeste. "Shit, no FBI number. Got to find her somewhere."

He went into the DMV program. "She's got to have a driver's license." Eckhaus leaned forward in his chair, stretching his back while the computer searched its database. "Shit, no record of a driver's license with Mississippi DMV." Eckhaus laughed.

"Maybe she's dead already. That nigger killed her. Doesn't mean I can't say she's the informant. I don't really need a body to show Pape.

"Might as well query LeGrand. See if there's any shagger mentioned in his file." He drew on his smoke as the computer churned, came to a halt, and spit out the information. "Imperial Wizard of the Mississippi KKK. Last inquiry 11-30-79. Hmm, yesterday. Who's interested in my man?" He hit a few keys accessing the prior inquiry. "Agent 1174. That's fucking Richmond. Why the hell would he be digging in old Klan shit? Not on any work plan of his that I've seen."

He left the file room and headed to his office, turning on the TV as he would on any other day, and listened to the report of the shocking murders of Public Defender Abraham Moskowitz and the Cook County Municipal Court Judge Bernard Shelton. Eckhaus lit a Camel with the butt of one he just finished and shrugged. "What're you going to do?" He crushed the butt in his ashtray. "Too damn early to page Pape now. I'll wait for awhile and give him the good news then. He was right about Napier's daughter. She's going to be the snitch."

\*\*\*

Junior woke shortly after eight. Patty was naked, clinging to him. He slipped out of bed and used the phone in the kitchen. "Kurt, it's me."

"You had a busy Friday night."

"How'd you know?"

"It's all over the papers, radio, TV. You take the VW?"

"Yeah."

"I figured. You need to talk to me, boy. Running off and doing things like that without thinking is dangerous. Anyway, when I saw the bug was gone I broke the front door and called the cops. Made it look like the car was stolen. They found it in the parking lot at 26th and California. But I guess you knew it was there. You better lay low in case somebody saw you. Where're you?"

"In Cicero with my girlfriend. My old place."

"You'd be better off here. I'll send one of the boys over to get you. Be there in about an hour. Play it safe don't tell her where you're staying. So get all the pussy you can 'til then."

Junior smiled. "Thanks, I'm going back to bed."

\*\*\*

At ten Eckhaus paged Pape and waited at his phone for two hours before it rang. "What the hell took so long?"

"Sorry, I just finished meeting with the RNC. They just left, had a flight scheduled to Maine right after the meeting."

"I confirmed what you told me last night. We need to meet in person."

"I'm leaving for O'Hare. Cab should be downstairs in ten minutes."

"That'll work. Have the cab bring you to the Federal Plaza. I'll meet you down there. We can talk for a few minutes and you can be on your way. In the center of the plaza there's a giant pink monstrosity. Some people say it looks like a steel flamingo. I'll meet you underneath it."

Fifteen minutes later Pape hopped out of his cab. Yesterday's Indian summer day had disappeared and the wind rustled his hair. He met Eckhaus in the shadow of the black steel and glass Dirksen Federal building underneath the sculpture. "Did you find something?"

"You were right. LeGrand was fucking Celeste Napier. That's why he paid her that money to sign the real estate contracts you mentioned. The guy who sits at the right hand of the director mentioned that the land deals were one of the items in the letter. Said it was hush, hush. Wouldn't tell me anything else."

Pape licked his lips. "That little bitch. We take care of her and she turns on us. She deserves whatever she gets."

Eckhaus handed Pape a folded sheet of paper. "This is the account you can send my money to."

Pape unfolded the paper. "Bermuda. You arranged that fast."

"We're at the point where we need to act quickly."

"The RNC is wiring me $200,000 tomorrow for polling, canvassing, and to help set up my organization. As soon as I get it I'll wire you $100,000. You'll get the rest when the job is done."

Eckhaus wanted to tell him to get fucked. He wanted all the money up front or Pape could do it himself. But if Celeste Napier was already dead there was nothing for him to do but fake it. In the worst case scenario he'd end up with a 100 G's. He could handle that. "I'm checking on her whereabouts and I got someone lined up to do the job. It's just a matter of time."

"Be careful, I can't be linked to her in any way. I've got to catch my plane." He walked through a group of Japanese tourists taking photographs of the Calder as he headed to his cab.

Eckhaus thought of the sunny beaches in Antigua, the possibility that he might not be spending this winter in Chicago, and the easiest $100,000 he ever made.

\*\*\*

William parked behind his father's maroon Mercedes in front of the ward office. He stepped out of his Camaro, walked past the Mercedes, and noticed a sign in the rear passenger windows. He did a double take. "For sale. Wonder why he's selling it? Just bought it six months ago." William laughed to himself. "Probably buying a new one. A bigger one."

He grabbed the door and stepped into the office. His father sat at his desk on the phone, behind him the city flag and the Stars and Stripes. Beauford wasn't wearing one of his tailored suits. Instead he had on a gray sweatshirt, jeans, and tennis shoes. His father waved him in.

\*\*\*

Beauford watched the young man coming in the door. He thought about his son. What it meant to have a son or could mean and the responsibility that he hadn't taken. The guidance he hadn't provided. The hope that a father invests in his son versus the way he had bankrupted their relationship. He was proud of him. His son had surpassed any dreams he may have had for him. He marveled at how William had the courage and values to recognize the importance of the relationship they didn't have. He wondered where that came from. He was ashamed to admit it; it wasn't from him. How did William perceive a subtle message as a desire to connect? Beauford wasn't even sure if he cast out such a message, but he was gratified that William had detected one. He tried to determine what his contribution to their relationship was and the only thing he could find was the tremendous burden he had put on his son —to know that your father was involved in the assassinations of King and Kennedy. How unfair life can be. He felt he had become the child and William the parent. He tried to remember the last time he had protected his son and the only time he could think of was that day long ago in Blackhawk Bayou when he pulled William away from his grandfather's dead body. Now William was protecting him.

\*\*\*

William walked to the desk, lifted a cardboard box off the chair in front of the desk and looked for a place to set it down. He noticed boxes stacked against the wall behind the desk. He placed the box beside the desk and noticed a half-filled bottle of Jack Daniel's in the waste paper basket.

Beauford hung up the phone. "Good morning, son."

"What's going on?"

"I moved out of the condo. It wasn't really me."

"Where're you going to live?"

"Here. In the upstairs apartment. I did it before."

"Why? That was quite a place. This is a big step down."

Beauford paused before answering. "I don't want to rush into this. Say too much too soon. Let's just say I'm trying to make some changes."

William tried to maintain his composure. He didn't want to delude himself that things were going to change. He had seen his father at his worst. Drunk, retching guilt and shame, and confessing involvement in a crime no black man could possibly live with. The only response he could honestly give him at this time was, "Okay."

Beauford leaned back in his chair and folded his hands behind his head. "So is this a social visit or a follow up on Thursday night? You know, cover all the bases, fill in the holes. However you guys say it."

"I haven't been around long enough to know how we say it. Someone would like to meet you?"

"Who's that?"

"Celeste Napier."

\*\*\*

Beauford went cold, laid his palms on his desk, leaned back, and exhaled. The woman who was the first step in his ruination wanted to see him. Why now, when he was starting to see things differently? He was trying to change and an obstacle has already been thrown in his path. Did she want to take him down again? "She's the last person I want to see."

William cleared his throat and scooted up the edge of his chair. "It's more than just her."

Beauford's brow furrowed. "What do you mean?"

"She's bringing your daughter."

"Daughter? We only…Just that one time…Can't be mine." He shook his head.

"She's light skinned."

Beauford leaned forward, the muscles in his neck tensing. "A mulatto."

"She gave a statement on your behalf to the county sheriff clearing you of the murder and kidnapping charges. She wouldn't lie about that. She wouldn't lie about the girl."

A grin broke across Beauford's face and he nodded. "She wants money." He leaned over the corner of his desk, pulled the Jack Daniel's bottle out of the wastebasket and set it in front of him. Beauford started rifling through his desk drawers looking for a glass.

"Never said a word about money. Said that her daughter has the right to meet her father. She originally told the girl that you didn't come home from Nam. Anyway, Celeste's trying to make something of her life. She's going to college."

"If she's honest why didn't she come forward sooner? Like eleven years ago when this all started?" He set two glasses on the table, filled one a third full, held the bottle over the second glass, and looked at William.

William nodded. "She didn't know what happened to you. Thought the Klan lynched you. Her father disowned her after he found out she was pregnant. Left her in Greenville in some flophouse. LeGrand, the mayor of Ruleville, was in Greenville and ran into her. He took her to his ex-wife. She ran a home for girls. She used the lady's name since then, Virden."

"You know more about my life than I do."

William took a sip of whiskey. "Not really. One thing that was interesting, the night LeGrand saw Celeste in Greenville she thinks she saw him meeting James Earl Ray."

"I told you LeGrand was the one that stopped them from killing my ass that night on Ruleville Bridge. He was the one that told me Marlee had been taken and gave me Reichardt's card. He was involved in this whole thing from the beginning."

"And they're both dead. We need to find somebody that can corroborate your story."

"Ain't no story. It's the truth. What happened to LeGrand?"

"He drowned in a fishing accident."

"You really think so?"

"I don't know and I don't know how to prove he didn't. I've got a deputy sheriff in Ruleville looking into it."

"So when does she want to get together?"

"I'm picking them up Monday at Midway at four. Why don't we meet at Michaels for dinner, that restaurant at the corner of Marquette and Kedzie."

Beauford thought about William and Marlee. He had orphaned them for eleven years and this little girl too. If he was going to step up he needed to do it now. Not go back to the old ways. "What's her name?"

"She calls her Missy. Don't know if that's her given name."

He picked up the bottle and glass and dropped them into the wastebasket. "I'll be there at 4:30."

# CHAPTER THIRTY-TWO

Eckhaus tapped a quarter-inch ash from his cigarette onto the mountain already in his ashtray and looked at William standing in front of him like an enlisted man in front of his drill sergeant.

William handed him three pages. "Here's my list of last week's activities."

Eckhaus examined the list, looking for LeGrand's name but didn't find it. He wondered what William was up to. Why would he query LeGrand and not mention it? Some brilliant philosopher once said there were no coincidences. If he mentioned LeGrand, William would wonder how he found out. An idea came to Eckhaus. A rather minor scam compared to the past few days.

Eckhaus opened his desk drawer and pulled out a manila folder containing the maintenance report on the cars assigned to his squad. He leaned back in his chair, faking reading a report. "The indices access report shows you queried someone named LeGrand. Don't see that on your activity report."

\*\*\*

*Son of a bitch.* William rubbed his fingers over his lips. He didn't know the administrative staff compiled a list of computer queries. "I've had so many names running through my head I guess I forgot to list him on my report."

"You guess. One of the keys to being a successful agent is detail. You can't tell a jury you forgot. A small error like that can destroy your credibility as a witness."

"Yes, sir. I'll be more careful in the future. Do you want me to update my report?"

"No, I'll make a notation on it. For the record how does LeGrand fit in with your ongoing investigations?"

William froze. Was it time to tell Eckhaus? Did he risk having the investigation pulled from him? But why wasn't Eckhaus asking him about the queries on Beauford Tisdale and Muhammad Hasan? They should be on the same report. Something wasn't right.

Eckhaus crushed his cigarette in the ashtray. "I asked you a question."

William's silence intensified his anxiety. He wanted to say he was checking on some lead that would probably develop into nothing. That he didn't want to waste Eckhaus' time with the allegations until he was able to corroborate them. If they checked out he'd give him all the details. But William knew he'd have to play dumb and stall. It was the only way to buy time. One mention of the King and Kennedy assassinations and it would be the last he'd ever see of this case. He had to ingrain himself in the investigation so they couldn't take it away from him. "I'm sorry. I'll have to check my notes. Then I can give you the lead on that."

\*\*\*

Eckhaus wanted to tell William he was walking on thin ice. He'd better focus on his cases and not go off on fishing expeditions or he might not make it through his probationary period. But if William had come across something on LeGrand and he pushed the kid he might alert him of its significance by coming on too strong.

His aching back had left him with interrupted sleep night after night and his tired blue eyes were veined in red. Eckhaus looked down at the report in the folder. He grabbed a pen, scribbled on the report as if making a notation, and shook his head. It was next to impossible that William could have stumbled onto anything that would tie into 1968. "All right. If you happen to figure how you came up with the name add it to your next activity report. You can go now."

\*\*\*

A handful of people including William waited at gate five for the Delta flight to arrive. William sat in one of the black plastic chairs at the gate. Across from him sat a man and woman in their fifties that looked like twins. They wore overalls, had fireplug builds that filled the chairs, hands folded resting on their laps, lips tight, and thumbs nervously circling each other in one direction and then the other. They looked like they would be more at home in Memphis where the connecting flight was originating from. Other people milled about, drifting in and out of the waiting area, sitting for a few minutes, and then going to check the arrival board.

William's expectations about the upcoming meeting wavered from disaster to gratification for his father. What if Celeste came down hard on his father? Wanted money? Back child support? Chided him for not returning to see her? What would that do to him?

He's trying to change. That could throw him back into isolation. Close up the connection that he was starting to develop with his father. He wasn't sure the meeting was worth the risk. But William had to weigh that against how useful she might be in terms of backing up his father's testimony. The irony played in William's mind that she could hurt his father, and the relationship William was starting to build with him, but if William alienated Celeste, her testimony corroborating his father's story might evaporate. He had no control over Celeste. She was hardheaded about Missy meeting her father and he didn't understand her motivation. Celeste had spent the last ten years establishing a life with Missy. Why was it so important that Missy meet her father now?

***

Celeste watched the wide-eyed excitement on her daughter's face as the plane descended into Midway. She pointed down at the ground. "Honey, look at the cars and trucks. They look like little toys. But they'll get bigger and bigger as we get close to the ground."

The child's face pressed against the glass and she jumped up and down.

"Sit down now. We've got to put your seat belt on." Celeste clicked the belt around Missy's waist. The thought lingered in her mind whether she would have demanded this meeting under normal circumstances. William had told her that Beauford wasn't the man she knew in Mississippi. She didn't know what Beauford was like now. Life had been hard for her and Missy but they had each other and that had been good enough until now. Ms. Virden had been good to them, but she was approaching seventy. Celeste prayed to God every day that things would work out for the best.

They landed and Celeste put on a red trench coat and slung a black vinyl purse over her shoulder. She walked down the ramp pulling a black carry-on, held Missy's teddy bear under her arm, and held tight to her daughter with the other hand. Missy had yellow bows in her tight curly brown hair, wore a blue wool coat and dragged a miniature carry-on with Disney characters printed on it. Entering the waiting area she saw William waiting for them.

For the sake of Missy, Celeste and William were courteous to each other, but the underlying current of tension was there. Celeste let go of the carry-on, grabbed the sleeve of William's bomber jacket and pulled him down to her lips. "Don't say anything about Missy meeting her father, because I haven't told her yet. Cause of what you said about him being different, I figured I better meet him first. Then I can decide if it's a good idea for Missy to meet him."

He nodded and grabbed their bags. They headed to his car and the meeting that each one had their fears about.

The gawking look of the old couple left little doubt that they were shocked that a racially mixed couple would act like that in public, let alone parade their mulatto child around.

\*\*\*

Beauford entered Michael's Restaurant wearing an off-the-rack blue suit and a white shirt. *I wear one of my tailor made, I'll look too rich. She'll try to hit me for money. I'm willing to pay some.* He walked past the pay phone and fake rubber tree in the vestibule and through the second set of glass doors and was greeted by the owner, Stavros Panakis.

Beauford caught Stavros in his normal pose, sitting on the stool behind the glass counter at the cash register, brushing crumbs from his favorite meal, a pastrami sandwich, off his baggy faded blue long-sleeve shirt and navy double-knit slacks.

"Hello, Mr. Alderman." Stavros said, followed by a low belch as he patted his stomach, double-checking that the money belt with the day's skim under his shirt was firmly fastened. He reached into the glass counter and pulled out a handful of Dutch Master's cigars and stuffed them into Beauford's suit coat pocket. "For you, yes?"

Beauford pulled the cigars out of his pocket and put them on the counter. "Not tonight, Stavros. Can I have a booth for four?" He pointed to the far end of the restaurant. "The one by the window over there. I'm waiting for some friends."

"You got it." Stavros waved to the skinny Mexican with the slick black hair. "Jose, clean booth and make set-up for four." He pointed to the booth farthest from the door. "Alderman expecting guests for dinner?"

Jose ran to the booth, slapped the dust off the plastic Tiffany lamp hanging over the black Formica table, sprayed the table and red leatherette booth with glass cleaner, dried it with a towel, and had place settings for four and glasses of ice water down before Beauford was at the booth.

Beauford sat down and pressed a dollar into Jose's hand.

"Gracias, senior." Jose bowed and backed away from the booth.

Stavros approached the table and placed four menus down. "Mr. Alderman, have special on the menu just for you, barbecue ribs. For you tonight, no?" A wide grin broke across Stavros' face as he extended his hands.

Beauford glanced at the clock on the wall. Twenty after four. They should be here soon. "Not yet. Let's wait until my friends arrive."

"Yes, your honor." Stavros returned to his pastrami sandwich.

Beauford fiddled with the menus. He didn't understand why Celeste wanted to see him after all this time. He was sure she didn't want him in his life. She should get a young man, someone her own age and move on, have a real family, more kids. Money crossed his mind again. *Some amount would be fair. I wouldn't mind helping out a little. She has raised the kid on her own all this time and maybe that would buy her silence.*

\*\*\*

Twenty minutes later William parked the Camaro on Kedzie a few doors north of the restaurant. He opened the door and put one foot on the asphalt.

Celeste grabbed William's shoulder. "Wait." She glanced at Missy in the back seat. "Honey, can you wait here with William for a little while. I have to go talk to a man first and then we can get a bit to eat."

Missy nodded and squeezed her teddy bear to her chest. William closed his door and settled into his seat.

"I'll be back in a little while, baby." Celeste left the car and headed to the restaurant.

\*\*\*

Beauford took a sip of water and watched the tall redhead come into the restaurant. She had grown from a perky teenager into an attractive woman. He strained to see if the little girl was hiding behind her.

Celeste approached the counter. "I'm supposed to meet Beauford Tisdale here."

"Tisdale? We have Beauford Richmond, the Alderman, yes?" Stavros pointed at him and Beauford waved. The Greek said, "Follow me, please," and led her to the booth. Stepping aside he directed Celeste to the seat opposite Beauford and winked at him. "Call please when ready to order, Mr. Alderman."

"Thank you, Stavros," Beauford said dismissing him. An awkward moment of silence followed as he looked at her and then glanced at his folded hands on the table. "Didn't you bring the little girl with you?"

"She's in the car with William. I thought it might be best if we spent some time alone first."

"That's probably a good idea."

Celeste unbuttoned her coat, slid it onto the booth beside her, and placed her purse on it. She wore a long-sleeve white blouse with a standup collar and a cameo necklace. "You look good, successful, Mr. Alderman."

"That's another story. I want to thank you for giving that statement to the police clearing me of those charges. It must have been difficult for you to relive that night."

She brushed her hair off her shoulder. "You're welcome. It was the right thing to do. That man called you Alderman Richmond. You don't go by Tisdale anymore?"

"Like I said that's another story." He waved his hand in front of his face, "To be honest with you I don't care to get into it. I have a question for you, though. I mean you and your daughter have a life, been on your own for ten years. I don't understand what brought you all the way up here? Is there something you need?"

"Missy has the right to meet her father. But I thought the Klan killed you, that's why I never tried to get in touch with you, let you know that you had a daughter. To be totally honest, I've been apprehensive about Missy meeting you. William told me that you weren't the same man that you were back in Mississippi. So I thought I better spend some time with you first. To make sure you're not some kind of monster that would hurt her."

He put his elbows on the table and formed a steeple with his fingers. "Well, I'm not the same man. I've been through a lot. More than any man should have to go through. Things happened, awful things that I can't discuss. But I'm trying to put it all behind me. William's helping me. If it wasn't for him I might not be here."

"I'm sorry to hear you've had such an awful time. But I can see things in your eyes that I saw a long time ago. There's still a gentleness about you that—"

Beauford interrupted her; he didn't want to hear any kind words from her, and feared what they might lead to. "Celeste, you're doing the right thing looking after Missy and getting an education. You deserve a good man in your life and Missy deserves a father and I can't been either of those to anyone. I can give you some money to help you out but I can't—"

"I didn't come up here to get money or get involved in a relationship with you. Time is running out."

"What do you mean?"

"I have uterine cancer. I'm trying to lead my life as if everything is fine. The doctors can't tell me how much time I have left. At least not yet." Her eyes welled and she picked up a napkin and dabbed them.

"I'm so sorry." He grabbed her hand.

"Beauford, you're the only hope I have and the only hope that Missy has. She's a wonderful little girl." Tears rolled down her cheeks and she covered her face with the napkin.

In his mind Beauford had failed miserably as a father. He was overwhelmed with the thought that he would ruin this little girl's life. This little girl who would have no one to depend on except him. His hands trembled.

Celeste put the napkin down. "I'm sorry."

Beauford couldn't look her in the face. He turned his head gazing out the window. He saw the gas jockey across the street running a squeegee across the windshield of a Chevy. *Her brother. Did William tell her?* He glanced down at the table and up at Celeste. "There's something you should know. Did William tell you that your brother is here in Chicago?"

Her eyes opened wide. "What?"

Beauford faced the window. "That's him. Over there by the pumps."

Celeste stared at the red headed man in the brown jump suit. "I don't believe it. That's Junior." She stood up bumping the table. "Excuse me," and ran to the door rushing through the incoming dinner rush.

Looking between the rush hour traffic she saw a young man pumping gas at the station across the street. He walked in and out of the light shining down from above the pumps. The shape of his face was familiar. His gait was like someone's she had known.

*** 

William's pager vibrated. He saw Daniels' number in the display and looked at his watch. "They've been in there for twenty minutes." He looked over his shoulder into the back seat. "Missy, I've got to call my office. Would it be okay if I left you here for a couple of minutes? I promise I'll be right back and I'll lock the doors so no one can get in."

Missy nodded, squeezing the teddy bear tighter against her chest.

William went to the pay phone in the vestibule of the restaurant and dialed the number. He saw his father but Celeste wasn't there. *She must have gone to the washroom.*

"FBI, Daniels."

"You paged me?" William asked watching his father leave the table heading to the bathroom.

"You sent an expedite request to the forensic lab?"

"Yes."

"How come I didn't know about it and if I didn't know about it, does Eckhaus?"

William leaned against the shelf supporting the pay phone and glanced out the window. He saw Celeste dashing across Kedzie, cars honking and screeching to a halt. "What the hell. I'm sorry. I've got to go. I'll call you back in a couple of minutes." He hung up the phone and stepped out the door. "What's she doing?"

***

Celeste saw the gas jockey glance at her and go back to his work. The traffic sounds must have caught his attention. She stepped onto the curb. Her pace slowed as she got closer, wanting to get a good look at him before she did anything foolish. She walked around the pumps. He was in full view. "Junior? Junior Napier?"

Junior jerked his head around at the sound of the unfamiliar voice calling his name. His first reaction was cops. But that wasn't a cop's voice and the accent was pure south. He stared at the woman. It was impossible. It couldn't be her. The past week had made him scared, cautious. Junior canted his head. "I know you?"

"Junior, it's me, Celeste."

"What the hell you doing up here?" He took the nozzle out of the car returning it to the pump and took five dollars from the customer.

"I came up here…"

***

Missy squeezed her teddy bear and bounced her legs together. She didn't know how much longer she could hold it. She told Teddy, "If I mess William's car he'll be mad at me. He doesn't like me. Please come get me, Momma." The cars honking and screeching got her attention and she saw her mother across the street talking to a man in the gas station. Missy dropped Teddy to the floor. She stood up in the back seat and pulled on the button trying to open the door. A warm feeling rushed down her leg. "Oh no, I peed, Teddy. I got to get Momma to clean up."

She crawled over the console into the front seat, jerked on the handle, and the door opened. Missy jumped out of the car onto the street. "Momma, here I come."

Cars screeched, collided, metal twisted, and Celeste and Junior looked in time to see Missy sliding across the hood of a car, into the windshield, and back onto the street. "Oh my God," Celeste screamed and ran into the street. She knelt on the pavement in oil and coolant that leaked from the cars, picking up her daughter in her arms. Her hands wet with Missy's blood.

The stench of burning rubber filled the air. Car doors slammed and drivers' shouted at each other. "It's your fault, you SOB."

William and Beauford ran out of the restaurant rushing to Celeste.

Junior stood over Celeste and Missy. "It's only a little half-breed. Why you so worked up?"

William grabbed Junior by the lapels of his overalls. "You asshole."

"William, go call for an ambulance," Celeste pleaded.

William ran back to the pay phone.

Junior put his hands on his hips. "Put the nigger down, Celeste. It ain't none of our business what happens to her."

"Shut up, Junior. This is my daughter." Celeste nodded at Beauford. "And this is her father."

"Don't talk like that. What would Daddy say?" Junior glanced at the black man kneeling next to Celeste and Missy. "I know that spook."

"He's Alderman Beauford Tisdale," Celeste said.

"Tisdale." Junior's brow wrinkled as the sirens from the police cars and the ambulance grew louder. The vehicles came to a halt and he retreated, widening the distance between him and the red-and-blue lights that flickered across the pavement. He knew it wasn't a good place for him to be and he had to sort out what he had just learned.

He went to the corner near the restaurant and watched Celeste get in the ambulance with Missy. He saw the younger black man help a crying Beauford to his feet. They walked into the restaurant, picked up a red coat and black purse, and headed to a

Camaro. Junior overheard the young black man tell Beauford, "Don't worry, Dad. Missy will be all right. The cars were slowing up for the traffic light." Junior backed into the shadows of the building. "Tisdale and his son. I found them, Dad. I found them."

## CHAPTER THIRTY-THREE

Paramedics pushed Missy's gurney down the drab green-gray hallway past the overflow of patients waiting for a seat in the triage unit. Celeste followed, forcing her way through the throng. The murmur of their conversations drifted around Celeste. Lingering in the air was the sterile smell of antiseptics. The sounds of pain and urgency pervaded the hallway. Sirens wailed from approaching ambulances and groaning patients suffering from drug overdoses, gunshot wounds, and knife stabbings were wheeled in on gurneys. Nurses, interns, and attending physicians rushed about. A woman screamed, "Oh, God," as she heard the words from a doctor, "I'm sorry. There was nothing we could do."

A paramedic backed off the gurney, calling out Missy's vitals as a nurse and intern took over. "Code red. Ten-year-old female hit by a car, unconscious, BP 120/80, pulse 77, lacerations and bruises on face, arms, and legs, no visible broken bones."

"Start the IV push," the intern ordered. "Up to trauma."

"I'm her mother. Can I stay with her?" Celeste pleaded.

"Follow us." They headed into an elevator and went to the third floor trauma unit.

The doors opened and the nurse pushed Missy's gurney into a cubicle holding five other patients. "On three. One, two, three." They lifted Missy off the gurney onto the examination table. A nurse slipped a collar on Missy's arm and checked her blood pressure again. "BP holding steady 117/78, pulse 75."

The intern placed the stethoscope on her chest and listened. "Airways clear." He flashed a light in her eyes. "Pupils normal and reactive. Bring in the CT."

Celeste's eyes were red. She stood a foot behind the intern. "Is she going to be all right?"

"There's a lot of tests we have to run before we can give you a definite answer."

A nurse pushed in the unit, centered it over Missy, and they stepped back. The machine hummed and clicked as they took several shots.

"She's stable right now. We'll get the film and have a diagnosis soon. You can stay here with her," the intern said.

"Thank you, Doctor." Celeste sat on the side of the bed and caressed Missy's hand. "You're going to be just fine, Honey." Missy lay there, motionless and silent.

\*\*\*

William weaved through the rush hour traffic. His father swayed from side to side in the passenger seat with Celeste's purse and coat on his lap. "How could you leave that little girl alone?" Beauford said, shaking his head.

"I'm sorry, really sorry, Dad. I got paged from the office. I asked her if she would be okay if I left for a few minutes to make a phone call. Told her I'd lock the doors and she'd be safe. I'm on the phone and I see Celeste running across the street. Missy must have got scared and chased after her."

"You got paged! You left that little girl alone because you got paged?"

They stopped at a red light and William's pager vibrated again. He glanced at the pager, it was Daniels' number again. The light turned green and William sped ahead. "What happened in the restaurant that made her rush out of the place."

"She told me she has cancer. That I was the only hope Missy has. I couldn't take it. Made me think of the way I left you and Marlee behind. What a miserable father I was. I saw Celeste's brother across the street in the gas station and told her. She bolted out of the restaurant and ran to him. Missy must have seen her and ran after her. I thought she was coming up here because she wanted money. But I was so wrong." He shook his head. "She's just trying to find a home for Missy to live in after…she dies. I proved how wrapped up I am in myself. I couldn't possibly think that she was coming here for any other reason but to take something from me."

"I thought the same thing. Anybody else would, too." His pager vibrated again. He looked and Eckhaus' number was displayed. "Shit."

"What is it?"

"The damn office keeps paging me. I'll call them from the hospital." William hoped that Daniels hadn't told Eckhaus about the lab request, but with the second page coming from Eckhaus that wasn't a good sign. He could kiss the case goodbye. He glanced at his father, wondering what he would think of Eckhaus. It was a certainty that they would meet now. He focused back on the road. "How bad is her cancer?"

"The doctors haven't told her how long she has. Her concern is finding someone who will take care of Missy. I'm the only one she has, except for her brother. You heard him back there. He sounded like his father. His old man was one of the Klansmen at the bayou that night I went to get Grandpa's body. He had to have something to do with Grandpa's murder. There's no doubt he wouldn't take Missy after disowning his own daughter."

"He's dead. He was bombing a church in Mississippi when one of our guys shot him."

"Peckerwood deserved it. Does Celeste know?"

"When I talked to her in Mississippi she told me. But I had all ready found the story in the paper down there." William pulled up to the emergency room door. "I'll drop you off here, go park, and meet you inside. Tell Celeste I'm sorry."

Beauford left the car and went to the admissions desk in the emergency room. "I'm the father of the little girl that was brought in, Missy Napier. She was hit by a car."

A nurse flipped her tortoise-shell glasses down from the top of her head and glanced at a large board on the wall while grabbing a chart from a rack. "Third floor trauma unit. Elevator around the corner." She lifted her glasses to her head and rushed to a cubicle.

Beauford took the elevator with two groaning patients on gurneys, two nurses, and an intern.

"GSW in the chest on this one," one of the nurses said to the other, pointing to one patient and then to the other. "His brother over here has knife a wound to the stomach. A little family quarrel." The doors opened and Beauford followed the group into a cubicle and saw Celeste stroking Missy's forehead in the last of six beds.

\*\*\*

Junior lurked in the shadows, longing for the security of his room in the gas station but didn't feel safe to cross the street until the policemen entered their cruisers and left, the tow trucks hauled away the last of the damaged vehicles, and the streets and sanitation crew hosed the blood and scrap metal off the road.

He pulled the collar up on his coveralls and hustled across the street, entering the station.

"Where the hell you been?" Frank Soder asked. "Some kid got hit by a car."

"Yeah, I saw." Junior entered his room closing the door behind him. He pulled the cardboard box onto the cot and rifled through the papers until he found his arrest report. Junior flipped the sheet and eyed the hit list. He grabbed a pencil and drew a dark line obliterating the name Alderman Richmond and circled Tisdale and son. He went to the file cabinet, pulled the 9 mm out of the drawer, extracted the magazine, and topped it off with a new bullet. A grin broke across his face.

\*\*\*

Beauford laid Celeste's coat and purse on the end of the examining table and put his hand on hers. "How is she?"

"She has a concussion, but she's going to be all right."

"Thank God."

She looked at his hand and slid her hand out from underneath his. "Why wasn't William with her?"

Beauford explained the situation to her.

"He couldn't wait. What could be so God damn important? I'll never leave her alone again for as long as I...." She stopped, realizing how cheated she felt, and changed the subject rather than contemplate her fate. "What happened to my brother?"

"Don't know. Didn't see him around when we left."

"I know the things he said sounded terrible. But he's my only family. Will you help me find him?"

"I can do that. Shouldn't be too hard. You're not considering….I mean the way he talked and working in a gas station. He can't take care of Missy."

"No, he's too much like our father. But he's still my family and I at least want to spend some time with him. I know this isn't fair but I need some peace of mind. If you can't see it in your heart to take Missy can you at least make sure that she gets a good foster home?"

"I promise you that's the least I'll do. I just don't want to take her if I don't feel right about myself. I'm afraid that I'd do her more harm than good."

She put her hand on top of his, "It means a lot to me to know that someone will look after her."

"I promise I'll do the best I can."

Celeste leaned forward to rest her head in her arms when she noticed her daughter's blood on her blouse and hands. "Can you watch her while I clean up?"

"Sure, go ahead," Beauford said.

She went to the bathroom and washed her hands in the sink and saw her reflection in the mirror. Her hair was disheveled; green eyes that once had a captivating spirit appeared listless, and skin paler that normal. Celeste wondered if the visible changes in her appearance were symptoms of her cancer or a result of her anxiety. She dreaded the thought of chemotherapy. She closed her eyes and pictured her future, one where she had only a few strands of straggly hair, sunken cheeks, and bulging eyes or, what if chemo wasn't an alternative? How could she tell Missy?

Guilt rushed at her from all sides; from one perspective she faced dying and leaving a young child behind. From another she realized that she had almost killed her child by leaving her with someone she hardly knew. How could she have been so careless? She grabbed several paper towels from the dispenser on the wall, soaked them, and tried to wipe Missy's blood from her blouse. Celeste ran her fingers through her hair trying to make it look presentable. She felt a heaviness deep inside.

It was that loneliness that had been gnawing at her soul since the night her father abandoned her in Greenville. The same night her father had killed her mother and the last time she had seen Junior, until tonight. Celeste longed to rid herself of the feeling that lingered within her and hoped connecting with the last living member of her family would resolve that issue.

*** 

William called Daniels from the pay phone in the lobby of the emergency room. All he got was Daniels' answering machine. "Shit, that means I've got to call Eckhaus." The phone rang four times.

"Eckhaus."

"It's Richmond, sir."

"What the fuck am I going to do with you, Richmond? I tell you what I expect of you and you still go off disregarding procedures. You just don't get it. There's no room for loose cannons. You're either on the team or you're not part of this organization."

"Yes, sir. Sorry, sir."

"What is this shit about you submitting a request to the lab and why did it take you twenty minutes to return my page?"

"I picked up some friends of the family at Midway and took them to have dinner with my father. A car hit the lady's daughter and we were on our way to the hospital when you paged. This was my first chance to call."

"You excel at making excuses."

"I swear, sir. That's the 100 percent truth."

"For your sake I hope that's true. And the lab request?"

"That's a long story."

"You can take all the time you'll need tomorrow morning. I get in at 6:30. I want you here waiting for me with Daniels to tell me about this lab request. You call Daniels and tell him to be here."

The phone clicked and William slammed the receiver into the switch hook, wishing it was Eckhaus' head. He hurried up to the trauma unit where he saw his father and Celeste sitting besides each other. "Is Missy all right?"

Celeste eyes welled with tears. "What do you think?"

William's eyes glanced to the floor. *I'm not going on the guilt trip you're trying to send me on. I told you not to come up here. You ran across the street to meet your long lost brother. That Nazi prick.*

Beauford stood, grabbed William's arm, and they walked to the exit. "She's got a concussion and some bruises, but she's going to be okay. Celeste is under a lot of stress. This just makes it worse."

"I understand. Tell her I'm sorry. I need to go see somebody. Do you want me to line up a ride for you?"

"No, go ahead. We can get a taxi and I'll pick Celeste up in the morning. I'm sure she'll want to come back here first thing."

*** 

William headed to Daniels' house in the far south suburbs arriving well after the family had finished supper. He pulled into the driveway of the aluminum sided bi-level. Through the picture window he saw the silhouette of the Daniels' family in front of the glow of the television.

As William approached the door the porch light came on and the front door opened. "I was wondering what happened to you. Why didn't you answer my pages?" Daniels said, standing in the doorway.

"You have some time. I need to talk to you."

"Come in." He looked over his shoulder at his family. "Dorothea, William's here."

Daniels' wife greeted him in the entry hall. "Would you like something to eat? Got leftover meatloaf I can warm up for you."

She reminded him of his mother when she was younger. Her soft-spoken voice comforted him. "Thanks, that would be great."

"Kids. In case you haven't noticed we have company," Daniels said.

The twin eight-year-old boys gave a quick turn from the television, waved, and returned their attention to the program they were watching.

"Kids, you've got to get some of your own to really appreciate them." He shook his head. "Honey, could you bring William's dinner downstairs. We need to talk about a few things without interruptions."

William followed Daniels downstairs to a half basement that had been remodeled into a rec room. He leaned against the pool table while Daniels went behind the bar made from the same birch colored paneling that covered the walls. Daniels grabbed two beers out of the fridge and set them on the bar. "You're doing a great job of pissing off the boss."

"How'd you find out about the lab request?"

"The lab always calls to document the receipt of evidence. That way you don't have to wonder if it was lost."

"Oh, didn't know."

"Bull, you know better than that." Daniels took a slug of his beer. "You trying to get your ass booted out of the Bureau?"

"Of course not. I had to find out more before I...."

Dorothea came down the stairs, "Meatloaf and green beans." She slid the plate and silverware on the bar.

"Thanks, Dorothea." William took in a deep breath. "Hmm, smells good."

"We might be down here awhile, Hon," Daniels said.

"I can take a hint, goodnight, boys." She kissed her husband on the cheek and returned to the twins and the television.

"How did Eckhaus find out about my lab request?"

"He saw me logging it in and was, to say the least, perturbed that you didn't have him sign off. Why'd you do it? No offense, but that was stupid. Does this request have anything to do with our Nazi friends?"

"No." William held the knife and fork in his hands and stared at the beer bottle. He didn't realize how difficult it would be for him to tell anyone. "The evidence I sent to the lab I got from my father." He pushed the plate away, suddenly not very hungry.

"And?"

"My father said he was forced to make a trip to Los Angeles in 1968 that assisted the people involved in the assassination of Robert F. Kennedy. The documents I sent to the lab are proof of his trip."

"I don't think I heard you right." Daniels looked at William and took a long swallow from his beer. "Our investigation proved that Sirhan acted on his own."

"Well, there's more. My father was used as a courier to deliver money to James Earl Ray. Which means that somehow the two assassinations were linked together." William spent the next forty-five minutes relaying his father's story to Daniels, ending with the arrival of Celeste and Missy today, and the accident.

"Anybody else know about this?"

"Not yet. Not until 6:30 tomorrow morning when we meet with Eckhaus."

\*\*\*

Eckhaus let himself in the door to the FBI office on the ninth floor. His mind and body headed in two different directions. He glowed in the anticipation of beheading William while his gut percolated from the effects of the long-term use of Vicodin and liquor.

The huge door closed behind him with a thud. The windows were covered with the predawn darkness. At the end of the hallway the glow from a desk lamp cast the shadows of two men. Eckhaus' heels clicked on the gray tiled floor as he walked toward them, gradually the murmur of the two men's unintelligible conversation became louder, until they stopped, and looked in his direction.

Eckhaus walked past William and Daniels. "Glad to see both of you could make it." He inserted a key into his office door, pushed the door open, entered, and automatically turned on the television. The low volume provided the white noise that helped take his mind off his back pain when the time and place for taking a shot of whiskey wasn't appropriate. He hung his navy-blue overcoat on the coat rack, sat in his rolling armchair of thickly padded leather, and waved at them to enter.

William and Daniels sat in the two wooden chairs in front of his desk. Eckhaus cleared his throat, "Richmond, as it stands right now, when it comes time to certify you at the end of your probationary period." He shook his head. "I can't do it, not unless I see a complete change in your attitude as it's manifested in the manner that you approach your work."

Daniels raised his hand, index finger pointed to the ceiling, "Sir, I think you may find some extenuating circumstances in what brought about some of the things you're considering when you mention William's approach to his work, specifically the lab request and computer queries."

Eckhaus' face reddened. "I've got news for you, Daniels, you're not here representing Richmond as his lawyer. You're my witness. I'm telling this kid he better shape up or ship out."

William swallowed. "Sir, I'm sorry I sent out the lab request without your approval and that I omitted the indices queries from my activity report. I was trying to corroborate some information I got from my father to decide if it was credible. Because it seems so far-fetched that I can hardly believe it myself."

"I hope this is all worth it." Eckhaus crossed his arms over his chest. "Because if this is a wild-goose chase that's all the more reason for your separation."

"My father said he was forced to transport some items to Los Angeles related to the assassination of Robert Kennedy. He gave me a couple of documents that would back up his statement and that's what I sent to the lab."

Eckhaus' eyes narrowed. He leaned forward putting one elbow on his desk and resting his chin on his hand. "What documents?"

"An airline ticket in the name of Muhammad Hasan and a matchbook with the same name hand printed in it from the...I forget which one, but a hotel in Knoxville."

Eckhaus took a deep breath. He knew he had to deep-six this before it went any further. He slipped a cigarette from a pack of Camels lying on his desk, lit it, and watched the gray smoke curl toward the ceiling. He laughed and said, "I find this totally preposterous, not only your father's statement but that you waste bureau time on this. Can you imagine the hundreds of thousands of hours that were spent investigating Senator Kennedy's assassination? Here you are, on the job five months, and you think you've discovered a conspiracy that was unheard of before? Let me call the director right now. This'll move to top priority on his desk." Eckhaus shook his head. "Was your old man drunk out of his mind when he made up this story?"

William licked his lips. "He had a few drinks that night."

Daniels rubbed the back of his neck and the air rushed out of his lungs. "You didn't tell me that."

"He had the ticket and the matchbook—" William pleaded.

Eckhaus crushed his cigarette in the ashtray and looked at his watch. "I'll be calling the lab in an hour to have those documents returned to me before this office becomes the laughingstock of the country. Richmond, you can leave. I have to talk to Daniels about your future. Let me give you some advice before you go. If you decide to stick it out, before your probationary period ends your time might be well spent looking at the want ads."

"It's not just the documents and my father's statement. An agent in LA interviewed him the night the senator was murdered. I queried the files and found the entry. I was surprised you didn't mention that from the indices access report."

"Indices access report?" Daniels said with a puzzled look on his face.

Eckhaus realized he had to buy time now so he could figure out what to do. He was no longer dealing with the fate of some fictitious informant. He now faced a real witness and two of his own agents that knew the tip of the iceberg, and he couldn't take the chance that they might go deeper. He thumped his fingers on his desk. "All right, I'll go out on the limb with you for now. Does anyone else know about these allegations?"

"No, sir," William said.

"Daniels, I want you to get a room in your name at the Palmer House. I don't want any reference made to anyone that the Bureau has anything to do with this room. Get Richmond's father and two of you debrief him. Don't leave until you're done. Right now this doesn't go any further than the three of us. When you've finished debriefing him let me know. It's almost seven. The finance clerk should be in. I'll go get a cash advance for the room. Both of you wait here." Eckhaus stood and walked toward the door.

"Sir, there's one more thing you should know about."

Eckhaus dreaded the day he was assigned the Pape murder. "And that is?"

"My father said he delivered cash to James Earl Ray the day King was assassinated."

Pain fired up Eckhaus' back like a bullet piercing his spine. He opened the door and grasped the frame to steady himself. He tried to control the muscles in his face concealing his grimace as if that would hide his involvement. "The more I hear the more unbelievable it is." He stepped out of the office closing the door behind him and leaned against the wall waiting for the pain to settle.

"That was a quick turn around," Daniels said. "First, he's canning you and now he's getting money so we can hide your father away. What's this about an indices access reports?"

"Yesterday morning I gave him my activity report for last week and my work plan. He goes over it and pulls this report out of his desk. I had queried LeGrand, the mayor of Ruleville, my father, and Hasan. Eckhaus checked this report he had and asked why LeGrand wasn't listed on my activity report since there was a record of me accessing him on the computer. I told him I forget to include his name. But he didn't mention anything about the queries for Tisdale and Hasan."

"I never heard of an indices access report."

The phone rang. Daniels looked at William. "I better get it. Might be Eckhaus calling about something. FBI, James Eckhaus' phone."

"Good morning, sir. This is Reginald Stamley, Barclay's Bank in Bermuda. Is James available?"

"He's stepped away from his desk. This is Special Agent Daniels. Can I take a message for him?"

"I guess one of you chaps will do as good as another. Wanted to inform him that we received a $100,000 wire transfer into the undercover account yesterday. I wouldn't want to be a politician the way you boys are putting them away."

"What do you mean?"

"The wire transfer came from the Mississippi Republican Campaign Fund in Jackson, Mississippi. You will get that information to James? Let's see, I wrote your name down here somewhere, Special Agent Daniels."

"Yes, Mr. Stamley."

"I trust it is all right that I told you about this?"

"Yes, sir. I'll relay it directly to agent Eckhaus."

"Well, good day, sir."

Daniels cradled the phone. "That's strange."

"What's that?" William asked.

"Nothing, it's probably on a need-to-know basis and you don't need any more trouble than you've got."

Eckhaus opened the door. "She's on leave and her replacement won't be in until nine. Call the hotel, reserve a room, and get his father over there right away."

"I took this call for you while you were out." Daniels handed Eckhaus the message.

Eckhaus felt like he was watching his world crumbling. He waved the telephone message in front of him. "Both of you know about this?"

"No, I took the call. I thought it might be you calling us. William has no knowledge of the subject matter of the message," Daniels said.

For Eckhaus the last few days had gone from being the best to the worst. He was counting on filing his retirement papers, getting the money from Pape, and spending the rest of the winter on the beach. Now there was so much more to do. His eyes wandered toward the window as he considered his options.

## CHAPTER THIRTY-FOUR

William left Eckhaus' office, went to his desk and telephoned his father in the apartment above the ward office. After several rings a weary voice answered the phone.

"Yeah."

"Dad, it's me."

"It's not even seven, kind of early isn't it?"

"Sorry, I just finished a meeting with my supervisor. He wants us to start debriefing you right away so he can determine what steps we should take."

"I'm supposed to pick up Celeste at 8:30 to take her to the hospital."

"I'll take care of her after I bring you downtown. Get showered, I'll pick you up in half an hour. We've got a room at the Palmer House Hotel so we don't have to do this at the office."

"Who's going to be at the hotel while you're running Celeste around?"

"Clarence Daniels, I mentioned him to you."

"Oh, yeah, the man that was like a father to you."

William had heard the reluctant tone in his father's voice. He realized that he would have to maintain a delicate balance between his father and the man that had been like a father to him.

William's thoughts shifted to Eckhaus; maybe he had been wrong about his boss. Eckhaus had been hard to work for, but

William had to admit he had pulled a few bonehead plays that were enough to set off anyone. Eckhaus had a world of experience; it felt good to have the boss on his side. And most importantly to William's surprise, he hadn't been kicked off the case. He rose from his chair and went to Daniels who had just finished making the hotel reservations on the phone.

"I'm picking up my father at 7:30, should be at the Palmer House by eight. The only thing is, he was supposed to take Celeste to the hospital at 8:30. I told him I'd do it. You think that's all right?"

"Go ahead, but don't tell the boss. He said he wanted both of us there, but he won't come by until I call him when we're finished. We've got room 330." Daniels dropped a couple of legal pads and a tape recorder into his briefcase. "I'll see you later."

William checked out with Eckhaus and gave him the room number.

He arrived at the ward office on time. William and his father started the trip downtown. "Daniels is a good man. You'll like him. He worked in Mississippi on some of those civil rights cases in the sixties." William considered telling his father that Daniels was the agent that killed Celeste's father, but he knew how touchy Daniels was about that.

"He's black, right?"

"Yes."

"That must have been tough."

"Yeah, he's got some stories. I'll drop you off at the hotel. He'll be in room 330. Then I'll take care of Celeste. I'll give her my pager number so if she needs anything she can get in touch."

"That's a good idea. I don't want her to feel stranded. She's at the Days Inn by the Midway. You said you're coming to the hotel after you drop off Celeste, right?"

"I'll be there as soon as I can."

"Thanks." He put his hand on William's shoulder. "I'd feel better about this if you were there."

With his father's touch a feeling of warmth flowed through William, but it suddenly turned cold. He realized that his efforts to bring them closer could result in his father going to jail. He was an accomplice in two of the most serious crimes in this country's history. William double-parked next to a long line of cabs at the entrance of the Palmer House on Monroe. He looked at the expression on his father's face and could tell he knew they were crossing a line from which they could never return.

A doorman in a red jacket opened the door and Beauford stepped out of the LTD. "Ain't you Alderman Richmond?"

"Yes, I am."

William watched his father standing under the marquee that ran the length of the hotel. Like stars on a clear night one-thousand lights shown down and in the bright lights his father's face turn from somber to joyful as he grasped the doorman's hand and shook it.

"I live on the east side of the ward. Good to see a brother in office." He slapped Beauford's back and then pushed his horn-rimmed glasses, held together by a piece of white tape across the nose piece, back up his nose. "You got my vote the next election."

"Thanks." He glanced at the gold nametag. "Robert, stop by the ward office if you need anything." Beauford palmed him a five-dollar tip.

"I will, Alderman. I will." He grinned.

William laughed as he watched his father. "Always the politician." He headed back to the motel to pick up Celeste and anticipated a much different trip. He felt sorry for her, knowing that the cancer and Missy's accident must weigh heavy on her. Maybe it wasn't pity for her as much as he just didn't know how to deal with the woman.

***

Eckhaus called the forensic lab in Washington, D.C. "I'd like to speak to the examiner that was assigned to an expedite request from the Chicago field office. Some one called yesterday verifying receipt of the evidence."

"One second," the receptionist said.

In a few seconds Eckhaus heard a familiar voice. "Special Agent Lovejoy."

"Frank, this is Jim Eckhaus from Chicago. How're you?"

"Great, Jim. Counting down my time. Less than a year to go and I'm out of here. How about you?"

"I'm sticking it out for a while yet. I was calling about an expedite request that you guys verified receipt of yesterday."

"Yeah, I started working on it first thing yesterday morning."

"Hope you didn't spend too much time on it because you can send it back," Eckhaus said.

"What?"

Eckhaus fed him a story he felt was at least partially true. "We've got a rookie agent who's a loose cannon. They don't screen the new recruits like they use to. I already told this guy he's not going to make it through his probationary period and now he has a personal vendetta against me."

"I was wondering what was going on. There were a couple sets of fingerprints and the only identifiable prints were a thumb and forefinger on the matchbook that matched yours."

Eckhaus closed his eyes and breathed a sigh of relief. "He knows I'm going to bounce him so he's trying to fabricate some kind of case against me."

"Why don't you send this to the Office of Professional Standards?"

"It's not worth it. I've only got a couple of years to go and I'd rather devote my time to my squad's cases than deal with those dipshits. I just want to get this kid out of my hair. Can you send the complete file directly back to me?"

"Sure enough, Jim."

\*\*\*

William pulled the Ford LTD up to the office of the motel, left the car, and called Celeste on the house phone inside.

"Hi, my father asked me to pick you up." William paused, it was none of her business what his father was really doing. "He had an emergency meeting with some city officials." He was sure if it wasn't for the fact that he was taking her to see Missy she would have told him to forget it.

"Oh, okay. I'll be down in a couple of minutes."

William returned to his car and waited with the engine running. A warm car would be one less thing she could complain about.

Celeste rushed out of the front door. Her red coat floating like a cape behind her. She stepped into the car. "You didn't ask, but Missy's doing much better."

The look in her eyes made him feel like she was still trying to lay blame on him. "Good." William wanted to keep his words to a minimum, less of a chance of getting into an argument.

She looked at the two-way radio mounted on the dash. "Is this an FBI car?"

"Yes." He wondered if she was going to try to cause him trouble, figuring that he was using the car for personal business.

"Do you mind if we make one stop before we go to the hospital?"

"Where?"

"I'd like to stop at that gas station and see if my brother's there."

Rather that comment on Junior, William headed south on Cicero. It was only slightly out of the way and would make him just a few insignificant minutes late. It was a quiet ride.

He pulled into the gas station. The only person he saw was a chubby skinhead behind the counter. "Let's talk to that kid and see what he can tell us."

William held the door open for Celeste. She walked up to the counter and turned on the charm, "Hi, I'm Celeste, Junior's sister. Is he around?"

The boy scratched his head and flustered a response. "Ah, no he a…he's not here right now."

"What's your name?" William asked, the boy seemed slow.

"Earl…Earl Soder." He stuttered the words out.

Celeste winked at the boy. "You must be the boss."

"Well, my dad owns the place." His puzzled expression turned to a smile. "But yeah, when he's not here I'm the boss."

"Good, then I'm talking to the right man. Do you have an address for my brother? You see, I'm up here from Mississippi visiting and I'd like to spend some time with him before I go home."

"He sleeps right here most the time," Earl said pointing to the door of the room behind the counter. "But he ain't here now."

"If you don't mind I'll leave a message for him in his room." Celeste walked behind the counter. "This is my friend, William. He's driving me around since I'm not familiar with the city." She opened the door and stepped inside.

William nodded at Earl, followed her inside, and closed the door. "Why do I feel like your chauffeur?"

"If that boy is anything like Junior it's probably best that I did the talkin'." Celeste sat on the cot, grabbed a sheet of paper off the filing cabinet and started writing a note to Junior.

William knelt at the cardboard box that was Junior's filing cabinet, rifled through it, and found the arrest report. "Looks like your brother had a little trouble with the law."

Celeste looked up. "Let me see that." She grabbed it from William's hand.

He noticed the scribbling on the backside as she read the report but figured it was just some nonsense. "Well, this is a coincidence. My little brother was in a car accident with your father last March."

"What? My father never mentioned it. Can I see that?" William read the report and set it down on the cot. After hearing his father's story the other night it seemed like fate had intertwined their two families, first in Mississippi for generations and now in Chicago. He wondered how and when this would end.

Celeste finished the note. "Let's go to the hospital."

They stood and William opened the door. Celeste walked out, her coattails breezing behind her, the note and arrest report floated off the cot like leaves, and settled onto the cement floor.

William knelt down to pickup the note and saw the words "Hit List" on the back of the arrest report. He glanced at Celeste, caught her winking at Earl, and read the names that had lines drawn though them, Shelton and Moskowitz, the judge and public defender that had been murdered. Next on the list was Alderman Richmond. The names that followed were circled, Tisdale and son. William stuffed the arrest report inside his coat pocket. He placed the note on the cot, hurried to Celeste, grabbing her arm, and led her out the door. "Missy is waiting for you." He couldn't tell her he found the hit list and risk that she might let Junior know. "We better get going. Let me know if you hear from your brother. Maybe after he settles down we might all want to get together, since we're all family." *Celeste might be the best path to arresting Junior,* he thought.

***

Beauford was stretched out on one of the single beds, sipping coffee from a Styrofoam cup, and eating donuts from a box on the nightstand. They had a room that faced the inner courtyard which gave him a view through the window of a brick wall. Daniels sat at a small circular table in front of the bed drilling him with questions. On the table was a mini cassette recorder that had been taping Beauford's story for almost an hour. Daniels had filled several pages of a legal tablet with notes.

There was a knock on the door, Daniels shut off the tape recorder, and opened the door expecting William. A startled expression crossed his face. "Didn't think you were coming until I called."

Eckhaus stepped into the room, nodded at Beauford, and looked for William. "Where's your protégé?"

Daniels waffled as to what he should tell him. The only reasonable explanation was the truth. He explained that William had taken Celeste to the hospital, relieving Beauford of that responsibility so they could start the debriefing, and that William would soon return.

***

Eckhaus felt the weight of the 9 mm Browning in the shoulder holster under his coat. "How long is he going to be?"

Daniels looked up from his notes. "I don't know exactly. With rush-hour traffic I'd say at least a half hour."

The thought crossed Eckhaus' mind. Should he do it now? William wasn't a witness. He couldn't testify to his father's knowledge. It would be hearsay, but he was still a threat. "Don't let me stop you. Go ahead. You mind if I take a look at your notes?" Eckhaus pulled on the base of his black leather gloves, removing the slack from around his fingers.

Daniels turned on the tape recorder. "Not at all, go ahead."

Eckhaus picked up the legal pad realizing he'd have to take the tape recorder with him. He drifted behind Daniels as he read the notes. Eckhaus turned his back to Beauford as he unbuttoned his overcoat. With a sudden move he swiveled, pulled out the pistol from behind the legal tablet, jabbing the barrel of a silencer against the back of Daniels' head.

***

Beauford's eyes bulged when he saw the man draw the long pistol out from under his shoulder and jab it into the back of agent's head. *What the hell?* He watched as Daniels turned from prey to predator in a microsecond. He twisted to his right, elbow flying.

Beauford heard a pfft.

Daniels' left ear split, blood spraying across the room. His momentum kept him turning and his elbow slammed against Eckhaus' right arm, crashing into his body. The table and chair spun to the floor, the tape recorder slamming down.

\*\*\*

A jolt of pain fired up Eckhaus' spine. His legs crumbled beneath him. He collapsed onto the faded green carpet and the yellow pages of the legal tablet scattered across the room. Eckhaus held the Browning across his body looking up at Daniels who was straddled over him on his knees. Blood poured down the side of Daniels' face.

Eckhaus raised the pistol as Daniels dived on top of him. With a whoosh the air rushed from Eckhaus' lungs. His eyes bulged as he gasped. The semi auto lodged between their bodies. Daniels' blood flooded Eckhaus' face, dripping into his eyes as they grappled for the pistol.

Eckhaus swiped across his face with his arm attempting to clear his eyes. Daniels raised himself and pounded his knee into his opponent's solar plexus as the pistol fired another shot. Daniels collapsed on top of Eckhaus, rolled to the side, and lay on his back. His head turned in Eckhaus' direction. The Browning lay on his supervisor's chest pointing at an entrance wound under his jaw, the exit wound on the top of his head, and gray matter and bloody tissue splattered against the wall.

Daniels raised himself to a sitting position and covered the remains of his left ear with his hand. He peered over the footboard of the bed and saw Beauford slumped on his side. "Beauford, you all right?"

Daniels stood and stumbled over to the bed. He shook Beauford's shoulder and turned him onto his back. His head lay in a pool of blood. A bullet had ripped through the right side of his nose leaving a gaping hole in his face. Daniels pressed his fingers on Beauford's jugular, but there was nothing to feel.

Daniels grabbed a handful of napkins from the donut box and covered the remnants of his ear. He picked up the phone, hit 911, and informed the operator of the situation. There was a knock on the door. "Oh, God, William."

***

William knocked harder. The smell of cordite filled his nostrils. "Open up, it's me," he shouted as he rattled the doorknob.

It finally opened. Daniels stood there, his hand full of napkins covered his ear and shirt soaked with blood.

William gasped. "What the...?"

"William, your father." Daniels shook his head and stepped aside.

William rushed in and saw his father lying on the blood-drenched bed spread. "God almighty, not now, not after all this." He looked around the small room and caught glimpses of the debris. Eckhaus was lying in front of the bed, mouth open, eyes protruding, hair and tissue sticking to the wall. Pistol in his hand and blood gurgling from his wound. Yellow sheets from the legal tablet strewn across the floor. The table was on its side, tape recorder lying next to it. The chair spilled over, one leg broken. Daniels sat on the foot of the bed cradling his forehead with one hand. William shook his head. "If it hadn't been for me he'd be alive. What the hell happened?"

Daniels looked at him. "I don't know."

# CHAPTER THIRTY-FIVE

William felt so removed that it was surreal, as though he was backstage watching actors. He leaned against the wall next to the door. The two patrolmen that answered the call stood outside the door limiting access to the room.

Evidence technicians took photographs of his father and Eckhaus and outlined their bodies with chalk. The paramedics wrapped Daniels' ear, stanching the flow of blood, while two homicide dicks started asking him questions. The coroner's investigators flopped two black body bags onto the floor and zipped Eckhaus and William's father into them. They tossed each bag onto a gurney, strapped it down, and wheeled them from the room.

Special Agent in Charge James McAlister and Assistant Special Agent in Charge Larry Brunson debated jurisdiction with a CPD lieutenant. Since the perpetrator was dead and the victims were an FBI agent and his witness, the feds won out. The homicide cops lumbered out of the room, lips pursed. Damage control had been initiated.

McAlister and Brunson moved to a corner of the room, arms crossed over their chests, and heads close together. William figured they were trying to limit any potential threats to their careers. He watched Brunson remove his wire-rimmed glasses and clean them with a handkerchief. William overheard him. "We've got to find out what they were doing here. Richmond didn't have a gun on him, wasn't self-defense."

McAlister leafed through Daniels' notes. "This is about some guy named Tisdale in Mississippi back in 1968." He flipped to the last few pages. "Something about him getting his father's body at a bayou and getting attacked by the Klan."

William approached the two men. "Sir," he said, speaking to McAlister, "if you don't mind I'd like to ride with Daniels to the hospital?"

"Sure, son. I'm sorry about your father." McAlister grabbed William's arm and drew him closer. "Obviously don't make any statements to anyone, press, CPD, or otherwise. We want to keep this in house. As soon as possible, like later today, we'll need to get together and start our internal investigation. Call me as soon as Daniels is dismissed from the ER."

"Yes, sir." William nodded.

"My condolences," Brunson said, flicking a piece of lint off the sleeve of his blue suit.

"Thank you, sir." William followed the gurney that Daniels was on into the hallway and down a freight elevator so they could escape the press in the main lobby. He jumped in the back of the waiting ambulance in the narrow alley behind the Palmer House. As they rushed off to Northwestern University Hospital, sirens blaring and red lights flashing on the brick walls, he asked, "How're you?"

"All right, just a slight ringing in my ear, or I should say what's left of my ear."

"McAlister wants to meet with us ASAP—today. What're we going to tell him?"

Daniels pulled the tape recorder out of his pocket and smiled. "The only thing on the notes and tape is background information and your father's activities in Mississippi. If we tell them what your father told you they'll label it as ridiculous and bury it." Daniels' smile faded to a look of concern. "I'm sorry about your dad. Something is very wrong here but they're going to massage this so it won't be an internal Bureau issue, but a story about one man who went berserk. I think the best thing to say is that your father contacted us but he didn't give us any idea of the subject matter. We figured it had to be political corruption. That'll satisfy them on that end. Then maybe we'll have time to figure out why Eckhaus did this."

\*\*\*

It was midmorning and Junior was riding high on his good fortune and for the second time since they awoke, Patty was riding high on him. He watched her bouncing up and down over his hips, teeth clenched, and red hair flying as she was about to come.

"Oh, God. Oh, God." She fell exhausted onto his chest, heart racing, panting in his ear. "I love you."

Junior's chest was heaving and he was physically exhausted, but his mind was overcome with joy from a much less vibrant act. With the simple swipe of a pencil he had cut three names off his list, the two Jews he had murdered and the cowardly nigger he would take care of that had adopted another name in an attempt to hide from his eventual fate. How bizarre it was that his sister was the person that blew his cover. Now, whether Celeste wanted to or not she would help him get Tisdale and his son. He looked up and nodded. *Its close dad, the Tisdales will be gone.* Patty rolled off of him and lay spent. "Stay here, I'll put on some coffee," he said.

Patty brushed the hair out of her face. "That's about all I can do."

Junior marched, sans clothes, into the kitchen, turned on the tap, and filled the percolator with water as the sun's rays seeped through the gap between the window frame and the tattered shade. He turned on the eight-inch black-and-white TV, pulled the shade, and watched it snap up to the top of the window. The sunlight burst into the room as he lifted the lid off the coffee can.

The words "News Bulletin" flashed across the screen. "We interrupt this program with word just in that Chicago Alderman Beauford Richmond has been shot to death. Initial reports indicate that an FBI agent shot the alderman. The agent also was killed. No further information has been released. We will resume our originally scheduled program but will interrupt when any additional information becomes available."

Junior dropped the coffee can spilling the grounds across the floor. "Holy shit." He rushed into the bedroom and shook Patty. "Wake up." He grinned at her. "That nigger that killed my mother. I just heard on the news that an FBI agent killed him." He laughed. "The agent's dead too, maybe it was the one that shot my father." He danced in a circle. "That would be great."

Patty smiled, pulled him down to her, and hugged him. "I don't want to talk about that stuff, niggers and FBI agents. We just made love."

"They killed my mother and father. I was gonna get revenge." He pushed her hand away and his voice became sullen. "Now I don't have to." He realized that the promise he made to his father had been stolen from him. He had been deprived of his reason for living. He lowered his chin and sighed. "Now I can't."

"Maybe things will be different now, just you and me." Patty tried to probe his mouth with her tongue but Junior turned his head. "What's wrong?"

"I made a promise to kill Tisdale. That nigger killed my mother and now he's gone." He rose to his knees and hurled a pillow across the room. "What if the dead FBI agent was the one that killed my old man. Be just my luck, I'll never get revenge…except for Tisdale's kid."

"What do you mean?"

"I swore to my old man over my mother's grave that I would kill Tisdale and his son. The son's the only one left now. I can't take a chance. I got to get him or for the rest of my life I'll feel like I let my old man down."

"Let well enough alone." She stroked his thigh trying to distract him. "The spook that killed your mother is dead. Ain't necessary to have any more killing."

"A promise is a promise. Ain't nothing else to say. I gotta go." Junior felt like a tightly coiled spring. He slid to the side of the bed, slipped on his underwear, jeans, and military boots. He leaned under the bed, pulled out his dagger and strapped it on. Junior walked to the dresser, grabbed the 9 mm, and folded his arms across his chest. He admired his reflection in the mirror, a swastika tattooed across the top of one pectoral and the words "Blood & Honor & Klan" over the other. Junior grabbed his sweatshirt. "I'll see you later. I got to finish this."

Patty jumped out of bed and grabbed his arm. "Don't go. I'm scared. I want you here with me. You might get hurt or if they catch you—you'll go back to jail."

"You don't have to worry about that. Ain't going to happen." He shook off her hand, pulled on his shirt and black leather jacket, and marched out of the apartment.

\*\*\*

By one o'clock William and Daniels were seated in McAlister's office facing the SAC. The office was adorned with all the accoutrements of a bureaucrat that had believed in self-hero worship. Framed photographs of McAlister and various officials, headlines from significant cases, and awards decorated the walls.

McAlister sat in a black overstuffed leather chair behind a large cherrywood desk and looked like he was mentally chewing over words, testing them. "Clarence, I realize you've been through a very difficult day. But I think it's in everyone's best interest, including the Bureau, to analyze this situation as quickly as possible so we can get this behind us." He nodded his head toward Daniels' ear. "How're you feeling?"

"They gave me a shot and some Vicodin, so everything's numb. I'm going to have to get reconstructive surgery on the ear. I was very lucky."

"Thank God for that. You were in contact with James more than anyone else. Do you have any idea why he might have done this?" He spread his hands apart. "Was there any indications of psychological problems, undo stress, anything at all that stands out in your mind?"

Daniels shook his head. "No, sir. I didn't notice anything unusual in his behavior."

There was a knock on the door, Brunson entered, closed the door behind him and sat in a wooden chair to McAlister's right. "I went through his office and car. Didn't find anything. I'll get his apartment tonight." He crossed one leg over the other, rested his elbows on the arms of the chair, and pressed his hands together forming a steeple.

McAlister nodded.

Brunson pointed at William. "Do you know if there had been any previous contact between your father and Eckhaus?"

William shook his head. "None that I'm aware of."

Brunson uncrossed his legs, braced his black shiny shoes against the base of McAlister's desk. "How was this meeting arranged and what was the purpose of it?"

"William's father told him he wanted to talk to us about something. He refused to give us any advance information. As you can see from my notes we were just getting into his personal history, some stuff about the Klan when Eckhaus came," Daniels said.

"Why did James go to the hotel and where was William?" McAlister said.

Daniels felt anger flaring in his chest. The tone of McAlister's voice got to him. As if in every question there was doubt of the credibility of the answer before it was given. "I don't know why Eckhaus came when he did. He told me to call him when we were finished." He nodded in William's direction. "His father had a commitment to take a friend to the hospital. William took care of that so I could start the debriefing and he returned to the room minutes after the shooting."

McAlister drummed his fingers on his desk. "The Office of Professional Standards is flying in an inspector from Washington tomorrow afternoon. Of course he'll want to speak to both of you." He looked at Daniels. "You two make sure you've got your story down. We've got to make this right. In the meantime, if you think of anything that may be related to the shooting tell us immediately. And, of course, as I previously told both of you, no comments to press or anyone else. Any questions?"

"Do you mind if William gives me a ride home? I could use the rest and my wife is concerned."

"Go ahead, just stay available in case we need to get in touch. William, how're your mother and family coping?"

"About as well as they can. My mother and father are divorced. My sister took it hard. I called them from the hospital."

"It was good that you made contact with them. Make sure you let us know about the funeral arrangements."

McAlister looked toward Brunson and Brunson shrugged. "Well, I guess that's it. The OPD will go through us to make arrangements to interview you guys. We'll notify you."

***

Junior pulled a Pontiac Grand Am into one of the repair bays. He got out of the car, walked past a stack of tires and a box of brake shoes, and went to the front counter. "Hey, Earl, anybody lookin' for me?"

"Ya know that Grand Am supposed to be done today?"

"Yeah, I know. That's why I brought it back." He cocked his head. "Anyone come by for me?"

"Ah, yeah. Your sister was here. She's real pretty, Junior. She ain't fucking that nigger is she?" His lips curled.

"Ah, shit. What'd he look like?"

"Young dude. Nice clothes. My Dad says they all got nice clothes but they ain't got a pot to piss in."

Junior put his hands on his hips. "Yeah, what did they want?"

"She left you a note?"

He reached out his hand. "Give it to me."

"Ain't got it." Earl pointed to the back office. "It's in your room."

"You let them in? Damn it, how many times have I told you never tell anyone I stay here? Never let anyone in there." Junior stomped around the counter and headed to his room.

"I'm sorry, Junior. Don't be mad at me. You know how I forget." The door slammed in Earl's face.

Junior saw the note lying on the cot. He sat down and read it.

Dear Brother,

I'm glad that after all this time we have finally found each other. This should be a time for celebration, but unfortunately I have some terrible news. I have cancer and I don't know how much time I have left but I would like to spend some time getting to know you. I know that you don't approve of Missy but she's a wonderful child. I hope you see fit in your heart not to judge me or her. I'm staying at the Days Inn near Midway. Please call. If I'm not there I'm at the hospital visiting Missy. You're my only living relative and it would mean so much to me to spend this special time together.

Love,
Celeste

The note fell from Junior's hand to the floor. He shook his head. "Yeah, I'll call you. Cause how else am I gonna finish what I gotta do."

***

William pulled the LTD out of the government garage.

"Go north on Lake Shore Drive. We're going to Eckhaus' place," Daniels said.

William's brow furrowed. He was experiencing thoughts he had not yet allowed himself to feel. The loss was creeping in and he knew if he hadn't pursued his desire to have a relationship with his father the man would be alive. "I thought you wanted to go home. I don't know if I can do this."

"We've got to do it now. Brunson will be there tonight. We've got to get to the apartment before he does if there's any chance of finding something that might help us get to the bottom of this. It's the only chance we have that might lead us to the truth. If we don't and Brunson finds something I have a feeling we'll never see it. McAlister's covering his ass for the sake of his career and the Bureau."

An icy rain started falling from the gray skies and it pinged on the roof of the car. "How're we going to get in? McAlister has Eckhaus' keys."

"My years in the black-bag squad were good for something."

They were heading up Lake Shore Drive toward Eckhaus' apartment on Marine Drive. Whitecaps broke the surface of the lake. William's pager vibrated. He glanced at the display. "I think its Celeste. She must have heard about my father. We're almost at Foster. I'll call her from Eckhaus' place." They pulled onto the Lawrence Avenue exit ramp as a blustery wind whistled through the barren trees in Lincoln Park.

They parked a half block away, entered the building, and took the elevator to the tenth floor. Daniels gave him a pair of latex gloves and slipped on a pair himself. William had been shocked by his father's secret life, wondered if there was more to be discovered, and how much worse it could be. What link could there be between a black farmer from Mississippi and a white FBI agent that would result in their deaths?

Daniels opened his briefcase and removed a small black pouch and handed the briefcase to William. He looked up and down the hallway. There was no one. He pulled the tension bar out of the pouch and inserted it into the top of the lock. He felt the first tumbler and eased in the raking bar. With each clockwise movement he pressed the tension bar deeper. In thirty seconds the lock opened. He pushed open the door. They stepped into the apartment and Daniels closed the door. He dropped his tools in the pouch, grabbed the briefcase from William and put the picks away.

William breathed in the stagnant smell of cigarettes.

Daniels said, "You take the bedroom and I'll check the living room."

William looked around the room. A gray blanket with cigarette burns lay wrinkled diagonally across the bed. On the nightstand was a half-full bottle of Jack Daniels, an empty Manhattan glass, and a brown plastic bottle of Vicodin. He pulled the drawer open. It was filled with loose change, a variety of pills, and .38 and 9 mm caliber ammunition. He closed the drawer and looked at the closet.

The sliding door was open revealing four suits, three blue and one brown, and a couple of gray sport coats with black slacks that hung from the rod. William started searching the pockets. "Empty, empty, empty." Peering down the clothes rod he saw the other half of the closet. Ten white shirts, half of them with ties all ready knotted around the collars. Three pairs of black shoes were on the floor. His pager vibrated again. It was the same number. William sat on the bed and used the phone on the nightstand.

"Pediatrics, ICU, may I help you?"

"My name's William Richmond. I was paged, probably by Celeste Napier."

"One second. I'll get her."

"William, is it true?" Celeste's voice cracked.

"I'm afraid so."

Celeste whimpered. "What happened?"

"We don't know all the facts yet. I'm working on it right now. I'll give you a call later? Maybe we'll know more then."

"What's going to happen to Missy now? You've got to help me."

"We'll help. I'll talk to you later, okay?"

"Okay. I'm sorry, William. I've got to get back to Missy." The line went dead.

William stood and inadvertently pulled the phone off the nightstand. A mini cassette slid from under the phone and tumbled down to the carpet. He placed the phone back on the nightstand and bent down. "I think I found something," he shouted.

Daniels came to the doorway. "What did you find?"

William held up the tape with a piece of scotch tape on it. "It was taped to the bottom of the telephone."

"Let's check it out." Daniels went to his briefcase and pulled out a tape recorder. They sat on the sofa as he slipped in the tape, and pressed the play button.

*"Hello, James. You're looking good."*

"Voice isn't familiar," Daniels said.

*"Your eyes aren't what they use to be."*

"That's Eckhaus," William said

The tape continued through some small talk.

*"Who's picking up the tab?"*

*"Courtesy of the Republican National Committee...."*

Daniels shut off the tape. "That phone call that I took for Eckhaus this morning in his office was Barclay's Bank in Bermuda confirming receipt of a $100,000 wire transfer from the Mississippi Republican Campaign Fund to an undercover account."

"You think he was working some kind of sting operation?" William asked.

"I don't know. It's possible. It could have been a case he brought with him from Washington. I'd like to know who the guy is he's talking to." Daniels pushed the play button.

More small talk until they heard Eckhaus say, *"There may be a problem. One that might interfere with your vice presidential candidacy."*

Daniels pushed the stop button. "I think I know who it is?"

"Who?"

"There's only one of Reagan's possible VP candidates that's got a little southern twang to his voice. Edward Pape, the Governor of Mississippi."

"Why would a guy like that be meeting with Eckhaus?"

"I don't know." Daniels pushed the play button.

They watched the wheels of the cassette turn and listened to Eckhaus say, *"I heard through the grapevine that an attorney had contacted headquarters. He has a client who claims to have information that would reveal that King's assassination was a conspiracy."*

Daniels stopped the tape. "Is it possible he's talking about your father?"

"I don't know. He didn't tell me about any attorney."

The tape continued. *"If I'm even remotely linked to this I'm ruined."*

Daniels stopped the tape again. "I think we just heard the Governor of Mississippi confess to being involved in the assassination of Martin Luther King." He swallowed and started the tape again.

*"LeGrand knew me and the only link to both of us was Sakich. But they're both dead."*

William leaned back in the sofa. "LeGrand, that's the guy my father said saved him that night at the bayou. Celeste said she thinks she saw LeGrand meet with James Earl Ray. Ever hear of Sakich?"

"Doesn't ring a bell."

The tape continued, Eckhaus saying, *"The only thing I heard is that it's a woman."* Eckhaus and Pape debated further on who she could be. Then Eckhaus said, *"That leaves two options. Buy her out or get rid of her."*

Pape responded, *"There's no guarantee if we give her the money that she won't come back later for more or decide to talk later."*

"Conspiracy to commit murder between an FBI agent and a governor." Daniels shook his head.

"Maybe calling my father a female informant was a way of providing cover for him. That's the only explanation for Eckhaus shooting him," William said.

"Could be. Let's hear what else they say."

Pape goes on, *"Can't you volunteer? It would be logical since you oversaw the first investigation. Don't forget you've something to be concerned about too."*

"Sounds like Eckhaus was involved in the conspiracy." William asked.

"As difficult as it is to believe, it sounds that way."

*"$200,000, the same the girl is asking for. For that I can get the job done, subsidize my pension, and you can become vice president."* Daniels shakes his head. "Eckhaus negotiated a price for killing an informant."

*"Your republican friends. They've got millions in campaign funds."* "And he tells Pape where he could get the money," William said.

They heard Eckhaus slurp the rest of his drink and open the door. Then Pape gets excited. *"Wait. That land in Mississippi. LeGrand paid that girl some cash to be a nominee on the transaction. What's her name? Shit. The daughter of the guy that led us to Ray."*

*"Those were your guys. I didn't know them."*

*"Napier. That's the guy's name. I can't think of the daughter's name. But you should be able to find her,"* Pape says.

*"What's Napier's first name and where's he live?"*

*"It's Jimmy. But he's dead. One of your boys shot him while he was bombing a black church."*

Daniels' eyes closed as he pictured the look on Napier's son after he shot his father.

The tape continued. *"LeGrand gave her money so he must have had something going on with her."*

*"I'll check her out. Get back to you."* Then the sound of the door closing, the ping of the elevator and the tape went quiet.

Daniels sighed. "I don't know how much is true and how much is bullshit. Were they involved in a conspiracy to murder King? We have the least amount of information on that but it seems the most credible. If it wasn't for the assassination why would any of these other things even be discussed? The alleged informant. The money Eckhaus is asking for. The money that was sent to the undercover account. And what about Celeste Napier? If there's somebody else out there that's still involved in this that thinks she's the informant are they going to try to kill her?"

They sat there in a daze.

Daniels looked at William. "This tape corroborates what your father told you. His story was the bottom part of the organization. The tape is the top half. But there's one major problem."

"What's that?"

"It's not admissible evidence. There's no legal foundation, no one alive that can testify as whose voices are on the tape, when and where the conversation took place. No one except Pape."

William stood. "That's great. We've got evidence incriminating the man that might be the next vice president of this country in the murder of Reverend King and there's nothing we can do with it?"

"I didn't say that." Daniels smirked. "Let's finish going through the apartment and get out of here. Brunson may be here any minute."

"There's one more thing." William pulled out Junior's arrest report from the inside pocket of his coat. "Look at this. Napier's kid, I think he's the one who murdered the judge and public defender over the weekend. Next on his list was my Dad, me, and you."

## CHAPTER THIRTY-SIX

That evening Junior went to the pay phone in Michael's Restaurant across the street from the gas station. He dropped in the change and punched in the number.

"Days Inn at Midway International Airport."

"Like to speak to Celeste Napier."

"One second."

"Hello."

"Celeste, It's me, Junior. Got your note. Don't know what to say." He paused and sighed. "Sorry you're so sick and I didn't mean to offend ya." Junior smiled, proud of his acting job.

"I'm glad you called. Everything in my life is falling apart. Missy getting hurt. Beauford killed. I needed to hear from you. You're my only living relative. I needed somebody I can be close to."

"I heard about Beauford on the news. Hope you can forgive me for the things I said. Wasn't right of me to say those things." Junior looked up at the ceiling. "Is your daughter okay?"

"She's doing well. She has a mild concussion. But other than that it's just bumps and bruises. Fortunately the cars were slowing for the light."

"That's good. She's lucky. They got those muscles that are real springy." He laughed under his breath, *shouldn't have said that.*

"It would be nice if we could get together before I head home."

"Don't make much money at the gas station so it's hard for me to take time off. Ya know when and where he's going to be laid out and buried?"

"William gave me the information earlier today. Hold on."

He heard the ruffle of paper.

"The wake is at Bethune's Funeral Parlor on Thursday from three until nine. Friday they'll be a service in the morning at ten at the funeral parlor. Then they'll take him to St. Mary's Cemetery at 87th and Pulaski for the burial."

"If I can't make one I'll try to make the other." He tore a page out of the phone book and scribbled down the information.

"How can I get in touch with you?" Celeste asked.

"Don't have a phone. Best thing to do is call the station and leave a message. Don't know the number offhand. It's in the book."

"All right I hope to see you at the visitation, Junior. We can talk little bit there. But I would like to spend some time with you besides that."

"You will. I promise." Junior hung up the phone and smirked.

***

In a matter of seconds her phone rang again. "Hello, Junior?"

"No, it's me, William. Did he call?"

"Yes, I just got off the phone with Junior and I thought that was him calling back. We had a real nice conversation. He apologized for the things he said the other night and he's going to try to make it to Beauford's wake or burial."

"Good, I'm glad to hear it went well." William thought, *if he comes, it won't be for my father, it'll be for me.* "Does anyone besides Junior and me know where you're staying?"

"No, why?"

"I don't want you to be alarmed with what I'm telling you because it's strictly a precaution. We don't think anyone else was involved in my father's death. But if there was, it's remotely possible that there could be a threat against you. Again, there's no solid information. I'm telling you this strictly as a precaution."

"What should I do? You don't think that Missy's accident was on purpose?"

"I have no reason to believe that it wasn't an accident."

"Should there be a guard at her door?"

"No, I don't think there's a threat. Did you ever have an attorney contact the FBI about the things you told me about my father, LeGrand, James Earl Ray or for any other reason?"

"What? No I've never talked to any attorney about anything. The only person I've ever talked to about that stuff is you. Why?"

"No reason in particular, just curious."

"You wouldn't ask me if there wasn't a reason."

"No, really. Listen, there are more important matters. How's Missy doing?"

"They're supposed to discharge Missy tomorrow morning. I'd like to get her tonight. She can spend the night here with me and you could get the room next door. I mean if there's any real concern about somebody wanting to hurt me."

"I don't think it's a good idea to take her out of the hospital early. If you want I can get a room next to yours, take you to the hospital first thing in the morning and you can stay with her until they release her."

"I would appreciate that."

"Where's Junior live?"

"He didn't say. Said he moves around. He probably stays with some girlfriends."

"If you talk to him again why don't you ask him?"

"Why?"

"He's your only living relative. You should know where he is so you can get in touch with him." William thought, *he's killed two people and he's looking for me. I'd rather surprise him than have him surprise me.*

"I'll get something from him at the visitation or the funeral service."

"Alright, I'll be there in about thirty minutes." He hung up the phone, turned off the tape recorder and looked at Daniels.

\*\*\*

A short while later William knocked on Celeste's door. The door opened a crack, held close by the chain. He saw a sandwich in her hand at her side. "I should've asked you if you needed any food."

"I stocked up on lunchmeat and other stuff. I'm okay."

"I was able to get the room next door so if you hear anything during the night page me, call the room or bang on the wall. I'll be there. I brought some work to keep me busy. I better settle in."

He tried to sleep that night but the violence and gore of the day haunted William. Between the nightmares of his father's death, the anticipation of someone attacking Celeste, and the knowledge that Junior maybe stalking him, he hardly slept. The following morning William knocked on her door. "It's me."

She opened the door leaving the chain hooked and peeked through the gap. "Hi."

"I'm ready anytime you are to go the hospital."

"All right." She paused, slid the chain off the door and opened it. A warm smile spread across her face. "Thanks for everything."

He noticed the change in her voice. He dropped her off at the hospital. "Talk to you later, I've to get to work. Keep me posted on how everything's going. You can page me."

***

The following day was Beauford's wake at Bethune's Funeral Parlor a few blocks north of Soder's Gas Station. William and Marlee stood by the closed, pewter-colored casket for the better part of the day. The room was flooded with floral displays of lilies and dahlias that filled the space on both sides of the casket and down the length of the pale walls. The scent of the flowers countered the heavy emotions of the one-thousand people that paid their respects as they passed by the casket of the man that had risen from a Mississippi farmer to a Chicago alderman.

The guests seemed to arrive within their own cliques. The mayor, police chief, and other city and county politicians gave low-key expressions on the surface that seemed sincere about Beauford's tragic death and what a great loss it was to the city. The irony was that many of them were subjects of investigations by the FBI agents that followed.

McAlister, Brunson and most of the agents from the Chicago office showed. It was a closely knit brotherhood with strongly held opinions but at a time like this they showed their support to the family.

Others like Dante Ippolito and Deputy Commissioner Falcone muttered curses as they knelt at the casket and tried to pick out which mourners might be agents. They were concerned about what Beauford was doing meeting with the FBI and what he had told them before his demise. They hoped that his passing was an insurance policy that meant their way of doing business would continue. There would just be a different palm to grease.

Then there were people like Robert, the doorman from the Palmer House, who felt a loss of a hero that had taken the time to shake a regular man's hand. One of his kind, that he saw taking large steps forward for his people.

And the family had their own thoughts. Marlee wondered what had happened to her father that had made him so remote. In her mind he wasn't dead. This was just a dream, she would wake up tomorrow morning, hear something about him on the radio or see him at some political affair.

Nathleen Richmond quietly knelt at the casket and remembered warm thoughts about the young man that she had loved in Mississippi. She noticed the white lady with the mulatto child and wondered who they were.

Celeste held Missy's hand and knelt in front of the casket. Her heart ached with the fear of what the future held for her daughter. Her eyes welled with tears as she drifted to the seats in the rear and waited to see if Junior would appear. But that never happened.

*** 

Shortly before 9:00 p.m. the funeral director announced that visitation had ended and ushered out the last guest. William walked up to the casket, rested one hand on it and thought about what his father had gone through. The long separation from his family. The turmoil his father had suffered that only he and Daniels knew about. William remembered when he was a child how he had both missed his father and hated him. He had suffered through the pain and rage of wondering why his father didn't love him. How, by chance, some minute gesture in the last week of his father's life had opened a door to renew their relationship and the utter irony that the same gesture closed the door on his life.

# CHAPTER THIRTY-SEVEN

It was a brisk sunny early December morning and a primer-gray Olds Cutlass was parked at the Dunkin' Donuts across the street from Bethune's Funeral Parlor. The driver watched the pallbearers carry Beauford's casket to the hearse. William, his arm around Marlee's shoulder, followed them. Nathleen was next and then a parade of politicians, constituents, FBI agents, and interested parties ranging from mistresses to hotel doormen. The Richmond's entered a gleaming black limousine, which was followed by three waxed and buffed flower cars. Two CPD motorcycles and a squad car with flashing red lights headed the long procession which was being recorded by news vans from the local network affiliates. The long line of cars went past Soder's Gas Station on its way past the ward office, and circled Marquette Park before heading to St. Mary's Cemetery. A mile square patch of grass, barren tall oaks and elms with a smattering of brown leaves spotted the grass. A large statue of the Virgin Mary overlooked thousands of gray headstones.

Junior pulled the Olds Cutlass into the rear of the procession. He spun the dial on the car radio looking for some heavy metal. He was looking for something to get his juices flowing, not a funeral dirge. He parked the car a safe distance from the burial site. The sweet smell of new-mown grass cut for the last time for the season filled the air as he took cover behind a headstone marked Goldstein. Junior watched the casket carried from the hearse to the grave. He saw William standing between his weeping sister and stone-faced mother. He put his arms around them as a black minister muttered unintelligible words that seemed to bring tears to everyone.

Junior extended his forefinger, raised his thumb, and rested his hand on the headstone. He looked down the imaginary barrel and sighted William in. "Fucking big man, protecting all your nigger bitches." Junior squeezed his index finger and his thumb fell like the hammer of a pistol crashing down on the firing pin. "It won't be long now. You be one dead nigger."

He scanned the crowd surrounding the grave and spotted his sister and the little girl. "Son of bitch. Celeste, what the hell's wrong with you. Your brain must of turned black after he raped you."

***

William lowered his arms as the minister finished his last words. Marlee stepped forward to lay a lily from one of the sprays onto the casket. He followed her and, as he touched the casket, William thought of the last time that his father touched him. That last sensation of intimacy he felt from his father. The only feeling of closeness he could remember. So much between them had gone unsaid and unrealized. They were so close to a new beginning but William had to push him into cooperating. He questioned why he pushed so hard. Did he really believe it was necessary so they could mend their relationship? Or once he learned his father's secrets had it become too tempting for William to exploit them for himself? He stepped back from the casket.

A parade of mourners passed the casket to say goodbye to Beauford for the last time, some crying, some smiling. Remembering the man in other times and places. Because of the sudden and violent nature of Beauford's death the family decided to forsake a dinner after the burial.

***

Junior watched Marlee. She kissed William on the cheek, hugged him, and returned with her mother to the black Cadillac limousine they had ridden in during the procession. His eyes shifted to William. Celeste and Missy approached him and the three of them got into a Camaro. Junior shook his head. "She's so weak. She switched from the old nigger to the young one. What am I gonna do with you, Sister? You and your mulatto child." He steadied the 9 mm in his waistband, turned and walked to the Olds Cutlass. "Don't deserve no respect. I know what Daddy would do."

Junior left the cemetery and parked down a residential street waiting for the limousine that held Marlee and her mother. He followed it back to the funeral parlor where the two of them got into a white Buick Skylark and headed home. He kept a safe distance.

***

Nathleen pulled the Skylark onto the apron of the driveway. She and Marlee left the car and entered the beige brick bungalow through the back door.

"I'm tired, Mom, I think I'll go up stairs and take a nap." She stopped at the base of the stairs. "I can't believe he's gone."

"When you don't live right it's just a matter of time before the Good Lord sees fit to take you away. He don't play." She opened the refrigerator and took out a plate of leftover ham. "You want some. A good sandwich will perk you up."

"No, thanks, I think the Good Lord wants me to take a nap."

They laughed. For Nathleen it was a pathway to turn away from the anger and betrayal she felt toward Beauford. Nathleen watched her daughter go upstairs. She sat at the kitchen table and finished making her sandwich while boiling water for tea.

***

A half block away Junior parked the Cutlass and prowled toward the corner bungalow carrying a couple of blank sheets of paper rolled in his hand. He was in a place he never imagined he would be, alone in the middle of a black neighborhood. His eyes were colorless and he felt pure venom rushing through his veins. He took the front stairs two at a time and pressed the doorbell hard twice.

The lady opened the interior door still wearing her mourning clothes, a black skirt and jacket over a gray blouse. She spoke through the storm door. "Can I help you?"

"Yes ma'am. I'm lookin' for Mrs. Richmond. My boss sent me. I'm from St. Mary's Cemetery and there's some forms he needs signed." He held up the rolled papers.

"I'm not his wife anymore. We're divorced."

"It was my fault these forms didn't get signed. My boss ain't gonna be too happy if I bring 'em back unsigned." He scratched his head. "I don't think it matters none that you ain't his wife anymore. If you can sign 'em I can be on my way."

Nathleen took in a deep breath. She unlocked the storm door, pushed it open, and reached for the papers. "All right, give them to me."

Junior glanced over his shoulder, checking the sidewalk and street. They were clear. He handed her the papers. The moment she grabbed them he shoved her into the living room. Junior put his foot behind her leg as he stepped forward and knocked Nathleen to the floor. He leaned over her prone body, raised his hand, and cracked her across the face. She moaned and lifted her hands to protect herself.

"You be quiet or they'll be a lot more pain for you." Junior closed the door and locked the dead bolt and returned to Nathleen, hovering over her. "Where's your daughter?"

"Don't hurt her. She's a good girl."

He clenched his fist and waved it in front of her face. "I ain't here to hurt nobody unless I got to. Where is she?"

"Upstairs in her bedroom taking a nap. Take me if you have to have somebody, just leave her alone. I won't tell no one." Her cheek started to bruise. "Then you can go and nobody will ever know."

Junior laughed and shook his head. "I ain't interested in fuckin' any nigger bitches." He pulled a roll of duct tape out of the pocket of his black leather coat, ripped off a piece, and covered Nathleen's mouth. "Roll over." He straddled over her and wrapped the tape around her wrists several times. Then he bound her ankles and knees, grabbed the back of her collar, and dragged her into the center of the living room. He yanked her hair, turned her head, and looked into her bulging eyes. "Now you be nice and quiet and me and your daughter will be right down." He pulled the dagger out

William wanted all of this to have never happened. As if somehow eleven years of their lives could be erased. But that couldn't happen and the violence of the assassinations, the riots and his father's death were reality. All William could do was pray for a reason that all this wasn't for naught.

and dimpled her cheek with the tip. "Don't do nothing to make me open up that sweet little girl. You understand?"

Nathleen nodded. Her eyes wide open.

"Good, be back in a second." He pushed her head into the beige carpet, sheathed the dagger, walked to the stairs and took them quietly. He pushed the first door open and there was Marlee. A white quilt pulled up to her neck. He looked across the room. A portable record player, a stack of 45's and LP's were on a stand next to the dresser. A poster of Earth, Wind and Fire hung on the wall. Her black dress from the funeral hung over a chair by a small wooden desk covered with homework.

Junior slid the dagger out of its sheath and approached. With each step his heart pounded faster. He could smell the sour stench of his anger. Marlee lay on her side, back facing him. He placed the cold steel against her neck. She spun around, eyes opened wide. Before she could let out a scream his hand covered her mouth. Junior lowered himself and whispered in her ear. "Your momma is tied up downstairs. If you don't want nothing to happen to her you be nice and quiet."

Marlee nodded. Her chest expanding and contracting.

He pushed himself up and sheathed the dagger. He took out the duct tape, and ripped off a piece with his teeth. Junior raised his hand from Marlee's mouth and covered her lips with the duct tape. He yanked the quilt off and looked at her lying there in white cotton panties and a bra. Junior slid his finger across the inside of her thigh dragging it up to the crotch of her panties. He thought, *maybe if there's time.* A hideous laugh came from deep inside him. He trussed her wrists behind her back with the duct tape. Junior yanked her out of bed and dragged her downstairs to the living room. "See, Momma. I told you I wouldn't hurt her." He shoved Marlee to the floor and wrapped tape around her ankles. He inhaled and proudly stood over his capture like a lion standing over an antelope.

***

William fell in line with the rest of the cars waiting to leave the cemetery.

At the exit Missy leaned forward from the back seat and whispered in Celeste's ear.

"She's hungry. Could we stop at McDonald's and get a burger?"

"I could use a bite myself." William pulled into the Golden Arches and they entered the restaurant.

A few minutes later they were walking to a table with a tray full of food. "Missy, this was a good idea." William stuffed a French fry into his mouth. "Oh, these are good."

A grin broke across Missy's face as she sat down and took a bite out of her hamburger.

"Did you happen to see my brother yesterday or today?" Celeste sipped her coke.

"No, I didn't see him at all."

"Hmm, I was wondering. He said he would try to make it one of the days."

William glanced down at his pager. "It's my mother, I'll be right back." He went to the pay phone.

"Hello."

"You alright, Mom? You sound upset."

"Something's wrong with Marlee. Can you come right away?"

"Yeah, we're ten minutes away. Be right there." William rushed back to their table. "Something's wrong with my sister. Let's finish eating in the car."

"Sure," Celeste said as they bagged up the food and returned to the Camaro. "What's wrong with her?"

"She didn't say. But my mother sounded upset."

"Was your sister close to your father?"

William sped out of the parking lot. "I think she was closer than the rest of us." It hurt William to admit it. "Every once in a while she would talk about him like they had met recently. She tried not to mention it. Didn't want to upset my mother."

\*\*\*

Junior took the phone away from Nathleen's ear and covered her mouth with the duct tape. He dragged Marlee into her mother's bedroom on the first floor, closed the door, and returned to Nathleen. "Does he have a key for the house?"

She lay on the floor motionless as her eyes were filled with tears.

Junior whipped out his dagger. "You want me to mess up your daughter's pretty face?" He grabbed Nathleen by her hair and jerked her head up. "Does he have a key?"

She nodded.

"That's better. Don't wanna have to cut your girl." He grabbed Nathleen and pulled her across the room into a rocking chair directly across from the front door. Slit the duct tape around her wrist and taped her forearms onto the arms of the rocking chair. "It won't be long now, Daddy." Junior went to the front door and peered through the small square window. In a few minutes he saw the Camaro park and William, Celeste, and Missy get out. "Fuck it, Celeste. Why you got to be so stupid. Something might happen that you ain't gonna like."

Junior saw them come up the stairs and backed into the corner of the entryway behind the door. He felt like jumping up and screaming, "Yes." It wouldn't be long now. His heart was racing. He watched William press the doorbell and wait. He pressed it again and knocked. He heard the keys enter the dead bolt lock and turn. The door opened.

"I'm worried. She didn't answer the door," William said as Celeste and Missy entered.

William stepped in just as Celeste saw Nathleen taped and gagged. She screamed. "Oh, my God," and ran to Nathleen, Missy followed.

Junior crashed the butt of the pistol down on William's head and he tumbled to the floor.

Missy cried, scared by her mother's scream.

Junior watched Celeste's gaze turn from Nathleen, down to William, and then to him. He closed the door and turned the dead bolt.

She focused on the 9 mm. "What're you doing?"

He took a step forward, standing over William's prone body, and pointed the pistol at the back of his head. "Keeping my promise to Daddy. Gonna be one less nigger in this world."

William spun, pulling out his Glock.

Junior jerked the trigger, firing two rounds. Shell casings jumped into the air. William's Glock skittered across the floor, stopping in front of Nathleen. William grabbed his right arm. Blood spilled from the flesh wound staining the elbow of his blue suit coat.

"Good. I'd rather kill you when I can look you in the eye. Not shoot you in the back of the head like a sick dog." He pointed the pistol at William's face. "Daddy, the promise is kept, goodbye nigger." A fire rumbled through Junior from his groin to his chest. There were three things he knew: A black man killed his mother, a black man killed his father, and he was going to avenge those deaths.

"Don't, Junior," Celeste pleaded. "What're you talking about Daddy for?"

Junior's eyes shifted up from William to Celeste. "This nigger's old man is the one that killed Momma and raped you. That's how you got that half-breed." He waved the pistol at Missy. The little girl was shaking, standing next to Nathleen in the rocker.

"That's a lie. Who told you that?"

"Daddy told me when we put Momma in the ground. I promised him over Momma's grave that I'd kill the Tisdale men to avenge Momma's killin'. And you found them for me." He glared down at William. He felt the resistance of the trigger against his finger.

"Daddy killed Momma, not Beauford." Celeste took a deep breath. "Beauford didn't rape me. I took him cause I...cause I hated Daddy so much."

Junior's rage fired like a hot furnace. "You make me sick. I thought about doing this and now I know its right. You shamed Daddy." He lifted the pistol. The barrel moved from William to Celeste. The tension grew in his trigger finger. The trigger slowly moved back. "Good-bye you lying nigger loving whore."

A shot fired. Celeste's eyes slammed shut. She grimaced. The sound blasted through the room. Cordite filled their nostrils. Blood gushed from the sucking chest wound. Junior collapsed next to William.

The Glock thudded to the floor from Missy's hands. She shook in a palsy. Tears rushed down her face. She wrapped her arms around her mother's legs. "That man was going to hurt you, Momma."

# CHAPTER THIRTY-EIGHT

Saturday morning William called Celeste in response to her page. "How's Missy?"

"She's a mess. Crying and shaking fits, tossing and turning all night. She's finally asleep," Celeste whispered. "I didn't tell her that Junior was my brother. I'm afraid that would be catastrophic."

"Good idea. You should probably take her for professional help."

"I will. I wanted to let you know that we're heading home later today. I'm sorry for the way things worked out. I hope me coming up didn't contribute to this awful mess."

William shook his head. *You don't know how awful this mess is.* "Taking Missy back to familiar surroundings is good idea. She'll be more comfortable there."

"When I get home I'll call and give you Mrs. Virden's number and if you don't mind I'll keep you informed on my condition."

"I meant it when I said we'll help out, so stay in touch."

"I've asked the funeral home that took care of your father to make arrangements to have Junior sent home when his body is released. I'll have him buried next to Mom and Dad. Maybe he'll find peace there. Thank you, William."

\*\*\*

The next call he made was to Daniels. "What are we gonna do?"

"You know that place we met on the lake. I'll see you there at one today," Daniels said.

William pulled into the planetarium parking lot. The annual Christmas show drew hordes of families. Kids stuffed into winter parkas, scarves wrapped around their faces as their parents held one in their arms and pulled another along.

He walked through the crowds and saw Daniels standing in back of the planetarium facing the lake. Gray skies met the steel-colored water blending into one. Daniels held onto a White Sox baseball cap as the wind attempted to put it in flight.

William zipped up his black leather bomber jacket. "All the little munchkins make great cover, but couldn't we have met inside somewhere?"

Daniels took a deep breath. "I think better in the fresh air and we've got a lot of thinking to do."

"Clue me in."

"First thing, we don't talk about anything on the phone. I can't help thinking that OPS, the brass or even worse somebody we don't know about is going to try to find out how much we know and what're we're going to do."

William pulled the collar up around his neck. "What is it we're going to do and when?"

"I got a call earlier today from McAlister. He made me the acting supervisory agent. That's going to tie me up for at least a couple of days and make it easier for him to keep tabs on me. But I want to move on this. Let's plan on heading south Friday. I'll put us both on leave." Daniels turned, faced the planetarium and spit. "No way Pape gets the VPs nomination."

William stuck his gloved hands into the pockets of his jacket. "How can we prevent that with the little we have?"

"I'm not sure. But we have to go down there to confront him—play the tape."

"It's not admissible and he'll know that. He was the attorney general."

"The threat of it might be enough to get him to change his mind."

"And if it isn't?"

Daniels shrugged. "We'll do what we have to."

\*\*\*

On Monday morning it was announced that Clarence Daniels was the acting supervisory special agent. He held a squad meeting with his agents in the bullpen area amongst the agents' desks standing against the wall of what used to be Eckhaus' office. "Just so everyone knows, Eckhaus' office is off limits to everyone until further notice by orders of the SAC. The door is locked so don't even try to get in. There won't be a service for him here. His body will be shipped to Montgomery, Alabama, where his father resides. If anyone is interested in sending a card or note to his father the address can be obtained from the SAC's secretary. It's very likely that you'll be seeing agents from the Office of Professional Standards around and they may even want to interview you. It goes without saying, but I will anyway, be cooperative and truthful and there shouldn't be any fallout for anyone. If anyone does have any information or insight to what happened, see me. Otherwise, let's get back to doing what we get paid for—working cases."

\*\*\*

Two hours after dusk on Friday Daniels and William approached the stairs of the state capital building in Jackson. Daniels wore a navy blazer, dark gray slacks, a gray tie and a patch over his left ear. William a black suit, the one he wore at his father's funeral, and a red tie.

"My cousin is a janitor. Told me the governor has been working late every night he's in town since the word got out he has a chance to be the VP candidate. He's meeting with some of his staff tonight," Daniels said.

"You're from Mississippi?"

"My daddy moved the family up to Detroit when I was barely two, but I've still got relatives down here. Cousin told me this use to be the site of the state pen. How's that for karma."

"Looks like the white house."

They marched up the stairs. Sitting at a small wooden desk in the lobby was a state trooper. Steam was rising from a

Styrofoam cup of coffee sitting on the desk, next to it a black telephone, two-way radio and a newspaper. Standing next to the trooper, leaning on a broom, was a slender black man in coveralls, wearing black frame glasses and white canvas shoes. Ten feet behind them was a tall Christmas tree fully decorated with hundreds of red, white and blue ornaments and white lights.

"Cousin Clarence, how you be?" the janitor said.

They shook hands and gave each other a hug.

"Just fine and you, Jasper?"

They exchanged the normal conversation about family members dead and alive.

Then Jasper nodded toward the white trooper, obviously approaching retirement. He had a gray comb-over, wore a faded uniform and had a potbelly hanging over a cracked black-patent-leather belt supporting an old six-shot Colt revolver.

"Trooper Jamison, this is my cousin from Chicago. Remember I tole you he might stop by tonight to visit me. Mind if I give him a private tour of the building? Ain't nobody around this late on a Friday to do it."

Jamison yawned and stretched his arms over head. "Go right ahead, Jasper. But make sure you boys don't cause no trouble now."

Their heels clicked on the shiny marble floor as Jasper walked them to a bank of elevators. An elevator pinged, gold doors opened, they stepped inside and watched them close. Jasper pushed the buttons for two and three. "His office is on the third floor. Big sign on the door. If he ask you how you got in please don't mention me." The elevator stopped on two and Jasper stepped out with his broom. "See you, Clarence," and he nodded at William.

They rode up to the next floor and stepped out. A matron with a pushcart full of supplies was shining the gold doorknob on the governor's door. Next to her a janitor was waxing the floor.

\*\*\*

Edward Pape sat in an overstuffed maroon leather chair behind an oak desk that dominated the room. Behind him to his right the stars and stripes and to his left the state flag. It was called Stars and Bars—three horizontal stripes, blue, white and red top to bottom in the field and in the canter of the flag was the Confederate battle flag. It was a perfect setting for a photo op.

His two closest advisors sat in armchairs in front of the governor's desk. Chief of Staff Brandon Arendale was a short thick man, dressed in a black double-breasted suit and had a face that was crossed like a road map with thin red lines. Campaign Manager Earl McClellan was slender, had an angular face and a curved spine. His blue suit coat hung over the back of his chair. Bright red suspenders that matched his bow tie contrasted with his chalky skin. Three glasses of bourbon and an open bottle sat on the desk. Cigar smoke curled to the ceiling from the cigars in the ashtray between their chairs as the threesome planned the best course of action to get the governor the vice presidential slot on the ticket.

Pape spun in his chair and admired the poster hanging on the wall in back of him between the flags. "Has a good ring to it, Ed Pape for Vice President. Give the people something to be proud of."

McClellan pointed to the poster. "It's a good picture, Ed."

"I'm the dark horse, no pun intended." They all laughed. "Give me some ideas to better my odds.'

Arendale puffed on his cigar and shook the ash off in the ashtray. "We've got to get some national name recognition for you."

Pape said, "Maybe a misinformation campaign? A few leaks of some scurrilous information on my competitors? Some Tricky Dick type stuff?"

Arendale and McClellan laughed.

"There's a lot of good politics to be learned from that man. I don't have to be the best candidate." Pape drew on his cigar, exhaled the smoke and held the stogie between his thumb and forefinger. He pulled it away from his lips and gazed at the red glow. "I just have to be the lesser of all the evils." He admired the Monte Cristo, rolled it between his fingers. "You can't beat a good Cuban."

The door opened. Pape looked up from his cigar, forehead wrinkled. Arendale and McClellan turned in their chairs. They saw two well-dressed black men. One had a patch over his left ear. The two advisors glanced back at Pape and then at the intruders.

"Ah, excuse me gentlemen. This is a private meeting and the capital is closed now anyway." Arendale waved his cigar.

"We need to talk to the Governor," Daniels said.

Pape shook his head. "Call my secretary on Monday and make an appointment. Now kindly leave and close the door behind you." He nodded at McClellan signaling him to get up and lock the door behind them.

Arendale raised his eyebrows. McClellan looked at the door again and back at Pape.

Daniels folded his arms across his chest

"This must be a fucking joke." Pape gestured with his cigar at the men and shook his head. "Can never do enough for them. Got a lot of nerve coming here at this hour."

"Let's call security. Get the troopers. They'll get them out," Arendale said.

They pulled out their badges and flashed them at the three men. "FBI," William said.

"Can't you see we're busy?" McClellan turned to the governor again and back at the men, gesturing with his hands extended. "Call the secretary Monday and make an appointment."

Pape crushed his cigar in the Waterford crystal ashtray to his right. "Brandon, make a note to my secretary to contact the SAC of the Jackson office tomorrow. I don't appreciate federal agents barging in at their convenience."

Arendale scribbled a notation in his planner.

William closed the door and turned the dead bolt lock. He and Daniels walked forward, stopping behind Pape's advisors.

"You guys look like the fife and bugle corp." Pape pointed to Daniels' bandaged ear. "Bureau must be short on agents if you guys got to be working." Pape laughed. "What can we do for the feds?"

"Actually Governor we're not working," Daniels said, leaning forward and placing his hands on the back of Arendale's chair. "This isn't business, it's personal and we have a message from Eckhaus."

Pape swallowed. "That's very amusing. Don't you think that I know that he's dead? Must be very hard on the bureau when something like that happens. A mentally unstable agent goes off the deep end. It affects the credibility of the entire agency." Pape leaned over, opened a humidor, and removed a cigar. "Would either of you gentlemen be interested Cubans, Monte Cristos? I won't tell if you don't?"

"Doesn't interest me," Daniels said. He looked at William, who shook his head.

Pape clipped off the end, lit the cigar and blew a gray cloud of smoke in William's direction. "Is this some kind of joke?"

Arendale frowned. "Edward, I don't care why these guys are here. As your attorney and chief of staff, I advise you not to answer any questions these agents may have for you."

"We're really not here to ask you any questions, Pape. We have a tape that Eckhaus made and we're going to play it for you," William said.

Daniels stepped between Arendale and McClellan and placed the mini cassette tape recorder on his desk. "Would you like me to start it now or do you prefer to wait for your associates to leave?"

Arendale stood, poked his finger into Daniels' chest. "This is ridiculous. You don't come barging into the governor's office interrupting an important meeting—"

"Brandon, Earl, it's late," Pape cut in. "Why don't you gentlemen go home to your charming wives? I'll call you tomorrow."

Arendale's face reddened. "I'm telling you, Edward, I won't be responsible—"

"Go." Pape gestured to the door.

The two men grabbed their briefcases and left the office, muttering.

William and Daniels sat in the empty chairs. Daniels leaned forward and pushed the play button. The three of them listened to the meeting between Pape and Eckhaus.

At the end of the tape Pape sat forward in his chair, rested his elbows on the desk. "Well, that's a very interesting tape. So what do you propose to do with it?"

Daniels grabbed the tape recorder, took out the tape, and tossed it on Pape's desk. "You'll announce tomorrow that you're withdrawing your name as a candidate for the vice presidency and resign as governor."

"That's ridiculous. I will not be extorted…"

Daniels reached for the tape.

Pape grabbed his hand. He felt Daniels' cold black eyes burrowing into his.

"Copies of this tape will be sent to all the major networks along with a brief narrative naming the parties involved and appropriate background information explaining the circumstances," Daniels said.

"Who's going to believe an FBI agent that went insane? He killed that alderman and then what? Committed suicide or was shot by that other agent. Whatever stories you guys fabricated. The FBI's reputation isn't what it used to be with things like that going on. I'll sue you and get such a following that it will sweep me into office."

Daniels pointed his thumb to his chest. "I'm the agent that killed Eckhaus."

William cleared his throat. "That alderman—"

"The quiet one speaks," Pape said, smirking.

"Was my father."

Pape tapped his cigar on the ashtray knocking off a quarter-inch of ash and shrugged his shoulders. "Sorry about that."

"Sure you are," William said. "There's more than just the tape. There's a $100,000 that was wired to an account in Bermuda from the Mississippi Republican Campaign Fund."

Pape intertwined his fingers behind his head. "I think I see where you're coming from. You certainly deserve much more for your sacrifices and the sacrifices of your ancestors." Pape paused to admire his political response and tried to determine an amount that would pacify his tormentors. "$50,000...,each. How would that do?"

Daniels grimaced. "You son of a..."

William grabbed Daniels' arm. "Your generosity is greatly appreciated. But it's hardly enough."

Daniels' mouth dropped open. He looked at William.

Pape leaned forward. "You're right. I'm sorry. I hope you weren't offended." He exhaled and crossed his right knee over his left. "If one G man is worth a $100,000, you guys are too."

William smiled. "That's better."

"It'll probably take a week or so." Pape drew on the cigar. "I mean, I assume you want cash."

"Checks would be fine. You can make mine payable to the United Negro College Fund." He looked at Daniels who took a deep breath and nodded. "You have a charity you'd like the governor to support?" William turned and looked back at the governor. "Of course you'll still be expected to resign that same day and withdraw your candidacy. This'll buy you a little time to deal with it. But let's not make it more than a week or we'll send the tapes out. Of course I'm sure you realize that if anything should happen to us there are several parties instructed to forward copies of the tape to the networks."

The Governor crushed his cigar in the ashtray. "You fucking niggers. You killed my son and now you're ruining me. Our family has been instrumental in helping you people. You think your ancestors ever thought they could be FBI agents? That's the appreciation you show?"

Daniels stood. "You can keep the tape."

William rose from his chair. They both turned and walked toward the door.

William stopped half-way, spun around and pointed his finger at Pape. "You son of a bitch, did you really think you can get away with killing Dr. King and Senator Kennedy?"

Daniels grabbed his elbow and pulled William toward the door.

Pape leaned over his desk and waved his fist at them. "Everything I've worked for. You'll be sorry you ever came here...." He went on shouting and waving his hands. Then heard the door shut and he realized he was alone.

Pape fell back into his chair, poured a glass of bourbon, drank it, and poured another. He felt his legacy crumbling faster than he could ever imagine. He spun around in his chair, grabbed his vice presidential poster, tore it down and flung it across the room. He gulped down his drink, and filled it again. The bottle clinking against the glass as his hand shook. "Motherfuckers, think they can stop me...."

\*\*\*

Daniels and William walked down the stairs of the capital building. They stopped and looked at the illuminated dome. The Stars and Bars, lighted by a flood light, was waving in the ink black sky.

"You really think this will change anything?" William asked.

Daniels put his arm on William's shoulder. "Not everything comes to a fair and just ending. I don't think we'll know the answer for a long time, maybe not ever. Let's go home." They got into William's Camaro and headed north.

\*\*\*

Pape thought about what he would have liked to have said at the convention. He stood behind his desk envisioning himself standing at a lectern in front of thousands of cheering supporters at the convention. "Yeah, this is my fucking campaign promise. I'll get all the niggers out of the great State of Mississippi. They can pick any state they want. No, I'll pick one for 'em. Give them North Dakota. Freeze their asses off." He drained the bourbon, filled his glass again, and crashed down into his chair almost missing it.

"My boy, Michael." He sobbed. "I failed you. You died in vain. And Tom's girl, hurt so bad he couldn't stand it. Sakich dead. Eckhaus dead. Our dream dead. The Pape legacy dead." He pulled another cigar from the humidor, clipped off the end, put it in his mouth, and flicked his lighter. There was no flame. He opened a drawer and removed a can of lighter fluid. He squeezed the can and fluid shot out onto a stack of campaign leaflets sitting on the corner of his desk.

"Ah shit. Fucking useless paper." He sealed the lighter, flicked it, and drew on his cigar. The tip glowed a bright red and he set it down in the ashtray. Pape lifted the bourbon to his lips, his hand trembling, and half the golden brown liquid spilled down his shirt. "It's over." He opened the bottom drawer, and pulled out a revolver and a box of ammo, and set them on his desk. He stared at the mini cassette with contempt.

"Fucking Eckhaus. Why'd you tape that?" He grabbed the pistol by the barrel, crashed the butt down smashing the cassette, and ripped the tape apart.

His fingers fumbled trying to open the box of ammo as the hands on the clock drifted late into the night and the liquor filled his veins. "Fuck you," Pape screamed. "No niggers are stopping me." He swept his arms across the desk and sent the campaign flyers, ammo, pistol, ashtray and cigar flying across the room. His eyelids drooped. "Tomorrow—show them. Get on the ticket— niggers will be sorry." He grabbed his left arm.

* * *

They were on the road for an hour when Daniels fell asleep. Driving on the highway late at night was a place where you can put things together, making a perfect world and then tearing it apart so your gut roils with pain. That's what William did for the next two-

and-half-hours, doubting everything they had done—seeing absolutely no good coming out of their efforts at a cost that was measured in blood. At three in the morning he pulled into a low-slung motel a few miles south of Memphis and shook Daniels. "Wake up. Let's get a couple of rooms here."

Daniels stretched his arms and yawned. "Where're we?"

"Just outside of Memphis." William pushed the door open

"I guess a bed will be better for my back than sleeping in this bucket seat."

The motel clerk was a bony old man with a huge gap between his tobacco-stained teeth. He looked at the small overnight bags they were carrying. "You boys traveling mighty light." A toothpick wiggled in his mouth.

"A short trip," William said, eyes red from the glare of oncoming headlights.

The clerk slammed two keys down on the counter. "Sixty bucks for rooms twenty one and twenty two, out the door and to the left. You boys want a wake up call?"

"Don't even think about it," Daniels said, tossing the cash on the counter.

They left the office, the silence of the early morning interrupted only by the sounds of their shoes scraping the cracked sidewalk. Daniels stopped at his door. "First man up wakes the other?"

William kept on walking. "Sure, as long as it's not before ten." He opened the door and stepped into the room. It looked like a throwback to the sixties. A green shag carpet, the television bolted onto a wrought-iron stand, and a swag lamp hanging in the corner over a small round table. He sat on one of the two single beds, threw his overnight bag onto the other bed, and listened to it squeak.

He spent the night tossing and turning. His right arm throbbing from the bullet wound. His mind raced through the emotional consternation of his life, wondering if they had done the right thing, if there was anything else they could have done. Wasn't there some way they could have prosecuted Pape? He settled on the only thing that calmed him. That would reduce the electric tension that spasm through his mind. Quit the bureau. Then he drifted into a sleep that seemed like it was interrupted a few minutes later by a ringing phone. He was sure it was part of a nightmare. It wasn't.

William looked at his watch, seven in the morning. "What the hell?" He picked up the phone. "Yeah?"

"We need to get back to Chicago?"

"Why damn it? I want to go back to sleep." He hung up the phone.

A few minutes later there was a knock at his door. "William, it's me, open up. We have to go."

William stumbled out of bed in his underwear and opened the door. The sunlight blinded him as he stared at the silhouette of Daniels. "I told you don't call me until ten." He stepped back from the door and collapsed on the bed.

Daniels stepped in and closed the door behind him. "I'm sorry, man. I woke up early. A couple in the next room was doing the wild thing all night with Johnny Cash supplying the background music. Thought I might as well check in with the wife. McAlister called last night looking for me. He told her that the squad is mine. Brunson wants to do a squad review ASAP to cover any questions DC has as a result of the Eckhaus thing. Anyway, she's wondering why the SAC didn't call me in Motown. I told her we're going to Detroit on a case. I figured it was better if no one knew we were coming down here. So, I've got to get back before too many questions come up about where we were. I'll drive. You can sleep in the car."

"Shit," William said, crawled out of bed and headed to the shower.

Daniels turned the TV on, sat in a rickety chair at the table, folded his arms across his chest and closed his eyes.

A few minutes later William came out of the bathroom with a towel wrapped around his waist. "I was so fucking naive to think we could stop him."

"You look like hell. Take a few days off. Get out of town. Go some place sunny and warm and drink a lot of rum. Get things off your mind for awhile." Daniels got up, walked to the TV, and turned the volume down. "Something else is bothering you besides everything that's happened the last few weeks?"

William sat on the bed and lowered his head to his chest. "I'm quitting. This hasn't been what it's supposed to be." He felt walled in by the circumstances. Images flashed through his mind. Images of good men that were dead—his grandfather, King, Kennedy, his father, and God knew who else. "There must have been something else we could have done?"

"Under the circumstances we did all we could. Don't make any quick decisions. Stick it out awhile. Things will get better. I'll get the squad moving in the right direction. I'll make things right."

"I don't know. What if Pape runs for office anyway? Are we really going to send those tapes?"

Daniels glanced away from William. "He's not going to run."

William gazed at Daniels. He seemed at peace, like he knew something William didn't. "How can you be so certain?"

Daniels nodded at the TV.

CNN was on. There was a streaming line underneath the talking head and then a picture of Pape filled the screen.

Daniels turned the volume up. The announcer went on. "As you have been reading it was just announced that the Governor of Mississippi, Edward Pape, suffered a severe stroke early this morning in the state capitol. Apparently he wasn't found until early this morning, which complicates any potential recovery. It's terrible timing for the Pape family and for the people of Mississippi, and possibly the entire nation because the governor was one of the leading candidates for the vice presidential spot on the Republican ticket. He could have been one heartbeat away from being the President of this country. Instead it looks like the end of the Pape legacy. We'll bring you additional updates as they come in."

They sat in silence. Then William stood and shut off the TV.

Daniels shook his head. "It's over now, over for good, probably for the best. If this had become public knowledge it would have changed the past. It might have done the country more harm than good to expose what your father told us. Maybe, letting what actually happened rest will change the future."

For William the world had changed. There was an empty place inside of him now, and he didn't know how, or if, he could fill it. Change happens that way. The empty place inside is a vacuum that fills with what you need, not necessarily what you want.

# EPILOGUE

It was the dog days of August 1980. The air was thick and heavy and the temperature in the nineties. William and Marlee walked in ankle deep water at the 12$^{th}$ Street beach. Between them was Missy skipping, holding each one of their hands. Celeste had spent her last months at Nathleen's and passed away in late spring. Nathleen had become the child's foster parent.

Edward Pape spent the rest of his life in a wheelchair. His left side paralyzed. His face contorted, drool running down his chin, barely able to speak. But with the full knowledge and awareness for the last ten years of his life that his hoped-for legacy would never be achieved.

William stayed with the FBI.

470 | Lee Williams

## REFERENCE NOTES

Page 33            Ray used the alias John Willard to register at Bessie Brewer's
                   Boarding house. Ibid., p.62.

Page 35            James Earl Ray had a habit of tugging on his right ear lobe.
                   This was adapted from Gerold Frank, *An American Death,* p
                   163.

Page 36            Physical description of Ray. He was in his early thirties,
                   slender, wore black-rimmed glasses and his blue eyes stood
                   out against his pale skin. He had a long narrow nose, brown
                   hair slicked back, and a receding hairline. Ibid., p. 162.

Page 38            Ray used a Remington Gamemaster 760 30.06 rifle to
                   assassinate King. Ibid., p. 34-38.

Page 39            Ray lived in Alton and Quincy in southern Illinois and served
                   in the Army in Germany. Ibid., p. 288-289.

Page 39            Ray was serving a twenty year sentence in the Missouri State
                   Pen for forging postal money orders. He worked in the kitchen
                   baking bread. He used to put sixty loaves in a box that was
                   sent to the prison farm. He jumped into a bread box and had a
                   someone stack the bread on top of him. He got to the farm and
                   walked away. His brother met me and drove me to Chicago.
                   Ibid., p.236-237.

Page 96            Ramon George Sneyd was an alias used by Ray. Ibid., 190.

Page 96 - 97       The description of Bessie Brewer's boarding house was
                   obtained from. Ibid., p. 58.

Page 100           Painted on the door of the bathroom door at Bessie Brewer's
                   boarding house was "toilet & bath." Ibid., p. 58.

Page 101           Ray drove a white Mustang. Ibid., 184.

Page 102           Ray wrapped the Remington 760 he shot King with in a green
                   bedspread and dropped it the doorway of Canipes Amusement.
                   Ibid., 97-98.

Page 104           The *Chicago Tribune* headline on April 5, 1698 was MLK
                   SLAIN-POLICE HUNT FOR KILLER.

## REFERENCE NOTES CONT.

Page 119        In 1816 the American Colonization Society was formed for the purpose of the return of free African Americans to what was considered greater freedom in Africa. The founding fathers of this country believed it was an acceptable movement. Thomas Jefferson proposed colonization of the blacks and even Abraham Lincoln contemplated it rather than risk dividing the country in two. In 1816 the American Colonization Society was formed in Washington, D.C. Its purpose was to emigrate freed blacks to Africa. Subsequently, the federal government and various state governments funded the society. Congress, under President James Monroe, provided $100,000 to purchase land in Africa. The land was purchased from Sierra Leone and named Liberia. The capital, Monrovia, was named after the president. At one time there were 13,000 immigrant blacks in Liberia. Wikipedia.

Page 128        Information regarding the damage, arrests and other details regarding the riots in the country after King's assassination were obtained from the *Chicago Tribune* issues of April 5, 6, and 8, 1968.

Page 139        On April 18, 1968 *The Chicago Sun Times* published the first photo of King's assassination.

Page 142        Radio reports of King's funeral and conspiracy allegations. Ibid., p. 126.

Page 143        Ray was seen in Loblaw's Groceteria in Toronto on April 23, 1968. Gerold Frank, *An American Death,* p184-185

Page 144        The April 20, 1968 issue of *The Chicago Sun Times* headline was GALT UNMASKED-Dr. KING SUSPECT ESCAPED CONVICT, article on page 1 and 14.

Page 147        Sirhan programmed to kill. Dan Moldea, *The Killing of Robert F. Kennedy*, p. 134.

Page 147 & 155  A white woman with dark hair put on a polka dot dress. Ibid., p. 40, 70-71.

Page 156        Quote of RFK California speech. ""We are a great country, an unselfish country, a compassionate country...." Ibid. p. 25-26.

## REFERENCE NOTES CONT.

Page 157    Dialogue during RFK Shooting "Kennedy, you son of bitch." Ibid., p. 93.

Page 167    *The Chicago Sun Times* headline of June 9, 1968 RAY IS CAPTURED.

Page 171    Sirhan Sirhan had no recollection of planning or committing the shooting of Robert Kennedy. Ibid., p.122, 125.

Page 188    On June 10, 1968, James Earl Ray was arraigned in London's Bow Street Magistrates Court, charged with possession of an illegal firearm and a false passport. He fought extradition and was ordered held in the Wandsworth Prison South London. Ibid., p. 377.

Page 198    On July 19, 1968 Ray waives extradition in London and is transported to Memphis. On July 19 Ray waived extradition. Shortly after midnight he was handed over to American authorities at London's Wandsworth prison and flown nonstop in an Air Force jet to Millington Naval Air Force Station where he landed at 3:48 a.m. Hampton Sides, *Hellhounds on His Trail*, p. 381.

Page 198    On July 22, 1968, Ray pled not guilty to the first-degree murder charge of killing Martin Luther King. *Chicago Tribune.*

Page 201    The trance Sirhan's Arab associates had put under had worked. He had no recollection of murdering Bobby Kennedy. Dan Moldea, *The Killing of Robert F. Kennedy*, p.122, 125.

Page 290    Headlines on *The Enterprise Tocsin* on the April 11, 1968 KING MURDERED and June 13, 1968 RAY ARRESTED IN ENGLAND.

www.ingramcontent.com/pod-product-compliance
Lightning Source LLC
Chambersburg PA
CBHW021209090426
42740CB00006B/168